Red Carpets
and
Other Banana Skins

Also by Rupert Everett

HELLO DARLING, ARE YOU WORKING?

THE HAIRDRESSERS OF ST TROPEZ

Red Carpets
and
Other Banana Skins

RUPERT EVERETT

Little, Brown

LITTLE, BROWN

First published in Great Britain in 2006 by Little, Brown

A CIP catalogue record for this book
is available from the British Library.

Hardback ISBN-13: 978-0-316-73222-2
Hardback ISBN-10: 0-316-73222-2
C format ISBN-13: 978-0-316-73223-9
C format ISBN-10: 0-316-73223-0

Typeset in Electra by M Rules
Printed and bound in Great Britain by
Clays Ltd, St Ives plc

Little, Brown Book Group
Brettenham House
Lancaster Place
London WC2E 7EN

A Member of the Hachette Livre Group of Companies

www.littlebrown.co.uk

Contents

1 Tales from the Crib   1
2 Innocence and Experience   9
3 Brancaster   14
4 Virgin Queen   19
5 Stage Beauty   30
6 London   40
7 Paris   58
8 Drama School   73
9 Suzy   86
10 Clubs and Drugs   90
11 John   94
12 Glasgow   103
13 The West End   115
14 Paula   121
15 Barbarian Queen   135
16 Natasha and *The Far Pavilions*   140
17 *Another Country*   151
18 *Dance with a Stranger*   157
19 The Lubed Desert   166
20 The Harris Hollywood House   172
21 Fred Hughes   183
22 New Year's Eve   188
23 Julie Andrews   193

24 Colombia 198

25 Bob Dylan 203

26 Rock Follies 211

27 France 215

28 Béatrice 223

29 St Tropez 228

30 *The Vortex* 233

31 Los Angeles 240

32 Windy Ridge 246

33 Russia 253

34 Ready to Wear 267

35 Miami 274

36 *My Best Friend's Wedding* 283

37 Sea Crest Apartments 290

38 The Hollywood Year 296

39 Goodbye, Roddy 312

40 *Unconditional Love* 322

41 Donatella's New Year's Eve Party 327

42 Charity Begins as Far Away as Possible 335

43 Goodbye, Albert, Goodbye, Mo 345

44 Talk to Me and Then Move In and Out
Real Slow 354

45 Haitian Hiatus 364

46 Viva la Diva 371

47 Dangerous Lesbians 375

48 Travels with My Father 381

49 The Old Ladies of the Woods 386

50 Goodbye, Hollywood 393

51 Wilma 398

52 Goodbye, Miami 404

Red Carpets

and

Other Banana Skins

CHAPTER I

Tales from the Crib

At several times in life one comes to a point of no return. The drama of this moment often escapes us. We walk into it unconcerned, not hearing all the closing doors slam behind us, not aware that suddenly we are cut adrift from the past and are loose on the high seas, charting a new course through undiscovered waters. I must have been six when it first happened to me. I was living with my mother and father, my brother and our nanny in an old pink farmhouse with a moat, surrounded by the cornfields of Essex. The local farmers had finished the harvest and that morning they were burning the stubble. We knew because my mother came charging into the house, after dropping my father off at the station.

'Nanny! Mrs Smithers! They're burning the stubble!'

Mayhem. I sat on the hall floor as the two women in my life careered around the house slamming doors, closing windows, drawing curtains. Footsteps pounded across the creaky floorboards above, shaking the whole house: my mother's purposeful gait, identifiable to her children a mile off, and Mrs Smithers', our darling cleaning lady, like a gentle elephant squeezed into my mother's hand-me-down court shoes. Snatches of conversation could be heard from the gables – a peal of laughter from my mother. And then silence. The sun battling through the curtains made the house feel like an aquarium during the burning of the stubble and, since my mother was a stickler for cleanliness, they could stay closed for days until the last fleck of black ash floated off through the sky. I loved it. Darkness made you feel naughty. And outside the inferno raged around us.

It was one of the highlights of our summer and we children were out there, under the gentle scrutiny of the local farmers from beginning to end, looking for hedgehogs and field mice to save from the fire and only leaving as dusk fell on the black glowing embers and the fields around our house had turned into giant tiger-skin rugs.

Meanwhile, inside the house that morning we settled down to the agreeable state of siege, and all sat in the kitchen as Mummy and Mrs Smithers reminisced about former 'stubbles', and Nanny made coffee and Ribena. 'That dratted ash can get through anything,' my mother could say a thousand times during the course of the next two weeks and Mrs Smithers would keep on nodding sagely like a toy bulldog on the back seat of a car.

So it came as quite a surprise that it was decided I should be taken to the cinema. 'What's the cinema?' I whined, lips a-quiver, ready for a tantrum. But there was no arguing, and no explanation.

'You'll see!' was the only answer.

So pretty soon we all bundled into our Hillman, Mummy at the wheel, me beside her with my own steering wheel, suction-stuck to the dashboard, and Nanny in the back, as we drove at a snail's pace through the howling flames down the chase that led to our house so that I could at least have a good look. I don't think Mummy knew that flames made petrol explode.

Until that year, 1965, we did not possess a television. The only images I saw were happening then and there in front of my very eyes. I had no concept of a world outside, and no desire to find one. When Churchill died my father went out and bought a large cumbersome set so that he and my mother could watch the funeral, and that was the first moving picture I ever saw. Grainy, incomprehensible and utterly boring, I thought, but then I turned around to see the tear-stained, enraptured faces of my parents and must have reconsidered. This television could get a lot of attention.

The Braintree cinema would be getting a lot of attention, too. It was unremarkable, one of those dismal buildings from the fifties with a curved brick front, Crittall windows and a shabby marquee. We parked the car and joined a long line that stretched around the cinema. None of us much liked queuing – my mum always had a million things to do, and I wanted to get back home to the stubble – and we nearly decided to leave. But fate was hell-bent and after half an hour of ranting (Mummy) and whining (me) we arrived at the box office.

And so my mother bought the fateful tickets and unknowingly guided me through a pair of swing doors into the rest of my life. Goodbye, Braintree! Suddenly we were in a magical, half-lit cavern of gigantic proportions. It must have been the hugest room in the world and at the end were the biggest pair of curtains I had ever seen. I loved curtains already, but these were something else. We were guided down the central aisle by a Braintree matron with a torch. What were all these chairs, and how did you sit on them?

'It's just like a loo seat, darling,' said my mother.

I sat down between Nanny and her, took one of their hands in each of mine and slowly accustomed myself to the light and my racing heart. Looking up through the gloom was a circle, a balcony and, hanging miles over our heads like a tired moon, a huge crusty chandelier half lit as if for a seance. The place smelt of cigarettes and damp with the odd breeze from the toilets of urine and disinfectant. And sex. Even if I didn't know what it was yet, an insalubrious mist hung over the provincial cinemas of yesteryear. This was the place you got to finger your girlfriend's quim.

'Quim' was a word the big 'yobbos' shouted from the circle at the Braintree girls as they waited in line for ice creams down in the stalls.

'Show us your quim, Karen!' they'd shout, and the girls would giggle coquettishly.

'What's a quim, Mummy?' I asked one morning during coffee.

'Your little toe, I think,' said my mother vaguely. Mrs Smithers and Nanny nearly choked. I realised right then that poor Mummy was not very much in touch.

But all that was for the evening show. Something much worse could happen at the matinée. Even that day, sprinkled among the little children with their mums and nans, was the odd old fossil, motionless and lizard-like in the playground fray of the stalls. ('Don't sit too close to Mr Barnard from Millens & Dawson, there's a good boy,' one might be told. But no one cared much in those days.) The kids' giggles and screams bounced off the walls of the half-filled theatre. There was endless movement. To the toilets, to the ice cream lady, and finally some child would go too far and be dragged out. All that noise and movement stopped suddenly as the lights dimmed from the tired moon above and the little sconces on the walls jerkily faded to dull embers, and we all turned as one towards this huge billowing curtain that was bigger than our house. It was lit from below and was a bright crimson at the bottom as if the sun were about to rise from the empty orchestra pit.

What was behind it? Where was it all coming from? The film's certificate was projected while the curtain was still closed. It seemed as if it were bursting through from the other side, and then those huge curtains silently swished open and *Mary Poppins* sprang across the footlights and into my heart.

The next ninety minutes were the most shocking, inspiring, funny, tragic, exhausting, draining and troubling of my entire life. First of all, when all the nannies blew away, I was terrified. Looking at Nanny for a second, her life and role suddenly came into a new perspective. This could be a dangerous job, I thought. And then when Mary Poppins flew effortlessly down into the film something changed for ever. Was it that Julie Andrews looked and behaved somewhat like my mother? Maybe. Or was it because I already loved my own nanny to death? Of course, I could definitely identify with the spit spot of it all. Julie's way of showing emotion was our way. Controlled but with feeling; practical but with warmth. As for Mr Banks, he *was* my dad. But I didn't want him to lose his job because of me. Yes – by halfway through the film I *was* Jane and Michael. I was learning at a fearful rate. I could identify with everything in the film. New horizons suddenly appeared. Maybe one could jump into the pavement. It had to be true, because everything else sort of was. After all, we drove past St Paul's Cathedral every time we went up to our London flat, so I suppose I must have felt that the film had been tailored specifically for me, but soon it all became too much. My brain was overloaded. When Mary Poppins left without saying goodbye, I was so distraught that I had to be taken out of the theatre and missed 'Let's Go Fly a Kite'.

The kids in the movie went off with their dad to the park and Mary Poppins decided to leave. That was where I started shouting, 'Jane! Michael! Quick! Go back to Cherry Tree Lane.' A light slap from my mother was no deterrent, especially as the parrot umbrella seemed to be reading my thoughts. 'They didn't even say goodbye,' it squawked at Mary Poppins.

'Nobody told them you were leaving!' I screamed back, by this time hysterical.

'Shut up,' said Mummy and Nanny, but I could not. I stood up and bellowed my heart and lungs out, and was dragged, kicking and screaming, from the cinema.

I was silent on the way home, listlessly looking at the glowing embers of the fields as we drove towards our house. Everyone tried to coax me back into my usual boisterous self, but there was nothing to be done. I was too upset to think.

Something had changed. I could feel it, but I couldn't express it. Actually, looking back, what had happened was that a giant and deranged ego had been born. Until that afternoon I had lived without question from day to night, from winter to spring, from anger to joy. I seamlessly inhabited every moment. There were no questions. But now I was on the game, looking for a personality, and my plumbing was all wrong. The hot was coming from where the cold should have been.

My mother was discarding an old tweed skirt (a pye r squared). It was my first act of madness. I was going to be Mary Poppins' daughter and this skirt was how I would pull it off. I rescued it from the dustbin and before long I was wearing it all the time. The place where I practised being the new 'me' was our climbing frame, which had a swing in the middle. I would sit on that swing in my red tweed skirt and black slip-on plimsolls, for hours on end, humming the hits I was learning from my new *Mary Poppins* LP. Nobody paid much attention. But something had started. From then on I was a regular at the Braintree Embassy. I must have seen *Mary Poppins* twenty times, and no sooner had my mother put her foot down and banned me from seeing it again than Julie responded to my desperate telepathic messages to her and came out with *The Sound of Music*.

On Saturdays in the winter months my father would go hunting, and our whole household was galvanised into a fever pitch to help. My mother would run around like a chicken with its head cut off. Cooking breakfast. Squeezing my dad into his breeches and boots. Getting the rest of us up. She was a regular tornado, storming around the house. Mr

King and later Mr Baker, our grooms, would begin to saddle up the horses. My brother would back up the car and attach the horsebox, and I would sit there humming show tunes wondering what I could do to get out of following the hunt with my mum and her best friend Mrs Barker. Wishful thinking. It was never going to happen. Finally the noise of my father's boots clunking across the hall downstairs signalled my mother's shrill alarm call. 'Roo! Come on. We're off.'

Everyone we knew hunted; at the meet the grown-ups drank cherry brandy on their horses. The hounds seethed around. Some of the women still rode side-saddle; many of the men wore pink coats, top hats and white stocks. (A stock was a long starched piece of fabric that wound around the neck and was tied in a certain way that always eluded my father.) My mum and Mrs Barker were the only mothers who did not hunt, and they stood around in their headscarves and wellies, while the Barker boys and I sat sullenly in the back of the car, cruelly imitating our mothers' inane chatter. ('Julia, darling, your crab mousse was divine. You *must* give me the recipe.' 'Oh, Sara, just put in a lot of Elnette to stiffen it.')

Then the huntsman would blow his horn and they would be off; Mrs Barker and Mummy would canter towards the car and we'd set off after the hunt. They hardly ever caught a fox. We would drive for miles down little lanes and farm tracks just to be there when the hunt galloped by. Sometimes there was drama. Mrs Motion was thrown off her horse and dragged for a hundred yards; she never came out of her coma. I remember it vividly. Her inert body – a black hump at the end of a field; and all of us running towards her. A doctor who was watching the hunt gave her an injection, which proved to be lethal. She should never have had one.

My brother was the first to start hunting. He hated it, but did it to please my father. I had no intention of pleasing anyone and made this as clear as I could, but I was made to go as well. I had a bitchy pony named Crisp. She used to lean round and nip me if I wasn't concentrating, and there was little love lost between us. I much preferred my brother's mare Netty, who was a lumbering old thing totally unruffled by anything. You could kick and kick and she wouldn't budge, but then slowly she would lurch into a stately canter that was not unpleasant. Crisp, on the other hand, was a plotting maniacal freak, and on my first time out ran away with me, overtaking the entire hunt. One of the golden rules of hunting is: no one rides in front of the Master and the hounds. No matter how hard I yanked on the reins, Crisp charged on. She was playing the game her way, determined to show me up. I could see out of the corner of my eye the ruddy disapproving faces of the local gentry as I sped past and could hear their various comments:

'Control your pony, you bloody little idiot!'

'Young Everett's being run away with!'

'Heels down, toes up!'

All very well, I thought, as I galloped past the Master and the hounds straight towards a gate that was taller than the little bitch Crisp herself. I knew just what was going on in her head. She was going to gallop as fast as she could and then stop dead when she got to the gate, throwing me over without her, and breaking my neck like poor Mrs Motion. There was no going back. It was time to drop the resistance and show her who was boss, so I let the reins go, kicked the shit out of her and we sailed over the gate to our mutual astonishment and that of the rest of the hunt. It should have been a moment of victory. But I felt humiliated and, vowing never to touch Crisp again, I jumped down and stomped off across the fields.

I only had two or three more hunting experiences. On the last one we finally caught a fox. The poor thing was torn apart by the hounds and then something even worse happened. I was the unwilling victim of a tribal initiation. Another tradition: any new hunter had to be 'bloodied' after they had witnessed their first kill.

'Young Everett. Come to the front,' said the Master to the huntsman and the word was passed back. There was nothing for it. I kicked old Netty into action and sullenly rode past the rest of the hunters who were all smiling at me benignly like the devil worshippers in *Rosemary's Baby*.

'Dismount, boy,' said the huntsman. Someone had cut off the fox's paw before it was torn to shreds. Raw and oozing, it was presented to the huntsman who then smeared it all over my face. Everyone laughed; there were a few claps, a couple of pats on my hat, congratulations from the Master – and the awful thing was that I felt really fabulous. Totally macho. Fitting in with the gang. My dad beamed at me from under his top hat. Mr King gave me a wink. My mother and Mrs Barker waved from a distance. I felt like one take-charge kind of guy. For a millisecond.

Then some of the blood got into my eye and I freaked. Never had a mood swing happened so fast – it even took me by surprise and suddenly I was spluttering and shrieking, but words would not come out. The blood was everywhere. I could taste it. I was literally seeing red. If I could have, I would definitely have blacked out, but instead (as usual) I abandoned poor bemused Netty and made another of my early dramatic exits. I never hunted again.

Looking back, however, those traumatic times seem like the romantic scenes from a nineteenth-century novel. The morning meets in front of the old houses around the county, mostly shrouded in mist and drizzle so that all you could see were the reds of the hunting coats, the silhouettes of the horses and the dripping gables of some Elizabethan manor. The hunting horses always beautifully turned out, clattering down driveways, waving their bandaged tails; you could hear them even if you couldn't see them. Did people shout 'Tally-ho'? I don't remember. I remember the smell. The chatter. The women with their veils, leaning over to tighten their horses' girths and somehow managing to hold a glass and a conversation at the same time – chatting and flirting with the men who drank from their flasks with their hands on their hips. There were a lot of affairs conducted from the raunchy position of the saddle and a lot of political talk; because this was the era of power cuts and 'Bloody Wilson!'

It could be a dangerous game, the hunt. When you put your kids into it you knew there were certain risks. We were to be tested against the elements. But that was good. It gave one a zest for life and adventure that you cannot get from a Gameboy or a computer in a world where everything comes second to safety. You had to take the bull by the horns and that was what they taught you when you went out hunting and you galloped off out of control. You held your whole life in that moment and if you fell – then that was that. But if you didn't . . .

Sometimes if the meet was near by we would hack home in the dusk down country lanes where the only noise would be our horses' hooves and the odd pheasant crashing through the hedgerows. Lights twinkled out from the cottages by the road and we all thought anxiously about high tea in front of the fire at home. Baked beans and poached eggs; toast and Marmite; whisky for my father as we all helped to pull off his boots before he disappeared to soak in a salt-filled bath.

CHAPTER 2

Innocence and Experience

My life started on the move. Our family, led by my father, was a restless one from the beginning. When I came along he was still a major in the Duke of Edinburgh's Wiltshire regiment, and so our first home was one of those weird red-brick army dwellings in a place called Hook in Hampshire. My first real memory is of travel: falling down the polished wooden stairs in our house. The trip seemed to go on for ever, and I must have gone head over heels because I could see the whole world turning upside down and then zooming in as my face crashed against the oak stairs. My parents both claim amnesia about this moment, but I know it happened. I think it did me serious damage. To this day I cannot totally straighten my arms; not to mention my ways.

My father left the army when I was three and we moved to London where he went to work for the notorious Marquis of Bristol who, in the thirties, had presided over a bunch of upper-class thugs nicknamed the Mayfair Gang. They stole jewellery. Now in 1961 he had moved into the import-export business.

Our house was in Cheyne Row, in Chelsea, opposite the Catholic church, but we didn't last long there, mostly because our labrador Susan couldn't figure out London at all and went into a serious depression. Anyway, soon my dad had changed jobs and was working for a firm of stockbrokers in the City. So, after nine months we all got back into the Hillman – me, Mummy, Nanny, Susan and my brother – and drove to a pretty clapboard cottage near Colchester. This was where I witnessed my first snog.

My nanny, Jenny Pepper, was extremely pretty. I loved her almost as much as I loved my mother. She had an auburn beehive and every day we went for our walk down a lane with steep banks on either side. After about a mile there was a crossroads where a tree trunk stood next to an old black-and-white striped wooden signpost. This place was one of my many 'houses' and I would hold tea parties for Nanny and Susan on the tree trunk, using acorn cups.

One day, Nanny's fancy man, Dave, came on the walk with us. He was good looking with greased-back hair and long black sideboards. They were walking on the road and I was scampering along the bank above. As we approached the tree stump I turned round, proffering acorn cups to Dave and Nanny, only to see Dave's tongue burrowing down inside Nanny's mouth like a huge slug. He looked as if he was going to eat her. Instant jealousy brought forth the most blood-curdling scream I could manage, but Dave just glanced at me as he continued to snog Nanny and raised his hand from her bum in a gesture of 'Wait a minute'.

I began to prepare myself for a major tantrum but something stopped me. This was interesting. I'd never seen Nanny so speechless. Her heavily mascaraed eyelashes were tightly shut to the rest of the world. She was in a trance. Dave had his hands in her beehive, on her bottom, all over, so I just sat down on the tree trunk and gaped. The thing that fascinated me was that they just weren't themselves; they were bewitched. But after the snog was over, it was as if it had never happened. They both came up to the tree trunk for tea; Nanny's face was raw from Dave's stubble. I tried reproaching them with my eyes as I passed round tea, but Dave wasn't having any nonsense, though Nanny looked down with a self-conscious giggle. Her beehive was all over the place. 'Cake, anyone?' I burbled with quiet wounded dignity, but in reality I was pretty excited. Now I knew this was what grown-ups did, and I was longing to join in.

At about the same time my mother took us boys aside and in serious tones warned us not to go into the woods above the farm because there was a funny man there who might take us to his house, give us sweets, put us on his kitchen table and play with our 'wees'. My brother looked horrified but I couldn't think of anything better. Travel, sweets and someone playing with my willy: I couldn't wait to trike up there. But no matter how often I slipped away from our house to tramp around the woods behind the farm, I never met a soul. (My poor old mum, though, was always inadvertently pushing the wrong buttons. Much later, when we were teenagers, her fantasies took on a darker twist. She told us to be careful of our bottoms on the streets in London because often men would come up behind one and give one an injection and one would be kidnapped and then one would never get home.)

My father put on his stiff collar, his City suit and his bowler hat on Monday mornings and left the house at eight-fifteen. He came back on Friday at about six. When I was five, my brother Simon was packed off to school, so that I was left alone with Mummy and Nanny, and my governess Miss Spooner who lived at Windy Ridge and came three mornings a week. These were, without doubt, the most glorious days of my life. And if Mummy, Nanny and Miss Spooner weren't enough, in the almshouses up the lane towards the church lived my best friend, Mr Brewer. He was eighty-nine years old. He loved dogs so I would go round with Susan. His sister Elsie lived in the house next door and she would knock on the wall with a spoon to let him know that dinner or tea was ready. The almshouses were low red-brick bedsits from a bygone age, with latticed windows and tiny doors, but then Mr and Miss Brewer were minuscule. Mr Brewer wore braces on his legs and Elsie rarely got out of her dressing gown. Their back gardens were jungles of flowers with two little tumbledown outdoor loos at the end. They were in bed by eight and Mr Brewer was up at six and off to the church where he was the verger. If my family was typical of the post-war rationing generation of the last century, then the Brewers belonged to the one before.

Life seemed to stretch out around me like the endless cornfields about our house. My father would come home from the City for the weekends. My brother would come home from school for the holidays. Our fortunes steadily increased and my father decided it was time for us to buy our own home. So one day we moved from the little clapboard farmhouse to the pink one with the moat. It was round about then that Nanny and Dave announced their wedding and her impending departure.

Bundled into the Hillman once more, Mummy tooted the horn as we drove past the almshouses. Out hobbled Mr Brewer from one door and old Elsie from the other. A pair of weathervanes announcing a change in temperature, they chatted philosophically about how we'd keep in touch and see each other soon, but of course, even though we were moving only fourteen miles away, we never saw them again. My last sight of Mr Brewer was vanishing in a cloud of dust through the back window of our departing car. He was leaning on his stick, waving. Elsie was hobbling into her house. Susan watched solemnly but I waved back excitedly as we disappeared around the corner.

Soon afterwards, the day of the wedding dawned and we all drove up to Castle Rising in Norfolk, where Nanny was from. As soon as we got to the church I could feel that chill wind of panic announcing the oncoming storm. I had a starring role as Nanny's pageboy in short red corduroy overalls. We all waited outside the church, my mum like Jackie O in a mini dress, big white earrings and an extraordinary pillbox hat attached to her bouffant, my dad suave in his morning suit. Rockabilly Dave stood with us outside the church as the organ tootled inside and finally Mr Pepper arrived with Nanny, lovely in her wedding dress. On cue the organ piped up into some rousing anthem and I was given Nanny's veil to hold. As the service began, everything fell into place. All the previous conversations when she'd tried to explain to me that she was leaving; all the warnings; all the little asides I had heard but not understood ('I think he's taking it rather well, don't you?' 'Yes, he doesn't seem to mind at all').

Mary Poppins was coming to life, except that I was not being spared the last scene. I was right in there, and I played my part to the hilt. I completely ruined her wedding day. First of all, I started asking questions, tugging at Nanny's dress as the vicar tried to get on with the service.

'Where are you going Nanny, anyway?' I whined.

'Shush,' said my mother from the second row.

But I wouldn't let up. My little quavering whines rose above the drone of the vicar and became more insistent each time I was told to be quiet. No one would answer; I had become invisible. So, as usual, I became hysterical: floods of molten tears burst out over my fat spoilt cheeks as I sat down in the aisle and bawled. My mum tried to take me away but I had hold of Nanny's veil and resisted arrest.

I was terribly upset and so was Nanny, because she loved me too. Dave, on the other hand, had had his fill, so he must have been relieved when the wedding march trumpeted his and Nanny's impending freedom. He began to walk her firmly out of the church, but I still had her by the veil, and I yanked at it with all my might. Freeze frame. My mum tried to prise it out of my hot furious little fists and poor Nanny was stuck there in the middle of the aisle, Dave pulling in one direction and me in the other. Were the guests amused? I'm not sure. A brief impasse ensued, but not for long. My father took over and hauled me out, and the wedding marched on. Poor Nanny was whisked into her car and off to the reception before I had a chance to wreak further havoc. My parents decided it would be too risky for us to go with them, so we drove off without a real goodbye, leaving Nanny to her new life, while we went to stay with my grandparents in nearby Brancaster.

For many years we kept in touch: always a card at Christmas and birthdays; and in the early days Nanny would visit us with her own babies, first one and then a second. But slowly, painlessly, we drifted apart. We moved again; Nanny and Dave split up; I went away to school. The common ground was being washed away. Waves of new experiences effaced the old footprints, and soon Nanny and me were a dot on the horizon.

CHAPTER 3

Brancaster

Through all the moves, the new schools, the holidays and my parents' business trips, the one constant in my life was the house I was born in, and my grandmother who looked after me there whenever my parents went away. My grandparents' house was the most romantic thing in my world. It was a Victorian rectory of flint and brick with steep slate roofs over ornate peeling green gables. It stood between the marshes and the gently rolling Norfolk hills. My grandfather planted a poplar wood to protect us from the rough winds off the North Sea and it was under those endlessly whispering trees that I was lulled to sleep every after- noon in my pram.

I was born on 29 May 1959 'sometime before tea'. No one can remember exactly when, and my birth certificate holds no clue. I was delivered by our local doctor, Jarvis Woodsend. My father was painting the garage doors as Dr Woodsend drove past and cheerfully called out, 'It's a boy, all eleven pounds of him.' My father fell off the ladder and cut himself. Those were the days. No epidural for my poor screaming mother. Just her mother, the midwife and Jarvis Woodsend, who had an appointment to play golf at half past four.

If things were quite relaxed in our house, at my grandparents' the clock was turned back and we lived by the standards of the Edwardian age. My grandfather was the alpha male of our family and I was terrified of him. He was not particularly interested in little children and in the dining room at 'the old rec' we sat with Nanny at a table apart from the grown-ups and talked in low voices if we had any sense. If we got too noisy my grandfather would make some crushing remark that could reduce us to tears, so we mostly kept quiet. But in a way, we were all in the same boat because he found his own children – my mother, Uncle David and Aunt Katherine – equally irritating at times. He loved my grandmother, his parrot Polly, books, sailing, the news and of course the Queen on Christmas Day. (That event still brings my entire family to a standstill.) For Grandpa, everything else was a distraction. Sometimes his mother, Great-Granny M, would come and stay, and we would have to go and kiss her goodnight in bed. It was frightening and exciting to kiss her bearded face and sometimes you could see her breast peeping through her nightdress. She was the bohemian in our strict naval family. One day Great-Granny M made an announcement: 'Roo is musical.'

We were all on our best behaviour when Grandpa was around, and our mutual fear and respect for him made for a kind of camaraderie in our old-fashioned family. He was a huge man, extremely antisocial, but also very funny when he wanted to be. Everyone was in awe of him, except my grandmother. They had been in love since they were children, and theirs was one of the most successful relationships I have ever seen. They were perfectly matched, both equally formidable, quite frosty to the outside world, and quite reserved with each other, but they were very happy together. And after my mother, Granny was the person I loved most in the world.

In the summer months we would go sailing in my grandfather's blue sailing boat, the *Wayfarer*. She was moored in a creek on the marsh next to her little pale blue tender, a rowing boat named *Sieve*. A sailing morning would begin with my grandfather announcing at breakfast (a meal, like all others, where you had better not be late) the predictions of his treasured best friend, the barometer. If high tide was at about noon and if the wind was of a favourable direction and strength, it would probably mean that we would be sailing. A flurry of militarised activity would ensue. The women disappeared to the kitchen to help Miss Cottrell, the cook, while the men, which included me, would set about organising the sail bags and batons for the *Wayfarer*, the rowlocks and oars for *Sieve*, and the binoculars and rugs for our picnic. Laden down with this seafaring treasure, our strange family caravan left by the west door of the house, across the lawn that sloped down towards the water garden where Granny kept her Muscovy ducks, through the poplar wood, over the bank and across the dyke that separated the low Norfolk farmlands from the sea. My grandfather strode ahead while the family chatted behind him. ('I thought Miss Cottrell looked a bit under the weather, this morning.' 'She's having a terrible problem with her left knee.' 'Will someone remember to close that gate?' 'Roo? You're the last.')

You were in another world once you stepped out onto the Norfolk marshes; our voices blew away on the salty wind into the huge grey sky. It blustered in your face and roared past your ears if you stood against it. When it stopped there was an eerie silence broken by the screech of a sandpiper high above and the gurgling of the incoming tide through the marsh below. The marshes stretched out as far as the eye could see. A track snaked through them towards the *Wayfarer*, past banks of sea grass and samphire, where boats lay, beached whales ludicrously dumped by the tide, sometimes tilted against a bank, sometimes sunk into the mud like alligators. There was an old black abandoned tugboat that had a chimney with a conical hat. It could have been Peggotty's house from *David Copperfield*. We would arrive at *Sieve* and in groups of twos and threes would be shunted to the *Wayfarer*: men first, of course, to get the boat ready, women and children second with the food.

Eventually, everything was 'shipshape' and we would all take our positions. Children would be laced into life jackets, while my grandfather sat at the helm in his straw hat giving orders, a grown-up at each side to man the foresail, and someone to release us from our mooring and pull up the anchor. Precision was the order of the day. The sails would flap noisily as they discovered the wind and we'd be off, tacking through the creeks, until we reached the ocean. As the *Wayfarer* took the wind and we careered towards the oncoming bank, my grandfather would shout, 'Ready about!' and we'd all duck down. The two grown-ups at the front were coiled springs on the foresail, waiting for my grandfather's word, and when, finally, he gave it – 'Leo!' – the boom would swing, the foresail flap, and at the last minute the *Wayfarer* would elegantly turn and head out for the open sea.

I always crouched on the floor out of the wind, and would spy on the faces of my family framed by the towering white sail against the sky, sitting up straight in the wind, chatting, laughing. Uncle David, a dutiful son in the old tradition, was a huge handsome man with jet-black hair and thick eyebrows; his relationship with my grandfather was almost military. He was not particularly encouraged as a young man, and neither was my Aunt Katherine, who was very shy. Never to be married. And my mother, Spikey, was the bully of the family. The sisters had been vaguely educated by nuns at Les Oiseaux convent somewhere in the North of England. Both girls converted to Catholicism and addressed one another as 'my child'.

Our destination was often Bird Island, a wildlife sanctuary that you could walk to at low tide. We would have our picnic there, huddled away from the wind in the dunes; the children would drink hot Bovril and play with shrimping nets, and the grown-ups would talk about mysterious incomprehensible things like Churchill and devaluation.

But what I liked more than sailing, which actually at the time I dreaded, was to have permission to stay at home with Nanny and Miss Cottrell and Mrs Ransom, the housekeeper. After the sailing party clattered out, a kind of tension evaporated like a huge sigh and the house was quiet. On these days I had the run of the place. I particularly loved sitting in the attics where old trunks full of my grandfather's naval regalia were piled up next to thousands of magazines from the forties and fifties. I would dress up and spend hours leafing through *Country Life* and *The Field* with their pictures of sexless debutantes and their antique houses for sale. The Christmas decorations were also kept in a box in the attic, stored in old newspaper; I would carefully unwrap them and stare for hours at my distorted reflection in the round silver and pink balls.

I had been born in a big grey room at the end of the house that looked out over the drive. It had a huge old Victorian wardrobe, and I would get inside it and play there for hours on end. I loved silence. Sitting there in the darkness of the half-closed cupboard, listening to the noises of the house. A far-off loo flushing; bathwater gushing down the old copper drains; the wood pigeons in the trees outside; my grandmother's car crunching across the gravel. It felt magical. Watching the world through the crack in the wardrobe door, everything was beautiful, even the dust that floated through the shafts of sunlight from the windows.

At teatime the family would return, banging around and running baths. From the snippets of conversation I could gather what kind of a day they'd had and soon Mummy or Nanny would call. I would tingle with pleasure at the sound of their voices. 'Roo? Where are you?' But I wouldn't move. Then I'd hear them coming. They knew all my haunts and so they would go from one hiding place to another, a tide of foot-steps and voices coming and going and then coming again, until finally the door of the room where I was born would open. I would shrink to the back of the wardrobe and hold my breath, but soon that door would open too, Nanny's familiar arms would reach in and pull me out from behind one of my grandmother's mothballed ballgowns, and we would go down together to the drawing room for tea.

CHAPTER 4

Virgin Queen

One day my mother and I went up to London to a shop called Gorringes where she bought me grey clothes: shorts, sweaters, shirts, socks – all grey, four pairs of each. I can't remember having any particular reaction, mild curiosity perhaps. I gambolled around as we bought a trunk and a little overnight case that I still have, but I was totally unaware that during the next few days the first significant part of my life would die and nothing would ever be the same.

During those last evenings of freedom my mum sewed labels into my new outfits and piled them up together in the spare room along with sheets, towels, a dressing gown and slippers. The labels had my name on them, followed by a number.

I was going away to school. Strangely enough, I was totally unfazed by this information. The night before we left, I packed and repacked my overnight case in a boisterous fever of excitement. My parents and brother were gathered around. Apparently I could not take the red tweed skirt. I thought that was a bit odd, but I let it pass in the general exuberance I was feeling at being an adult.

'You're being very grown-up about this, I must say,' remarked my mother.

'Well, I am seven,' I replied proudly.

But my brother watched through his tortoiseshell glasses with the cynical eyes of one informed by the past.

The next morning we got into the car to make the five-hour drive to Basingstoke in Hampshire. Again, not a twinge; I said goodbye to Susan. She knew but I didn't. She gazed at me soulfully as I dollied past on my way to the luggage-crammed Hillman.

During the drive the others became quieter and quieter. Finally after several hours we turned a corner and my brother said, 'We're here.' We drove down a long avenue lined with huge ancient trees full of rooks' nests and my heart began to beat with an unknown drug: adrenalin. Suddenly we were in a row of cars also laden down with trunks and bikes. Glum, malicious boys stared out from within. We got to the entrance: huge stone columns straddled by heraldic lions and thick black wrought-iron gates, beckoning one into hell. My heart jumped into my mouth and sheer terror surged through my body as a grey-flint stately home rose up before us at the end of a sweeping drive.

We hit a sort of traffic jam of upper-class couples driving back to London. Why were some of the women crying? We parked the car and got out. Instinct told me to stay close to my mother. I could hardly breathe, I was asphyxiated by panic. There were boys everywhere, all shapes and sizes, running in and out of the school in gangs, shouting and screaming. The unfamiliar smell of floor polish and school loos hung in the air. A continuous stream of cars came and went, cracking across the gravel. Boys buried themselves in their mothers' coats. Others stood defiantly apart, little heads bowed. Teachers, most of them retired army officers and well-to-do spinsters, mingled through the crowd as if it were a village fête. I was mesmerised. This could not be. My mother would never leave me in a place like this.

We were met by a shuffling man with a pipe – the headmaster, Mr Trappes-Lomax. He was shrouded in a wispy microclimate of foul-smelling smoke, and his wife Mary (Mrs Trappes-Lomax to us) was dressed for the Second World War. They introduced us to Matron Walters, a little old hunchbacked hag who, dragging herself one banister at a time, took us upstairs to see the dormitories. More unruly boys roamed the upstairs passages of this once gracious home, pulling their trunks and tuck-boxes across the old wooden floors past rooms filled with rows of black wrought-iron cots covered with bare mattresses. My dormitory was St Anthony's. My mother put my little night case on my bed, and before I could open my mouth Mr Trappes-Lomax suggested that my brother took me down to the school dining room for tea while he escorted my parents to 'the drawing room' for a glass of sherry. My grasp on my mother's hand turned into a sweaty vice-like grip.

'Darling,' she said, as she unprised my hand from hers, her voice carefully casual, 'we'll probably go while you're having tea so I'll kiss you goodbye now.'

And then all the energy that had been building up exploded in torrents of the deepest pain I have ever experienced. Tears flash-flooded down my face, drenching my little grey shirt. I begged and begged not to be left, or at least for my parents to wait till after tea. Finally, she agreed. My brother took me down into the bowels of the evil-smelling prison, through endless passages crowded with boys – me blinded by my tears, him grim, weary and silent.

Inside the huge refectory, the din and energy were terrifying. Separated from my brother (he was at the ten-year-olds' table), I was given a little cake with white icing and sat in abject grief until finally the meal ended and we raced through the school, trying to find my mother and father.

We caught them outside the front door near the Hillman. My dad patted me on the back and said, 'Good luck,' as he got into the car, but my mother stood there, guilty, uncertain and tear-stained in her Jackie O hat. 'Don't cry or I'll cry too,' she said, as she hugged me for the last time. My mind was racing. There must be something I could say to bring an end to this madness.

But all I could think of was: 'What will Susan say?'

'She'll understand. I'll tell her you'll be back any minute now at half-term.'

'It isn't any minute now,' I said with a tide of fresh tears.

'Come on!' said the major.

She stumbled into the car and shut the door. I looked down at the tears splashing on to my shoes: new sandals from Startrite. Last week I had loved them, but now they were just another part of the plot against me. I couldn't look up. I didn't want to see the betrayal in my mother's eyes. My brother took my hand and nudged me as my mother unwound the window and waved.

'What are you looking at, darling?' She was crying and her mascara had run.

'My shoes,' I said. And I looked up, but the car had already moved off.

We watched the Hillman glide down the long avenue towards the gates, my mother looking back at us and waving, my father's face firmly fixed on the road ahead. Still holding hands – frozen between one world and the next – my brother and I stared at the tail lights with a terrible intensity as they disappeared around the corner. Maybe they would wink a sudden reprieve, the whole image would dissolve and we would be back at home at the end of a nasty dream. As long as we could see them we were still in some kind of contact. But with their last glimmer died all hope and we were left to make our own way through the rest of our lives in the tradition of our Empire-ruling forebears.

But where was the fucking Empire?

What was it about the English upper classes of that era that drove them to procreate and then abandon their children to the tempestuous dangers of boarding school? In the days of Empire, the British ruling class had to make sure that all colonial officials were hard cases. Thus boarding schools were born. A child with a soft vulnerable heart soon had it calcified by abandonment, bullying, beatings and buggery: the rigours of prep and public school. He was soon conditioned, so that by the time he became a faceless gnome in the 'diplomatic' he was without feelings of the normal sort and could be utterly ruthless in the service of his or her Britannic Majesty.

But why us? The Empire was over. There was no need for us to be boiled alive, but our parents were paranoid Conservatives. Their Moses was Enoch Powell and my early years were full of catchphrases like 'Rivers of blood'; 'We didn't fight a war for this'; 'It was much better when . . .' Actually it was not. It was much more fun with Twiggy and the Beatles, whooping it up in a miniskirt and an afghan coat. But not for the Everetts. We were as conventional as they came. And so there I was, one chilly April evening in 1967, a 'new boy' at Farleigh House School, Farleigh Wallop, Basingstoke, Hants.

That first night the lights were turned off at six-thirty although it wasn't dark outside. A wood pigeon cooed dreamily from a nearby tree as all the little boys sobbed in their beds. We were heartbroken but soon most of us passed out from exhaustion. Only a boy called Wilson wailed all night. The next morning we woke and remembered where we were with a deep shudder and the sobs began with renewed anguish as Matron Walters herded us down to breakfast. Now we were on our own in a vicious, jeering jungle of boys.

In those far-off days there was definitely a St Trinian's feel to the English prep school. To start with, teachers were not subjected to particularly rigorous training or investigation. The war had left an abundance of army officers who took to the blackboard, and Farleigh House was a school run by a motley crew of washed-up Empire rulers. The school had been the seat of the Wallop family, whose circumstances were reduced after the war (even though they quickly became rich again by developing half of Basingstoke), and was pioneered by a Captain Trappes-Lomax, a man without the faintest hint of a qualification. He started the school in the late fifties and died of a heart attack in 1965, while he was having a bath. His brother, the pipe-smoking Mr Steven Trappes-Lomax, stepped valiantly into his sibling's shoes. Mr Stevens, as he was known, was a terrifying figure to the boys. He had a moustache like Hitler and soft googly eyes that blinked a lot. He wore a musty, tobacco-smoked tweed jacket and was prone to make spot checks on the dormitories at night. His tall, slightly hunched silhouette stalked the dark night-time corridors with his torch. If there was 'fooling in dorm' the suspects would be rounded up and told to come down to 'the drawing room' in fifteen minutes, where one's punishment would be administered, carried out with full country-house decorum. First offenders were congenially shown the ropes: 'If you'd be so good as to bend over that chair, I'm afraid I'm going to give you six.'

It was always two, four or six. The 'gymmie' was one of old Mr Trappes-Lomax's faded lace-up plimsolls and was kept in a bottom drawer next to the chair. Six of the best was agony through your pyjamas, and it was therefore preferable to be summoned after breakfast the next morning. Then at least a bit of blotting paper between butt cheek and pants could soften the blow.

Our mornings began at seven-twenty. Matron Walters' Edwardian walking shoes could be heard clunking around in the passage, getting ready for a ludicrous daily procedure known as 'temperatures'. She would storm into the freezing dormitory and open the curtains.

Bleary-eyed boys shuffled out to the thermometers. Each boy had his own, marked with name and number, and we would stand in line, half asleep in our dressing gowns, for the two allotted minutes before she would take them out of our mouths, squint at the mercury, shake the thermometer and send us off. No sooner had we learnt the ropes than elaborate plans would be hatched to give ourselves temperatures and thus a morning in the sick room. We used to put our thermometers in hot water and groan, but unfortunately Bilgo, as she was called, was blind as a bat and we would be sent on our way anyhow.

Down to the chapel for prayers or, if it was a holiday of obligation, mass, and then breakfast, after which Mr Stevens would read out a list of those he wanted to see in the drawing room for a session with the gymmie. We were obliged to take a shit after breakfast and then sign something called the tick board. A tick if one had shat, a cross if one had not. So there was mayhem every morning in the main hallway between boys lining up for the few loos, other boys lining up outside the drawing room waiting for punishment, and others running around pretending to be aeroplanes etc. It was a three-course meal of prayer followed by defecation and punishment, but all this ended as 'the clanger' – a kind of town crier's bell – was rung by some smug prefect and classes would begin. If you had, against all the odds, managed to get a morning in the sick room, which would absolve you from the downstairs rituals, you could achieve a feeling of intense peace as the bell clanged and echoed through the vast house and the constant din of children suddenly evaporated. Footsteps everywhere. Doors slammed and then silence. If the sick room was empty, you could secretly unfold your *Beano* and settle down in the clean sheets to wait for Matron and a Haliborange vitamin pill.

My name was Everett Two. My brother was Everett One. Our first names were sacred to the memories of our mothers and were never used until they called us by them as the school train squealed to a halt at Waterloo. CJ, my form master, was very dapper. He'd been a priest or was about to become one, I can't remember which, but he had a black cigarette holder, black thick dandruffy hair and a miniature black poodle whose name escapes me. He was mostly a gentle man, though a couple of terms later, when he became headmaster, he was subject to fits of rage and gymmie-happy mornings in the drawing room.

MAJ was an exhausted old gentleman who taught English. He had caught malaria in the tropics when he was young and as a result moved very slowly. Between classes, there was always an explosion of play in the form room until someone would hiss, 'He's coming!' and we would all scamper back to our little desks and be quiet. MAJ entered a room with languid dramatic flair. He always travelled with an acolyte from his last class who carried a large woman's wicker basket for him, in which MAJ kept his books, an apple and the morning paper. In the sudden hush we could hear the drinks-party banter between him and his little pilot fish.

'My sister saw your grandmother last week in Burnham Market.'

'Oh really, sir? How is your sister?'

'In terribly good form. Now where are we?'

And then in he'd sweep. The acolyte would put the basket on the table and be discharged, and class would begin. MAJ was a kind man. When I left Farleigh under a slight cloud and was miserable in some crammer on the south coast, he wrote me one of the sweetest letters I have ever received. He was a real character, extremely eccentric, but he could get nasty. Once, during English composition, I had written a sentence in my exercise book which ended with '. . . And off they went.' The only problem was that I'd written 'of' instead of 'off'.

MAJ went ballistic. 'What have you written, Everett Two?' his shrill and menacing voice screamed into my ear.

' "And off they went", sir.' I replied, followed by an enormous whack across the head with a ruler.

'No, you haven't, you silly boy. What have you written?'

I looked at the page and couldn't think what my mistake had been, so I repeated, ' "And off they went", sir.' Bang went the ruler again.

And so this dialogue continued, gathering a violent momentum with each question and erroneous answer. MAJ could really go for it. He grabbed me by the hair, slapped me over the back of the head and almost rubbed my nose in my book. It was terrifying. 'What have you written?' He was red and screaming now, frothing at the mouth. I remember looking at the page in my exercise book, unable to think, not daring to speak, waiting for the next blow. When someone was getting it, the atmosphere became electric; the class would be quiet and tense; no one moved a muscle for fear that the storm would divert itself onto someone else before it blew out. Luckily for us, MAJ was quite frail and his blood was thin from the malaria so that after a bit he would have to sit down. He would clutch his basket and take a quinine pill, and things would slowly go back to normal.

But actually Farleigh House was a lovely school and I was very happy there. At some point during my first winter term it began to snow. I remember being stunned. It fell past the high arched windows of form two, and fluttered silently across the park in front of the house. It didn't let up for days. The country came to a standstill and to make matters worse, or better for the boys, the power cuts began. At four o'clock our whole school was plunged into darkness, and candles and oil lamps would be lit while outside the silent storm swirled into glorious drifts for us to play in the next day at break. It was just like the *Beano Christmas Annual*. Boys huddled around candles telling ghost stories. The huge stately home with its corridors, back staircases and high ceilings became the set for a horror film, full of dark cavernous shadows where the bullies of the school would lurk and pounce out on us weeds as we scuttled from one candlelit pool to another.

The chapel was mesmerising after sunset. Candles blazed in their silver sconces on the altar and when our bushy-browed priest raised the monstrance containing the host and held it above his head to bless us, a huge medieval shadow leapt up the wall behind him like Satan about to lunge at us and we all gasped as one. It was Catholicism at its very best: a converted dining room, donated family silver, an Irish priest in red satin; wide-eyed boys with the names of the counties their families owned; and, strangely enough, God. In the quartz sky and the crystal ground; in the breathtaking madness of upper-class Catholic ritual; in Mr Wilson's power cuts. But most of all, God was still in us boys, in our wide-eyed wonder at everything we were seeing. We forgot our miseries and ambitions, the cruel abandonments, and just lived in blissful excitement.

It was during this time that I went to confession and, choosing my words very carefully, revealed to the Father behind the grille that I had been 'vulgar'. I could see him smiling to himself in the shadows of the sacristy. I suppose he thought I'd said something rude but the vulgarity I was talking about was of a very different nature. There seemed little point in correcting the misunderstanding and so I was absolved with a penance of only three Hail Marys. Absolution was never far away. Confession, like defecation, was regimented at Farleigh House.

Our music teacher was another ex-soldier, but this time from the ranks, Mr Paul Issitt. He had been a regimental bandleader and could play every instrument and he had a kind of barrack-room familiarity that we loved. I was fascinated and followed him as though he were Jesus. He was bald with a huge beaky nose and sometimes when he opened his mouth one could glimpse the most elaborate silver scaffolding supporting the roof of his mouth. His sidekick, or girlfriend, was the divine Miss Jellyman. She was a beautiful woman with short auburn hair but she was confined by polio to a wheelchair and had little lifeless legs like sausages. She worked in the school office as a secretary in the mornings and then taught the clarinet in the afternoons before being wheeled up the avenue by Mr Issitt to the estate cottage they shared with MAJ.

They arrived at Farleigh at the same time as me. Soon Mr Issitt had formed an orchestra and we were putting on *The Mikado*. Strangely enough I had no urge to play Yum Yum or Pitti Sing and was blissfully happy next to Miss Jellyman in my role as second clarinet. I did have a sort of pang when Miss J produced some greasepaint on the day of the dress rehearsal and Mr Issitt showed the boys how to put on their make-up. The smell of it was intoxicating. The show was a triumph. My best friend Noel Two sang 'Tit Willow' and I accompanied him on the clarinet.

The music room became my headquarters, and quite soon I had the job of pushing Miss Jellyman to lunch every day from the main house to the prefab dining room in the old kitchen gardens. I was terribly proud of this great responsibility – I adored Miss Jellyman – and received a packet of supplementary fruit gums every week. Mr Issitt taught me piano and I learnt fast. In no time I was playing the organ at mass on Sundays and benediction on Fridays. My favourite part was communion when everyone shuffled up to the altar to receive the sacrament and I had to play something quiet and moody. 'Where is Love?' from *Oliver* was my favourite but show tunes raised some eyebrows from the more fundamentalist staff members. Mr Stevens finally drew the line one morning after I had played an artful medley on the theme of 'Somewhere Over the Rainbow' as the sacrament was taken from the tabernacle.

The holidays were heralded by the trunks coming down from the attics and hysteria fell upon the school. Nobody could sleep. Boys talked all night about their dreams for the hols. Our teachers and their rules relaxed. Stories were read instead of lessons being taught, until finally the morning arrived when two huge coaches crackled down the drive. We all piled in while Mr Stevens smoked his pipe benignly at the front door, Mrs Stevens by his side. They waved as we rumbled off through those huge grey gates of hell, down the avenue towards Basingstoke station. Mr Issitt and Miss Jellyman waved from their cottage gate, MAJ from his, and suddenly it was over.

It was April 1967 when I started at Farleigh House. My eighth birthday was on 29 May and my mother sent me a large multicoloured cake. It became infested with ants, but I ate it anyway. I sliced it with care, and ants scuttled out carrying huge crumbs on their heads. Nobody minded. We weren't going to sacrifice good cake for a few ants! I shared it with my new friends and made it last for weeks.

I stayed at Farleigh House until I was twelve. Terms and holidays came and went. Our little hearts hardened with each beat. We cried less and grew fast. Like jellies we began to set in the moulds of class, religion and nation, and if life before boarding school had been time-less, then the clock began to tick with the school years and time played its usual tricks. Holidays rushed by and term time dragged along. The groundwork for a life of anxiety was being laid. The joy of returning home would be fringed with subconscious panic as one counted off the days left until the beginning of the next term.

During those first years at Farleigh I became extremely religious and spent hours praying for a visitation from Our Lady. I wanted to be a saint with my own basilica. In the holidays I vainly knelt for hours underneath an apple tree in the orchard at home. I was waiting for Mary to come floating down and tell me terrible secrets concerning the fate of humankind that I would then have to impart to the pope him-self, thereby, of course, avoiding school. Obviously, nothing happened except that during my last year, when I was twelve, I failed all the exams that were meant to get me into my next school – public school – and was removed from Farleigh House in the dead of night and sent to a crammer at Seaford in Sussex. I was miserable and so were my parents. Something was wrong but who knew what? I lasted six weeks.

Then I was sent to a school called Milton Abbey in Dorset where I was even more miserable. I managed to scream my way out of that after a couple of months and was removed in the middle of the term and allowed to come home while my parents regrouped. Finally, at the end of the summer they managed to get me a place in the Catholic monastery, Ampleforth College, in Yorkshire. I was thirteen. My brother was already there and had run away twice. It did not seem very promising.

CHAPTER 5

Stage Beauty

Ampleforth Abbey was a drizzly Dickensian village nestled against the steep wooded banks of a huge and beautiful valley on the Yorkshire moors. The Abbey church itself dominated its surroundings. It had been built in the twenties or thirties and was like a child's drawing of an old gothic cathedral. The original school was older, made of honey-coloured stone with towers, steep slate roofs and huge latticed windows. The oldest part, St Oswald's House, was sliding down the valley and had to be held up by huge wooden buttresses. Wind wailed around the school, rooks cawed in the woods, and the low heavy boom of the Abbey bells could be heard far away on the moor. If Farleigh House had coaxed and conditioned us into the religious prison, then Ampleforth College was there to throw away the key.

Inside was a labyrinth of vaulted passageways and classrooms, dorms and washrooms, noticeboards and lockers. The place was in turns either totally deserted or bursting with rush-hour traffic. All roads lead to Rome and our school was a delta of meandering tributaries, leading inevitably towards the monastery itself where no boy could set foot without initiation. An invisible line divided the worldly and the other-worldly. The noise and bustle of the school fell sharply away as the silent monastery stretched out before one, where monks in their black habits could be glimpsed gliding through the gloomy cloisters as if on wheels.

Needless to say, I was in the choir, and we were the only boys allowed to set foot inside the hallowed ground. On Sunday mornings before high mass we marched from the music school in our red cassocks and virgin-white surplices as the loudest of the Abbey bells throbbed through the air, shaking the windows. We were led by Mr Bowman, the music teacher (who, to the horror of some of the parents, had sideboards and, worse, wore high-heeled suede boots under his cassock), to a door in the side of the monastery where the shrouded monks waited for us in long blood-curdling lines, a black Ku Klux Klan. Ampleforth was Catholic ritual on a grand scale. On a cue from the Abbot we were led into the vast church by acolytes swinging silver bowls on chains billowing with incense. The hooded monks appeared out of a scented mist as the organ took off and nine hundred boys stood as one and launched into a rousing rendition of 'Jerusalem' or some other piece of propaganda.

It was all very clever. You felt as if you belonged to something big; your spine tingled with an Arthurian sense of destiny; and the plan was that you left Ampleforth a raunchy eighteen-year-old boy bursting with testosterone, a fully formed Empire builder with the added twist of a Catholic agenda. After ten years of prep and public school you were part of the gang; and if you weren't, then you were a freak or a fairy. Luckily for me, I was both.

But Ampleforth was effective. I learnt who I was. Or at least who I wasn't. I was not going to be part of that gang. I was probably going to be homosexual and that meant I was going to have to learn how to act.

The theatre was another Victorian pile built into the side of the hill. It had a musty sexy smell and underneath the stage was the green room, the domain of Algy Haughton, the theatre teacher. He had long white hair, a handlebar moustache and lived in a caravan with his wife Rosemary and their hundreds of children. He was a hippie, I suppose, because when he left a few terms later, he moved to a commune called Lothlorien. He presided over the green room like a latter-day actor-manager behind a huge theatrical desk covered with scripts and papers. The drop-outs and freaks of the school gathered around him, sitting on the weird furniture that had been clumsily constructed for various

bygone productions. A mock throne stood next to an enormous chaise
longue under Mrs Haughton's ingenious velvet drapes. It was freezing
in the green room and there was only a double-pronged electric fire to
warm Fagin's gang but this didn't make any difference. There was a
kettle, a huge tin of Nescafé and, if you were lucky, a sticky jar of powdered milk. Games and classes could be safely skipped by hiding in the
green room; smoking, drinking and sex could take place without the
risk of discovery. If anyone was coming you could first hear a faraway
boom as the enormous oak door of the theatre foyer slammed shut, followed by distant echoing footsteps, closer and closer, until finally an
awkward shuffle down the narrow stairs that led to the green-room
door. And if that wasn't enough, one could lock the door from inside
and bolt through another door onto the rugby fields below.

The first play I was in was *Julius Caesar*. I played Cinna the poet. It
was a small part, involving only being beaten up by the rabble and
running screaming from the theatre. It was an easy role and the only
male one I was to play during my entire Ampleforth career. The leading lady was a boy called Wadham. He was one year older than me and
exuded an icy professionalism. He played Calphurnia, Caesar's wife.
Everyone seemed to shrink in his presence. I looked at him and I knew:
this was a great actress. I had to make him my friend.

I went unremarked as Cinna the poet but next term the exhibition
play – the one that was to be performed for the parents at the end of the
summer term – was to be A *Midsummer Night's Dream* and I landed
the role of Titania, Queen of the Fairies.

Rehearsals took place after house supper, which was at about six-
thirty in the evening. I would race down the hill from my house to the
theatre with my heart in my mouth. Never would show business be
more exciting. I literally lived and breathed the play. Wadham was
making a rare appearance as a male and gave us his Puck. We quickly
became friends and forged what was to become a legendary team: the
Lunts of the Ampleforth Theatre. The strange thing was I couldn't act
at all. Algy Haughton was worried, I could see. He told me where to
move and how to say my lines and I followed his instructions reli-
giously but there was no life in my performance whatsoever.

The week of the production arrived and still I had made no progress.
Rosemary, Algy's wife, made the costumes. Mine was a lovely apple-

green acrylic bodystocking and matching skirt, an ingenious crown woven out of coat hangers topped with large emerald sequins, a gauze train (which got jammed in the green-room door on the first night and never made it onto the stage) and a very fetching peach-blond wig. During my last fitting she tried to cajole me into a performance.

'This is Algy's last show, Everett. You must try and give your best. We need to feel more energy. We need to see the fairy in you.'

'All right,' I replied glumly.

'Show them you're a queen.'

'Okay.'

I was on the verge of tears. I loved the Haughtons and I wanted to make them proud but I was so self-conscious that as soon as I got on stage, I totally lost all sense of myself.

'I can do it when I'm on my own, Mrs H. It's just . . .' I trailed off, my chin a-quiver.

'Don't worry. Just do your best.'

The noise of an audience entering a theatre on the first night of a production produces one of the most extreme sensations I have ever felt. Drugs, sex, punishment and love all pale by comparison. Maybe waiting for the result of an HIV test is similar. The rest of your life just falls away. Your heart bangs in your chest as if it is about to explode. You can hardly speak. When the lights go down, an expectant hush descends on the house and you stand in the wings, taut and breathless. You are totally alone but at the same time you're completely merged into the whole human machine of the event. The stagehands, the actors, the dressers: everyone watches the stage intently as it plunges into darkness and you can feel the breeze against your face as the heavy velvet curtain flies out. There is an electricity of concentration that makes one believe in weird things like the power of prayer. It is quite extraordinary. And so was what happened next.

Stripped of most of my costume, I was literally bundled up the stairs and into the wings while desperately trying to dislodge my train from the fucking green-room door. That train *was* my performance and I wasn't going anywhere without it, but the others had their way and naked but for the bodystocking I found myself tumbling onto the stage. I froze. An uncomfortable silence followed. I could feel a sort of collective gasp backstage. What next? I just gaped at the audience. I had reached rock bottom. All I could think of was Mrs Haughton. Her words echoed through my frazzled brain: 'Show them you're a fairy. They want to see a queen. Fairy. Queen. Queen. Fairy.'

And then suddenly from out of the static emptiness inside my head came a terrifying high-pitched giggle. It flew out of my mouth – God knows where it came from – and then it stopped. I looked at the audience, aghast. There was a split second of silence and then the strangest thing happened. The house broke into rapturous applause. Well, maybe not rapturous applause, but I got a laugh. Its energy nearly knocked me over. There was no looking back. I literally took off. Possessed, I gallivanted around the stage, ignoring all of Algy's carefully plotted moves and intonations, and cackled up a frenetic vaudeville performance, the like of which no one had ever seen before and hopefully never will again. My fellow actors looked appalled. Wadham stared icily down from his perch on our forest tree but I didn't give a fuck. The audience loved it: I was under their control and they were under mine and that's how it should be. Never did a Titania get so many laughs. I had the house in stitches, and I couldn't get enough of it.

The interval came. I was lying in my bower on top of Barnes who played Bottom, probably at this point waving at the audience. When the curtain came down, Algy and Rosemary rushed onto the stage as if in some Hollywood movie starring Bette Davis. They couldn't believe their eyes. They were ecstatic. I had transformed in the bat of an eye from an awkward child into a stage monster. Wadham came down from his tree and grudgingly admitted that I was 'super'. Maybe I wasn't a traditional Titania, but at least I was something. I think the review in the next term's *Ampleforth Journal* pretty much summed it up. The critic agreed that I had been good, but he said that my performance 'left one with the distinct impression that what Titania really needed was a good spanking'.

The writer of that review was called Ian Davie, a legendary English teacher whose nickname was Dirty Davie. He was a portly gentleman of sixty-odd years, who walked on tiptoe as if he were trying to see into the neighbour's garden. He adored gossip, and was truly fascinated by the boys and their jumpy, erratic progression through puberty towards manhood. He had informants in every dormitory and knew exactly who was doing what and where and to whom. He hated games and loved the theatre. His laughter ranged from a drag falsetto to deep bass and back again in sweeping arpeggios. It was completely infectious. In fact everything about him was catching. He was the single biggest influence of my school days. He would hold forth in his little room of an evening, over coffee and biscuits, with a lofty Wildean turn of phrase that thrilled and inspired his chosen disciples. He was, quite possibly, the kind of teacher who would be struck off today, but he educated in the literal sense of the word. He led you out. He knew what I was about and nudged and cajoled me to become myself.

'I hear you were raped again as you flitted through St Oswald's washroom yesterday evening on your late-night trawl,' he would say as he passed one a chocolate digestive. 'You really must stop encouraging poor X. His passion for you is making him unmanageable in class. You must get your mother to send you a new dressing gown. The one you have is too décolleté. Remember what happened to Diana Dors.'

'She bit off more than she could chew, sir?' (I had a huge overbite and was often compared to that great siren.)

New words, new ideas and a healthy disrespect for everything were the order of the day. And when Algy Haughton retired to Lothlorien, Mr Davie was appointed head of the theatre. He announced that the next year's exhibition play would be Schiller's *Mary Stuart*. I was to take the title role and Wadham was to give his Virgin Queen. Meanwhile, he delegated to another of our clique, a brilliant boy called Dominic Pearce, a production of Noël Coward's *Blithe Spirit*. Noel Two, who it may be remembered played Koko in my prep school's production of *The Mikado*, was also in the play, and Barnes who had shone as Bottom played Madame Arcati. My character, Elvira, was a ghost who had died in front of the fire in her nightie, and so during the next holidays I dragged my bemused mother around the sales to get just the right negligee, holding various outfits against me.

'You'll never get a wink of sleep in that,' said my mother testily.

'Mummy, I'm not going to be in bed, I'm going to be on stage!' I shrieked. I was losing my patience with this woman.

Our kitchen at home was taken over as I tried to dye my new negligee a ghostly grey, and I managed to ruin one of my mother's prize saucepans, but I felt quite smug at the end of the holidays when, along with my school uniform laid out on a bed next to my open trunk, lay a pair of tights and a negligee with my name tags sewn in.

The play was a triumph for Wadham and me. I was perfectly suited to play the skittish Elvira, and Wadham was a chilling dowager. It was my favourite term, and we bubbled over with joy. I erected a dressing room for myself on the theatre's fire escape, complete with signed photos, wig stands, three telephones, and an electric buzzer on the floor so that when I received guests I could press it with my foot and pretend to field phone calls from all my imaginary agents. Wadham and I subscribed to *PCR*, the professional casting magazine, and when *The Boys from Brazil* was going into production Wadham sent a photograph of himself as Queen Elizabeth I to the casting director. We were obsessed by Franco Zeffirelli and would write each other letters from him, inviting us to Cinecittà to take part in a new film. Finally, though, Father Charles, the fire monitor, dismantled my dressing room and I was back with the boys in the green room.

Homosexuality bloomed like a poisonous flower, a deadly nightshade that came out after dark for secret assignations in the shadows of the bell tower or the trees beneath which lay yesterday's monks in the monastic graveyard. Thus in my mind the image of sex was entwined with death. I discovered myself under the blanket of a cold night sky on a bed of skulls and shrivelled hands locked together in prayer clutching their rotting rosary beads. The religion was lashing out at me: I dreamt endlessly of the Last Judgement; I would be naked in the cemetery and the monks would rise up from their graves and drag me down to hell. Thanks to this expensive Catholic education my mind was being split down the middle like a watermelon. During the day I was one person and at night I became someone else. During the term I was one thing and during the holidays I was another. I wanted to be an actor. I was sure, but I had a sense of dread because I was clearly such a sinner. One only had to dip into Genesis to know that Yahweh could be a pretty vengeful queen. The monks would cheerfully tell us: 'Some of you will be chosen by God. You *will* have a vocation. You cannot fight it. It falls upon you.' Was God scouting from his cloud? Would he zap me into a monk in a musty habit trudging off to matins and not a bubbly soubrette in some West End dressing room?

Mary Stuart was my swan song. Encouraged by Mr Davie I had

decided to leave Ampleforth. I couldn't wait to get out: I'd had enough
of priests, and I'd had enough of upper-class blobs. Sadly, I was not a
great Mary Stuart. I had no depth. Wadham, on the other hand, was
sensational as the Virgin Queen. The stage was divided between his
side, upon which we had built a spectacular Elizabethan window, and
my side, which was Fotheringhay Castle with a spiral staircase and an
ominous cardboard door through which I made my final exit.

The play was a symbolic moment. Mary took holy communion one
last time before going to her death. The play was my last communion
with Ampleforth. I was going to die to the past if it was the last thing I did.
I wanted to wipe away every clue that connected me to it. But there was
a hitch: on the last night of the play – the big one – someone had forgotten to set the plumed quill on stage with which Wadham was to sign
my death warrant. I was waiting on my side in my snood, my crucifix
clutched to my breast, watching him go through the agonising decision
of whether to kill me or not. Noel Two, playing Burleigh, had the death
warrant in his hand and was pushing her/him to sign. Finally in a mar-
vellously haughty moment Wadham grabbed the warrant from Noel
Two, but there was no plume on the table. Wadham was momentarily
nonplussed, but being a consummate professional said to Judd, a rather
irritating boy who was playing a herald, 'Boy, where is the royal plume?'

Judd quivered. He had not been taught improvisation. Nobody
moved. People gathered in the wings, aghast. This was the high point of
the play. You could have heard a pin drop. And no plume, even though
the whole plot hinged on it.

'Go!' boomed the Virgin Queen. 'Fetch me a plume!'

Judd scuttled off and came back on stage with a blue Bic biro, which
he gave to Wadham with a flourish. Wadham looked at the biro for a
second and then burst out laughing. Then Noel Two laughed, and
then everyone laughed. Laughing on stage, which is called corpsing, is
sheer delight. You know you've got to stop, but you can't. It gets worse
and worse. Everyone avoids everyone else's eyes and calm is eventually
restored, but one glance at a fellow actor can set the whole thing off
again. Well, we couldn't stop. The audience of our parents politely
pretended not to notice. Finally Wadham managed to pull himself
together, wiped his eyes and signed the death warrant. I braced myself
for my last communion and my final moment on the Ampleforth stage.

I managed to stop myself giggling but as the priest put the host in my mouth, the image of Wadham signing my death warrant with the biro flashed upon me, and I spluttered with suppressed laughter. The host shot out of my mouth onto the floor.

There was a huge collective gasp. None of us knew whether to pick it up or what, because, remember, in the Catholic Church the host *is* Jesus' body and there are all sorts of rules concerning it, and one is that you are not allowed to touch it under any circumstances. Only your tongue can, which raised the question: would Mary lick it up off the ground at this point? Our audience was well versed in Catholic ritual, so they understood my dilemma and started to laugh. I was literally crying. My false eyelashes were halfway down my cheeks on a river of mascara and I'm afraid to say that Mary went to her death on the wave of a huge round of applause.

It was 1975, the year Pol Pot christened zero in Cambodia and the grown-ups talked endlessly about Vietnam. But all that meant nothing to me then. I was just sixteen, three years into the five-year sentence of public school, and I couldn't wait to get out. That weekend I had to persuade my parents to let me leave and pursue a career on the stage. I had expected enormous resistance from my father, but when I asked he just said yes. My mother, on the other hand, behaved like the chorus in a Greek tragedy: 'If you leave school now your life will be a disaster.' She set about persuading my dad to renege on our deal. But once my father had made up his mind, there was no changing it. He knew that I had blind ambition. He had it himself. He knew the best thing to do was to test it, keep our fingers crossed and see what happened. My mum, on the other hand, knew virtually nothing about life and couldn't see that what I really needed was to be set free. She was going to fight me all the way.

Goodbye means nothing when you are young and impatient. The future is there, just out of reach, the only thing that counts. Nothing and nobody means anything by comparison. I went to say goodbye to Mr Davie. It was late afternoon on the last day of term. The setting sun poured through his open window and the gleeful shouts of jubilant marauding boys on the eve of freedom wafted up from the yard below. We chatted about this and that for a while and then fell silent. The kettle boiled. We silently made coffee.

'One last chocolate biscuit?' said Mr Davie. He hid it, but I knew he was sad. He had taken me out of my chrysalis and now I was ready to fly out of the window without even looking back.

I hurriedly finished my coffee, got up and stood at the door. I could hardly contain myself. He sat back in his chair, a wise old Buddha with his hands smoothing his large stomach. Smiling, he gave a little wave: 'Toodaloo.' He blew me a kiss and I flew out on it.

CHAPTER 6

London

London crept onto my consciousness in a series of grainy snapshots. In 1962 my father left the army and we all dutifully piled into the Hillman to set off for Chelsea and the pursuit of his dreams. We didn't last there very long – perhaps the Marquis of Bristol and his import-export business were too heady a wine for a man hitherto contained within the granite colonnades of the staff college at Sandhurst. Soon the memory of town was hidden with the rest of the world behind the trees at the end of our garden in Essex. But as time went on this small corner of London came back into my life in a game of hide and seek. Each time closer, more vivid. I would turn around and find myself there again.

Between the river and the King's Road, between Oakley Street and World's End, lies one of London's sweetest villages: St Thomas More's Chelsea. Hardly anything remains from Tudor times but two or three eighteenth-century streets still stand. Cheyne Row and Upper Cheyne Row flank an ugly Catholic church, The Holy Redeemer, and behind them lie a little warren of lanes. Nineteenth-century London squeezes in on every side, and now the noise of the Embankment is a constant anxious rumble, creating tiny vibrations in every cup, saucer and windowpane. But back then, Chelsea was a quiet bohemian back-water, misty in winter and lazy in the summer; and the King's Road was a suburban high street of greengrocers and the odd art shop.

The Holy Redeemer, with its mesmerising and aristocratic priest, Father De Zulueta (Zulu to his flock; he later drowned off the coast of Spain), was the thriving centre of a rather grand Catholic community in the sixties. I don't know whether this was a contributing factor to my parents' decision to live near by. More likely, it was because my mother's second cousin Sylvia, a formidable family spinster, lived around the corner with her huge water-retaining legs. Either way, one of my first scratchy recollections is of being carried across the street for high mass on Sunday. Aunt Sylvia and my mother walked ahead, in black lace scarves and gloves. Nanny, Simon and I followed behind as our father locked up the house. If I shut my eyes, I can still hear the organ, the church bells, and see Zulu on the steps in his billowing cassock, receiving the faithful as if he were at a dreary cocktail party in the House of Lords.

On weekday mornings my mother and I would drop my brother off at school on the corner of Glebe Place, while my father, whose job fell through the day we arrived in Chelsea, sat in his little study, afraid to leave the house. In those days a man without a job was not to be trusted.

In the afternoons Nanny took us to a garden in some square and sat with the other nannies under the trees while we played on the grass. In my memory London was lit for an endless summer. Rows of prams stood in the shade. Couples sat on rugs and deckchairs. A jungle of lilacs, rhododendrons and towering plane trees were held at bay from the street by cranky uneven railings caked with layers of black paint. The noise of the odd taxi chugging round the square, the distant hum of the city and the gossip of nannies accompanied me as I chatted quietly to myself and picked bunches of daisies for Nanny.

But our labrador, Susan, put an end to our London sojourn by her inability to relieve herself anywhere but inside the house. She would squat with a troubled look at the top of the stairs. It was her dirty protest and it drove my mother to distraction. But Susan wasn't the only one unsuited to a life in town. My parents were country folk at heart and pretty soon the removal van returned and took our family back on the road. For the next five years London turned into a word. The reality – the experience – was almost entirely lost. It was the word that explained my father's absence at work in the City, but as a small schoolboy I came across it again, as if for the first time, from a different perspective. It became an endless jumble of streets falling away through the back window of the taxis that took us boys from stations to dentists, and from dentists to other stations, and so back to the safety and calm of the country. As the school train pulled into Waterloo or King's Cross, our mothers could be seen at the barrier as we craned out of the windows and waved frantically. The noise and smell of London, and an animal need to reclaim our mothers' bodies, crashed over us and made our eyes tear as we leapt out before the train had stopped and ran down the platform towards them. On the journey back to school we sat in the cab with our tails between our legs, and the streets fell away in half the time, swallowing with them the bliss and comfort of the holidays.

Either way, trunks and tuck-boxes were crammed in beside us and my mother presided like a peahen on a moving nest. She always wore gloves and a hat in London. Any contact with the street was always blurred by the protective mothbally swish of her mink coat and accompanied by the smart clip of her high heels.

But when my brother was deemed old enough, we would no longer be met at the end of term, either by her, my father or by the mysterious Christopher Lucy who was sometimes sent to take us to my father's office for lunch. We were to make our way from Waterloo to Liverpool Street on the tube alone. These were our first tentative steps into the wild and we both loved them.

First we took 'the drain' to Bank and then changed to the eastbound Central Line. Our hearts were in our mouths. My brother pretended his was not but I knew by the intense way he studied the signs that it was. I still couldn't read much but I stood beside him in blatant imitation, acting as if I could. It was another turning point. As we climbed onto the escalator a hot dusty metallic wind blew up in our faces, the sexy breath of a city coming in for a first deep kiss. Down on the platform I held on tight to my brother's hand. The ominous black hole of the tunnel seemed to beckon. We flinched against the walls at the rumble of the oncoming train and then we gingerly edged our way into a packed carriage. For a moment I thought I saw Christopher Lucy watching us from behind a *Financial Times*, but when I looked again he was gone.

The lights flickered and the carriage jolted into the tunnel. Bodies pressed against each other in frozen embraces. Businessmen and secretaries lost in their thoughts as the lights leapt back on. The claustrophobia was delightful and terrifying at the same time. It made me want to scream. Hands hung by my face: big hairy ones squeezed into gold wedding bands; delicate worn ones with cracked nail varnish on the ends of fingers bruised from typing. All clutching at something: a briefcase, a handbag, the *Evening News* or a pack of Players turning in restless fingers.

At Bank we followed the swarm of bodies through a maze of tunnels and escalators towards the Central Line. My brother was our grandfather and we were on the *Wayfarer*. He held on to my hand as if it were a tiller and he ploughed intently through the sea of commuters, grim and vigilant. For the first, but certainly not the last, time in my life I had the feeling of being followed: a strange sensation of heat on the nape of my neck. I turned around but everyone was following. This was another London, coming towards me and not falling away . . .

Finally as we arrived in the vast grimy space of Liverpool Street station with its sing-song directions to the fleshpot destinations of Clacton, Frinton-on-Sea and Colchester, my father popped out from behind a wall like the White Rabbit and Christopher Lucy appeared from the rear. My brother and I let out huge moans of frustration, tinged with relief. The two men shook hands as if they were at the end of a military manoeuvre.

'Good work, Lucy,' said my dad.

'Thanks, Major,' said Christopher, and he disappeared into the crowd.

During my second year at Ampleforth I made friends with a boy called Dominic Bohne. 'Boney' lived in Fulham with his mother who was a painter; she had a glorious mane of jungle-red hair and dressed in long cheesecloth skirts. Her boyfriend was one of Boney's elder brother's best friends from school. It was a scandal. They all lived together in a small flat, Boney, his mother, his sister, his brother, and the brother's best friend. It seemed unbelievably sexy to me, but obviously my mother took a very dim view of it all and during the holidays always tried her best to sabotage my trips to Fulham. Boney and I never went to the Great American Disaster or Harrods like other public schoolboys of our age. We hung out instead in Biba and Kensington

Market, and bought patchouli oil and joss sticks, and tried on high-heeled boots and embroidered knee-length Indian shirts. We listened to Mahler and *Sister Morphine*. I spent all my pocket money.

Boney had long hair that was parted in the middle. A career of imitation began and I grew mine. On one of my trips to Fulham, Boney's sister dared me to feel inside her knickers. The three of us were sharing a room together. My shaking hand went up her thigh only to come across a piece of string coming out from inside her . . .

'What on earth—' I said, visibly recoiling. I was still terrifically proper. Boney and his sister broke out into peals of laughter, and then he pulled up her nightie in a practical, matter-of-fact way that shocked and impressed me.

'Well, you want to have a look, don't you?' said Boney.

'Oh, gosh,' I said, as we all studied the white string. 'It looks like the fuse to a bomb.'

'You can pull it out if you want,' said Boney nonchalantly.

'I don't think I will, actually,' I replied, somewhat stiffly (but not where it counted).

Boney's sister and me began a sweet cuddly affair, but it was Boney I really loved, though not in a sexual way; he was a haughty beauty and I was his acolyte. I felt like a different person in the gloriously anarchic world of their flat in Fulham. Sometimes, at night, I would watch Boney and his sister while they slept, the orange light from the street cutting across their pretty faces, casting shadows under their lashes. They were indifferent to the creaks and groans in the adjoining bedroom. They seemed to accept everything. Nothing was suppressed. I tried to imagine a similar episode taking place in my family: lying awake in a next-door room as my mother was bonked by Anthony Brew, my brother's best friend. What would happen? My brother would be found hanging from a rafter in the stables and I would have left home with our forty-five-year-old groom whom I quite fancied (and who, I was sure, fancied me). Our family's life ruined for ever: care for me, prison for Mummy and a life of shame for the major. And then, laughing out loud in the middle of the night, I suddenly realised that I wasn't just in Fulham; I had gone to a place where my family couldn't get me back.

I loved Boney, his family and London. I always rushed to their flat from Fulham Broadway station, across the humpback bridge into that maze of endless identical streets, in a kind of ecstasy. The triangular blue skyscraper of Lillie Road presided over the low chimneypots; for me, it was the Statue of Liberty. Later, when Boney and I ventured out together, and the street was already cold and dark, the skyscraper caught and held the light, in a time zone of its own, splashed orange by the setting sun under a huge pink and white sky. It didn't matter where we were going – the corner shop, Chinatown, the World's End: it was all flashing lights and freedom.

Returning once from a visit to the Bohnes, breezing down the platform of Witham station towards my perplexed mama, wearing what my father called 'that bloody sari', I embarked upon that process of isolation that precedes a full-blown teenage revolution. Family life was suddenly claustrophobic; it seemed as though time were running out. I had one thought in my head: I had to leave Ampleforth. London was a closing door, and I had to bolt through it before it slammed. With a mad click in my head I set off at a frenetic pace.

And so I finally moved to the metropolis in September 1975. My mother had very carefully selected my digs, in the home of Mr and Mrs White of Cathcart Road in Earl's Court, just behind the Fulham Road. Friends of friends with children of my age. For £16 a week I was lodged and fed. My mother had craftily contrived that weekends would be extra, but I had no intention of going home. I had £6 a week and a bicycle. My little room was on the top floor and pretty soon it was swathed in Indian finery from Barkers bargain basement (Biba had closed down) and drenched in a smog of sandalwood joss sticks.

Mrs White was a great cook and often entertained. Not being a member of the family, I would have my supper in the little television room between the kitchen and the dining room next door. It was very cosy: the polite burble and clink of the party through the wall; *The Two Ronnies* on the telly; the White family dogs Samson and Biscuit at my feet, waiting for leftovers and a late-night walk.

I was enrolled in a rather louche sixth-form college called Mander Portman & Woodward, situated near by in Rosary Gardens. No one ever met Mr Mander, but Rodney Portman and Peter Woodward were more like stockbrokers than headmasters, and lounged about their office in City suits and brightly coloured braces. They were on to a good thing: they'd rented a large ugly house and found a lot of rather amusing characters as teachers (guns for hire, with their own lives and ambitions beyond teaching). Once they had given the place a coat of white paint, covered the floors with a good solid hair-cord carpet, and got some tables and chairs – bingo: they had a school.

I studied History of Art and English and, as far as I could see, so did almost everyone else. They were the easiest subjects: three lessons per course per week, and the rest of your time was your own. My new schoolmates were the unruly rich. Some had been asked to leave their public schools, some had left of their own accord, and some seemed hardly to have been educated at all.

I enjoyed every moment of it and grew nearly a foot in a year, as if liberated from the constraints of boarding school. I was the only boy in a class of seven girls. I looked forward to tutorials, much as one anticipates a really good party.

Flora McEwan was a tall, beautiful sixteen-year-old, with rosy cheeks and an infectious laugh that showed her teeth and gums to great effect. She had come straight from a convent in Ascot and lived with her family in the street parallel to mine. She jogged beside me as I rode my bike on the way to school. She looked undeniably eccentric, galloping through The Boltons across the Brompton Road, but I looked pretty kooky too in my grandfather's knee-length naval cape, striped wool football socks under rolled-up trousers, and a long purple Dr Who scarf.

Emma de Vere Hunt, was straight out of the pages of St Trinian's. She was wafer thin, with long blonde hair and a gash of red lips on a birdlike face. She wore the tightest jeans imaginable, a tailored tweed jacket and perched on scarlet stiletto boots that matched the pack of Marlboros clutched in her long red fingernails. Much more sophisticated than the rest of us, she sauntered round the school as though she owned the place. For one thing, she had been at Holland Park Comprehensive where you might not have got A levels in class but you could certainly get Class A at any level.

Her boyfriend was one of the misunderstood rebel heroes of our day, a man whose very name made upper-class mothers shudder: the beautiful and damned Charlie Tennant. He was the son of Colin Tennant who owned the island of Mustique, and his mother had been my mother's bridesmaid. He would wait for Emma after school in dirty black drainpipes and a leather jacket. He had golden-blond hair and was very good looking; but he had a stoop before he should have done and at twenty-one he had been through it all. He was saddled with terrible obsessive-compulsive disorders at a time before they had really been medically identified. Sometimes he would make ten attempts to jump over some unseen boundary as he tried to enter a room, or turn round and round in a kind of agony before getting into a taxi, waiting for some invisible green light to go off in his head. It was sad to watch as there was nothing you could do to help. Drugs eased things for Charlie, though not much. The matrons of Belgravia might shrink at the mention of his name, but actually he was extremely shy and well mannered, almost painstakingly courteous. We all worshipped him, of course.

Charlie Nicholl taught us English Literature. He must have been twenty-five years old, a better-looking Bob Dylan. The girls changed completely as soon as he walked into the room. Suddenly no one laughed at my jokes. Les girls studied their Chaucer with a deadly attention. In-depth discussions on 'text' continued well after the end of class. They all fancied the pants off him, and he them. I might as well have been dead.

I tried to explain that Charlie was probably a communist and that, come the revolution, he would be sticking their pubic hair to their faces as beards on their way to the guillotine.

'Only after fucking us, hopefully,' giggled Emma de Vere Hunt through a haze of smoke. 'Anyway, I don't have any pubic hair.' She winked knowingly at the others.

'Well, you will by the time the revolution comes!' I replied.

'Not while there's a razor around, sweetie,' she retorted and all the girls cracked up. I was out of my depth.

Years later I went to meet a writer whose book I wanted to option for a movie. I was staying in Rome at the time and he was living in Livorno. We arranged to meet halfway at Harry's Bar in Florence. My train arrived late, so I ran past the Ponte Vecchio like a crazy ostrich, and was sweaty and breathless as I walked into the restaurant. Who should be sitting at a corner table but Charlie Nicholl. Older, fuller, more Dylan than ever, the author of one of the best books I had ever read.

'Always late, Rupert!' he said with a déjà-vu half-smile and slightly raised eyebrows. Over lunch we talked about his book but a host of forgotten memories made it hard for me to listen. For a start, I remembered his last school report. He read my mind.

'I'm sorry if that last report seemed rather harsh,' he said finally over coffee.

'That's all right, Charlie. I expect I deserved it.'

'Well, you were a bit of a . . .'

'Twat?'

Unfortunately I was never able to get Charlie's book set up, although it is one of the most thrilling, funny and touching books I have ever read.

Meanwhile, that autumn of 1975 the nights got longer, the temperature dropped and the city braced itself. The walk to school was blustery and grey, and there was a smell of burning leaves in the squares and parks. I was living in London but it still felt like a closing door. At the end of a day at MPW, I lingered in the hallway as everyone wrapped scarves and coats around themselves and exchanged details of the night's promise before jumping into the deep cold stream, the hurrying mass, to be swept away by the tube or the bus to their real lives, to which this one was only an inconvenient sideshow. The school would suddenly be quiet. Finally, always the last to leave, I would cycle home to eat my dinner in front of the telly as the Whites entertained next door.

I had plenty to do. My mother made sure of that. I learnt the piano on Thursdays and went to practise at the home of a family friend on Tuesdays. Greta was a Maltese Rita Hayworth and I adored her. She had known my parents when they were engaged in Valetta back in 1952. She was extremely wealthy and lived in one of the last unconverted Mayfair mansions in Hill Street, off Berkeley Square. I would sit for hours in the vast ballroom on the first floor, where the piano was, before going down for lunch with her and her little girl Felicia at the huge round table in the dining room below. In the corner of the ballroom was an old gramophone with piles of seventy-eights beside it. I would put on *Horowitz Meets Rachmaninov* and play inaccurately along. Horowitz's piano and Greta's were in a semitone of disagreement. If I think of myself that first winter, a lonely sixteen-year-old just bicycling around London, or lying awake at night, or being the clown at school, or sitting round the table with Greta and Felicia swapping news, it is to the ghostly discordant echo of Horowitz and me taking the slow movement together of the Second Piano Concerto. The crackly string section would soar up towards the ceiling of the huge old room, the three chandeliers would shake as an underground train passed deep below the house, and I would be lost in an instant gratification that no amount of serious practice could ever achieve.

But life was about to begin. Mrs White would look into the telly room as her dinner party clambered down the stairs from the drawing room. She always wore long satin skirts that stopped abruptly at her shapely ankles and her sensibly heeled court shoes with bows. A ruffled white silk shirt was tucked into the skirt, clusters were attached to her ears, and her hairstyle, which the Princess of Wales was about to make famous, completed the classic look of a handsome upper-middle-class English mother in the full (toilet) flush of a fallen Empire.

'Everything all right?' she would say as Mr White went shuffling past in his dinner jacket, a couple of bottles of claret under each arm. Samson and Biscuit would wag their tails and look at me. We had a secret bond. When the grown-ups had settled down for dinner, the three of us would embark upon the crispy night. Samson was a big black half-breed with a white stripe on his chest; Biscuit, a slightly older golden retriever, bore more than a passing resemblance to her mistress and certainly took her part as we began to explore further and further into the night-time city. One too many unfamiliar corners away from Cathcart Road, she would stop in her tracks and look at Samson and me. Her raised ears, a patiently rotating tail and an unwavering stare got no sympathy from us; I would look to Samson and he would look to me. We understood each other perfectly. 'Drag the bitch, if she won't come,' said Samson and he would canter off down the uncharted street.

One night before Christmas, we were walking past a converted greengrocers on the Fulham Road called Wolseys Wine Bar, and there, in the big front window, sat Ralph Kerr at a table with a guttering candle stuck in a bottle. He had been in the year above me at Ampleforth and was in his second year at MPW, having failed his A levels on his first attempt and was spending another year to take them again. He was legendary in the school for having been found by Rodney

Portman in the pub one day nursing a huge glass of red wine (his tipple of choice).

'Don't you do Maths?' wondered Rodney vaguely, as he settled down with a G and T and the paper.

'Yes,' replied Ralph.

'Because I rather thought the Maths A level was going on kind of now,' said Rodney.

'Yes,' replied Ralph again.

'Well, shouldn't you *be* there?'

'I suppose I should, really,' said Ralph, philosophically.

He was quite small, with curly brown hair and the soft eyes of one of those girls who saw Our Lady on a tree in Portugal but then wished they hadn't. He wore an enormous black overcoat and always carried an umbrella. Now he was sitting in the window of Wolseys like a character from Toulouse-Lautrec. In the half-lit background behind the bar stood a man with an afro in a silver-sequinned dress. He was drying glasses. The place was empty: just tables, chairs, candles, Ralph and the man in the dress. A lopsided Christmas tree flashed its lights half-heartedly. Ralph saw me walking by and raised his glass in a grim silent toast; I took the dogs home and then went back to the bar.

For the next two years I spent nearly every evening at Wolseys in the company of Ralph. The barman in the sequin dress turned out to be a Scotsman called Alastair who lived in Edna O'Brien's basement round the corner in Carlyle Square. He came from Burnt Island and was the first all-out freaky queen I had ever met. Sometimes, if he was really drunk, he would take his dentures out and lurch upon us at our table, his crumpled lips ranting a Glaswegian slang I was only to understand later, but the meaning of which was already fairly clear. (Some things went down smoother without teeth.) Alastair could be quite scary on these occasions but Ralph never lost his cool as we were confronted by this toothless drag gargoyle in the candlelight. He would simply do as he always did in moments of uncertainty: pour another glass of wine. This time for Alastair, whose name he loved to say backwards.

'Riatsala, a glass of wine perhaps?' he would say politely as if Alastair had just said 'What a lovely herbaceous border' instead of 'See ye'se, see mae, see mae maith, ahl gie'yese u gummie.' (It was to be five years before I heard the word 'gummie' again, and the person proposing it was down on his knees in a Glasgow alley.)

But Alastair would always remember himself, be temporarily diverted and back off. Under his supervision Ralph and I became a regular pair of sixteen-year-old drunks without really knowing it. I had never before or since been a regular in a bar, but I must say it brings with it a warm community connection and a lovely befuddled distortion to one's life. It stands there in the mind's eye – a kingdom above the clouds, Shangri-La glimmering through the thick forest of your day, waiting to take you in. There is just enough easy camaraderie and just enough sense of space for the seasoned regular to say as much or as little as he likes.

That winter we could both inevitably be found after dinner in the window of Wolseys watching the world go by. Ralph was the first person I met who simply liked to sit and look. He was endlessly diverted by the comings and goings in the street; I learnt from him how to sit still. Sometimes we would go on to Up All Night, a late-night burger joint, or to Françoise's, a nightclub in the King's Road. Everything was paid for on the never-never of our flapping chequebooks. Ralph's was a huge one, music-hall size, big enough to see from the upper circle of a theatre. We both got heavily into debt.

For all that, I gained a sense of security from Ralph and his family. He lived with his sister, Bizza, in Upper Cheyne Row opposite the Holy Redeemer. Their parents lived in a little alley further down the street, and they were all looked after by Amelia, a grumpy old Portuguese lady in slippers. I claimed them as my own, proving myself, yet again, to be one of those birds that jump into a neighbour's nest when nobody is looking. They must have known I was being incredibly pushy, but they never made me feel bad. They probably thought that I needed looking after, and in a sense I did. I loved being with them. Bizza would play Joni Mitchell songs on her guitar, and I would stay for dinner without being asked. The parents would arrive from over the road and we all sat in the dining room as the mysterious corner cupboard shook and there was a rumbling from below as Amelia's soup rose through the floor like a magic trick, steaming and victorious (having been suitably thinned to accommodate the extra guest).

Some nights at Wolseys, Alastair's flatmate would arrive. He was called Danny and was dressed from head to toe in shiny black leather, his gaunt unshaven face hidden in the shadow of a peaked leather cap. He wore high boots with spurs, and was a strange and troubling sight. The leather squeaked as he sat down at a table and the chains that adorned him clanked like Marley's ghost. I was electrified, but took good care not to show Ralph or Alastair. One night in spring I was walking Samson (Biscuit was safely in the country, otherwise she might have dragged me home) and I saw Danny in the distance, turning up Redcliffe Gardens towards Earl's Court. His sharp black silhouette was an urban panther stalking through the dancing lights and shadows of the trees. He stopped gracefully to light a cigarette. I was mesmerised. Without knowing it, I had stumbled into the essential hungry gay image of those times. An empty street, a lone predator, and something about to happen. Samson and I followed at a safe distance. After about five minutes Danny went through the side door of a pub. When we caught up I stood on my toes to look through the half-frosted window inside while Samson had a long piss against the wall. The room was packed: in the smoky haze stood construction workers, cowboys, skinheads and other clanking, squeaking leather-clad men. One was dressed entirely in bin liners. (Nicky Haslam, as it happened.)

'Are you a detective?' said a voice behind me. I shot around. It was Danny. He was leaning against a lamp-post. Under the cap his face was a midnight blue, and his jaw pulsed in the orange streetlight. I visibly gasped. Samson bristled.

'What's going on in there?' I squeaked. 'Is it a fancy dress party?' My mind was racing ahead. How was I going to explain this in Wolseys tomorrow night?

Danny laughed, slightly unpleasantly. 'Yeah, it's a kind of fancy dress party. Why don't you come in?'

'I don't think I should,' I said awkwardly, though I was longing to. 'I've got a dog, you see. We were just out for a walk.'

'Yeah, yeah, yeah. I know what you were doing,' sneered Danny.

'No, you don't,' I said, going purple.

'Okay, I don't,' he said and walked back into the pub without another word.

What unusual behaviour, I thought, intrigued. I took one last peek through the window and watched him make his way through the crowd. He was godlike. Soviet Reality in Earl's Court. He turned around and I ducked. Samson and I ran all the way home.

And so I developed a secret life. The pub was called the Coleherne. It was full of men into dressing up. All shapes and sizes, ages and classes left their identities at home as they squeezed into their night-time personae. There was an innocent feeling to the place. If you were good-looking, you probably didn't quite know it; if you were older you probably didn't much mind. There was something in everyone. In those days, just for being there, you counted. It was a different world. There was still a cherished, half-criminal stamp on being gay. Not so long ago homosexual practice had, after all, been illegal, and in that spring of 1976, sex was still very much conducted alfresco. Parks, disused basement areas, garages and alleyways were the unnamed but known places of worship, and being gay felt like being a part of an ancient Masonic lodge. You were outside the culture, and you loved it.

I had a series of noms de plume and pretty soon I was a regular at the Coleherne, and also the Boltons, the pub across the road. It struck a different chord and was more of a marketplace for young runaway boys. But it was all dressing up to me. I moved effortlessly between the two and a basement club, called the Catacombs.

At some point, biking from one latitude to another within that shimmering pink triangle, indulging, as I almost invariably did when alone, in waking dreams of the legendary screen career that was waiting to unfold before me, I was beckoned from a passing Rolls-Royce and joined instead, for a brief amateur career, the ranks of the oldest profession. In the prevailing winds of change I was simply fulfilling my duty as a Thatcher youth. 'Get on your bike and work,' was Norman Tebbit's message to the unemployed. (He was Thatcher's gruesome henchman.) I got off mine and jumped into a passing limousine. However, more than enough has been said about my brief foray into commerce, both by myself and others, so I will only quote my bank manager, Mr Humphreys, in a letter dated 18 April 1976:

I have noted with pleasure that your current account is no longer in debit and stood at £9.46 as of this morning. We will be pleased to issue you with a new chequebook as soon as the monthly transfer of £10 from your father comes in. Keep up the good work.
   J.C. Humphreys
    Manager

But I wasn't the only one in that neighbourhood setting out on a career of complicated late-night love trysts under an assumed name. If the Boltons and the Coleherne ring some distant bell in the reader's mind, it is because there was another princess tying on her pointe shoes at that time, getting ready to spring a few years later from the wings of Earl's Court onto the world stage. Lady Di and her giggling flatmates lived in Coleherne Court.

I witnessed one of those early uncertain walks in the public eye that she took from her flat to her car, surrounded by the school of sharks that would eventually undo her. I was going out for breakfast early one morning with Ronald, a toothless biker who had a poppers factory in his basement off the Coleherne Road. He was extremely thin, living the dream, wearing caps, jackets, studs, handcuffs and a handlebar moustache. His jeans and chaps were more or less painted onto his body, showing off to great effect the 'definite added plus' to his already burgeoning charms. As we came around the corner into the Old Brompton Road there were shouts and screams and people running in all directions. It was as though a bomb had gone off. Suddenly, from a hundred yards away, Lady Di was striding towards us, the billowing engine of a runaway train all set to knock us down. She was already branding the gestures and expressions that we would come to love and hate and then love again over the next fifteen years: the unreadable smile, the apologetic but shifty air, the hand through the hair.

Actually the scene had all the premonitory violence of the crash to come. The photographers were sprinting backwards, shouting her name. I dodged out of their path but Ronald, who would have been an activist had he survived, could not or would not stand aside in the pile-up that followed. Three or four paparazzi banged into him as they dashed past. One fell to the ground, knocking down a second. Ronald was about to explode, but as Lady Di and the others came upon him, she grimaced affectionately, with that ease for instant connection that made her a star, looked him up and down, clocking the cock and the handcuffs, before blushing slightly and smiling naughtily at him through half-closed eyes.

It all happened in a second, but Ronald was hooked, and the next day he was in all the papers. Sometimes just a corner of him, sometimes his back, a huge red hanky stuffed in the pocket of his jeans, but mostly full on, blurry, but definitely there. And for anyone in the know, (probably everyone) the 'added plus' could be seen, grainy, like a mysterious mountain range on Mars. Ronald kept the cuttings by his bed till the day he died, which was not long after. They said he had tuberculosis, but it was a mysterious death – one of the first I heard of – that fluttered the nerve endings of our collective subconscious. Someone was walking on our graves. Whenever I see that famous calling-card picture of the Princess of Wales outside the primary school in the Boltons, the baby almost allegorically placed on her hip, the sun shining through the floral print dress, leaving nothing to her future subjects' imagination, I always think of Ron, and the brief moment they shared.

I saw her once again, at the funeral of Gianni Versace. Everything had happened. Now her face was grim and set in stone. Elton John sobbed uncontrollably beside her, but there were no tears left inside Diana. No more apologetic smiles, no limpid, laughing eyes glancing down at the packages of the passing trade. The rosy future of twenty years ago had gone up in smoke. She sat upright with her arm around Elton and her steely gaze fixed on the small gold box containing Gianni's ashes. She died two weeks later.

But I am getting ahead of myself. That summer of 1976 I scraped through my exams at MPW and was recalled home by my mother. I told her that I wasn't coming, that I had other plans. She countered by cutting my pocket money, but it didn't matter. I already had somewhere to stay and Mr Humphreys was under control. I had made friends with Jody Fenton, a girl at school, and she let me go and live in the cottage she shared with her sister in Markham Street off the King's Road. It had not rained since March. Now it was June and suddenly the famous heatwave was upon us. My life exploded in every direction.

The curtains flapped in the hot breeze from the street. Rod Stewart played endlessly; Jody looked a bit like him and was obsessed. Her room was next to mine under the eaves. A noisy fan stood in the doorway between us, turning from one dishevelled bed to the other but giving us very little respite from the blasting heat. At some point in the late morning one of us would plough through the debris of old knickers and half-filled cups down to the kitchen to make coffee (instant).

Then we would lounge on our beds for another couple of hours, smoking, chatting, dozing off, before coming round again to join in a rousing chorus of 'Tonight's the Night'.

Life was perfect: nothing to do all day and each morning hotter than the last. The city's parks and squares turned a golden brown. Dust clouds and diesel fumes made trucks billow on the main roads. The air was sticky and sexy. And the heatwave kept on coming. London was driven to a fever pitch. No one could sleep and no one could work. Sex was on everybody's mind. I spent all night out and came in each morning just before dawn.

On Saturdays the punks arrived on the King's Road. Thousands of kids poured out of the tube at Sloane Square and terrorised the local community. Where had these people come from? There had been no warning, which made them all the more shocking, because there had been no reference to these wreckers either in the previous year's fashion plates or in the general press. Punk was completely fresh, an invading army. Mohican warriors riddled with safety pins bumped drunkenly into scuttling housewives who cursed under their breath. Boys in black bondage trousers and dirty kilts snogged fat slutty drunk girls with their baby-pink hair stiff with egg whites. Chelsea pensioners looked on in mute rows from the bus stops. There was puke on the pavements and brawling outside the pubs. It was revolution. The upper class reeled in horror at this encroachment on their sacred turf.

One Saturday Mrs Fane, our neighbour, was coming back from Mrs Beaton's Bakery on the King's Road with a baguette sticking out of her shopping bag. A passing beauty with a padlock around his neck whipped it out and started eating. Mrs Fane, a tiny woman, but with a reasonable experience in holding back the rabble during partition, turned on this big drunken lug, pulling herself up to her full five foot three.

'Give me my loaf, you bloody yob,' she said, as Jody and I watched from our room.

'Shut your shitty arse, cunt,' replied her new friend nonchalantly.

Mrs Fane nearly retched, but then, gritting her teeth, she swung her shopping bag over her head and socked the boy hard in the face with it.

'Cor. That hurt,' he whined.

Then she grabbed her loaf and marched off, thrusting it half broken back into the shopping bag as though it were a sword. 'You should be in prison. We didn't fight a bloody war for this,' she shouted as she slammed her front door and the whole street shook.

Punk in the heatwave was the trailer to a new England. They were the advancing rabble, wobbling in the shimmering desert smog towards the World's End, and the end of the world as we knew it. Their Boudicca, unbeknown to them, was another peach blonde with a lot of egg white in her beehive: Margaret Thatcher. She would be the Main Attraction; they were the razorblades on the wheels of her chariot. They both wanted to get their hands on the past and slash it to pieces. Punks wanted to fight on the high streets and shatter the windows of the greengrocers. Maggie the grocer's daughter was going to close those grocers down and put up Tesco's. They wanted anarchy and so did she.

The Chelsea hoorays packed up and went to the country at the weekends. Those who stayed had their own anarchic agenda. Punk, for the upper-class rebel, was heroin. For the five years before both groups finally burnt out, we hooray junkies watched the working-class fray from the safety of the stands, scratching ourselves with distant half-smiles, dilated pupils and a swag bag of silver stolen from home while our parents were away.

CHAPTER 7

Paris

Mothers have an uncanny instinct for danger. Even far away, and totally ignorant of any world outside her own, my darling mother knew that the thunderclouds were rolling close. When she looked at me, she saw a Dorian Gray and his portrait at the same time. My youth was still there, but whispering around it was an older darker creature that she neither knew nor liked. Her instinct was to lock me up in a tower and throw away the key. She knew this was impossible, but she also knew, or thought she knew, that the danger I was in came from London, a place she had never trusted. And so she hatched a new plan. I was to spend three months in Paris learning French.

I was appalled and did everything I could to wriggle out of the trip, but she was would not back down. A girl called Dominique had been to stay with us five years ago on one of those exchange trips everyone dreaded. My brother was meant to go back with her at the end of the trip. He had flatly refused. Now this old credit was claimed. Trunk calls were made (after 6 p.m. of course) to Mme Feuillatte, Dominique's mother, and pretty soon it was all arranged. Little did my poor mama know that she was sending me into the very eye of the storm she had been hoping to avoid.

The boat train to Paris left at ten o'clock at night from Victoria station, to make its midnight connection with the ferry at Newhaven. My father took me to dinner in the restaurant at the station hotel and saw me off on the platform just as he used to do when I was a child on the way to summer holidays in Scotland. It was romantic to take the boat train: you stood in the footsteps of your nineteenth-century heroes, and nothing much had changed. The lights swung in the breeze from the high Victorian arches that stretched along the platform. The tracks ran off beyond them into the dark unknown. All you could see were flashing red and green lamps and the distant glow of the city you were about to leave. In those days travel really felt like travel, and going abroad was leaving your life behind. Victoria at night was your last taste of England, full of sad cinematic goodbyes, extraordinarily lit in ghostly sepia night-for-day that confused the odd pigeon flapping around in the girders. The disembodied voice of some genteel medium from Bromley read the tea leaves from a high office overlooking the tracks. Her voice echoed across the station. Bing bong! One journey ended as another began, and you were briefly suspended between the past and the future in an exotic emotional limbo.

I leant out of the train window and looked down at my father on the platform. He seemed impossibly ancient, standing there in his overcoat, bowler hat, briefcase and brolly, although in reality he was only a little older than I am as I write this today.

'Mummy is awfully keen for this to work out,' he said warningly.

'Relax, both of you!' I replied. The new me was dangerously abrupt.

'Well, as you know, Mummy can't.'

At an unseen cue, the stragglers embraced and finally jumped on board. Doors slammed all the way down the train and the stationmaster blew his whistle.

'*Bonne chance*,' said Daddy, in a French devoid of any attempt at accent. 'Write, won't you?' He stuck his chin forward and chuckled. It was his gesture of affection, and I returned it.

With a metallic squeal we set off, but it seemed as though the platform was moving and not the train. The major, along with the other waving friends and relations, simply slid on a kind of conveyor belt back through the barrier and into the past, where as far as I was concerned they all belonged. The train clanked and jerked out of the old station across the river, the street lamps twinkling beneath us on the Embankment, the essence of London, moons held in the wrought-iron claws of Empire, laced with strings of bulbs that stretched all the way to Big Ben and threw white squiggly lines across the Thames.

There was an actor in the British theatre who was legendary not so much for his acting as for his magical ability to catch every first night in the country. If he didn't manage to attend the actual performance, then on the noticeboard backstage his familiar spidery handwriting could be spotted on cards from foreign parts to all the members of the cast. Everyone knew him, or thought they did. In fact he was, and still is, a mystery character, but one whose presence was essential for a play's success. His name was Vernon Dobtcheff.

He invariably wore black: polo neck, fedora and spectacles. Even if you were filming on location in French Guiana, you would most likely come across him in a local bar, on his way to somewhere, another location perhaps, or simply picking up some dry cleaning. He played small parts – spies and hit men – so he worked a lot during the Cold War. (Things may have quietened down a bit since the Wall came down.) I met him that night on the boat train to Paris. Without knowing, I was being beckoned into show business by its patron saint.

Squeezing my cases along the packed carriages, I finally came across an empty seat. 'Is anyone sitting there?' I asked.

A man in a large black hat looked up from a newspaper and surveyed me through thick lenses. His nose was larger than John Gielgud's. 'You are, one hopes,' he said in a fine baritone.

He observed me from behind his paper as I stuffed my case into the rack above the window; I could tell he was checking out my bum and I wiggled it around as if I were in a *Carry On* film. When I finally settled down he dropped his paper with a flourish. It was curtain up.

'I'm Vernon,' he said and offered me a bejewelled hand. We chatted pleasantly during the trip and when we arrived at Newhaven, he said with an old-world chivalry and a coquettish twinkle, 'If you need a place to lay your weary head, I have a cabin with two beds.'

I was quite tired from the night before so I cautiously accepted the offer, wondering what exactly might be involved. Nothing much, as it turned out. I lay down on one of the beds. Vernon took off his hat and his glasses. He was naked without them, a baby bird with scraps of fluffy hair. The little bedside light between us threw his shadow against the wall. His nose was a giant beak. He produced a bottle of whisky from a rather macabre black holdall and poured some into a couple of toothmugs. As we toasted each other from our beds, the boat horn boomed our imminent departure and suddenly the whole cabin began to shake with the vibration of the engine. I kicked off my shoes and settled down to sleep. Vernon blinked blindly at me, said, '*Repose-toi bien,*' and switched off the light.

I woke once during the night. The light was back on. He was in his specs again, slowly licking his fingers before turning a page of the book he was reading. He looked over and winked. I went back to sleep.

Later, at about four o'clock in the morning, he shook me gently and we made our way together to the French train. It was freezing and inside the windows were misted up and dripping. I slumped unconscious into my seat but received another gentle prod as we approached Paris. By now the window had cleared and I looked blearily out.

The huge white domes of the Sacré Coeur glowed in the distance on a hill in front of a deep blue sky complete with stars and a sickle moon. It could have been the backdrop in a provincial theatre. The train edged respectfully towards this surreal vision in a giant curve as the sky bleached and turned pink. The stars and the moon gave way to an early morning jet; and the man in the black hat watched me with the amused smile of a fairy godmother.

I know it sounds hackneyed, but I felt an uncanny sense of recognition as I watched the approaching city, jerkily framed by the train window that early October morning. Everything in my whole life fell away in the face of it, like the sound cutting out during the intense denouement of a film, leaving only the protagonist's heartbeat. We pulled into the Gare du Nord and as the doors opened the last English dust particle dissolved in the hot rubbery breath of the Parisian station. I walked down the platform with Vernon, who asked me if I knew where I was going. I was about to answer when a tall handsome woman in a fur coat waved from the buffers. It was Mme Feuillatte. We kissed hello, although we had never met before, and I was about to introduce her to Vernon, but when I turned around he was gone. A moment later I could see his departing figure sliding down an escalator, waving like Sally Bowles at the end of *Cabaret*. We left the station and got into her car.

Mme Feuillatte drove me across Paris in her Citroën; the noise of the car on cobbles was more confusing to me than driving on the wrong side of the road. We beeped our way across the Arc de Triomphe and over the other side to Neuilly where the Feuillattes lived. In those days Neuilly was the exclusive nest of the grande bourgeoisie. It was feathered by industrialists and property developers with political connections, and they were making a lot of money. Mitterrand's socialist agenda was no deterrent. This was the heyday of the offshore company. Chirac was their man and they lived like princes. Boulevard Maurice Barrés was quite simply the best address, a quiet road running along the edge of the Bois de Boulogne. The large honey-coloured buildings stood back from the street in their own private gardens and the park stretched out in front as far as the eye could see.

Looking at Madame as we chatted for the last time in English, she could have been a photograph by Helmut Newton come to life. She had a handsome pampered face, beautifully made up under a tight blonde chignon, and the expressionless regard of someone who had recently committed murder and was simply going through the motions. Huge emerald and diamond clips clung to her ears. She wore a priceless fur coat with quite possibly nothing underneath but the sheer silk stockings on her beautiful legs.

Inside the house, we stood side by side in silence as the antique lift with its double doors and windows wobbled awkwardly to the first floor. Up close she smelt delicious, from another planet. She stalked ahead of me through the large apartment, now speaking in French, her heels leaving their mark on the deep rust-coloured carpets. Huge windows looked out over the Bois; cartoons by Raphael hung on the oak-panelled walls between them. A series of double doors connected the hall, the drawing room, Madame's bedroom and the dining room. Thus, her large fur-covered bed could be seen from every room, the unattainable high altar that Monsieur's guests could glance at sideways as Madame herself served them another glass of 'Feuillatte' champagne.

A delicious smell of coffee wafted through a swing door that led to the other side of the apartment where the children lived and Monsieur had his office. Two pretty Indonesian girls in starched aprons worked in a tiny kitchen; their grey nylon dresses sparkled and snapped with electricity if you passed too close (probably Madame's deterrent).

I was to sleep in Monsieur's office, which was decorated like one of the tunnels at Charles de Gaulle airport. A huge black and white photograph of Monsieur presided over the desk. He was very Chirac, a bull of a man with dyed black hair and big murderer's hands. I could imagine Madame dropping her coat on the floor and walking obediently to the bedroom, nude on her heels, as Monsieur followed, with his big fat cock sticking out of his suit.

This industrial French bourgeoisie made our own rationing-obsessed middle class look positively downtrodden. Partly because they were overtly sexual, whereas we were covertly sexual. They prepared for days in advance for lavish 'at home' evenings of *échangisme*; we groped the wives of our friends on the dance floor at Annabel's, and possibly had a quick rabbity fling in a taxi on the way home. They looked for perfection in everything and were not afraid to spend. We shopped at Peter Jones and drowned in cheap plonk. They were tremendous show-offs: food, furniture, clothes, hair, cars and holidays had to be perfect. And it was. I have still to taste a better cup of coffee than that served by the electrical maids in Neuilly, or to eat a better-cooked piece of 'rosbif' than Madame's.

She sat me down to breakfast that first day and then I hardly saw her again for the next three months. As for Dominique, she was my brother's age and we hardly ever met either. So from then on I was more or less left to my own devices, which suited me perfectly. I had been enrolled by my mother at the Alliance Française, a school in the Latin quarter. I went there once.

That first afternoon Madame suggested that I went for a walk in the Bois de Boulogne. The Bois was not like an English park. There were few lawns edged with herbaceous borders; no bandstands; just miles and miles of tall spindly trees in the muddy ground under the low Parisian sky. The whole area had a run-down feeling to it that was not unpleasant. And even if it had never really recovered from the Impressionist era, the Bois was still in many ways the pumping heart of Paris. Wide alleys were the arteries that carved through it and fed the Parisians to the woods. The glorious restaurants and pavilions of the nineteenth century stood crumbling beside them, their lakeside terraces still laced with Chinese lanterns in a hopeless attempt to retain their Proustian ambience. Veins of sandy bridle paths wound off into the woods, and the deeper you went inside, the muddier and rougher were the tracks, turning finally into webs of barely perceptible goat paths, the capillaries that delivered one into secret bowers of dripping rhododendrons. Here, fantasy could become reality; all of Paris knew the Bois and had been transported, at some time or other, by the flow of lust from the lights of the *grands boulevards* into the dark heart of the nighttime woods.

That afternoon I passed a small truck. It was rocking slightly to a muffled Brazilian samba coming from within. As I approached, the back door opened. Out hopped a small bald man in a green loden coat. He looked about and then strode purposefully into the thicket as if he were late for a meeting. The door slammed behind him and pretty soon some curtains that covered the windscreen were thrown open to reveal a woman of gigantic proportions at the wheel. She started the engine and the truck moved off, but only fifty yards down the road, before it stopped. The door opened again and out came a pair of legs in shiny black boots with stiletto heels.

Delphine was well over six foot. A tiger-skin bikini top barely contained her enormous breasts that looked ready to explode. These giant constructions seemed to overwhelm her body, which was as thin as a rake and bent comically under the load. She had a jungle of black hair, and as she teetered around the outside of the truck with a cigarette in her mouth, she was trying to negotiate herself into a floor-length fur coat, which wasn't easy. Her arms could hardly stretch away from the breasts and the breasts seemed to want to go down the sleeves as well. With one hand she held a breast back as the other prodded and pushed its way down the sleeve. The long sinewy muscles of a mountain goat strained across her armpits and up her neck like an anatomical drawing. She craned forward so that her hair didn't get caught in the coat, and then up so that her cigarette did not burn or burst the boobs. And all this while walking through mud, balanced on six-inch heels. Finally in the coat, which was riddled with cigarette burns the size of bullet holes, she threw open the back doors of the truck. This girl had class. Inside was a boudoir with pink satin walls, a glitter ball suspended from the ceiling and a mattress covered in leopard skin on the floor. This was my first look at the Brazilian she-man in all the glory of her unnatural habitat. It was also the first time I heard Jobim. The song was 'Desafinado'.

'Love is like a never-ending melody . . .' You bet, Delphine seemed to be saying, as she settled seductively against the side of the truck.

'*Tu as envie, chou?*' she asked in a thick Brazilian French that I did not understand.

'Sorry?' I said.

'Ahh, English baby. You wanna get fucked by Delphine?'

'Who's Delphine?'

'This.' And she opened the coat and revealed, straining against the same tiger-skin bikini, an enormous cock. 'And baby, don't ever forget. I got sugar too,' she added, turning around to reveal a thin flat bum.

And so I made my first friend in France. Delphine ruled the Bois, or at least her part of it, with a rod of iron. Literally. Hers was a famous erection. She was hysterically funny in her makeshift English. She came from a town in Brazil called Belo Horizonte (Beautiful Horizon). Now she lived in Pigalle in a *chambre de bonne* with the tiniest window you had ever seen. I called it 'limited horizons', and as she laughed you could see her father, the chubby butcher with twinkly eyes whose picture was on the wall. She possessed the innate wisdom of the semi-literate hooker, but she was reckless and dangerously vulnerable. In short, she was a mess. Sometimes I would spend the afternoon in the cab of the truck and listen to her spanking businessmen; she would insult them in Portuguese, but she had a terrible cough and sometimes when she got carried away, the whole thing would turn into a tubercular fit and she would have to call off the show. She loved to chase the dragon: smoke heroin on a piece of silver foil. I would prepare it for her while she was working, ready for whenever she would stick her head through the little hatch.

'God, give me strength,' she would rasp, and I would hand her the foil and a little makeshift pipe, then light a match underneath, and she would suck the heavy smoke deep into her lungs. In the brief moment of silence while she held her breath, the noise of the woods bled in. Her poor victim shuffled about in the back of the truck. A car drove past. She would look at me solemnly through a caked thatch of lashes, and then exhale in a Marilyn kiss pose, like the exhaust pipe of an old car, before shutting the hatch door and getting on with the job. Sometimes there were flecks of blood on the tinfoil pipe. When I pointed this out, she replied, 'I'm very Camille, darling, didn't you know?'

Once, a man left without paying, and ran off into the night. She jumped into the driving seat of the camion and tried to run him over. I had rarely laughed so much in my life because she was serious. It was terrifying. The man had a head start, but she soon found him. He dodged left and right in front of the headlights. Delphine was screaming blue murder. Finally he escaped into the trees, but only after a tussle between her and me over the steering wheel. She stopped the car and slapped me so hard that I bled.

'Now who's Camille?' I muttered.

'Never interfere!' she screamed. Her face was suddenly the butcher's, but the eyes weren't twinkling. She was unrecognisable and demonic; she shook me and spat insults in three languages before pushing me out of the truck and driving off.

But we made up, and with Delphine at the wheel I learnt all about the Bois. Whatever you wanted, you could get it in those woods. Sometimes when she was too stoned or it was raining too hard, we would drive around, listening to Brazilian love songs and watch the people at play (or work, depending on your perspective). Like many hookers Delphine was constantly fascinated by her job. Sometimes we parked the truck on the corner of Avenue Foch and ate chocolate as we observed the wife swappers at work. Or we cruised the homos for rent at Porte Dauphine. She knew them all, and sometimes if I liked one she would call him over, tell him I was her little brother from Beautiful Horizons, and we would make out in the back of the camion while she drove around and Jobim sang.

Once she took me to a tree stump deep in the woods where the ancient tarts congregated round a small bonfire. She was delivering smack. These witches sat around all night laughing and smoking, six or seven of them, old girls keeping their hands in. According to Delphine, they had a surprising degree of success. Groups of kids would seek them out for a dare; the old girls were philosophical and played along. After all, it beat 'ashtray work'. Twenty years later, when my best friend was murdered in the Bois, it was the old girls who were the last to see her. But that's another story.

For now, it was the forest from *A Midsummer Night's Dream*. Heaven and hell; boys and girls; transsexuals and she-men; dealers, mobsters and policemen. Everyone had their own little bit of turf. The Feuillattes lent me a bicycle and I would beetle around the Bois as the season changed, the leaves fell, and all the love nests and hideaways were exposed. The cold weather arrived, but it didn't stop anyone. The *tenue* was *décolletée* come rain or shine. You could only tell the season by the clouds of breath coming from a girl's lips.

Flora McEwen, my friend from MPW, was living in Paris as well, and three times a week we arrived late for life class at an art school in Montparnasse. We did rapid sketches of a strange lady with a hennaed bob, a huge scar right up her stomach and a very unruly bush. I was still a delinquent young hooray on a looting session, and I am ashamed to say I laughed out loud at some of the poses attempted by Madame. She was quite chunky, at least fifty, and entirely uninhibited. One day she arched balletically on all fours, before looking up expectantly through her bob at the naked light bulb hanging high above and her open bottom gave a little sigh of disbelief right in my face.

Flora lived seven storeys up an oval-shaped back staircase that smelt of old apples and polished wood. She had a new camera, and one afternoon, after art class, both of us utterly broke, crouched in her little room – it was tiny and we were giraffes – we hatched a plot that I would become a supermodel. The more we thought about it, the better the idea seemed. The next afternoon we went all over the city, while I posed and Flora clicked away. Luckily for me, given my extravagantly inept posing technique, she hadn't quite got the hang of how to use the focus, and in most of the pictures that we collected breathlessly a week later, I was no more than an insignificant blur.

But we were exuberant; drunk on ourselves, each other and living in Paris, we thought the pictures were brilliant. I made them into a little book and, armed with my new portfolio, Flora and I attacked the boutiques of Paris. (We had never heard of model agencies.) Our first stop was the Pierre Cardin Men's Boutique. We went in and Flora immediately summoned the manager. Although she had not been head girl at her convent, it was a role she could have played with flying colours.

'Hello, my boyfriend *est un lord anglais*. He might be able to model for you.'

'Oh?' replied the manager stiffly.

'Oui,' continued Flora. *'Il est là studying art avec moi à L'École du Louvre, et voilà.'*

Over to me. I rushed forward with my book. The bewildered manager leafed through it.

'Pas mal, huh?' said Flora persuasively. I tried to look languorous, as I leant against the counter, although things weren't going according to plan as the manager, obviously amused, asked the rest of the staff for their opinion.

'J'ai fait ça avec du flash,' explained Flora about a picture in which only a pair of red eyes could be seen on a white haze.

The manager told us to go up to the head office around the corner, but obviously called to warn them of our imminent arrival, as we never got beyond the concierge. We had no more luck elsewhere. I was turned down by everyone, and the rejections made me feel suicidal; my whole sense of self seemed to slip away.

'I feel absolutely hideous now,' I confessed to Flora, thoroughly crushed.

'You're not hideous,' she said, 'you're just weird looking. Your time will come. Anyway, stop complaining. You're a bore once you start going on.'

'Oh, thanks, Flora,' I said, deeply put out. But she was right.

Flora's cousin Katie was in Paris too. She had a pet mouse that she kept in her pocket, and a boyfriend who worked in the toilets of a discotheque called Le Club Sept. The club was owned by Fabrice Emaer, the king of the Parisian night. There were a string of other establishments on the same street – Le Pimms next door, and across the road Le Piano Bar, run by France's first air hostess, a tipsy lady named Isolde – but the crowd was always trying to get into Le Sept. They were held at bay by a ferocious black lady by the name of Jenny Bel'Air, the queen of the door people, and you didn't want to mess with her. Jenny could make or break you with the bat of an eyelid and, like all door people, she had the memory of an elephant.

Le Sept was a tiny underground place lit by a flashing roof of neon striplights in pinks and blues. The walls were mirrors and so the effect was totally disorienting; you never knew when the club ended and the walls began. There was a bar at one end with a giant bucket of crushed ice in which nestled bottles of champagne and vials of poppers. Katie would sit on the floor by the toilets with her boy, Pascal, and I would head for the dance floor in my white satin Acrobat drainpipes.

One night, Yves Saint Laurent was sitting with Rudolf Nureyev, Andy Warhol, Catherine Deneuve and Betty Catroux. She was Yves' muse: the woman he wanted to be. Yves and Rudi were whispering intimately in each other's ears; Deneuve looked listlessly into the crowd; Andy and Betty were laughing at some private joke and pointing at Yves. I yearned to be them, or at least to be with them; they were so near, and yet so far. They shone ethereally above the bobbing heads on the dance floor: polished, beautiful, at the peak of their form, lit for the whole club to worship. The silhouettes of waiters passed in front of them with fresh bottles and ice buckets. Fabrice stood by the table with his arms folded, chatting amiably through a cigarette in his mouth. Betty was his muse too, and when she threw back her famous blonde mane and laughed, the others clapped in adoration. In the middle of all the movement, Deneuve's sculpted face was jarringly vacant and pulled the focus from the group as she stared at some world unseen by the rest of the club.

And then, when 'Carwash' began to play, Saint Laurent and Nureyev jumped up and came hand in hand onto the dance floor. They started jiving together, as I wiggled my way towards them and danced for five ecstatic minutes by their side. When the backing girls sang 'Toot toot beep beep' they raised their hands and wagged their fingers in unison. Nureyev was wearing thigh-length boots and YSL was in black tie. The next time the chorus came around I joined in too and wagged my finger at Nureyev who took my hand and twirled me round and round. The flashing neon, the mirrored walls and the most famous ballet dancer in the world spiralled around me for what seemed like an eternity.

After that, I spent nearly every night at Le Sept, and although I never made friends with anybody famous (though not for lack of trying) I did meet some weird freaks along the way. One was a tall thin Vietnamese boy called Kim. He was very quiet, always dancing, and when he laughed he covered his mouth with his hand. Like me, he was new to

France, having escaped Saigon in '75 with his family. His father had been shot dead by the communists, and in desperation his mother had married a surly colonial French colonel who got them out and with whom they now lived in a kind of slavery. Kim and I had rebellion in common, although his would go far further than mine. (We had no idea that we were at the beginning of a long journey together that would end in his death twenty years later, but at that time ours was an unremarkable friendship, and one I would never have remembered but for that image of Kim laughing, one of those little bookmarks one makes in the subconscious, for no particular reason. Years after, almost unrecognisable to ourselves and to each other, another hand on a different mouth rang a strange faraway bell, and the book fell open at the same page.)

Needless to say I didn't learn a word of French in the din of Le Sept, nor in my bed every day till the early afternoon, nor in life class, and only rudimentary sex French in the Bois. But I lived happily speaking the language of love: an intense love for the city, and being a foreigner there; for sex, for religion, even for the Feuillattes. Paris was at its breathtaking best at the end of the seventies, a crumbling post-war romantic thriller full of mystery and intrigue. Behind the arched green doors onto the streets lay a thousand hidden universes, each with their own smells and sounds. In the mornings these doors were briefly thrown open to the world as the concierges swept the courtyards and watered the rows of potted geraniums. Their high-pitched voices, the sounds of their vacuum cleaners, and Johnny Halliday on their radios were the morning trio that bounced off the walls and awoke you to a stranger's embrace in an unknown bed. Being from nowhere, with no place to go, you drifted back into a dreamless sleep pressed against the warm morning body of another, who like you was asking no questions, and were only awoken again by the tomb-like afternoon silence and the solitary click of the buzzer on that big green door that beckoned you back out into the Parisian jungle. And when you hit the street, and everyone was returning from the day's work, you never felt more alive. Everything was beautiful: the peeling white shutters in the late afternoon sun; the smell of the drains; the little tied parcels of fitted carpet guiding the gushing water down the street.

But it was all about to change. Chirac was soon to be mayor, and he had already ripped out one of the oldest parts of the city, Les Halles. In its place, that winter of 1976, was a gigantic hole, like a huge grave. Not only was the old medieval city to be buried in it, but so also were most of the people I was dancing with that winter. When it was finally flattened over, a whole way of life had been flattened as well.

Christmas approached, and it was time to leave. Delphine gave me a card with a picture of herself as a curly-haired little boy. I sat with her one last afternoon in the camion. It began to rain. It streamed down the windows and beat on the roof. Delphine drifted off. She answered my questions in a dreamy voice with half-opened eyes. She only moved to cough or scratch. I was planning to come back in February, so it wasn't one of those sad goodbyes. In fact we never said goodbye at all. The conversation petered out; I removed a cigarette from her half-open mouth. She let out a grateful snore of acknowledgement and I gently let myself out into the rain. I never saw her again.

She was shot by a farmer in Normandy. On a whim she decided to get out of Paris and had taken the camion to a village near the coast. Her presence was not appreciated by the local agricultural community, and one morning she was found lying in the truck, riddled this time not with cigarette burns but with bullets from a shotgun.

Madame Feuillatte dropped me back at the station and kissed me on both cheeks. As she turned to go, I heard a familiar voice behind me.

'Ah, there you are, dearest boy. Everything went according to plan, I trust. *Tu parles couramment français, maintenant?*' Vernon Dobtcheff appeared as if he had been in the other room. 'What a coincidence, eh?' he said with a wicked grin.

'Yes, but what happened to you?' I asked, still slightly peeved to have been left so abruptly three months earlier.

'Ah,' replied Vernon with a twinkle. 'Places to go. People to see. Actually, I had to collect some laundry before catching the train to Prague. And now, dear boy, we should hurry. That is, if you are coming home?'

'I don't really want to,' I replied. 'I want to stay here.'

'Well, you're not. Come on, we don't want to miss our train, do we?' And so Vernon delivered me back to London.

I forgot all about him until five years later. Ian McKellen brought him to see a play I was in at the Greenwich Theatre in London. It was only then that I learnt who he really was. 'This is Vernon Dobtcheff,' said Ian. 'He is famous in the theatre.'

'Oh, don't worry, Ian,' breezed Vernon with a lascivious wink. 'No need to introduce. Rupert and I go back a long way.'

Ian raised his eyebrows and pursed his lips. 'You're a sly old thing, aren't you?' he said later and then I knew. I was in.

CHAPTER 8

Drama School

There is a grim area of London called Swiss Cottage. In the late seventies it was a kind of dividing line between the centre of the city and its surrounding suburbs. Now it is more or less part of the West End. Its high street is the Finchley Road, which at some point became the main exit from the city to the north, and so Swiss Cottage was cut in half by two dangerous torrents of traffic that left a marooned island in the middle, which was occupied by the Swiss Cottage pub, a rambling mock chalet complete with window boxes, gingham curtains, oak beams and fake chimneys, a gloomy landmark for Londoners returning from the weekend. Its twinkly lamps of fake cheer rise above the flow of tail lights on a Sunday night, and remind one of empty flats, lonely old ladies and imminent death.

On either bank of the constant stream of traffic, poor split Swiss Cottage rose and fell in waves of bedsits and rooming houses. There was a feeling of collapse on those wide avenues of large ugly houses. It was a land of broken dreams, inhabited by Jewish immigrants from Austria and Poland. They were people who had lost everything; first-hand experience of war was still present on their faces, etched in a kind of frozen horror. They met in the Cosmo coffee shop on Finchley Road and always came to the shows at the drama school.

The Central School of Speech and Drama stood back from the Finchley Road and from the world itself. It was a white building with blue doors; its windows were dark and empty. It might have been the headquarters of a spiritualist society, were it not for the odd show song jangling from a half-tuned piano in an upper room, or the disembodied voice of a dance teacher counting. ('And one and two and three and *turn.*') There was a sad, dilapidated feeling to the place.

On the day of my audition, 4 February 1977, hundreds of young hopefuls were congregated in the foyer. A little old medium in a chiffon scarf introduced herself as Vinkie Gray, registrar, and ticked off names on a clipboard. There was an extraordinary tension in the room. Was it ectoplasm or blind ambition? From the first moment we were all turned on, little electric lights strutting our stuff, prancing and performing like show ponies straight out of the horsebox. We came from all walks of life but shared the same dream of world domination. We had all been the funniest person in our class, the best looking in our village. This was the next step. Rejection was unimaginable at this stage, but what had seemed so easy, so certain in front of the mirror at home was suddenly confused by a new element: competition.

One by one we were taken to a large studio at the top of the building to perform our Shakespeare speech. The staff sat behind a long trestle table, about a dozen of them. There was a hushed religious feeling in the room; they were theatrical Jesus and his performing apostles at the Last Supper. In the middle sat their leader, a small perfectly formed man named George Hall. He had an intricately groomed beard and moustache, above a black polo neck, jazz trousers and ballet pumps, and when he walked an invisible string seemed to suspend him from the top of his head.

Next to him was Barbara Caister, the head of movement, a Welsh lady with a beer gut and bare feet, a ravaged beauty going through the motions. Later that day, she taught us the secret of movement. It was called 'the whoosh-ka'. My God, I remember thinking. I came here to learn how to act like Garbo at the end of *Queen Christina* (actually, I already knew), not how to do a whoosh-ka. But in case you want to try it at home, it goes like this. Feet together. Hands stretched high above your head. And . . . drop from the lower back down to the ground (whoo). Bounce up a bit, rounding the lower back as you go (sh), before flying up to start the whole head-spinning process again (ka).

It was demonstrated to us by a top student from the graduation year, a flat-footed queen with a steamed-pudding face. Up and down he went, Barbara standing beside him beaming like a magician who had just sawn someone in half. It was not very impressive.

Bardy Thomas was the head of voice. She had a pinched, mean face that was not disguised by a romper outfit and Pebbles hair. Over the next two years, she didn't try particularly hard to camouflage her dislike for me. Now, after my audition, she laid her cards on the table.

'Rupert,' she said, all smiles and clipboard. 'Could you just make the sound O for me?'

'Oh?' I replied, my nasal upper-class twang suddenly naked in the acoustic of the high room. Bardy looked to the others and sighed. They nodded sagely.

'No,' she explained, patiently. 'That was not an O. That was "Eh-oh". I want you to say O.'

'Eh-oh?' I was puzzled.

'No. O.' She made her lips into a big circle.

'Eh-oh,' I drawled.

'O!' she shouted.

'Eh-oh!' I shouted back.

'You see, Rupert,' cut in George Hall, 'you have a very thick upper-class accent. We're just a bit worried that it may be, er . . .'

'Impenetrable,' finished Bardy. 'He can't pronounce his ch's either. Say church!'

'Sshchursh?' I whimpered.

'See, he's got a shushy S,' said Bardy, as she scratched away on her clipboard. Years of wearing a brace had pushed my tongue into the wrong position. My dreams were crumbling. Bardy turned to the others. They all looked worried.

'I'm sure with a bit of practice, I can get it right,' I said.

'It's not that easy,' she snapped.

Later in the day George Hall took the floor and taught us a breathing exercise. It was called, 'I give you the cake! I take it away.' He was like a Vaudeville star from the last century; only the hat and cane were missing. But he was quite a performer. 'Okay. This may seem absolutely dotty,' he said with huge eyes as he painted a shimmering rainbow around him with his hands. 'Totally bizarre! You're going to think: he's absolutely craaaazy!'

We all laughed. He was good. He put everything into it.

'Imagine I am giving you a cake and when I tell you about it you're really excited. Like this! I give you the cake?' Suddenly his arms shot out to present the imaginary confection. He gasped ecstatically, a huge intake of breath held in the ribs, his face a cartoon of mock excitement. He looked deranged. 'And now,' he said after this dramatic pause, 'I take it away!' His whole body deflated with an enormous sigh.

We were a bit puzzled. After all, no one had ever talked to us like this before, and we were not aware that there was a mechanism to breathing. We just did it. But soon George was standing in front of us conducting.

'I give you the cake?'

We breathed in with excitement.

'I take it away!'

We breathed out with a big groan.

And so the day went on. We were observed in movement, singing ('The Lambeth Walk') and acting. We stood with our arms stretching towards the sun and we rolled ourselves up into little balls. We watched each other suspiciously out of the corners of our eyes while we were trying to be spontaneously magnetic, and at the end of the day we were herded into another room by Vinkie Gray while the spiritualists decided our fate. There were about a hundred of us, and places for fifteen. It was an agonising two hours. The whole of life hung in the balance. Finally Vinkie tottered back in with her clipboard and read the names of the people who had been accepted. I was one of them. With a couple of exceptions, it was the happiest day of my career.

They gave me the cake, but two years into the course they took it away.

Meanwhile, my father bought a house in Chelsea, off the King's Road, in a pretty cul-de-sac of nursery-coloured cottages called Bywater Street. I was given the basement, and my parents lived upstairs during the week when they came up from the country. They removed the stairs between the basement and the ground floor and replaced them with a trapdoor which in times of diplomatic strain over the next few years (there were many) they barricaded against invasion with crates of champagne.

Bywater Street was my first home and I loved it, although the basement was so low I could hardly stand up. There was a little front room with the flat's only window. Its view was the white brick wall of the area, and a mysterious hole through which hosts of thick grey slugs oozed in the summer months. There was a tiny kitchen, an even tinier bathroom with a bath so small one had to perform Houdiniesque contortions to get in; and the little back yard had been converted into two minuscule bedrooms. I was to have lodgers. In the major's world everything had to be cost effective and these lodgers would provide me with an allowance.

In September the school year began. Finally I was at drama school and soon I had a pair of lodgers, two Southern belles, Betsy and Ginger. Betsy was from North Carolina and was at Central with me, and Ginger from Virginia was at another drama school, Webber Douglas. They slept on bunk beds in one room and I slept on a mattress in the dank airless cupboard next door. The place was a mess. But we didn't care. We stayed up all night and left for school early each morning.

The morning peace would be broken by the jangle of Betsy's alarm clock, and within a minute the flat was mayhem. We were fountains of energy, or we were out cold. There was nothing in between. The kettle and the music went on together. We sang along to every song, still at that age when songs appeared to have been written specially for us. 'Baker Street', 'I Will Survive' and 'Native New Yorker' blared across the street in high rotation. We danced around the flat with our toothbrushes in our mouths, mugs in our hands. If it was warm we put on our tights and T-shirts all ready for the morning movement class, and within twenty minutes the door had slammed, shaking the whole house, and we were clambering up the area steps in our tights and helmets onto Betsy's scooter and heading for Swiss Cottage, singing all the way.

You're no tramp,
but you're no lady,
talkin' that street talk

It was a six-day week at Central, and a three-month term. We rehearsed a play, studied movement, voice and singing. We had make-up class, improvisation, and twice a week we spent the whole morning at the zoo, studying animals. At the end of the term we had 'shows' followed by 'crits'. We performed the play we had rehearsed, followed by five minutes of the animal we had chosen and a twenty-minute group improvisation to music.

Theatrical Jesus and the touring disciples sat behind the trestle table on the last day and pronounced judgement on your term's work in front of the whole year. It was a useless exercise in authority, but they seemed to enjoy it.

After my initial enthusiasm, it seemed to me that there was barely any difference between this bastion of the theatrical establishment and Ampleforth. One wore tights and a jockstrap at Central instead of rugger socks and shorts. 'Poof' became 'darling' but that was about it. The teaching was uniformly flat and uninspired. Both places were institutions and had the bad breath of tradition, authority and class obsession. Just as no one at public school was taken seriously if they had working-class origins, so in the drama school you were simply a joke if you were upper class. Emotion and creativity were the domain of the poor; buffoonery was the hooray's lot. The British theatre was in the third generation of its working-class revolution. The relative innocence of *Look Back in Anger* in 1956, and the star-studded casts presented by Tony Richardson and George Devine during the initial heyday of the Royal Court Theatre, had slowly crystallised into something much harder and more menacing; so that by the mid-sixties audiences were appalled to watch a baby being stoned to death on the stage at the Court in Edward Bond's brilliant play *Saved*. In those days – unimaginable in today's grab-it culture – being part of the theatre was similar to joining the priesthood. There was a vocational commitment involved, a missionary zeal. Vanessa and Corin Redgrave lurked at the stage doors of our regional theatres with leaflets describing the horrors of touring in the Urals. In hushed voices, huddled in the local pubs and occasionally in the canteen of our drama school, they described the Workers Revolutionary Party to receptive impressionable actors, who were mostly out of work and desperately reaching for identity. They were fertile soil for the seeds of revolution (not so dissimilar, in a way, from today's disenchanted mujahedin). Someone would run into the changing room and shout, 'Vanessa Redgrave is in the canteen!' and we would all run out and stand around awkwardly as Big Van talked earnestly to a puzzled George Hall. She always looked utterly spent and was not, I felt, a great advertisement for Utopia.

The strange thing was that I became a kind of buffoon. That was the power of peer pressure. You either had to get down on all fours and change everything about yourself or you bowed to the prevailing winds and became what people thought you were anyway.

For the time being, I got myself an evening job tearing tickets in the Donmar Warehouse theatre in Covent Garden. The play was *Macbeth*, starring Ian McKellen and Judi Dench; Trevor Nunn was the director, and the production was brilliant. The actors sat in a circle on orange boxes. There was no set, just a naked light bulb and an old metal sheet hanging from the roof that made thunder when shaken. Ian and Judi were spine chilling as the Macbeths and working at the Donmar was another of the high points of my career. I loved that job; I couldn't wait to get there every night. I tore the tickets, sold the programmes and was thoroughly smug with the punters. As soon as the three-minute buzzer rang, I herded them unceremoniously into the makeshift theatre and closed the black felt curtains behind them with a self-important swish. Any latecomers were subjected to my withering disapproval and, depending on my mood, I would either let them go in during the scene change, or not. Sometimes I just sent them home. I was drunk on being part of the group. I stole half the money I made selling the programmes and learnt more about acting than any number of whoosh-kas could ever teach me.

But it was not all plain sailing. By the end of the first week I received a complaint via the house manager from the leading actor that I was putting him off. I used to look, perhaps a shade too intensely, through the crack in those felt curtains, like an imprisoned wife in purdah, making eyes at Ian McKellen on the stage as his clothes were torn from him by the little witches in their dirty lace mittens.

I suppose I was a kind of modern-day Eve Harrington (the aspiring actress in *All About Eve*). Like Eve, I lied about everything. My age. My name. My background. I was a real number. I'd already seen this production of *Macbeth* a year earlier, during the blistering summer of 1976 while I was on a student course at Stratford-on-Avon, and for the first time in my life I became an obsessive fan. It was fun, but it was a full-time job. I hung around the stage door at night with all the other freaks. We huddled in a pool of light like lost souls. They were almost inevitably women. Some, the amateurs, washed in and out on the tide, but hidden among them were the fabulous diehards, eccentric ladies whose lives had been changed by seeing the play. Being a fan meant that you could utterly abandon your own life. You were 'born again'. Your whole existence became the play and the brief contact you had with your saviour at the stage door. The star was a flickering mirage that meant everything to you and nothing to him. You blinked and he was gone. He blinked but you were still there. It was a long high mass with a short moment of communion.

When Ian appeared, the ladies whined and snivelled, arms outstretched for the miracle of physical contact. In the brief moment of climax, cards, cakes and keepsakes fell on him like a plague of locusts and then it was over. My technique was more menacing. I positioned myself to full advantage, stood back and stared. I never asked him to sign anything. (I learnt, much later, just how effective this tactic could be.) Ian disappeared into the night and the ladies shuffled off, clucking. When they were all gone I dived after him into the darkness, darting in and out of the shadows like the hero in an Enid Blyton novel as I tracked my star on the walk home or to the pub. Sometimes, if I woke early enough (I had ripped a copy of the rehearsal schedule off the wall backstage so I knew his every move), I even waited for him to leave his house in the mornings and tracked him to the rehearsal room. If he spotted me, I pretended I had lost something in the rubbish. I was quite macabre. Then six months later I was passing by the Donmar Warehouse in Covent Garden and saw a poster announcing *Macbeth* as part of the coming season. I couldn't believe my luck. I dashed inside and got the job tearing tickets.

Pretty soon I had manoeuvred my way into a backstage position where I got to kneel by the side of the stage and take the three little voodoo dolls from Judi Dench's hands as she rushed into the wings after the mad scene. Then I had to take the dolls into the dressing rooms during the interval and set them by her place ready for the next scene. I acted very businesslike on these trips, but still managed to look sultry as I passed through the men's dressing room where Ian inevitably sat half naked and smoking in front of the mirror. The stalker was in the house! I think he was initially quite freaked out, but I kept my head down and bided my time. After all, there was a whole season ahead.

It was one of the most exciting jobs I have ever had. Creeping around in the wings of a theatre while the show was on, listening for the changing nuances of performance, feeling the disparate audience being drawn slowly together, was like being on drugs for me. My heart lived in my mouth and so it was a tight squeeze when I finally managed to manoeuvre my way on to the back of Ian McKellen's scooter and sped off towards a late-night tête à tête in Camberwell. I remember the look of fury on the face of his other most persistent fan, Sue. I had tortured this girl since my elevation to ticket-tearer. She was tall, slightly hunched, with pebble glasses, a high forehead, and long scarves that wound around her neck and dragged behind her on the floor. She was actually quite sweet, although sometimes she lashed out at Ian and had to be restrained. I will never forget the look of utter disbelief on her face as I nonchalantly strapped on Ian's spare helmet, a tartan Sherlock Holmes deerstalker and put my hands around his waist before riding off into the night. You could have knocked her over with a feather.

But she needn't have worried. There is an unbridgeable gulf between the fan and the friend. The fan cannot live without the framework of the play, and outside the security of tickets and programmes and latecomers I was a rabbit caught in the headlights of a car (or a scooter, in this case). I was a different person around him, and however valiantly he tried to cajole me out of my speechless state, I was stuck in a relationship that was divided by footlights.

Once, a year or so later, we were at his house and he was sorting out his make-up for some show he was preparing. The actor's paint palette is (or was) a scuffed suitcase full of smeared greasepaint sticks, beard glue, nose putty, hairpins and make-up remover. Its smell is the essential *eau de théâtre*. On the last night of a play, in the weird rush to get out of the theatre and back to ordinary life, these tools of disguise are thrown back into the box, along with telegrams and good luck cards ripped from the mirror, only to resurface later on another table in another town for another disguise. During a rummage through a make-up box, old times are briefly recalled as the cards and telegrams are reread with a smile, and then thrown out as the make-up is cleaned and reorganised. This was one of those times. The *Macbeth* season had ended. It was a Saturday afternoon. We drank a bottle of wine. I rearranged the make-up sticks and he sorted out his beards and sideburns. I loved greasepaint. Every colour had a number: 5 was an ivory foundation; 9 was a clay-coloured highlight; Carmine Lake was a dark burgundy for wrinkles and eye bags. Soon, we drunkenly began to make ourselves up. I painted on a Ziggy Stardust look with a lightning bolt across my face. He was a chalk-white geisha. We sprayed ourselves with fixative and then Ian suggested we play rock stars and fans. Unfortunately, improvisation was not proving to be my strongest suit at Central, let alone in my hero's flat, and this latest reversal of roles, far from freeing me up, as Ian had perhaps imagined, made me feel incredibly self-conscious. Suddenly, I was standing there on the sofa with a stringless guitar over a painted body, while Ian was writhing about on the floor screaming. This man could certainly improvise! After a moment he stopped.

'Go on then. Say something!' he said, but my mind was a blank.

Finally I put one arm out, struck an imaginary chord and lamely whimpered, 'Good evening, Camberwell!' before bursting into floods of tears.

Meanwhile the *Macbeth* season ended, and I became a dresser at the Aldwych Theatre, the other RSC venue in London. I dressed Charles Dance, John Nettles and, for a brief moment, Alan Howard. It was not a very savoury job. The play was *Coriolanus* and there was a lot of fighting. I had to pick up my artiste's sweaty underwear each night and take it upstairs to the wardrobe to be washed. It felt like a bit of a come-down after picking up Judi's voodoo dolls, but I still had an inane thrill just being inside a theatre.

In the dressing room next door to me worked another dresser, Joe McKenna, a tiny thin boy from Glasgow, a child star who was growing up. He was seventeen but still looked twelve, and he was trying to get into a drama school in London. The first time I saw him he was dancing down the Strand, on his way to the theatre, wearing a pair of beige shorts, a white short-sleeved shirt with a bow tie, knee-length socks and sandals. In his hand was a tin lunchbox, and he was literally swinging around a lamp-post.

I was soon to discover that Joe was more famous than some of the uptight RSC actors he dressed, due to the fact that he had played Ken Barlow's son on the legendary TV soap *Coronation Street*. Sometimes, as he was leaving the stage door of the Aldwych, fans would rush up to him instead of the leading actor, and ask for autographs. We became best friends, and every night we took the number 11 bus home, while I regaled him with stories about my life. Some were true and others were not. Joe was very suspicious and never believed a word I told him. I did make up some terrible lies, the most ornate of which was that I was conducting an affair with Rudolf Nureyev, who was performing at that time at the English National Opera. I would rather grandly get off the bus by St Martin's Lane and tell Joe I was off to meet Rudolf. One night he followed me. I was stalking with the other fans outside the stage door. Rudolf came out in thigh boots and a pork pie hat. We fans crowded around him as he made his way towards his bright yellow sports car. He winked at me as he got in. I smiled hopelessly. Then he roared off and the fans dissolved back into the real world. Suddenly, who should I see across the road, hiding behind a car, but Joe? We faced each other across the street. There was an awkward moment of silence, and then Joe proceeded to lay into me in a guttural Glaswegian, previously shrink wrapped, and all the more shocking because it bore only a vague similarity to Sing-Song Joe of Dressing Room D. He stormed off towards the Strand.

'Not a word of the fucking truth comes out of your mouth!' he screamed. I ran to catch up with him. I could hardly breathe. It is, after all, utterly exasperating to be caught out in the face of such a fantastical lie. My voice quavered; I was on the verge of tears.

'Listen, Joe,' I gasped, 'I may have lied about this. But not every thing's a lie.'

'Oh yeah,' said Joe wheeling around. 'What's true then?'

'Well,' I said, trying to sound reasonable, 'I am a member of the Embassy Club.'

'Big fucking deal. You're a fucking liar.' And he marched through the traffic on the Strand. A number 11 bus was just pulling out from the bus stop. Joe darted through the cars and managed to jump on it as it was moving off.

'You're pure shite,' he shouted from the bus, a fairly mad sight it must be said, in his retro child-star garb.

'Okay, so I'm not having an affair with Rudolf Nureyev,' I said, running to catch up, shouting to be heard, 'but I am shagging Ian McKellen, I swear!'

It was too late. The bus lurched off towards Trafalgar Square, Joe staring glacially down at me, victorious, as they swung around the corner.

We soon got over that hump, although it turned out to be a preview to the fairly bumpy ride our relationship endured over the following years. But when you're young you can forget and forgive anything; and as no one in the wardrobe department liked us much (least of all the wardrobe master, a mean queen with a falsetto), we had to stick together. We were probably utterly exhausting to have around. Joe was a T. Rex fan and always had to be told to stop singing.

One day the child actor who played Coriolanus' son forgot to show up. Maxine Audley, a famous, now totally forgotten, actress played the grandmother. She was an extraordinary star from a bygone generation: she had played alongside Olivier; she was a kind of legend; she liked a bit of a tipple; and she was fabulous to watch from the wings. She was like Sarah Bernhardt or something out of the nineteenth century. 'Oh darling,' she'd rasp at Joe and me as we hung around in the wings during the show. 'Could you be a poppet and fetch my fan?'

So we were very excited when she suggested that Joe play Coriolanus's child. I could already see him typing it up on his CV. I, of course, dropped everything. None of our actors got any service at all that day; I devoted myself to Joe, making sure his costume fitted, running up to the wardrobe to get stockings. I was very supportive, but then I had to be: I was still back-pedalling from Rudolfgate. When Joe went on stage, I took a picture from the wings with a camera that had a flash and the whole company went ballistic; I got my first warning.

After Joe's stage triumph, he took two weeks off to be in *Coronation Street* again and I went up to visit him in Manchester where he was filming. Joe showed me around the set of the Rovers Return, the most famous pub in British television; he pretended to be Marc Bolan coming in for a drink and I played Bet Lynch. Then we adjourned to the green room and rehearsed his lines for the next show in campy American accents. We were just having a laugh, but suddenly Rita Fairclough threw her newspaper down and stormed up to us. 'You little piece of shit,' she said to Joe. 'You think you're too good for us. Pay a bit of respect. This is your bread and butter.' And she jabbed at Joe's chest with her lacquered fingers, as she launched into a five-minute tirade. Elsie Tanner even looked up from her newspaper. Joe went white and then burst into tears but Rita was relentless. Finally we left the room and I thought Joe was about to faint. And then Elsie swayed over to us. 'Don't worry, pet,' she cooed confidentially. 'Some stars shine brighter than others.' She winked and moved on; but this was to become our mantra.

We were too big for the Aldwych and in the end we were both fired within a month of each other. Joe's downfall came as a surprise. One afternoon during the matinée he was walking along towards the wardrobe on the top floor of the theatre. Downstairs Alan Howard was having his famous moment on the stage. Never have I seen an actor milk a scene as much as Alan Howard did in *Coriolanus*. Basically his mother (Maxine) has inadvertently undone him. She brings his child to the stage (Joe). It is the emotional high point of the evening. The rest is bloodshed. On a good night, you could hear a pin drop.

'Oh Mother, Mother!' whined Alan Howard in an incredibly strangled stage cry. It was really effective. I loved it. 'What have you done?'

In the silence that followed, the ghostly voice of Joe could be heard, like the Phantom, from somewhere above the chandelier in the middle of the theatre:

'She's my woman of gold, and she ain't very old, uh-uh-uh
She's faster than most and she lives by the coast, uh-uh-uh.'

The audience exploded with mirth and Joe was fired then and there. He had to finish the evening performance and never come back. Between shows we went shopping for balloons and streamers and wine, and Joe gave a party in his dressing room. No one could believe his nerve, but everyone came anyway.

My own demise happened a week later. The Embassy Club was having a Roman centurion party, and I had my eye on Alan Howard's Act Two red leather costume, which was a very butch gladiator's outfit. I slipped into his room and nicked it on the night of the party but forgot all about it the next day when I showed up, still drunk, for work. Needless to say, I left at the end of the week.

CHAPTER 9

Suzy

There was a beautiful girl in the year above me at Central called Suzy. Everyone agreed: she had star quality. She had red hair and an aquiline nose, and had already been trained as an opera singer. We were all in awe of her; she was quite haughty and remote. And yet at some point in the beginning of my second year, at a drama school party, Suzy and I began to kiss. She was the first girl I really slept with. She lived in a freezing ground-floor flat in Belsize Park, with a gas fire fixed into the wall that had to be fed money to work, and even then there was only a vague halo of warmth around it. Cups of coffee steamed like cauldrons and in the mornings it was almost impossible to force oneself out of Suzy's bed. The windows would be frozen into crystal patterns and water from the hot tap steamed out of the bathroom in thick white clouds through which Suzy would emerge, naked. She had an eye for drama. She was already going out with another boy, who surprised us one morning in bed when he arrived with a box of chocolates. Suzy was asleep but I woke up as he tiptoed across the room. He made a whispering gesture to me and I snuggled into her back, watching him as he carefully placed the chocolates on the end of the bed and withdrew. I luxuriated for a few moments in the feeling of power, and wiggled my toes against the box so that it crackled like a stocking present at

Christmas, and then I guided Suzy's feet towards them. Sure enough, she said: 'Is it Christmas?'

The second time we had sex, it lasted about three minutes. 'Are you all right?' I asked guiltily, trying to gauge her reaction, but Suzy's face gave little away.

'That was great,' she said, without a trace of enthusiasm, and leant over to light a cigarette.

I loved being with her. She was much more sophisticated than the rest of us and made life at drama school exciting. One night at the end of the summer we were drunk in the Swiss Cottage pub, and she suggested that we go swimming in the ponds in the middle of Hampstead Heath. We ran up the hill into the woods. Suzy threw off her clothes and dived into the thick black water, emerging far out in the middle of the pond. 'Come on, you weed!' she shouted, but I hesitated. It was dark and deep, but I was drunk and loving Suzy, so I undressed and jumped through a hoop of terror into the freezing water. Spluttering to the surface, in a blind panic, with nothing but depth below, I swam towards the ghostly image of Suzy, as if my life depended on it.

'Look – I've found the raft.' Her voice bounced across the pond. She was fearless and held me in her arms, laughing, as I shivered. We hauled ourselves up onto the raft and dissolved into the darkness. There was no beginning or end to it. Just the vague grey shape of Suzy's body and the noise of the water beneath. But soon our eyes became accustomed to the dark and the moon came out from behind the clouds and we played around for hours. Jumping off, kissing and jumping off. All sorts of experiments . . . Could we do it while treading water? How far was it to the bottom? Finally, spent, we leant our heads and shoulders on the raft and paddled our legs in silence. The water gurgled against the sides. Suzy was a beautiful statue, her pale vacant eyes shone back at the moon, her hair clung in thick snakes to her neck, and her breasts disappeared into the murky water, the nipples just visible, outlined in little silver ripples. A moorhen awoke and flapped about on the bank. The moon was blurry and low. The dark rustling trees bent over us and the blanket of water felt soft and protective now, as a breeze swept across it, lacing us in little pink waves. Everything turned into one thing and for a second or an hour we lost ourselves in it. But the brain always drags you away from those life-changing moments of oneness. Questions like, What am I doing here? and Where is this going? break the spell, and the real world retreats as the mechanics of illusion kick-start like an old generator after a power cut. In silence we swam to the shore and walked home.

As the evenings drew in we waited for each other secretly after school and walked to her flat and then to dinner in the little Indian restaurant around the corner. It was one of those typical places, a long thin room with red flocked walls, starched pink tablecloths and a lopsided picture of the Taj Mahal. Dinner for two cost £5.30.

One night, sprawled at another table, was a handsome man of about fifty-five in a crumpled pinstripe suit and a mop of black and white hair. He was leglessly drunk, booming orders and insults to the poor long-suffering waiter in a strange breathy vibrato that was pitched for the upper circle. Suzy and I watched him, entranced. In his intoxicated ramble he always came back to the same point, a single insult, a mantra, and he laboured over every syllable of it, so drunk that the muscles in his lips shook with the effort as he tried to form the words and throw them out: 'Your father mowed my father's lawn.' The mower's son winked at us and grinned as the drunken man got up from his chair and lurched across the room towards the loo with his napkin in his hand like a dandy from a Restoration play. When he saw Suzy, he stopped dramatically in his tracks. 'But soft,' he stage-whispered. 'What light from yonder window breaks?' The waiter tried to push him on towards the gents' but the man was having none of it.

'Get off me, flea!' he boomed and sat down. And so began the first of many evenings in the company of James Villiers, a theatrical legend whom nobody remembers; two eager students waiting in the wings and an old shot actor stumbling off the stage. We adored him, and he worshipped us. At least at night he did. On the rare occasions we met him during the day, passing each other on Haverstock Hill, or at the bank in Swiss Cottage (where, ashen-faced, he would fumble around in his pockets for an elusive chequebook like a silent screen comedian), he didn't have the first clue who we were. We were part of the night; we came with the flocked wallpaper, the drunk's dream of forgotten youth. For us, he almost became the reason we were together. We worked best through his eyes. He fancied Suzy and I think she fancied him. He

Left: My parents' wedding.

Middle: My christening looks like an Ealing film. Great-Granny M looks as though she already knows my secret.

Bottom: With my mother, my older brother Simon, and Susan.

Right: Me with our dogs
in Norfolk.

Above: On the beach in
Malta with Grandpa.

Left: My brother and me.

On the hunting fields.

Leaving for school for the first time.

Bianca and me, now and then.

Out and about. Clockwise: Cher, Joanna Kirby, Celestia Fox.

Above: With Albert Finney and Kenneth Branagh at the opening of *Another Country* at the Queens Theatre.

Right: Converted by Gordon Jackson.

Below: With the Fox brothers and Celestia's cigarette.

Above: In the punt with Cary Elwes.

Left: With Colin Firth.

Below: And in the pub with
Piers Flint-Shipman.

With Tina at
Mr Chow's in
Knightsbridge.

With Ruth Ellis
(Miranda Richardson)
at Pinewood.

With Meinir Brock
on the make-up bus.

would question us about school and acting and nod sagely to our replies, drifting off as we aired our grievances. He couldn't really listen. But when he lost the thread of the conversation, he was always ready with a familiar refrain. With us it was: 'If I were a producer . . .' His Rs rolled and so did his eyes. 'You, Suzy, would play Juliet, and you, Rupert, would be Romeo. But I am sorry to say, the cake was not cut thus.'

Once, as we were carrying him home, we passed what looked like a rolled-up carpet on the street. 'Wait! Is that Ronnie Fraser?' said Villiers. Fraser was another legendary drunk. Sometimes the two men would dine together in the Indian restaurant, and even the bullet-proof waiters would take cover. The place would come to a standstill and we all settled down to an evening's entertainment from these two oblivious lunatics. They sat across from one another against the repertory backdrop of flocked walls and the lopsided Taj Mahal. They shouted and screamed at each other; laughed and wept seconds later. They got under one another's skin. Jimmie usually went too far, and Ronnie would storm out, slamming the door of the restaurant, leaving the clientele on the edges of their seats, at which point Villiers would turn to the entire room and perform a sensational paralytic monologue about just how mad and drunk Fraser had become. But five minutes later the other would be back (as if nothing had happened) and the double-act would resume. This time Jimmie would play silent and wounded, and Fraser would turn to the audience in a comfortable aside and say, 'Did he have a stroke while I was out?' It was magic. Real theatre.

CHAPTER 10

Clubs and Drugs

There was a raid on a tiny bar near the World's End called the Gigolo. Suddenly the lights went on, the music cut out and the police were everywhere. Everyone ran for the exit. Nobody wanted to be booked or spend the night in jail. Police and queers collided; a poor fey queen was flattened against the wall, leaving a dirty protest of foundation and mascara streaked against the frosted mirrors, as the rest of us managed to squeeze through the mayhem and out into the street where more policemen were waiting to take pot-shots. One guy was tackled to the ground, his drink still in his hand, then it went flying into the air and the ice and lemon landed on a policeman's foot.

'Watch it, poof!' I heard the copper say as I ran to the corner of The Vale and stopped to catch my breath and watch. It was my first raid, as exhilarating as it was frightening. A paddy wagon and two police cars flashed and screamed. You'd have thought a bomb had exploded instead of a few queens having a grope, but this game of tag with the law was the queer reality of the day. I waited on the corner contemplating my next move as a silver-haired man in a smart black overcoat came striding down the road from the club. As others were rounded up and shoved into the paddy wagon, this man's very demeanour of entitlement seemed to forbid the long arm of the law from reaching out. He stopped by a rather beaten-up Triumph Vitesse which he unlocked; utterly unruffled, he got in, wound down the window and leant out.

'Perhaps you'll find what you're looking for at the Sombrero,' he said (the Sombrero was a famous discotheque in Kensington). I willingly jumped in. We drove in silence for a moment, past the police cars and the club. People were still being hauled from within. The paddy wagon pulled out sharply in front of us; the white-haired man punched the horn and muttered under his breath. 'What a business!' he said dryly. 'My name's James, by the way.'

'Thank God we weren't caught,' I said.

'Yes,' he replied suavely. 'It would have been rather boring.'

I later discovered that James occupied a rather lofty diplomatic position.

At the Sombrero, news of the raid had already arrived, and we were given free drinks by a barman who seemed to know James quite well. Other refugees staggered in and soon it turned into quite a party. Anecdotes were swapped; stories were embroidered as we all walked hand in hand into the gay mythology of the times. The Gigolo raid became a date like 1066; subsequent stories would begin with, 'I remember, because it was the day Tina Sparkle was arrested at the Gigolo.'

It never opened its doors again, and the owner spent several months inside on its account. But James and I became friends. He lived in a tall thin house in Belgravia. It transpired that we had more in common than we thought. He used to escort my aunt to debutante balls. At weekends Belgravia stopped dead in its tracks. Its large glacial houses were shuttered and bolted. The streets emptied of cars in a mass exodus to the country. Hardly a soul was abroad. The silence had the claustrophobic tinge of a Sunday even when it was Saturday. Only deviants and inverts stayed behind. Walking down a deserted Elizabeth Street with James on a Saturday afternoon, one would come across some ducal figure emerging from a chalky mansion on the corner of one of the big squares.

'Afternoon, James.'

'Good afternoon, Jeremy.'

'Are you doing anything this evening?'

'I thought Rupert and I might go to our club.'

'Oh, lucky Rupert! I'm afraid Darren is insisting we go to that rubber thing at Mile End. I'm rather dreading it.'

On Saturday evenings we met for drinks at his house. If it was summer we sat on the roof terrace under the branches of a huge plane tree, the only living souls in the patchwork quilt of little gardens. In my fantasy James was a secret agent. He drank Pernod, wore jeans and a tweed jacket, jodhpur boots and a scarf around his neck. He was extremely educated, but the impressive thing about him was that he seemed equally at ease in the House of Lords or a Dockland dive bar. In a way, this was typical of the gay scene of the times. While the country was still locked in the rigours of the class system, the gay scene – by nature of its illegality – was not. Apart from the sex (forbidden outside the four walls of a private residence), this was the great thing about it. Convicts chatted with barristers, plumbers made appointments with earls. The present-day star system of hookers, porno stars and bodies beautiful had not been pioneered. People were quite generous with each other, none more so than James. We saw Lindsay Kemp as Salome together; we became joint members of the Embassy Club in Bond Street. I met Derek Jarman through him, and when I wanted to buy a biker jacket and leather trousers, it was James who lent me the money.

The night of the royal wedding found us sitting on his terrace. It was a beautiful summer evening with a warm breeze that tasted of iron and chestnut trees, but even inside the fortress of a quiet Belgravia garden you could feel the restless crowds moving around the city. There were parties on every street corner, fireworks soaring above the rooftops, pubs overflowing onto the streets. Nobody was indoors.

It is not in the queer DNA to take part in public events and national celebrations so we decided instead to visit a louche club in Leicester Square called the Subway. It had once been the famous Four Hundred, immortalised by Evelyn Waugh and Noël Coward, the smartest nightclub in London for thirty years between the wars. It was christened in the twenties by the Bright Young Things, who manically danced there before 'sitting the next one out' at the surrounding tables to watch the slow collapse of the Empire, the destruction of the great aristocratic mansions and finally the Blitz, all playing out in front of them on the dance floor. From a tender romantic kiss as the band played 'A Nightingale Sang in Berkeley Square' to the desperate embrace of 'We'll Meet Again!' those walls held it all. Now men fucked each other as Gloria Gaynor sang 'I Will Survive'. Many of them wouldn't.

We squeezed into James's Vitesse, but the nearer we got to Buckingham

Palace, the more crowded the streets became and soon we had to abandon the car and walk. It felt as if the whole of England was out that evening in an expression of nationalistic unity not seen since the end of the war. Suddenly maypoles were erected on village greens, oxen were roasted on giant spits and it was Merrie England all over again, or at least a kind of Disney version. This crowd seemed to come directly from a Chaucerian rental agency. Wives of Bath with hands on their haunches threw back their heads and laughed. Snaggle-toothed vicars downed beer and danced. All those children's stories that had been branded onto our collective sub-conscious had turned flesh: the fairy princess; the frog prince; the kingdom saved from evil; happily ever after . . .

The Mall was packed with rosy drunken English faces, eagerly watching the balcony of the floodlit palace. Above them on high white flagpoles flapped the symbols and insignias that had suppressed them for centuries. It was the beginning of a new age, but not the one anyone had in mind. With that night the last thread of our medieval past snapped. Of course, the apple was poisoned and someone had cast a spell. The princess would short-circuit. The kingdom would be sold. And for us, the poor queers skulking around the perimeter that night, flapping in the breeze with the Union Jack and George and the Dragon, was another flag, a lethal marker only visible under a micro-scope. It was already unfurled in the old Four Hundred, silently exploding like the massive firework display that rained down from the sky as we finally arrived in Leicester Square.

And every time I walked down the stairs into the inferno of the Subway, I thought of the Ampleforth Christmas show in 1973 and smiled. *Blithe Spirit* by Noël Coward. I am wearing grey tights and a negligee as Elvira the dead wife. My arms are outstretched. Wadham is beside me as Ruth, another dead wife. He has flour in his hair to make him look ghostly. There is a cloud of ectoplasm every time he shakes his head. It is very effective and I am quite jealous. Barnes is Madame Arcati and Noel Two is Edith the maid. They are huddled around a table incanting. Finally we have been exorcised, and Wadham and me begin to float off into the ether. As we disappear through the french windows, in a sing-song voice I tell my still-living ex-husband about one final infidelity. 'Charles! I went to the Four Hundred several times with George Frobisher. And I must say, I enjoyed myself enormously.'

John

John Jermyn came from bad blood. As I mentioned before, his father, the Marquis of Bristol, was the impresario of a band of amateur criminals in the mid-1930s called the Mayfair Gang, an assortment of aristocratic rascals and cockney thugs in the Ealing Comedy mould. A rich silly woman with a weakness for the bottle was their perfect prey. She would be wined and dined by a suave gang member, and then taken to a nightclub where other members of the gang were ready at the next table, to be wooed with more drinks and exciting talk. Her hand would be held and its rings would be slipped off. Her handbag would slowly begin to move across the table while she wasn't looking and then suddenly disappear. The group at the next table would pay and leave. The suave gang member would, of course, stick by the lady through the meltdown that followed. It was simple yet effective. (Today, in Brazil, they have perfected this technique. It has a name: Goodnight Cinderella.) The Mayfair Gang were roguish and brash, yet by today's standards they seem quite innocent. They were only caught out when their plans became too grandiose and they attempted to rob the jewellers Cartier. According to legend, Victor Bristol was the last man to be publicly flogged; actually his punishment was rather less dramatic.

It's funny how life goes around in circles. My father left the army in

1961 to go and work for the import-export business that Bristol had set up with a mutual friend, a man named Ian Dundonald. (my godfather). Another friend of Bristol's and Dundonald's was a retired admiral who had been given the job of running the Chilean navy. The two men seized on this rather questionable opportunity and went into business, using the Chilean navy as both a means of carriage and of avoiding the delicate issues of Customs and Excise. If it all sounds like something one might have read in a Graham Greene novel, this was simply how business was conducted in post-war London. Insider dealing had not been invented then and if a chap from the old school just happened to have landed a 'whacking good job' running the Chilean navy and if that chap – who was 'a very solid fellow, by the way' – had had some interesting contacts with some other 'reliable chaps over there', then everything fell swiftly into place. Naval manoeuvres could be scheduled for the Pacific, with a 'fascinating visit to the Hollywood Studios' while one was docked in Los Angeles, and a few containers could be dropped off at the same time with no questions asked. That was how fortunes could be made in those days. Unfortunately for my father, no sooner had he arrived in London than he lost the job. Why, history does not relate, though doubtless he was just too straight for something as ambiguous as Victor Bristol's business.

Seventeen years later, his eldest son John inherited £12 million at the age of eighteen. His estranged father was already on to a third wife, a former secretary named Yvonne, and lived in Monte Carlo. There was nothing to stop the young earl Jermyn from diving off the deep end. He immediately acquired a large house on the west side of Brompton Square in Knightsbridge, having also inherited the use of his Palladian family seat, Ickworth Hall in Suffolk, and bought an enormous old motor yacht called *Braemar*: all this before he was twenty. And so began a rollercoaster ride that took him from London to Paris to prison and from riches to rehab to ruin. Disaster was to hit John again and again over the years. Divorce, suicide, addiction and death were his unhappy cards. But all this was for later. In the golden heyday of the late seventies, this terrible future was a mere whisper, the odd shiver you feel when somebody walks on your grave.

As part of his permanent entourage John had his own interior decorator. He was called Mrs Renwick, and he doubled as a kind of social secretary. He had a savage tongue, slicked-back hair and black-framed specs, and spent John's money like water on his addiction for ruched swags and draped tables. John's Minister for the Environment was a young stockbroker called Nick Somerville, a short, ashen-faced man with big dark rings under his eyes, who was always on the verge of nodding off. No one in John's inner circle had any money and pretty soon whether we liked it or not (and mostly we did) we were reduced to vassals. This incurred much backbiting among the court and frustration for John, so people went in and out of favour with the tide. Some, like Somerville, had squid-like tentacles and managed to withstand the crashing of the waves about them, clinging to a rock as the ocean was sucked away.

It was all quite eighteenth century in a way; except instead of a vicar and a tutor, John had a decorator and a trader. He enjoyed it all thoroughly and presided over the group of rakes and junkies like a mafia boss niggling and dividing them. On an evening excursion to dinner, whole restaurants could come to a standstill as drunken arguments broke out among the group, normally started by a girl called Clarissa. Everyone in the court had a taste for live performance. Waiters would be insulted or asked to join the party; and when other guests in the restaurant complained, John would infuriate them further by instructing the waiters to offer them pay-offs. ('Give them a couple of hundred quid and tell them to fuck off.') Sometimes everyone would disappear to the bathroom, leaving a table of steaming uneaten plates, but John would pay for all damage at the end of the evening in rolls of fifty-pound notes. The clientele would regard him icily as the group left the room. He was not a popular man in London.

Somerville brought me to John's house during my first year in drama school; John had just split up with his first boyfriend, Robin, whose pastel portrait hung in the bedroom at Brompton Square. This room was like the deathbed scene from *Camille*. Mrs Renwick had outdone herself: a towering four-poster bed swathed in layers of thick brocaded curtains stood in a pool of light. A coat of arms was set into the upholstered bedhead, reminding you whom you were sleeping with (in case you ever forgot), and plumes and a coronet tickled the ceiling from the top of the canopy. John would topple like a giggly beached whale onto the bed while Robin's rather ghastly portrait stared accusingly down.

The whole house was like the set for an opera or the home of a poofie Arab. Mrs Renwick had gone to town. Newly restored family portraits shone on walls of shot silk; curtains and bell ropes, blinds and lace had to be waded through to get to a window; polished antique furniture and sensational silver were cunningly lit by Mrs Renwick in seductive pools of shimmering light. (This was the first time I came across a dimmer switch.)

But the house gave one the same feeling of unease that Victorians must have felt on entering the home of Oscar Wilde in Tite Street. The ruby opulence was stifling. It was like an over-ripe fruit about to flop off the tree and splatter on the ground. Actually, there were many parallels between John and Wilde. Of course, John wasn't brilliant; actually, he was barely educated, but like Oscar he a was gaudy show-off, a parody of himself. Once you got to know him, though, underneath the pompous self-indulgence there was a pathos that was enormously touching. He was like one of those ne'er-do-well characters in a Restoration play. You understand from the beginning that they are going to get their come-uppance, but they make you smile with affection as they prance around the stage. Their exuberance is addictive and the vanity that blinds them is an exaggerated version of our own so that we cannot help but be moved by their defeat.

John wore pale suits, pink shirts and thick ties from 'Mrs' Nutter, with diamond and ruby cufflinks. His hair was blow-dried like a poodle, and his pointed nose was the only feature that still remained sharp in a face that had grown over itself with excess. He had sweet naughty eyes and was always clean-shaven, no matter how grave the night before had been. In short he was a curious, compelling mixture of order and debauchery. His conversation was a similarly eccentric mélange of upper-class camp and country-house slang. There were words he adored ('twinkie', for example; as in 'He is the most frightful twinkie' or 'I think you're being a bit of a twinkie'). Everyone was given female status, and almost all adjectives began with the words 'Mrs Most'; thus each man in John's world was a woman with a double-barrelled name ('You're Mrs Most Moody today').

Sometimes at the weekends, if I was rehearsing late on a Friday night, John's chauffeur, Foley, dressed in full livery, would arrive at Central with an enormous custom-made Bristol sedan. He would park it in front of the school, then march in and give the keys to its bewildered registrar, Vinkie Gray. Later, I would drive down to Ickworth in this giant car; but I was blind as a bat and had a pair of glasses with only one lens. These were dangerous times.

Weekends at Ickworth were always a source of fascination, where lucky (or unlucky) members of the local gentry rubbed shoulders with London junkies. Extraordinary stories circulated round the drawing rooms of Suffolk (projectile vomiting at dinner; John passing out at the table). Some colonel's wife had somehow got locked into a bedroom with a young couple who began to have sex in front of her and then tried to make her join in.

Yet despite appearances to the contrary, John was still very much an eligible bachelor, and many a young lady and her mother were prepared to overlook a few 'eccentricities' in order to become the mistress of Ickworth. The all-out favourite among John's friends was an American heiress called Marianne Hinton. She was a large girl who towered over John, but she had a sense of humour and was smart enough not to try to cut him off from his friends. She mounted a spirited campaign for several years and it was generally assumed she had been booked, but John could never make up his mind. Finally he upped and left for a life of tax exile.

John moved to Paris. He rented a beautiful apartment on the rue de Bellechasse in St Germain. Mrs Renwick constructed another *belle époque* mirage around John and he seemed more like Oscar Wilde than ever. He was lonely in Paris, and had only the faithful Foley for company; and although friends would visit for weekends, they were growing older and had to look to their own livelihoods. I went over a lot, and we would drive around in his huge car, like a Range Rover but bigger, with a megaphone on the roof, so that John could talk into a little mike in the car and terrorise the passers-by. If there was too much traffic he would shout, 'Fucking collaborators. Get a fucking move on.' Needless to say the French were not impressed.

One night we came back late from the Club Sept with a boy and a girl. John had fancied the 'twinkie' for a while, who finally agreed to accompany us to the apartment, but there was a catch. He was bringing his sister; she had arrived last night from Montpellier. John, as usual, had lost all his brash bravado in the grip of a crush, and became like a big dog that had been taken to the vet for an injection. We all piled into the giant four-poster and pretty soon passed out. A little later John nudged me awake; the brother and sister were hard at it.

'Meet me down in the kitchen in five minutes,' he whispered and lumbered off the bed.

Ten minutes later I found him naked but for a fur coat, decanting a bottle of port in the kitchen. He was furious. 'This is the absolute limit,' he said. 'These people have no manners.'

'Do you want me to get rid of them?' I said.

'No. Foley can do that. I've got a better idea. Let's get out of this hell-hole.'

I put on a pair of trousers and a T-shirt; John stayed in his fur coat. We let ourselves quietly out of the front door. Things were getting pretty heated with the family in the bedroom. 'I hope they don't steal everything,' I said.

'Don't worry, it's insured. And anyway, it's all fake.'

We jumped into John's Ferrari that was parked in the yard and drove at breakneck speed through the deserted streets towards the *périphérique*. Finally we quit Paris and were on the autoroute going east. 'Where are we going?' I said, as the first streaks of pink appeared in the sky and mountains stood in the distance.

'Did you know that dawn is when you can tell the world goes round?' John replied solemnly.

'What do you mean?'

'Look!'

Long thin clouds were scattered across the sky, black with pink edges. The horizon was a bumpy line; as we drove towards it the clouds got pinker, the sky got whiter, and suddenly the sun appeared straight ahead and began to rise. It was true! You could feel the earth rolling towards it. The sun rose and the earth fell away. We were driving round a spinning rock. I turned to John, laughing. And that's the image I will always carry of him. Furiously driving, who knew where, in a fur coat and dark glasses; his face bathed in that weird liquid orange light that sunbeams splash onto the ridges of mountains first thing in the morning. Beautiful and sad, it lasts a moment before flattening out into the reality of another day.

He turned to me, earnestly, and said, 'You see, I'm not just a pretty face. It's all a question of mindset.'

We drove all the way to Florence, through the snow-covered Alps, speeding through the Mont Blanc tunnel at 130 miles per hour. Finally, we sat in an Italian autostop, drinking coffee and laughing about the night's events, but I could tell he was still upset about the boy. 'I must admit,' he said, 'I'm Mrs Most Miffed.'

John's boat *Braemar* was tied up for a while in Nassau, and the first holiday I ever really went on that was not with my family or an exchange trip to France was to visit him in the Bahamas in August 1977. At the airport in Nassau I bumped into an old school acquaintance, Damian Harris, whose family lived on Paradise Island, the little spit in front of Nassau harbour. He gave me a lift to John's boat, moored in the exclusive bay of Lyford Cay on the western tip of the island. It was, and is, one of the stuffiest enclaves on the planet, yet entering its gates was like going into a work camp. Double fences topped with coils of evil-looking barbed wire encircled the whole estate, which included a golf course, a private port, a clubhouse and a hospital. John's boat lay alone that summer in the dock, looking very out of place; like her owner, she was from a different world. Prussia had still been Prussia when *Braemar* left Bremen. Her natural habitat was the flat grey Baltic sea, and even though she had been given a thorough 'tweaking' by Mrs Renwick, nobody had re-upholstered the engine, and as *Braemar* left the port to cruise she blew up. We were towed back in and spent the rest of the trip making journeys in our heads instead.

Nassau was a very different place in those days. It was the essence of James Bond. An air of mystery had hung over the Bahamas since the days when the Duke and Duchess of Windsor had been banished there during the war. The big fish on the island at the time was a man called Sir Harry Oakes. He befriended the Windsors and drew them into some questionable business ventures before being murdered in 1943. Nothing much had changed since then. It still had the lazy colonial feel of a forgotten backwater. Little whitewashed stones marked the sides of the roads and red pillar-boxes stood guard on the street corners. The town rose up from the port in a gentle slope of brightly coloured wooden houses. Huge liners stopped by a couple of times a week. Their horns made the air throb, and their funnels towered above the town.

On the other side of the harbour was Paradise Island where *Braemar* finally managed to limp. We anchored in front of the Harrises' house to take part in their big summer party.

Damian's father was the famous hell-raiser movie star Richard Harris. That year he was at the peak of his career, and married to one of the It girls of the time, Ann Turkel, a leggy Californian babe who always looked as though she had stepped off the set of a Tarzan movie. The Harris house was one of the most romantic places I have ever been. You could only get to it by boat. From Nassau harbour you could just make out its pale blue gables, but otherwise it was shrouded from general scrutiny by its own jungle that grew right up and into the house, huge palm fronds leaning nosily into the verandas and scratching against the upstairs windows. A coral stone path made a tunnel from the house through the trees to the pretty white wooden pontoon at the water's edge where Richard's powerful speedboats were moored, like the private navy of a James Bond villain.

It was one of those houses you could see right through as you walked towards it, from the veranda through the large panelled drawing room to the garden and the ocean on the other side. From the cool darkness of the house the lawn and the sea were a shimmering mirage of emerald and turquoise. In the evenings lamps twinkled on the jetty, lighting the way up to the house, and to speed across the harbour towards it on a clear evening, in a trail of phosphorescence, in that curious-smelling breeze around a port – salty and rancid at the same time – was a near-perfect experience. As the boat wheeled around and came alongside the dock, the house shone out from the trees like an open doll's house.

Richard was mesmerising. There was no point competing with him for attention. His performance ran 24/7. Even when he wasn't performing, as in sleeping, it was still a performance. I remember coming into the drawing room at Nassau one afternoon while he was napping on the big sofa. It was great theatre. His huge toes wiggled. The nails were regular foot fangs. The hands and feet were mannerist like Michelangelo's *David* (although unlike *David*, so were other parts) but there was also an older medieval quality, a stone jouster knight that had slipped off his tomb. In repose his face was slack; the jaw had fallen open. His large mouth was stretched wide. Straggly blond hair stood up and waved to the overhead ceiling fan. Loud snores from the depths of that huge ribcage caused his lips to vibrate. It looked as if he had a semi hard-on. I watched spellbound for ages until a voice said, 'Have you lost something, Rupert?' It was Richard. As he opened his eyes, I mumbled some excuse and rushed from the room, mortified. But he loved it, and recounted to all and sundry how I had watched him enraptured for a full half-hour. 'You were probably studying me for some acting tips,' he said.

CHAPTER 12

Glasgow

I had been at Central for two years and things had gone from bad to worse. I always got the parts of old men. My teachers said it was so that I could come to terms with my enormous height; but actually, this was bullshit. They just gave me the dud roles so that they could concentrate their interests on the richer talent. So I slogged my way through the grandfather in *The Night of the Iguana*, the father in *Hobson's Choice* and some old family retainer in *Cymbeline*. But it seemed like a waste of time; I became a troublemaker, and then stopped showing up altogether. Eventually, I was thrown out. 'We are not saying that there isn't some corner of the theatre that you might fit into,' said George Hall, after each of the teaching staff had had their five minutes tearing apart my performance and attitude. 'We just don't see your future here next year.'

I was paralysed. I went home and slept for three days.

In those days, the theatre was a closed shop; you had to have an Equity card in order to get a job. But you couldn't have an Equity card unless you had a job. It was a chicken and egg situation. You had to apply to the repertory companies, the provincial theatres around the country. Each of these theatres had two union cards to give out per year. So every September hundreds of students, graduates from the thousand

and one drama schools, waddled like little recently hatched turtles, vulnerable and inexperienced, towards this ocean of opportunity, but very few made it to the sea. Some made it as far as Seaford, for one season, but most were undone in the initial struggle. You wrote a thousand letters of application with stamped, addressed envelopes and 'head shots' inside. The reps all held auditions in London, but if you had been chucked out of your drama school, as I had, then you found yourself completely off the schedule. And so you travelled up and down the country on draughty trains, rehearsing your Shakespeare piece under your breath. The freezing platform was your stage and you paced back and forth waiting for delayed connections.

'No deeper wrinkles yet?'

Inevitably late, you were bustled onto the stage of some gloomy provincial theatre. Sometimes that stage was lit and the auditorium was a black hole. You squinted through a sort of conversation with a disembodied voice. Your heart was pulsing on your neck and you could hardly breathe. These would be some of the loneliest moments of your life. That brave attempt to be king for a moment on a stage; you could barely hear yourself above the din of ambition and the paralysis of fear. Shakespeare's beautiful music was most definitely lost on your shrill hysterical lips. Sometimes the lights were up in the auditorium, and sitting, like a dream version of one of the 'old fossils' from the Braintree cinema, munching on a sandwich, was a director who watched you through jaundiced eyes from the stalls. There was never much reaction. Perhaps, on a particularly bad day, a sandwich would freeze for a moment in a half-opened mouth, but these men were used to us.

I spent all the money I had on this audition process. It was very demoralising. I remember writing to the director Val May. Naturally, I assumed this 'new exciting talent in Derby' was a lady and wrote a very polite letter opening with 'Dear Miss May'. I got a snippy reply in my valuable stamped addressed envelope, saying, 'Mr May does not accept applications that are wrongly addressed.' Well, I never! Val was short for Valerie in my book; Val was Valerie Singleton from *Blue Peter*. I knew that men had sex with each other, but still had no idea that some men were called Val. I learnt the hard way. And what about my poor stamp?

I was turned down everywhere. It looked as if they were right at Central. However, I consoled myself with the fact that all these theatres were fairly tragic. As far as I was concerned there was only one place with any real individuality in the country, and that was where I wanted to go: the Citizens Theatre in Glasgow. For my audition I threw out all my old pieces. No more Richard II, no more Hamlet . . . I would try more of a Sally Bowles approach.

The Citizens Theatre held open auditions at the Round House theatre in London. A tiny little Glaswegian lady with a squeaky voice showed me into a room, as a large American girl squeezed past us holding a skipping rope. 'It's been a pleasure,' trilled the girl, and the small Scottish lady scowled back. Three aliens, thin as stick insects, sat in a row laughing hysterically as I came in. One of them, the youngest, a good-looking man of about thirty-five, was wiping tears from his eyes. The man in the middle looked considerably older and was not laughing with such abandon as the other two. He had a shock of grey hair and the manner of a deranged army officer's wife at a tea party. His name was Giles, and he ran the theatre. 'My dear,' he said. 'How lovely. What have you brought for us?'

'Nina from *The Seagull*,' I said, at which point the third man, huge and rather scruffy, who had been getting up to leave, abruptly sat down.

'This I have to see!' It was the first reaction of my entire career.

The Citizens Theatre was situated in one of the roughest parts of Glasgow, the Gorbals. By the time I got there the whole area had been torn down. Now it was a vast wasteland cut in half by the railway tracks, which were built on a low aqueduct of grimy old arches that ploughed through the Gorbals towards Motherwell and the south. The sandstone tenements from the nineteenth century had been replaced by grim modern towers that stood apart from one another, surrounded by a muddy no man's land upon which the odd corner shop still stood defiant on the vague traces of former streets. Trains from Central station clattered through this inner-city desert and at night they flew past, the lights from the carriage windows throwing exciting shadows against the grimy brickwork of the Victorian sidings. Villainous pubs twinkled out from under the arches below and figures from Lowry were briefly caught in the strobe effects of the passing trains. It was like the picture on the cover of a paperback thriller.

The theatre was on Gorbals Street. It had formerly been the Palace, one of the top music-hall venues in the country, with four giant statues presiding over a big white façade. Now it had been stripped of all its external glamour and was a sad solitary warehouse, with only a bus stop for company. But inside that unpromising hangar was a beautiful nineteenth-century auditorium, decorated like a Chinese restaurant in red, black and gold with pale pink cherubs: a mirage refuge from the bombsite outside. It was cheaper than the pictures. And warmer. So it was an unusual crowd, to say the least, that picked their way through the singing drunks who sheltered by the stage door. They were quite unlike any other audience I have ever seen.

But when the house lights went down and the curtain came up, even those punters who had chosen the Citizens over the bingo were momentarily gobsmacked. The most extraordinary visions of opulence and decadence flickered across the footlights; actors like animals performed in a style unknown to the rest of the theatrical establishment (let alone Glasgow). Faces caked in white greasepaint, clothed for a film by Visconti, they howled and squirmed half naked around amazing sets of classical ruins or beautiful drawing rooms, their declamatory style varying from the opera to the soap opera, seemingly incompatible, but, to my young entranced eyes, utterly mesmerising.

A short while after my audition I travelled up to Glasgow to stay with Joe McKenna, and we went along to the Citizens one rainy night to see a play about Diaghilev called *Chinchilla*. It was the first time I had seen this place about which I had built up such a fantasy. We crossed the Clyde on the Jamaica Bridge. A man lay on the pavement. His face was bloody. His hands grasped the rails as though he were being swept away.

'Gie's a hon, pal, aver th'ege?' he slurred.

'Sorry?' I replied politely.

'Wull'ye no gie's a hon o'er?'

'Just keep walking,' said Joe firmly.

'What was he saying? Maybe we should get help.'

'No, darling,' said Joe. 'He just wants to know if you'll help him jump into the Clyde.'

I will never forget that first image of the Gorbals. A half-built mosque; the burnt-out carcass of a car in a circle of parched grass; a menacing group of kids running around with a football. And the theatre, blurry in the drizzle, more like a Methodist church than a bacchanalian performance centre. A huge poster on its rough stone wall proclaimed: 'All seats 40p.'

'This doesn't look much like a place where the actors all have sex in the showers after the show,' I grumbled to Joe, in reference to one of the (untrue) myths surrounding the theatre.

'I'm sure you'll change all that,' replied Joe, tartly, and we went into the theatre. An old lady tore my ticket (she would be my co-star in the next production) and I sashayed with Joe through another swing door into the rest of my life. During the interval I went to see the three directors in their little front office near the stalls bar and was offered a job as an extra in their next production that was starting in a week's time. I couldn't believe my luck. Joe and I celebrated all night in a club called Cinders.

The play for which I was contracted was a typical Glasgow endeavour: an adaptation of the complete works of Proust called A *Waste of Time*. It was written by David McDonald, one of the three men I had met at my audition, and was directed and designed by one of the others, the man with the tears in his eyes, Philip Prowse. They needed dukes, and could find none among the stagehands and cleaners who usually did the extra work. Just by luck I was there at the right time and got my large foot in the door. I was paid £17 a week, and went to live with my Uncle David and his wife Aunt Pixie in their house by Loch Lomond, half an hour outside the city. Of all my family, it was Pixie who really supported me in those days, waking me if I was late for rehearsals, leaving meals in the oven when I returned late at night, and sitting up to chat about life at the theatre over a cup of tea. The rest of my poor family still bristled uncomfortably at my new career, but not Aunt Pixie. She seemed as excited as I was, and that meant everything.

Philip Prowse was a bit like a defrocked Zen monk. He was icy calm, with an ethereal voice and very long fingers, with which he restlessly twiddled a large mole on the front of his neck, or the assistant stage manager if he was within twiddling distance. He had a crew-cut and piercing blue eyes, and was a kind of visionary. He had started his career as a designer and had only begun directing a few years earlier. His roots were in the ballet and the opera, and his staging of plays was very different from anything one saw on the English stage. The only work comparable to his was done in Europe by people like Peter Stein or Patrice Chéreau, but Europe didn't rate in the Great Britain of the seventies. Like everything unEnglish it was simply a joke, and Philip was widely distrusted (and disliked) by the British establishment. His was a design-oriented theatre where the look of a performance was as important as the sound and feel of it. Added to this, he had a strange uncompromising view of humanity, and he tutored savage perform-ances from his actors. He was not a believer in cosy emotional resolutions. An actor could perform a scene with heart-wrenching vul-nerability, and then turn proudly to Philip. 'What did you think?' he would ask hopefully.

'I wanted to be sick, my dear. I felt it was utterly bogus. But I may be wrong.' Of course he never was. (Even when he was.)

He saw all human beings as self-interested manipulators and wanted to see that on the stage. Sometimes the actors couldn't accommodate all this, being drawn to emotionalism as bees are to honey. They were uncomfortable letting go of the accessibility of a warm performance, and were unable or unwilling to grasp Philip's world-view. These actors came across as wooden in performance and were not invited back.

We got along straightaway, and Philip became one of my closest friends. In the years that followed I was to become his unmanageable parody. But for the time being the most valuable thing had happened: a creative contact had been made, and a foundation for my life as an actor had been laid. This is as much as you can hope for at the start of a career: to admire a director's work, their angle, and to find some kind of parallel in yourself, so that when they talk about how they see something, whatever it is – a gesture, an attitude, the seemingly incom-prehensible movement from one emotion to another – you are able without much effort to perform it.

In one of Philip's productions an extra could walk away with the show. There were probably fifteen non-speaking roles in the Proust play: dukes, footmen, mothers and grandmothers. We were moved around the stage in a brilliant choreography, punctuating the action, and pointing the focus from one timeframe to another, so that we all had the opportunity to grab the attention of the entire piece.

A Waste of Time was an amazing production. For anyone unfamiliar with Proust, in a nutshell the books are a catalogue of memories inspired by an afternoon recital in Paris after the First World War. In the wizened old faces of duchesses and courtesans, musicians and artists, the author, by now a bedridden recluse on a rare excursion into society, is reminded, in nine intensely detailed volumes, of their various journeys through time. Tangled paths, long overgrown, are rediscovered and charted by Proust in a book that changed the face of literature. If you can get yourself into them, they become hypnotic, and are really moving and funny. A few films have been made from some of the different volumes. Pinter wrote a brilliant screenplay of all the books for Joseph Losey to direct. But to my knowledge ours was the only theatrical production ever attempted and it was a work of genius.

In the darkened auditorium a huge black veil billowed inside a gilt picture frame that spanned the entire proscenium. As the lights began to fade, liveried footmen carrying dripping candelabra could be vaguely discerned, moving behind it like reflections on a flat lake. Other ghostly figures began to appear: silhouettes in top hats, a group of old ladies around a table, and high up at the back, just visible, like a distant memory across a gulf of time, was a lady on a throne. As the audience fell silent and the house lights quivered out, she could be heard reciting in French. The black veil was pulled aside to reveal the frozen tableau of an afternoon salon at Madame la Duchesse de Guermante's house in Paris. Hunched old men with walking sticks, and women in beautiful afternoon dresses, watched entranced as an actress called Rachel performed *Phèdre* by Racine. Proust was played by an actor, now dead, called Stephen Dartnell. He was forty years old, deathly white; he stared out into the audience.

'*Vaines précautions! Cruelle destinée!*' moaned the actress. '*Par mon époux lui-même à Trézène amenée.*'

And strangely enough they loved it, but like Cinderella at the ball, the Glaswegian audience had a curfew, and the silver slipper on the stage shattered into a stampeding shoal of Dolcis wedges at twenty past ten, just before the last bus left from outside the theatre. Unfortunately, *A Waste of Time* was nearly four hours long. At a certain point in the play (ten-fifteen) a character called Swann, abandoned and dying, realises that the love he had dedicated his whole life to was nothing more than a mirage (ten-seventeen). A famous moment in Proust: the end of a long obsession. Swann has come to tell his friends, the Duc and Duchesse de Guermantes, that he is dying and leaving Paris, but they are late for a party, for which the Duchesse has made the mistake of wearing black shoes with a red dress, and they don't want to hear. Swann puts on his hat, picks up his stick and is about to leave (ten-eighteen, but sometimes, if Andy the actor was milking it, ten-nineteen) He turns back to his friends with a last thought: 'To think that I have wasted the whole of my life on a woman who was simply not my style.'

In the silence afterwards, you could hear a pin drop. Andy Wilde was an excellent Swann, but as he left the stage, half the audience ran from the building and we would often finish the performance alone. But no one cared: there was an intensity about that play that everyone felt. It's difficult to describe a theatrical production. It exists for the moment it is on the stage, and even then, it's different for everyone who sees it. As the curtain falls, the final tableau dissolves into the ether. A few pictures might remain to jog the memory, but photographs are performances of their own, and so the magic of theatre is its life, yet also its death. Both are contained and celebrated in the moment of applause. The curtain goes up again. The actors take their bows. It's over. So I won't go on.

The week before going back up to Glasgow to begin, I gatecrashed Nicky Haslam's party for Andy Warhol at the newly refurbished Casserole, the restaurant above the Gigolo. I stole a beautiful suede jacket by Claude Montana from the shop where I had been working in Beauchamp Place, and also borrowed a garnet necklace (without asking) from the bedroom of Maria St Just, the mother of one of my best friends. I went over to my friend Hugo Guinness's house, where some junkie acquaintance of one of his sister's had left a bottle of methadone on the nursery table while they all went downstairs for a drink with Mr and Mrs Guinness in the library. Both Hugo and I were utterly reckless; diving off the deep end. We didn't know or care exactly what methadone was ('It's a downer, no?' we agreed vaguely), but like the medicine bottle in *Mary Poppins* it stood there beckoning us, looking absolutely delicious. So with an ear to the nursery staircase, we both took an enormous swig, filled the bottle up with water and set off down the backstairs to crash the party.

The restaurant was packed. There was nowhere to sit but I was about to fall down, so I squeezed on to the edge of a banquette and had a quick nap. A few minutes later I opened my eyes to find three extraordinary faces looking at me with amusement. Lady Diana Cooper wore a hat like a medium's lampshade with long white tassels. Next to her sat Andy Warhol under a weird peroxide wig, plonked the wrong way round on his head, and Bianca Jagger was sleek and glowing beside me with delicious smelling pomade in her hair. We introduced ourselves and I apologised with half-open eyes for the intrusion.

'What are you on?' asked Lady Diana from inside the lampshade.

'Morphine, I think,' I said.

'Oh, isn't it marvellous?' replied the old lady in a jolly voice. 'Doesn't one just want to curl up and have a lovely scratch? I was on it throughout the war, Andy.'

'Aww, gee, that's great,' said Andy.

And so I became friends with Bianca Jagger. She was beautiful. She'd just cut her hair short and was wearing a green Halston trouser suit. Nicky was not entirely pleased, but Andy and Bianca were entranced.

At a certain point Andy took Bianca's lipstick and wrote on my forehead, 'I love you.' A photographer took a snapshot. I thought no more about it, but the following Monday, after the first day of rehearsals in Glasgow, I was the leading story in the *Daily Mail's* Nigel Dempster column, beneath the headline, 'Spotlight on Bianca's new leading man'. My first brush with publicity left me with a spiralling sense of panic that should have made me think twice about the life I was so busy plotting for myself. Dempster revealed that I was a confirmed bachelor (journalistic patois for 'screaming queen'), and I can remember writhing around in my bed, worrying about the various reactions of my family and the company I had joined that morning. Dempster also mentioned that I was working at the famous Glasgow Citizens. The next day all hell broke loose among the Scottish press, and that evening I was asked to go and see Giles in his office. Philip and David were there too. Tears prepared themselves behind my eyes as I gloomily resigned myself to being fired.

'My dear,' said Giles. 'I have had the *Evening Times*, the *Herald*, the *Scotsman* and *The Stage* on the phone. They all want to talk to you. What on earth is going on?'

I explained the situation.

'What was she wearing?' said Philip.

'A green Halston trouser suit,' I replied.

'How ghastly. I wonder if it was made in ultrasuede?'

'I don't think that is really our problem, Philip,' said Giles. 'What are we going to do about all these journalists? We'd better have a press conference.'

I went white. How was I going to get along with the rest of the company, being the extra that I was, *and* give a press conference? Actors are quite touchy about these things. But Giles seemed quite determined, so eventually it was organised. I had by then made friends with the actress Di Trevis. She advised me to tell the press all sorts of lies: that Bianca and I were both macrobiotic and were planning a trip to the source of the Nile, and that she, Di, was my 'constant companion'. Unaware of the repercussions, I repeated what she said more or less verbatim. Over the next few weeks hysterical articles appeared in the Scottish press, and were repeated around the world. Bianca was furious, but everyone in Glasgow laughed.

A *Waste of Time* went on tour and I was promoted to a speaking part, and thus finally got my Equity card. Soon afterwards, while we were playing at the opera house in Amsterdam, I went blind. On the night before the official performance in front of Queen Juliana, I put my head into the water of a Jacuzzi thick with detergent and developed an acute case of conjunctivitis. The next day I could not open my eyes. The trouble was that there were no understudies. There was a crisis meeting and it was decided that instead of cancelling the performance, it could be reblocked by Philip during the intervals, so that I could be led from one position to another. Luckily I was playing Charles Morel, the pianist, so mostly I was seated at the piano, but Giles was deeply unamused. Philip, on the other hand, took it all in his stride.

'My dear,' he said, 'all piano tuners are blind.'

'Yes,' replied Giles tersely, 'but few concert pianists are.'

Before each act Philip re-rehearsed the scenes I was in, but while we were going through the extremely complicated third act, the bell went and we never got to finish, so that when it came for my big speech I stood up and, feeling no helping hands to guide me, began a perilous journey down a small flight of steps towards the front of the stage. The whole cast (and, I like to think, Queen Juliana) held their breath as I headed like a lemming over the edge but at the last moment I miraculously stopped and delivered my speech standing on the lip of the stage with a fifteen-foot drop into the orchestra pit right in front of me.

The amazing thing was that everyone thought I was pretending. Legend has it that as I left the stage for the last time I opened my eyes and winked at an attractive stagehand. In fact, I did not. But it just shows what a plotting maniacal queen I must have become that people entertained the idea that I could dream up and pull off such a gigantic scam.

I adored Glasgow and returned often over the next fifteen years. The jobs I enjoyed best and did best happened there. There was always a drama at the Citizens. You couldn't wait to get into the theatre at night before the show. A formidable lady named Rose Cull ran the canteen, which was like a prison staff room – shiny custard-coloured walls, a pool table and a TV. She was a stocky Irish redhead with small shrewd eyes that swivelled from one breathless queen to another, and she had a voice that could rise above the din of a shipyard, let alone the Citizens' canteen. She'd put her big hands on her hips and call us 'a bonch ae fockin' shirt lifters' but she came to every show even if she didn't understand a word, always sitting in the same seat, upright in her coat, her handbag on her knees, and her eyes glued to the stage, where you could hear her roar with laughter during the most serious moments. She was a lovely woman, and her canteen was a marvellous place, a melting pot of stagehands, wardrobe fairies, actors and front-of-house staff. Philip and David presided over the proceedings like the generals of a benign dictatorship, and Giles flitted around, suddenly swooping in on one. ('Darling, could I have a quick word?') You could score anything there from drugs to a washing machine. Conversation moved seamlessly from football to Flaubert or Proust to pornography. There were no holds barred. No one was patronised, neither the fey queen nor the illiterate thug; everyone was quite fascinated by everyone else.

I loved to sit there in the afternoons during the run-up to the show. Rose's little son, dressed in his grey shorts from school, played pool with the big lads. People drifted in and out in various stages of undress or disguise. Trains rattled by outside. A cardinal in deep red robes and caked in white foundation might be sprawled on the black leather couch lost in conversation with a rockabilly stagehand. Uncle Derek, who played the piano during the panto and was the living expert on Liszt, invariably arrived late 'coming thru' from Edinburgh.

By seven o'clock the place was jammed and only quietened down as the strains of *Coronation Street* cut through the din, at which point we turned as one towards the screen. But the start of the *Street* unfortunately coincided with the Act One beginners' call for the play. With groans and lingering looks, ladies in evening gowns and men in white tie and tails left for the stage, leaving Philip, David and Rose wrapped up in the Rovers Return as though they were in a box at Bayreuth.

CHAPTER 13

The West End

At some point during the second run of the Proust play in Glasgow, Lindy, my recently acquired agent in London, sent me a script called *Another Country*, about an English public school in the thirties. The leading role was seventeen-year-old Guy, a thinly disguised schoolboy version of the famous British spy Guy Burgess, who had dismayed the whole of Britain in the fifties by defecting to Russia. In those days, no one in stuffy England understood why someone who had everything – class, looks, and position – could betray their country. Julian Mitchell's play offers a compelling formula for treason: when Guy Bennet is found out to be gay, and therefore barred from joining the exclusive school fraternity – a governing elite of older boys – he turns against the world that has turned against him and plans a life of revenge. It is a compelling theme, full of haunting parallels, and a beautifully written play. As I turned the pages, sitting in the mayhem of the afternoon canteen at Glasgow, everything drained away as I saw with a rather scary clarity how my whole life might unfold were I to land the leading role.

I took the night train to London after the show on a Saturday night; leaning out of the window as we clanked over the Clyde, Glasgow felt like mine now. I was a part of it – and I had an overwhelming desire to jump off. We passed slowly behind the theatre, through the Gorbals, looking impossibly romantic, bathed in that ghostly orange glow of the Glasgow street lights. As we picked up speed ruined warehouses flashed past, close to the tracks, suddenly bouncing the roar of the train back into the open window, while the floodlit sky-rises rolled back into the distance, giving way to motorways and ring roads swathed in pools of mist on the horizon. We hurled through Motherwell and plunged into the cold damp air of the Scottish lowlands. Unable to get comfortable on the tiny bunk, exhausted but wired, I felt as if I was being swept along, going in the wrong direction; that something more complicated and dangerous was taking place than simply another audition for another play. I didn't sleep all night.

Julian Mitchell and Stuart Burge (the play's director) were an odd couple and the Greenwich Theatre was an odd place. Seagulls squawked around the rigging of the *Cutty Sark* down by the river; its masts could be seen from the theatre, sticking out over the rooftops. It felt a bit like Jane Austen's Portsmouth. Genteel village architecture ran down the hill towards the water. Teashops with bow windows swarmed with tourists who clambered around the area all day, but at night Greenwich was reclaimed by its gangs of Teddy boys, and you had to take care on the way to the station.

The theatre was a Grade One listless building run by Alan Strachan, a timid fellow in glasses. Julian Mitchell was a big man with an orange beard and an explosion of hair from his nose and ears, as if a bomb had gone off inside his head. He was extremely charming, always laughing, and had mischievous blue eyes. Beside him, Stuart Burge seemed to be dwarfed by the energy of his scribe and sat next to Julian rather like a tree that had been bent from years in a howling wind. He was small with a lazy eye under a mop of grey hair. He was also very sweet, quite shy and an extremely good director. I read some scenes from the play. Julian played the other parts. Stuart gave me some direction and that was it. I took the shuttle back to Glasgow in time for the evening show. Lindy called me the next day to tell me I had got the part.

After the sophistication of the Glasgow company, the first day of rehearsal for *Another Country* required a bit of an adjustment. The other actors in the play were mostly people who had come from TV as kids. There is something quite alarming about a child actor; but there is something even more alarming about them when he or she is no longer a child. Where do they go next? How do they make the leap? How do they shrug off their stage mums, who have lived and breathed through every tap rehearsal, every sprouting of a pube? The child wants to grow up but at the same time his subconscious is trying to freeze-dry him as it holds onto the elusive image of departing youth by its fingernails. The result, I concluded (erroneously) that first morning, was that an ageing child star had a quality about him not unlike an egg in aspic, or in the worst case a foetus staring glumly out from a bottle of alcohol. They still looked sixteen but were in fact thirty-four. There was an extraordinary boy called Gary playing a character named Wharton who was supposed to be thirteen. Gary was older than me, but tiny. Actually, he turned out to be quite brilliant. He was from the North, more of a stand-up comedian than an actor, a regular Tommy Cooper, cracking impenetrable jokes. But when he stepped out onto the stage he became a delicate little upper-class weed. Unfortunately for him, as we all morphed into our schoolboy personas, he was the obvious candidate for bullying. But it was pretty difficult bullying a Northern comic, and Gary endlessly bounced back with another joke.

Menzies, the part of the arch-diplomat of the school, was played by another child star actor, David Parfitt. He was a legend at the age of fourteen as the son of Wendy Craig on the hit TV show, *And Mother Makes Three*. Now he was ageless, like Tintin. As the play took its grip, he became his character and was always the mediator in the star wars that were to follow. He stopped acting after *Another Country* and became an extremely successful and sharkish producer.

Needless to say, I felt myself to be entirely superior to all these mere children, but not nearly as superior as another of the actors in the play seemed to be, a young man called Piers Flint-Shipman. He played the third member of our 'study', a typical empire ruler called Devenish. In the journey that *Another Country* took from out of town, through the West End to the silver screen, Piers and I were the only actors who managed to keep our grip on the swerving juggernaut that swung everyone else off during the drive from can't to Cannes. We became very close friends. He had recently left Eton, lived on Park Lane, and had a thin handsome face that blushed easily and seemed to be almost entirely immobile. During the first weeks of rehearsal he kept very much to himself, haughty and detached. Then one afternoon in rehearsal someone was humming a jingle from a popular TV commercial. 'It's tasty, tasty, very very tasty. It's ve-ry ta-sty.' Suddenly Piers lit up. After that he was the life and soul of the party, and his thawing out was the cue for us all to drop our various gimmicks, games and agendas, and come together as a company. All at once, to Stuart and Julian's delight, we became a class of schoolboys. The danger was that in the year that followed we became quite unmanageable (obviously, me in particular).

When you rehearse a play you quite often lose the plot – its plot. You become so wrapped up in the construction of your character, the production that is *you*, that you forget the play is meant to be a comedy, or a tragedy, or whatever it is, and sometimes when the audience comes in for the first time you are overwhelmed by their reaction and you fall to pieces. Thus, we had all forgotten that *Another Country* was primarily a comedy. It had begun to seem unutterably dreary to us as we slogged our way through it time after time. Stuart was a very thorough director, and he knew that our success relied on being drilled so that we did not fall apart when the audience took over.

However, no amount of rehearsal could have prepared us for the reaction we got on the first preview. From the very beginning the audience were swept away by the play. It was a curious feeling. We couldn't believe it. They laughed at almost every line. I remember looking at Piers out of the corner of my eye as a huge round of applause crashed over him after one of his lines during the first scene. He went pink with pleasure. We all watched from the wings during scenes we weren't in like children around a blazing campfire. It was utterly intoxicating. The audience were entranced, and the first night of the play was a riotous success. This was partly due to the fact that Piers' mother was best friends with the *Daily Mail* critic Jack Tinker, and his review was a giant full-page rave, but so were all the others. Success has its own momentum and life turned into a Hollywood movie from the forties (the sort when newspaper articles spin around on a black screen, as the show moves from out of town onto Broadway). We were a hit, the theatrical version of a boy band.

In the Embassy Club I had become friends with the casting director Celestia Fox. Her husband Robert was a producer and I invited them to come and see the show. The next day Robert decided to take it into the

West End. Kenneth Branagh took over the role of Judd, the other lead; and the virgin queen himself, Wadham from Ampleforth got the part of the head boy. I was elated. During the 'get-in' at the Queen's Theatre, an event that goes on all night, he and I hid in the empty upper circle and watched as the set was put onto the stage and the spotlights were trained into their correct positions.

It was strange and moving to be sitting there together. At school we had written one another letters pretending to be West End producers offering each other contracts, and sent them through the internal mail system. I remember my housemaster, Father Dominic, frowning as he once handed me an envelope with 'from the desk of Franco Zefirelly' written in a florid hand ('Zeffirelli with an I' was Father Dominic's only comment). We had dreamt in Technicolor of a moment like this; but would it, could it, live up to the childish expectations of Mary Stuart and Queen Elizabeth? Only time would tell.

On the afternoon before the first night there was a press call; after that we were free until the performance. Piers and I went out and looked at the front of the theatre. There we were in lights; my face was fifteen feet high on the front of the building. We walked down Shaftesbury Avenue to a bar called Phino's bar underneath the Phoenix Theatre. On the way we picked up some programmes from our show. It was then I noticed, looking at the cast list, that Piers had changed his name. He was now called Freddy Alexander. 'God, Piers, you can't change your name – you die if you change your name after your first job,' I said, referring to one of those countless theatrical superstitions that actors swore by.

'I don't care,' said Freddy. 'Piers Flint-Shipman just doesn't say it.'

'Doesn't say what?'

'Doesn't say screaming fans wet with desire.'

We drank two or three strong cocktails and walked back to the theatre.

The play was a triumph, without doubt one of the defining moments of my life, yet strangely enough it's pretty much a blur. The theatre was packed to the rafters; and when we came on at the end for the curtain calls, the audience stood up and the applause came and came in deafening waves, crashing against us. I looked at Piers. As usual he had turned red. I didn't dare catch Wadham's eyes. We might have forgotten ourselves and curtsied to the audience, as was our habit during all the curtain calls of our childhood. I could see Robert and Celestia with huge smiles across their faces. Julian Mitchell and his boyfriend Richard were leading the applause. My father and mother couldn't believe their eyes. All the grief was suddenly worth while. We were bathed in affection.

But a successful moment in life is hard to grasp when looking back. On the night, a whole future seems to be sitting in the palm of your hand, there for the taking. But the further away in time you move from the moment of triumph, the hollower it becomes. Soon it seems to be no more than the precursor for the next period of struggle, viewed with caution. When I think of that night now, I first of all remember Piers, Freddy from then on, who did die, less than two years later. Just before the opening of the film of *Another Country* he was killed on a motorway in France by a suicidal man who drove into the oncoming traffic. And second, more defining to me, or anyway as defining as the success of *Another Country* could ever be, and definitely sewn into my senses' memory of that night, with its applause that kept on going all the way through that long summer season on the stage at the Queen's Theatre: that night marked the end of the carefree, spontaneous way of life for us poor, barely legal queers. With the discovery that sex could kill, and in those days specifically gay sex, a new reflex in society was born. Little things: parents held their children closer when you came into a room; your plate was separately washed in a kitchen after lunch. The Christians and Conservatives began craftily to move the goalposts of public (im)morality. In particular, the Catholic Church surfed the crisis, making the most of fear and ignorance, and calling it conscience. Aids for them was like North Sea oil for Mrs Thatcher: the ticket to eternity. All that is wound around *Another Country*.

But I can still hear that applause and pan across our young bobbing faces all flushed in the fabulous lunacy of a moment's success. Was Kenneth already thinking of adapting the entire works of Shakespeare to the screen that night? And David Parfitt, did he know he was going to be Ken's producer? Piers was certainly not the type to have an inkling about his own death (he would have found that extremely common). The Foxes' marriage was to last two more years. And me: I thought I had it all down. But actually I didn't have the first clue what was really going on.

CHAPTER 14

Paula

Paula Yates and Bob Geldof came to see *Another Country* one night early in the run. They were friends of Robert and Celestia. Bob had just performed in Alan Parker's adaptation of Pink Floyd's *The Wall*, a film cast by Celestia; and, according to Alan, Bob had a cock so big that he needed a wheelbarrow to carry it around in. These are the fragments of conversation upon which whole legends emerge. But one didn't need to have coffee with Alan Parker to know that Bob had a big dick. Everything about him announced the fact: the incredibly thin body, the large pushy nose, the jungle smell of the man and, of course, the delight he evidently felt at the sound of his own voice, this was not the neurotic missionary zeal of a man with a button dick. Oh, no! Bob felt the unbridled joy of a stallion cantering around a field of long grass. There was an easy dialogue between his loins and his frontal lobe, as he played for his audience the preludes and fugues of his own opinions. He never listened. But this is not a put-down. Actually, it is the recipe for success. Bob was definitely sexy in a good old-fashioned Rimbaud (the poet) kind of a way, and all set to become a legend one way or another. He was dirty, he was mesmerising, he drove into you with the force of an electric screwdriver and he famously liked to be paid in cash.

Paula was his perfect foil. Or at least that's how it looked. On the one hand she was a typical English rock chick, the ideal consort for tomorrow's Che, with her shock of peroxide hair, a white candyfloss quiff, and a wardrobe of beautiful clothes made by Antony Price. She had a thin voice with a flat Uni dialect, and she clung to her man like a sweet little cartoon octopus. Literally. Her four extremities were coiled around him. But she was no bimbo, although she loved it if you thought she was. She was intelligent. She was a journalist. And she was the subject of a bizarre urban legend. She was rumoured to be the product of a famous rape.

The cast of characters from which she sprang was a rather macabre world of quiz hosts and TV preachers in the fifties. It was a kind of *Alice in BBC Land* where nobody turned out to be what they said they were. Her so-called father, the alleged rapist of the story, was the TV evangelist Jess Yates. Her mother was a fluffy-brained actress called Helene Thornton, who could not act and was not raped. At least, not by her husband. According to her, the story is even *more* bizarre. She believes that she was drugged by Jess Yates and raped by his friend Hughie Greene, which gives a whole new meaning to the words 'Opportunity Knocks'. It was later revealed by DNA testing (and at a time when Paula's sense of self was at an all-time low) that her real father was indeed Hughie Greene. If you have not heard of Hughie Greene, it will be almost impossible to explain how depressing it was for a girl like Paula to discover that she was his daughter. (He was a household name in the sixties, a macabre TV monster with the cheery bedside manner of a killer gynaecologist.) Being the product of the 'rape' brought with it, at least, a certain glamour, a sense of drama that Paula loved. But discovering that you were the child of Hughie Greene would have made you wonder who you were at the best of times, and it came as a death stroke when Paula's world was already caving in. But this was all for later.

That first night when we went out for dinner, to Langan's Brasserie, everything was still ahead. Paula was going to interview me for *Cosmopolitan* the next day, so the dinner was to break the ice. She wasn't classically beautiful, and yet she was startlingly attractive. She had a fragility that was erotic to men. She could break if you squeezed her too hard. She had a tiny waist that you could put your hands around and your fingers would nearly touch. This was her most extraordinary feature, because it gave the man she let hold her a sense of protective power, so that even if you were gay you could not help but feel turned on. Then she had a beautiful neck. It was long and slender and inspired the same head rush – a man could break it with one hand. It rose from lovely boy's shoulders and the flat chest of a young Bloomsbury lesbian. Her face had the illusion of beauty, but in fact it was wonky all over. Her forehead was round like Tweetie Pie. She had a pretty nose, little girl's eyes, but her lips gave everything away.

I think lips are more telling than eyes, and Paula's were as expressive as a cardiogram. They were small and pointed at the top, and however sultry she was hell-bent on being – and sometimes she was hell-bent – the lips could never quite control the mirth inside her, while there was still mirth. And they hid her sweet uneven teeth. When the lips and teeth carried the rest of her away, her voice could become lower and boyish. Half Mata Hari and half Marti Caine (an old-school Northern music hall comic), she moved between the two states as guilelessly as a child, and it was easy to fall in love with her.

The next day we began our interview. She had a curious technique. She began by undressing me like a doll. In those days I was so thin I wore five of everything – socks, tracksuits, T-shirts – and in the name of research, they all came off, one by one.

'What have you got here?' she squeaked.

'Another pair of socks?'

Pretty soon I was down to my underwear and she was sitting on top of me. Her skirts and petticoats were like an overflowing bubble bath, snapping with electricity, and at some point the interview ended and a strange love affair of utter misfits began.

She was married. I was gay. These constraints operated like a kind of safety net and there were no obstacles between us. We were released from the endless struggle to 'become' something, and the result was that we found a freedom in each other's company that was missing in the rest of our lives. We were both narcissists. We both loved to act up, and we adored being looked at. Our secret was safe with everyone.

During those early days she would come to my dressing room between shows, and everyone around the theatre craned their heads out of their doors to see her go past. Her arrival down the stairs was announced by the rustle of petticoats, the click of Manolo heels and the odd little gasp. She loved a dramatic entrance and had invented her own brand. She would stand in the doorway to the dressing room like a vision from some bygone production: Tinkerbell, perhaps, on the way to the stage. She always had flowers. The references for her life were all cinematic: Celia Johnson in *Brief Encounter* or Elizabeth Taylor in *A Place in the Sun*.

I remember watching that incredible film with her one Sunday afternoon in my little basement. Everywhere was closed. London was the most depressing city on the planet on a Sunday and people like Paula and me, whose lives were about getting ready and going out, were liable to crash. So we watched the film, and at the end, when Taylor comes to see Montgomery Clift on death row and she says, 'It seems like we're always saying goodbye,' I looked over at Paula. She was silently mouthing the words. She was like one of those hairless cats with a tuft. Motionless. Mouth half open. Almost purring. Drinking in the film. This was the kind of emotion she liked and responded to; abandonment and tearful farewells made her feel cosy. She wanted every moment to be the last. And that's how she entered a dressing room. She bit her lip. She loved to bite her lip. Then, in a breathy voice borrowed from Marilyn, but infused with all the drama of Elizabeth dropping in to say goodbye to Monty on his way to the electric chair, she would say, 'Hi, big boy . . .' It was pure genius.

Sometimes she came with her current sidekick, Hazel O'Connor. Then she wore construction boots under the couture. They reminded me of a pair of cartoon cats from a Disney film, spilling out of the stage door and preening onto the streets of Soho. Everyone would stop and stare as they rubbed themselves against lamp-posts and legs on our way for tea at Patisserie Valerie's, where in those days one might find Derek Jarman in a creative huddle with Tilda Swinton, or John Maybury recovering from a suicide attempt.

Just as the summers of childhood were hot, in my mind it was always autumn in the Soho of before. Old Compton Street was the hookers' high street, under a blustery sky, and full of shops selling cheese and coffee and wine. The smell of ground beans merged with the taxi fumes and was particular to that street. In the mornings, retired ladies of the night walked blind poodles for their sleeping protégées. In the surrounding streets, the front doors of the houses were studded with buzzers advertising the various talents of the models who lived upstairs, and at night the proverbial red lights glowed in the upper windows like sanctuary lamps shrouded by makeshift curtains. In the early evening anxious men in mackintoshes came and went. Later Soho was silent. The red lights went out one by one. Groups of drunks staggered through the spitting rain from the French pub to the Colony Room, and a lady called Elena closed the restaurant on Greek Street where Ossie Clark's sister, Auntie Kay, sang 'Gloomy Sunday' to a piano. All that was left by one o'clock were the lights of the empty theatres, endless forgotten names in reds and blues reflected in puddles on rainy Shaftesbury Avenue.

When I finished the run of *Another Country* I went straight into another play with Gordon Jackson at the Lyric Theatre in Hammersmith (it was about two priests and was called *Mass Appeal*). Gordon was a lovely man, and so was his wife Rona. They had no idea who Paula was or that she was with Bob, whoever he was, or that I was gay for that matter, but they saw us together a lot, and so assumed that we were an item. They would ask us out for dinner, and Rona would tell Paula about the pitfalls of being married to an actor, and Gordon would advise me about when it was the right time to take out a mortgage. (Never.) One night, when we had both been feeling fairly suicidal, Rona asked us when we were going to tie the knot. It was typical of our shared sense of drama that our immediate reactions were to think that she was talking about making a noose. Gordon threw back his head and roared with laughter. 'Will ye hark on these young?' he said to Rona.

'Soon,' screeched Paula, back-pedalling. She liked the way we looked to Gordon and Rona, and so did I. They thought we were a lovely couple, and we thought they were as well, and during our various encounters – when we were sometimes joined by a painfully shy Kenneth Williams, Gordon's best friend – the potential for living according to the norm was certainly not lost on me. It was effortless being one of the guys.

'She's quite sensitive, isn't she?' broached Rona evenly once while Paula was in the loo.

'She's just high strung, Rona,' admonished Gordon. 'So were you at that age.'

Rona's eyebrows rose ever so slightly, her face retired into her neck and her cheeks puffed for a moment.

Yet Paula was desperately fragile, and with any kind of confrontation she was channelled back before your very eyes into a nine-year-old child. She turned red, her voice stuck in her throat beneath the bitten lip, and her eyes sparkled with tears. It was then that her neck and shoulders looked their loveliest. But she was unbreakable at the same time. In the tradition of the great fragile rocks – Marilyn, Lady Diana, Frances Farmer – this combination was likely to drive a man mad. Already fragility has the aroma for some men that poppers have for others. They see it, they want it, they think they can ride it, but when they find it is unbreakable, that's when the murder starts.

But no man was going to break Paula. It had been done before any of us knew her, probably on the set of *Opportunity Knocks* or some afternoon quiz show. She had picked herself up and stuck the bits together on her own. But some bits were in the wrong place.

Considering the bluntness of my ambition, and the strength of my desire to succeed at any cost, it is puzzling how strangely I behaved once I had made it onto the West End stage. My name was in lights. Actually it wasn't, but my face (or one of them) surveyed Shaftesbury Avenue with a haughty regard. You could see it sneering from Cambridge Circus. Like in the movies, my address was Dressing Room A, although this came not without a struggle. Robert had wanted it to be a green room. I was apoplectic. Finally, after studiously arriving late from a series of quick changes in my original upstairs dressing room, panting onto the stage during the technical rehearsal, mouthing to some unseen authority in the auditorium that I would never make it to the stage in time, he succumbed and I moved into the star suite for the duration of the run. I was ecstatic. For about five minutes. Then I got bored. Suddenly the six months of the run turned into an endless tunnel. On paper, eight shows a week seemed like a cakewalk. The reality was much tougher.

The midweek matinée was my Achilles heel, that hangover from the days of Empire when trains steamed into the metropolis spilling out ladies from the country for a morning's shopping at the Army and Navy, followed by lunch and a matinée. In those glorious days, tea trays were served and the afternoon's performance was accompanied by the clatter of cups and saucers. Matinées were packed to the rafters. But that was then. For some reason this terrible tradition still exists even though for the most part there are rarely more than fifty or sixty people at a midweek matinée, and of those that are there, not all of them are all there.

So I quickly discovered the actor's worst nightmare: going to the theatre at two o'clock on a Wednesday afternoon. It didn't matter that I was just starting out. By the fourth week of the run I felt as though I had been in the business since Roman times. Walking down the street towards the theatre, never had the light of day looked more appealing. The descent into musty darkness, to the bowels of the earth, and the dusty smell of the dressing room seemed like live burial. The debris of last night's high-spirited escape always littered the room. Cigarette ends overflowed off saucers. Rancid dregs lay in unwashed wine glasses. You stared at yourself glumly in the mirror. Only last month those naked light bulbs around the edge were the symbol of everything you loved. Now you wanted to take them out one by one and eat them. Your view of yourself was framed by dusty, curling, stained telegrams that you had stuck on the glass. They accused you of being brilliant, and you believed them.

At some point the tannoy came on, and the stage manager announced the half-hour call and the opening of the house. A feeling of utter hopelessness engulfed you as a solitary cough echoed from the auditorium. Over the next half-hour you heard fifty or sixty people shuffle into the house. The murmur of conversation in an empty theatre was wrist slitting. You couldn't even lift the make-up stick off the table. Ten cigarettes later you were in the wings, and after some perfunctory greetings with the rest of the cast you had to pull yourself together and bounce onto the stage. All of your nerve endings braced themselves for the big push as you strained to hit the same notes at the same pitch, but it was going to be an emotional cop-out, a dead performance, and you knew it. You looked out over the house beyond the glare of the spotlights and saw row after row of empty seats stretching up into the darkness. A batlike screech or two suggested the presence of the utterly deaf. Then you must pretend that it was the first time you had ever said your line for the eightieth time.

I began to play elaborate practical jokes. I invented whole new sections of dialogue. I appeared in wigs. I performed in French. What was I thinking? On the day of Yom Kippur, Piers and I dressed up as rabbis, and after our first scene we dashed through the pass door into the theatre, jumped into our beards and hats, and then went into the royal box, and laughed uproariously at every joke made by Wadham. Of course, the whole cast on stage became hysterical and, as anyone will tell you, laughing during a play when you ought not to is more enjoyable than orgasm, scoring a goal, taking communion, or all of them together.

There was a tea party scene in *Another Country* that often came to a standstill. An older actor in the show, David William, who played the fey uncle of one of the boys (Piers), was easy to get going on stage, and soon tears of anguish and pleasure would be pouring down his powdered cheeks. Once Piers bought a special lump of sugar from the magic shop in Drury Lane that dissolved into a huge beetle once it hit hot water. We placed it in the sugar bowl during the interval while nobody was looking, and then sure enough, David took the lump and we waited breathlessly as he stirred his tea and sang his lines.

His was a campy part. He sat with his knees crossed, his cup and saucer in one hand, a teaspoon in the other. He incanted up towards the balcony, eyes wide, and a Swanson grimace. 'Thlonk' went the lump of sugar. David stirred archly, always staring up towards the gods (he was old school). Without looking he raised the cup to his lips, only glancing down as the two made contact. Surpassing our wildest expectations, he literally screamed and threw the teacup over his shoulder. Apparently the beetle had jumped out from the bottom of the cup. After that, the scene came to a standstill and we had to start again. At the end of the show a white-faced author came backstage, assembled the cast and gave us a severe dressing down. David William never squeaked about the beetle and we all performed like little nuns that night for the evening show.

One dreary matinée day, I started hearing voices. For some reason I had arrived early, and the stage and wings were empty. 'Yoohoo!' sang an unseen lady. I looked around. 'Yoohoo!' she sang again, very close by, but there was no one there. Was I hearing the theatre ghost?

'He can't see us. How terribly funny,' said a man's voice.

I got quite nervous. Then I saw a hole in the brick wall of the stage. It was about as big as a door handle. The voices seemed to be coming from the other side. I looked through and there was an enormous eye, soon afterwards replaced by a pair of red shiny lips outlined in black.

'There you are,' they said. 'We've been trying to get through to you for ages. My name's Maria.'

It was Maria Aitken, a noted actress who had just moved into the Globe theatre next door. We exchanged pleasantries, arranged to have tea between the shows, and soon struck up an immediate 24/7 friendship that exasperated everyone else we knew. From then on I was always in the next-door theatre. I even had my own little make-up set in Maria's room so that I could get changed there. This kind of behaviour was considered sacrilegious in the ritualised world of the theatre, and Betty, Maria's dresser, hated me on sight. 'He's no good, he'll get you into trouble,' she moaned, but Maria didn't need me to get her into trouble. She came from a troublesome family. When I told my mother of our rapport, her face drained of colour. Then she reminded me of the bad blood between our two families.

One of my father's great friends was an old soldier, General Alexander. This man lived in Yorkshire, not far from Ampleforth, with his wife Marabel, and my parents would sometimes stay with them during the holiday weekends. They were a typical military couple: out of uniform and out of touch. At some point while I was still at school, General Alexander had the misfortune to meet Jonathan Aitken, Maria's elder brother. He was an ambitious young journalist, hoping to become a politician; Alexander was an old drunk who made the mistake of talking to him about an official secret of no very great proportion at a dinner party one night. The older man showed the party some documents pertaining to some event in Ghana in the fifties. Aitken saw an opportunity. He asked Alexander whether he could borrow the papers to read at home that night since he was fascinated by the subject. Alexander agreed. A week later the whole thing was in the *Sunday Times*.

Over the next five years, Alexander was court-martialled, divorced and ruined, finally ending his life in a little caravan. At one point, driven crazy by the impending scandal, Marabel asked Aitken to tea and bugged the room rather hopelessly, in order to trap Jonathan into saying something with which she could blackmail him afterwards. I remember hearing this story as a child. It was legendary. 'Bloody gutsy of old Marabel. Such a shame he never came out with anything,' the officers said over port after lunch at home. The tape recorder was hidden under a few copies of *Country Life* and clicked loudly when the tape inside ran out. Aitken made political headway out of the story, and you can imagine my family's pleasure when he received his come-uppance many years later. Unfortunately, Alexander was already dead by then.

The streets behind Shaftesbury Avenue were a rabbit warren of stage doors through which I could be spotted emerging in my schoolboy costume and my geisha make-up, darting from one to another on my rounds. Philip Prowse had arrived with Glenda Jackson at the Lyric Theatre two doors down; Simon Callow was playing in the Duke of York's; and Derek Jarman lived at Phoenix House around the corner, so I had a wonderful summer. I swapped box-office banter with my fellow thespians over the phone during the half-hour before the show. I learnt all the jargon. Glenda started doing 'twofers' pretty quick into the run (two tickets for the price of one) and Maria was papering the house no sooner than she had moved in (freebies). Simon Callow lied insanely and always claimed there to be standing room only for the upper circle. We, on the other hand, went from strength to strength.

Robert and I fell out over dinner towards the end of the run. He wanted me to renew my contract with the play, and I, by now, was a hungry baby successivore, my first meal digested, baying for my next snack. He told me I was mad to leave a hit show. I told him I didn't care. Actually it ended up well for Robert, because the next actor who played my role was Daniel Day-Lewis, who received a better review than I had ever got, saying I was basically tinsel by comparison. Robert had it blown up and printed word for word on the front of the theatre and so, for a short time, embassies were closed and diplomatic relations between the two of us were severed. But it was a short-lived falling-out.

Paula met Michael Hutchence from the band INXS on the set of *The Big Breakfast* one morning in 1993. People who were there that day said that you could cut the atmosphere with a knife; there wasn't just sexual tension in the air, but also a feeling of collision. Two runaway trains were crashing into each other. Paula's life was ready to explode; Michael came along and she exploded onto him. They should probably never have met; the relationship was highly unsuitable for both of them. Michael was with Helena Christensen, and Paula had three children with Bob, and yet they could barely contain themselves. It was a black hole that sucked them both in. They were the Cathy and

Heathcliff of the ecstasy generation. The stage was set for the melo-drama to unfold.

Paula and I met shortly afterwards in Valotti's teashop on Shaftesbury Avenue. It was one of the last establishments of its kind, a place where actors and dressers ate beans on toast in a rush between the matinée and the evening performance, and now it was closing down. We were surrounded by a TV crew who were filming the event for Paula's show, and the sparrow-like Italian cockney waitress and her sidekick, the big Polish redhead, were in a state of rare excitement. Paula was beautiful that day and tinged with hysteria; her little pale lashes framed eyes that glowed like a vampire from a Hammer horror film. But she was in great spirits, ecstatically happy and during our interview playfully dug her stiletto into my groin under the table. Sitting there in the tiny booth that afternoon, I remember thinking that Valotti's was the perfect backdrop for Paula, though she would never have thought so herself. Against its red and yellow squeezy bottles of ketchup and mustard, its stainless-steel sugar bowls and cracked white teacups, she'd never looked so good. She had filled out, turning into a busty barmaid, yet still with that strange fragility, the latest in a line of English blondes, from Dusty Springfield to Diana Dors and Bet Lynch. She was sexy and fatal. She put all her energy into that. But she also had a fish and chips with extra vinegar side to her, and that was her secret recipe.

I had only met Michael once. Shortly before he died they came to a play that Philip Prowse and I were doing at the Lyric Theatre in Hammersmith. I was playing Mrs Goforth in *The Milk Train Doesn't Stop Here Anymore* by Tennessee Williams. It couldn't have been a fur-ther cry from my last appearance on those ancient (but relocated) boards when I had played a bounding exuberant young priest opposite Gordon Jackson. Now I was a cancerous old swamp bitch in the classi-cal Tennessee tradition. The play marked my first foray into the limelight after the success of *My Best Friend's Wedding* and the first night was a colourful affair. Michael and Paula, losing the plot, brought their baby daughter Tiger with them, and they sat in front of my par-ents. Tiger gurgled and giggled through the show, and I thought I must be dreaming.

They were sweet but detached afterwards. It was a strange place to meet, because neither of us had been there since the days of Gordon and Rona Jackson all those years ago. We were adults now, strangers to ourselves then; standing in the same place now, but we couldn't get back. Paula was giggly. Michael smiled. I was jumpy. At the dinner afterwards, there definitely seemed to be an aura of tragedy about them. Their faces looked as though they were seeing something else happening in the room. The air was thick around them. They had been swept too far out and were looking at us all from a long way off. Maybe, deep inside, they knew they were reaching the end of their journey. Each moment was just the one before the one before the last. What was a first-night party for the rest of us was just one in the series of sad farewells that Paula had dreamt of all those years ago watching A *Place in the Sun*.

Soon everyone knew that their relationship had turned into a runaway train. Events had outdone them. They had the first spilling nanny who spoke to a delighted press of Polaroids and opium under the bed. Bob and Paula fought. That delighted the press even more. And then Hughie Greene turned out to be Paula's father. Things hardly got better in Fleet Street. She held it together as long as she had Michael. The world around them shifted and subsided. People took sides. Trusted friends turned. And then Michael hanged himself from the bathroom door of a hotel room in Sydney. Was it sex or suicide? Either way, Paula didn't recover. Her last act was from *Hamlet*; her Ophelia would drown in a river of flash bulbs. I remember seeing a spread in *Hello!* magazine the year before she died. She was photographed on the beach at Hastings where she had a small house. The pictures were very moving. And like Valotti's earlier, Hastings, with its gloomy south coast Englishness, its old people's homes and its marauding yobs, was a perfect poignant background for Paula. She was putting up a valiant last stand, crouched out of the wind by the breakers, a lonely figure on a pebble beach beside the brown sea. After Michael's death her every stumble was catalogued. She was shot and had nowhere to hide. Somehow death was inevitable.

One October morning in 1997 I was in bed in New York and the telephone rang. It was Bob. We had not spoken in nearly twenty years. 'Paula's dead,' he said, 'and you've got to come and read a poem at the funeral. She wouldn't forgive you if you don't.'

The funeral was at Faversham, the beautiful medieval abbey

surrounded by council flats that Bob had bought for Paula in those heady days when everything seemed as if it could never go wrong, and if it did there was all the time in the world to fix it. Then they had been the Arthur and Guinevere of the New Labour movement; common with a grand touch, and Faversham a kind of Camelot. Bob's Round Table was the cream of international celebrity, though actually Paula had been the inspiration of the Live Aid movement. She was the one who stuck a collection box onto the fridge in Clapham after watching a documentary about Ethiopia.

It was a long and winding road from the kitchen in Clapham to the cloister at Faversham where she posed in that scarlet wedding dress surrounded by stars, every one a potential Lancelot. She had escaped from Camelot but now she was back. The Round Table were all there to welcome her home: Paul Young, Nick Cave, Jools Holland; older, a touch tubbier, more cautious, standing in awkward groups in the October sunshine. Paula wasn't the only one to have sailed too close to the wind. The nineties had eaten a lot of us alive.

Would she have laughed or cried to see her mother with whom she hadn't spoken for five years, meeting Tiger for the first time? She would definitely have done a quick rotation in her grave as Sabrina Guinness arrived in the church. The two women had disliked each other enormously.

Nobody wanted to talk much. There was nothing cheery about the event, which is unusual for funerals. Annie Lennox walked up and down at the end of the garden all alone, looking like *The Scream* by Munch. Soon the hearse rolled through the gates, accompanied by a blinding explosion of flash bulbs. The paparazzi had done her proud and were hanging out of the trees on the lane that led to the house. The white coffin, covered in tiger lilies, was carried into the chapel and the service began. It was beautiful. Bob had thought of everything and it was very moving to watch him. Whatever anyone might say, Paula had been the love of his life. Now he had her back feet first. Bono sang 'Blue Skies' accompanied by Jools. At the end of the service they put on a track of Paula singing 'These Boots Are Made for Walking'. I had completely forgotten it, but then I remembered seeing her the day after she had recorded it. We had been shopping in the World's End, and she had bought me a leather jacket. Her disembodied voice filled the old church: breathless, thin. She was no singer, but there she was again over the hiss of static, suddenly alive. Our hearts leapt for a moment at the trick of sound and it was hard to listen to that silly song through chorus after chorus, but finally she said, 'Come on, boots, walk.' The pallbearers, big-fingered mafioso types, lumbered from their seats and picked up the coffin as Paula broke into a final chorus and her physical remains left the church to be burnt at the crematorium.

CHAPTER 15

Barbarian Queen

In the four years since leaving drama school I had played a few small parts on TV, and had made a short film that would be my only (so far) near brush with an Oscar. It was called A *Shocking Accident* and won Best Short.

But my first serious car-to-the-airport kind of job was called *Arthur the King*. A reworking of the Arthurian legend from the pen of NBC in America, our film began with Dyan Cannon on a coach trip to Stonehenge under which lived Merlin, played by Edward Woodward (the actor whose name Noël Coward thought sounded like 'a fart in the bath'), who had left open what can only be described as a kind of spiritual window. Naturally Dyan falls in. She discovers that Merlin and his wife (Lucy Gutteridge) are stuck in a time warp under Stonehenge and spend their days (eternity) watching out-takes of life at Camelot on a screen hidden behind some stalactites. Malcolm McDowell was Arthur. Candice Bergen was Morgan Le Fay. I was Lancelot du Lac. In my woven gown, with my long dark hair and my painfully thin physique, I looked like a combination of Snow White and Anne Frank.

I was terrible as Lancelot. As a debut there were none of those early first signs one reads about in the biographies of others when a cinematographer swings down on a crane and says, 'You got it, kid.' Ours, a man named Dennis, asked me, during a pause while he adjusted his lamps, 'Why do you stand bent?'

'I don't know, Dennis,' I replied.

'You're all scrunched up,' he said, and made a horrible little grimace of imitation.

'Oh,' I said, outwardly nonchalant, but inside on red alert. 'Scrunched up' is not the phrase you are looking for from the director of photography (always known as the DP).

Being part of a film crew on location is not unlike being at a public school. Gangs form. The class macho lays his claim (Malcolm). The school jokester takes his part (Patrick Ryecart, nicknamed by his agent the Duke of Darling) and within the first week the school weed is identified. The assistants are the monitors, buxom hairdressers double as matrons, and our benign headmaster was a sweet little man from the Rank days by the name of Clive Donner.

Liam Neeson played Grak, the king of the barbarians, and he and I had a big stage fight at the end of the film. We rehearsed it for weeks. We had to fence, use poles, bend iron bars and gouge each other's eyes out, before I finally got him round his huge size-eighteen neck with my bony little hands and said the immortal line, 'Die, barbarian!' We were an incongruous match for a skirmish. Liam could have snapped me in half with a flick of those huge sausage-fingered hands. But he was one of the sweetest actors in those days when we were all starting out, and everyone adored him. He was a gentle giant, very much one of the Irish boys, and they attacked the world of acting differently from us uptight Brits. The Irish actor was a gypsy traveller; the Brits were civil servants by comparison. They packed light, smoked like chimneys and always made the day into a laugh. Later in California, Liam gave up drinking and changed considerably. Hollywood inevitably irons out the wrinkles in an actor's psyche, and after a few years in the lubed desert we are all homogenised. But the Liam of the early eighties was a happy-go-lucky semi-tramp with a gentle Belfast lilt and forget-me-not blue boxer's eyes. He was very much a man, and went out with one of the great sirens of the day, Helen Mirren, yet he was totally unfazed by hanging out with a queen. And of course, he loved a drink; but then in those days, everyone did. After shooting was over for the day, the whole crew adjourned to the hotel bar and we wouldn't move until the early hours of the following morning.

Our hotel was cut into the hills high above Dubrovnik. (It was to receive a direct hit in the war later on.) The view was incredible. Formal gardens on terraces threaded down towards the sea. I loved getting up for work in the mornings, bleary-eyed, still drunk. The sky was mauve and scribbled over with pink. The Adriatic was black. Far below, the waves crashed silently against the walls of the medieval city; in the distance, out to sea, was a craggy chain of little islands, on one of them, the ruins of a castle. There was a silence in the early morning that was not just about the absence of noise.

The make-up and wardrobe departments were downstairs in Tito's old summer palace. There, the Italian hairdressers brewed delicious coffee; you could smell it as you walked down the corridor. You shut your eyes in the make-up chair and were lulled into a semi-conscious state by the murmur of Italian and the moans of hairdryers and actors. People came and went. Assistants with voices like squaddies updated the room on the plan and the weather. Idle chatter about the scandals of yesterday awoke you with a smile. The glamorous 'barge ladies' were the subjects of our schoolboy fantasies. They had come for a couple of days to sail Arthur to Avalon (weather permitting) but the sea was proving too choppy for our barge. It was fairly makeshift and looked like a float from the Rio carnival. Each night someone claimed to have had one of the barge girls, or all of them. At some point Clive, the director, arrived decked out in a huge waterproof outfit, a colonel addressing his troops before battle. And soon we were ready. Tissues were placed around our collars to stop the make-up from staining our tunics. They made us look ultra sissy. The girls wore hairnets and giant rollers. Everyone was buzzing on coffee and cigarettes, and spirits were high as we all climbed onto our horses and rode out into the Croatian mists. By the afternoon the rain would normally bring work to a standstill and we would sit in little caravans high in the mountains, drinking the local beer, talking and falling silent. Mesmerised by the noise of the rain on the roof of the trailer, we would soon fall asleep, only to be roughly woken by a dripping assistant and told that work was over for the day.

In one long punishing scene I had to vault a wall into Grak's castle and pull myself up through a hole in a ceiling. I was on my way to save

Guinevere who was in chains upstairs, but unfortunately I was intercepted by Grak. Liam had developed a marvellous growl for the role that was like Muttley from *Wacky Races*.

'I've come for the queen, barbarian!' I squeaked on take one before jumping onto the end of Liam's jousting tool. 'Hee hee hee,' he giggled as he swung me around on it. I had to grapple it from him, which was more or less impossible, and then snap it in two. Five minutes of sword fighting ensued: jumping on the table, throwing myself down on Liam, pummelling his face with the handle of my sword before killing him with a good stabbing in the stomach. Then I had to go over to Guinevere and pull her chains off her. There was one chain made of rubber for me to break. The rest were real. I started tugging at the wrong one. Obviously it wouldn't break, so then I tried another and it snapped rather easily.

'That was fan-fucking-tastic,' said Clive at the end. Dennis walked past me to trim a lamp with a patronising smirk on his face. I was so exhausted by the time we came to the second take that I was becoming confused. 'I've come for the barbarian, queen!' I shrieked, and the whole set collapsed into hysteria.

I loved Candice Bergen. She was funny, beautiful and quite detached. We got along immediately. One night at dinner she gave me the most important advice of my career.

'Rupert, I didn't know whether I should tell you this,' she said, 'but I think I will.' She paused dramatically, and suddenly I was shot through with adrenalin, terrified that she was about to say that I couldn't act. When a friend tells you to give up, you know you're in trouble. 'You have lip tension,' she said. 'I know, because I had it myself.'

Of course I thought she was talking rubbish. Until the next day, when Dennis said, 'You always look as though you were about to say the word mower. Can't you relax?' Suddenly I caught myself in the lens of the camera. Candice and Dennis were right. A giant M was forming on my lips. Actually, I was tense all over.

At the end of the film I had my big moment. My face peeping out of my helmet, I walked towards Arthur's barge, tingling with drama. My cloak billowed in the freezing wind off the Adriatic. The barge ladies were covered with goose pimples and thinly disguised love bites. They had been in the bar late the night before. 'Goodbye, Arthur. As long as men dream, your spirit will never die.' I had rehearsed the line a million different ways but it was a lame duck and I could never get it off the ground. Malcolm had had a late night too. He was fast asleep and gave a little snore. I stifled a giggle and left the barge. Magically, it began to glide away. The barge ladies stood tall, their silk robes hugging their beautiful curves, their faces staring vacantly towards Windermere and the Bond film they were all joining next week. The crew watched, breathless. The props guys fanned smoke into the wind, frogmen pushed the barge from under the water, and suddenly – clunk – they hit a rock. There was a snapping sound and one of the corners sank into the freezing water. The girls screamed and Arthur jumped off his bier. Clive yelled through his megaphone, 'Back to one. That was a total fuck-up!' If not Tennyson exactly, it was an insightful epitaph for our film. But nobody cared. Christmas approached, and we all packed our trunks and dreamt about the Christmas holidays.

Arthur the King was renamed *Merlin and the Sword* and went straight to video. A copy can sometimes be found in those weird stalls at a Sunday market hidden among other disaster films, three for the price of one.

We had no illusions. Only Gladys, the wife of the producer, had 'chills' during every scene. But it was a cheerful film, and we all hugged like old friends at Heathrow before going home to the nightmare of a family Christmas.

CHAPTER 16

Natasha and *The Far Pavilions*

One of my best friends at that time was a girl called Natasha Grenfell. She lived on the other side of the King's Road in a flat in Ormonde Gate. It was one of the untidiest places I have ever seen. She never rose before lunch and was bleary-eyed and puffy until the evening, when she transformed herself and stepped out for dinner. Her father was a gentle, aristocratic manic-depressive called Peter St Just and her mother was the famous Maria Britneva, or Lady St Just to us, a tiny Russian woman with a clawing energy and a shadowy past. Despite a background in the theatre, and before that as a dancer (she was apparently known as the 'little grasshopper' as a child), she was grander than an archduchess. She terrorised us as teenagers. As far as she was concerned we were a worthless lot of spineless druggies. She was probably right. Weekends at their beautiful dilapidated Palladian mansion, Wilbury, would be slothful affairs punctuated by Maria bursting into rooms where Natasha and her friends sprawled about watching TV, and ordering them to perform chores around the house. We quickly learnt to always be carrying a log so that we looked as though we were about to lay a fire. Screaming matches between Maria and her daughters bubbled to the surface at meals around the huge dining room table. Lord St Just surveyed them from one end of the table as though he was watching the cricket. Occasionally he raised an eyebrow as a wicket was scored but otherwise he ate his meal and kept quiet. The latest Australian couple would be pale and pinched as they served up lunch, probably having just been called 'little fools' by Maria in the kitchen. They often packed and left in the midst of the meal, at which point a state of crisis was declared and, after whispered consultations, Natasha's guests would shuffle gingerly to their cars and hotfoot it back to London.

Maria was a fabulous monster but inspired as much love as she did hate. I adored her. County folk in Wiltshire found her impossibly grand and distrusted her connections to several highbrow international queens for whom she doubled as a kind of muse and high priestess during their various trips into town. Tennessee Williams was her best friend. According to Maria, he had based the character of 'the Cat' in *Cat on a Hot Tin Roof* on her, and no matter what her detractors could say to the contrary there was more than a marked similarity between the two women. Maria *was* a Tennessee Williams character. (On his death she became the executor of Tennessee's estate and it was only through her that I managed to get permission to play Mrs Goforth in *The Milk Train Doesn't Stop Here Anymore*.) Whatever else, Maria was a fiercely loyal friend and her special attachments included Gore Vidal and Franco Zeffirelli.

Zeffirelli was Natasha's godfather, and when I heard he would be coming to her eighteenth-birthday ball at Wilbury, I became hysterical with excitement. I arrived at the ball dressed from head to foot in black leather and proceeded to scour the house for a sighting of the great maestro fairy. Sadly, when at last he approached me, I had no idea whom I was talking to and simply thought, in the arrogance of youth, that he was just another antique dealer friend of Maria's who was trying to get into my pants. I glanced down my nose at him a couple of times and answered his questions with a perfunctory 'yes' or 'no', staring resolutely ahead onto the dance floor where young men in dinner jackets and girls in billowing ballgowns were gyrating and pogoing to a music other than that which was playing in the room. Zeffirelli stalked off. I nearly fainted when I realised my mistake.

Maria loved her daughters with a deep and dangerous passion. She was hell-bent on motivating them, but unfortunately for her their make-up contained more than a vein of their father's depressive nature, not to mention a healthy dose of that genetic Russian predilection for sitting around gloomily drinking tea. Maria's tirades only helped Natasha to hide deeper inside herself.

My family moved from Essex to Wiltshire in 1979 and from Enford, where we lived, to Wilbury was a fifteen-minute drive across tiny country lanes over the Salisbury Plain. Natasha and I beetled dangerously back and forth when the pressure of our mothers became too much.

One weekend, just after my return from Yugoslavia, there was an especially explosive lunch at Wilbury. It was Boxing Day, and Maria was being particularly poisonous. Natasha and I went out for a walk. I was leaving for India in the New Year on another miniseries called *The Far Pavilions*. I was home, but I'd already escaped. Natasha had not. A cold winter night was settling in. The old house stood grey and forlorn behind us. The raised voices and tears of five minutes ago dissolved in the damp silence of the sleeping countryside. The sky was still white but there was no light. Pheasants flew over, their weird strangled shrieks echoing through the woods. Natasha was in a black mood. At the end of the huge unkempt lawn was a dogs' cemetery. Surrounded by broken park fencing, little crosses marked the graves of generations of pugs and retrievers. The names of the dead were engraved upon them. Froggy Footman. Mishka. Kabanos. Later Maria herself was to be buried there.

Suddenly screams and shouts shattered the silence. A car screeched down the drive. We looked at each other and walked quickly into the trees.

'The Australians have left, can you beat it?' Maria's voice bounced between the house and the woods.

We turned around. She was tiny in the large windows of the library. Behind her the Christmas tree glittered and sparkled with tinsel and blinking fairy lights. She might have just jumped off it. You had to smile because she never stopped. The harangue continued as we trudged back to help with the washing up. Coming around the house we could see her hurtling past windows like a crazy witch. We both laughed, but as we got to the front door Natasha suddenly took my arm and looked at me with an unusual earnestness. 'Don't you need some kind of assistant when you go to India?'

The Far Pavilions was a romantic novel about the British Raj in the nineteenth century. It was a story of star-crossed lovers, an Indian *Romeo and Juliet*. The handsome English officer was played by Ben Cross and his Indian princess was Amy Irving. Togged up in a floor-length wig, her piercing blue eyes rimmed with kohl, she looked more like a follower of Charles Manson than the daughter of a maharajah. A star-studded cast assembled in Jaipur, the pink city of Rajasthan. My character was called Gorgeous George. He was an Anglo-Indian civil servant who sadly committed suicide in the first episode. But I didn't care.

I was young. I was working. I was going to India.

So in that February, 1983, I set off with Natasha for Bombay and a small holiday in Goa before joining the production.

Nothing prepares you for India. Of all the arrivals it is the most exotic, and the most destabilising. The whole rug of life is pulled from under your feet. From the airport we took a taxi into the city. We hadn't slept all night and could hardly keep our eyes open, but there is something about the colour of the dawn and the smell of the air that kept even Natasha awake on the long bumpy ride to Bombay. The road was a cacophony of hooting taxis and trucks. Scooters bearing entire families darted through the traffic; the women sat side-saddle with expressionless faces under saris that fluttered behind them. Cows lumbered across the road, cars swerved to avoid them, and the scooters flew on by. As the sky blanched, thin boys in loincloths washed by the side of the road, and fires glowed from the dark interiors of the roadside huts. We ploughed through this ocean of poverty in silence and were soon on more familiar ground, the India of Lutyens, and the collapsing traces of Empire. By the end of the journey we were in a kind of trance. Seeing India for the first time is a shock to the system, impossible to rationalise. The brain freezes, although Natasha's was already in the fridge.

We stayed at the Taj Hotel, which overlooks the ocean and the triumphal arch through which the viceroys marched on their way back from England. We slept all day and came out at night with the rats that made the ground look as though it was moving. We took a rickshaw and delved into the depths of the city. The driver gave us something to smoke. We were young, green, greedy hoorays and we didn't ask what was in it, because in the Embassy Club one never said no to anything.

Soon we were in a sort of red-light district. The street was mayhem. Women looked down through prison bars from upstairs rooms. They wore fuchsia and emerald and turquoise. Little rickety staircases led to their cells. The light, the colours and the noise were overwhelming. It was as if someone had turned the dials up too high on the TV.

'Darling, that joint was really weird,' said Natasha after a few minutes. We were stuck in a sort of human traffic jam. 'Am I really stoned or is there a hand coming up between my legs?'

We looked down and sure enough, there was a small grinning boy clinging to the undercarriage of the rickshaw. Or was there? When we looked back, he'd gone. The street was a dark seething crowd of men and since we were at a standstill, they began to crowd in towards us, curious and menacing. One man tried to drag me from the rickshaw, pointing in the direction of an imprisoned beauty upstairs. We both clutched the sides, suddenly terrified that we were going to fall into the blur of eyes, teeth, shiny hair and untucked shirts that surrounded us. I looked at Natasha. She was sweating. We were tripping. Or were we? You could never tell in India; everything was so extreme. But the experience was like a nightmare with some ghastly moral. The ladies of the night looked coldly down from their cages as the hands of men reached up from hell to drag us down. The crowd was pushing our rickshaw from side to side. Someone grabbed at Natasha's purse, but they underestimated her. She was certainly not going to let go of her wallet while she was still conscious.

Finally we escaped down a narrow alleyway and were soon being pedalled through dark wide streets covered with sleeping bodies. The driver rang his bell as we wove through the narrow passage left by the half-dead untouchables. Rats jumped across them and nibbled at their feet. The odd man or woman sat upright and listlessly watched as we passed. Now the din of the busy streets was a distant scary echo like a riot, a revolution coming from far away.

The next day we took the old ferry boat to Goa. Natasha put her back out carrying a suitcase so it looked as though I would have to be the assistant after all. The port was another impossible Victorian puzzle swarming with life. It was a two-day journey by boat. We had a cabin, but most of the travellers lived below with the cargo and we were rather jealous. A mix of Indians and hippies strung hammocks to the ceiling, sat cross-legged in circles, drank tea and listened to music. But even on the upper deck, it was a glorious trip. We lay in our cabin, luxuriating in the throb of the engine and the feeling of having disappeared from our lives. We had both given the slip to our overbearing mothers. Neither of them would be able to find us now, steaming down the coast of India. We sat in a dirty dining room at meals and played cards with some hippies from Manchester after dinner. Later, drunk and liberated, we lay awake all night and talked.

In Goa the body of St Francis Xavier was on display in a peeling old cathedral where the local Indian women dressed like Italian peasants. They swept the floors, trimmed the candles and said their rosaries (the Hail Mary in Hindu sounded like bees swarming). Many people had come to see the saint. Some of them moved across the church on their knees. His face was miraculously preserved, shiny as shoe leather from too much kissing. Some thoughtful nuns had plonked a curly old rug on his head. It looked as though it were made from pubic hair. His lips had receded and gave him a saucy grin that was not altogether saintly.

'He looks a bit like Bunny Rogers,' said Natasha. Bunny was a wealthy old queen who gave the famous 'Mauve Ball' every year in London. We both got the giggles. The bees looked ready to swarm.

At night we trekked for miles through the jungle, guided by the distant thud of music, to caverns under vast canopies of bamboo where the hippies had their raves. Men with handlebar moustaches and biker jackets sat around drinking beer, and acid casualties writhed to the music in the embrace of invisible tree spirits. Returning from a glade where a German woman in a sari ran the bar, I found Natasha dancing alone. It was a glorious sight. Everything had changed, but Natasha was the same. She could have been back in the south hall at Wilbury at her coming-out ball, moving from foot to foot in a sort of trance, her signature Silk Cut in one hand, its packet clutched in the other. A semi-bald man with long wispy hair and a pot belly danced up to her and started to rub his groin against her and nuzzle her neck. 'Actually,' said Natasha rather half-heartedly after a few minutes, 'I'm with my boyfriend.'

The Rambagh Palace in Jaipur was a gigantic Victorian city of vanilla and white, a beautiful monstrosity. When its famous maharajah died it was turned into a hotel, although the maharani, who was put in prison by Mrs Gandhi, still lived in a house at the bottom of the garden. Our bedroom was a large room panelled in dark shiny mahogany, which had been the maharani's library and looked over an inner courtyard.

The dining room was huge, a former state receiving room, the walls covered in pale green silk that had seen better days. Fans like sails swung from the ceiling and their breeze sent shivers across the tables below. Silverware jangled and napkins fluttered. Musicians played on a podium. Our first night was a star-studded occasion. John Gielgud and his boyfriend Keith were eating silently at a corner table. Sir John was the epitome of the theatrical knight: perfect posture in a linen jacket, a pristine shirt and a slightly florid scarf. His boyfriend wore gold chains and medallions under a deeply open shirt. Then Omar Sharif walked in and the band, which comprised two zithers and some bongos, launched into a rousing version of 'Lara's Theme'. Poor Omar, probably exhausted from a gruelling day at work, in hundreds of degrees of heat, had to wave and bow to the enraptured tourists as he made his way towards his table. You could tell from the hooded eyes above the beaming smile that he had been through this in every converted palace, wherever there was a band, and was quite used to it. Ben Cross and Amy Irving came in and sat with us at our table. Afterwards we all went to the bar. Everyone seemed to be much more interested in Natasha than me, and I began to feel more like the assistant than ever. Robert Hardy and his wife knew Maria, and of course Sir John was one of Maria's oldest friends. They had been in a play together in the fifties, when legend has it that Maria smothered Edith Evans with a pillow during a scene because she was upstaging Sir John.

We went outside. There was a full moon. Formal gardens spread out beneath the palace – hard red earth, fountains, and box hedges in patterns. A snake charmer sat cross-legged on the terrace playing a little flute. There were mountains in the distance. Peacocks stood in the moonlight. Their howls awoke me later that night in the pitch black of the maharani's library, and for a moment I had no idea who or where I was. But Natasha's sleeping form soon took shape in the darkness, grainy and reassuring, guiding me back like the three-two-one of a hypnotist, and everything fell into place. A peacock howled again. I looked at my watch. Four-thirty. It was time to get up.

Pat and Meinir were a famous make-up and hair team. Pat was make-up and came from Glasgow, but you could hardly tell. She and I made instant friends (and at the risk of playing into the hands of my detractors, she has been one of the most important relationships of my career. We have worked together ever since). Meinir was from Wales and made no attempt to cover her linguistic tracks. She was a great storyteller, rolling her eyes and her Rs. As she got more heated, she became quite guttural and would suddenly switch to Welsh. At this point you knew you were in trouble. She was moody; Pat was even-keeled. They were yin and yang, a really funny double act and the best in the business. They also loved a drink. The fridge in the make-up tent was crammed full of champagne and special favourites would receive a glass of Buck's Fizz as they stepped into the chair of a morning.

I should probably have been a silent screen star but I can't help thinking that there isn't much point in hair and make-up these days. Cinematographers don't light faces any more and actors all look drained and ready for rehab. (If only they were.) The fashion photo has become more deliberate, more tricked and retouched, but the moving picture presents the human face at its most banal. Skin has the texture of tea bags. Eyes are rheumy. Lips curve into nasty dribble drains. Even the stunning girls look as if they have emphysema. But in the old days, not so very long ago, when an actor had a close-up nobody could get anywhere near them because they would be surrounded by a forest of lamps on stands. Little lights called 'inky dinks' made your eyes look full of something other than blind ambition and fear. Carefully placed 'fills' and 'keys', 'wendy lamps' and 'blondes' gave your face the shape and contour of the cinema animal. A famous DP called Jack Cardiff lit *The Far Pavilions*. He was legendary – he had shot *The African Queen* – and he tinkered around with his light meter and his eyeglass. No one nagged him about the time. There were no monitors so everyone huddled around the action like moths at a flame. Walking onto the set, or later, when we got back to England, onto the sound stage, my heart always missed a beat. You went from the drab suburban drizzle to a dark dusty cavern with a face in the middle surrounded by lights. It was the face of someone you probably knew, but now it was different, possessed. Eyes were shrouded in deep mauve clouds and their lashes threw shadows across the cheekbones. A softening chin was firmed by a charcoal line thrown from a key light high above, and a girl's cheek was lightly bruised in its shadow. Pat and Meinir would stand absorbed outside the pool of light, brushes and sprays, powders and lipsticks at the ready, waiting for Jack Cardiff to give them some last-minute instructions. There was a religious feeling: a miracle was being performed before our eyes.

While I was in India, Nicky Haslam was redecorating my house in Bywater Street, and when we returned from Jaipur in April the building work wasn't finished. I had nowhere to live, so I went to stay with Amy Irving and her assistant Cindy in their suite at Blakes Hotel.

It was a Saturday afternoon, and I had an out-of-body experience. We all talk about premonitions, but do we really have them? We remember we haven't called someone and as we pick up the phone they call us, but this was different.

As I turned on the TV, I knew before the picture appeared that something was about to happen. Amy was running a bath in the room next door. She was talking on the phone. Suddenly everything crowded in – her voice, the bathwater – as if I was fainting or passing out drunk. In those days the picture came up before the sound, fuzzy at first, and then settled. The face of a boy I knew appeared out of the haze: John. He was talking, silently mouthing words. Adrenalin surged through my body and my head pounded. We'd had an on-off affair for four or five years but I hadn't seen him for a while. Why was he looking old and drawn like a Trappist monk? He was younger than me, just twenty-one. The sound came up, with the measured voice of a BBC announcer: 'John is one of the first people in this country to develop the killer cancer that attacks the immune system and does not seem to respond to any treatment.'

Aids had arrived in London, like a hurricane from across the sea. We had heard the odd story from New York, or San Francisco, but information was always cluttered and chaotic, and anyone who had contracted Aids in the States had been terrorised into hiding.

'Don't sleep with any Americans, whatever you do,' we said to each other rather half-heartedly, but the wind got stronger as the eye approached. Now it was here, facing me in the sitting room at Blakes. John talked simply and with dignity. I remembered his smile the first time we met. Now his lips were stretched across his mouth in an anguished grin as he patiently explained his situation to the woman who was interviewing him. She turned to the viewers and listed all the many ways of contracting the illness. John and I had done them all; so had I and a lot of others. I turned the TV off and sat for a moment, frozen. Nothing that mattered before was relevant now: the opulence of Blakes, or my career. All that remained was fear. I heard myself casually shout to Amy that I was going out for a little while, and I called John Creightmore.

John was an old-school theatrical GP. He lived in a high thin house on Cadogan Place that had been given to him for his lifetime by the old Lord Cadogan, one of his patients. It had not been redecorated since the war, and John saw his patients in the drawing room on the first floor. It was a mixture of *Pygmalion* and *Sunday, Bloody Sunday* and John was not unlike Peter Finch.

We sat for an hour as a spring dusk fell on the gardens outside and the traffic rumbled in the distance. Every so often the house shook as the underground train passed beneath and the little crystal sconces jingled on the mantelpiece. I cried and shook and was inconsolable, but John was a soothing doctor, almost like a vet with a frightened animal, and soon I had calmed down and was facing the facts. It seemed to me to be pretty clear that I would have the disease, but as John explained, as yet there was no real way of telling. Reliable testing had not been pioneered. Then the telephone rang.

'Stephen Beagley from the Royal Ballet has a temperature. Come with me,' John suggested. He packed his stethoscope into his briefcase and we got into his car and drove to Covent Garden. I sat in the stage door while John went to nurse his dancer. Fairies and bluebirds passed by on their way to the stage. The old stage doorman made announcements into a microphone that echoed through the building. 'Miss Taphouse. You have a phone call at the stage door.' Far away, the orchestra struck up, the timpani sounding hollow through the tannoy. Two ballerinas smoked cigarettes and complained about one of the male dancers. Their feet were in fifth position. John came back up with Stephen behind him in tights and glittering make-up. He was a coiled spring of male energy. A god. We chatted for a moment, then Stephen was called to the stage.

John and I walked through Soho and had dinner at Chez Victor's before driving home. It was after eleven o'clock when I got back to Blakes. Amy was still getting into her bath and talking on the phone. She waved. I went to my room, got into bed and took the sleeping pill given to me by John.

'Hon. The car is coming for us at five-forty-five. Do you want to come with?' she shouted.

'Yes, please,' I shouted back.

'How was your day?'

'Uneventful,' I replied. My first Aids-related lie, I thought wryly, turned over and fell into a dreamless sleep.

CHAPTER 17

Another Country

Another Country was shot in a huge old stately home that had been converted into a borstal. It was a beautiful seventeenth-century house built around a courtyard, surrounded by the flat ripe cornfields of Northamptonshire; a strange house with some beautiful staterooms and others full of urinals. It retained a repressed prison energy, smelling of floor polish and toilets, and to my overexcitable mind it still rang with the time-locked screams of male rape. In short, it was the perfect location for our film.

It was the hot July of 1983, Mrs Thatcher was on her throne, and I was climbing onto mine, for the most productive year of my career. I moved into a pub in a nearby village. My room had a creaky four-poster bed with a moth-eaten canopy. Old flowery wallpaper buckled and peeled off the walls. It looked over a pretty garden and miles of waving corn. In another room down the hall lived the costume designer, Penny Rose, an eccentric no-nonsense lady with a very old dog. The rest of the cast were stuck in a motel on the motorway. Robert and Celestia rented a house near the location and we made the film in six weeks for a budget of £1.5 million. Robert's co-producer was Alan Marshall. He was the last of the old school, and had been Alan Parker's partner for twenty years. He looked and sounded like a south London wide boy, but in fact he was a bearded huggable bear. He was straightforward; his background was in editing, and he brought with him the whole Parker world, if not the maestro himself, in Peter Biziou, the cinematographer, and the production designer Brian Morris. Between them and Penny Rose, the tone of the film was firmly etched in that English school of directors that came from advertising in the early seventies: Parker, Scott, Lyne and Hudson. Theirs was the golden-brown look of the Hovis bread commercial, and Marshall artfully set the stage for a young and talented, but nevertheless inexperienced, director, Marek Kanievska.

Marek was an eccentric Pole, only ten years older than most of the actors and quite unlike the normal British director of those times. He was not class obsessed and did not put himself on a pedestal. He was intrigued by the youthful hysteria of his cast, and encouraged us to play up as much as possible. He was addicted to complicated tracking shots, where the camera is put on a kind of railway and moves around during the action, like a silent voyeur. These shots drove Marshall mad, mostly because they ate hours out of our day. 'It won't cut together, Marek,' he shouted, storming onto the set, as Marek doggedly prepared another meander behind a vase of flowers. 'You've got a screw loose, you're not even shooting the action.'

'Yes, I am.'

'No, you're not. You're shooting a vase of blooming flowers. You're not the full quid, Marek, are you?' Marek feigned deafness. 'God! He's not even listening. What's Polish for quid?'

'Zloty,' said Robert, who always kept out of the fray.

'You're not the full zloty,' shouted Marshall, and the whole set cracked up. Even Marshall had to laugh, and from then on Marek was known as Zloty. They fought all the time, but Marshall had Zloty's best interests at heart. He brought the film in on time, under budget, and Marek directed it beautifully; *Another Country* was the best-made film of my career.

Piers – or Freddy as he was now known – and I were the only two actors who had ridden the rapids of the stage show of *Another Country* through to the final event. We were the real-life, self-appointed prefects on the set, swaggering around and torturing the other actors. Freddy was everything the old school abhorred. Unapologetic for his independent

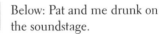

Above: Mummy and me.

Left: God knows what
we were thinking. With
Bob Dylan and Fiona,
by David Bailey.

Below: Pat and me drunk on
the soundstage.

Rupi in Colombia.

Marriage to Ornella Muti.

Left: Tonguing with Ruby at the premiere of *Hearts of Fire*.

Below: In bed with Paula.

Right: With Béatrice on the Croissette at Cannes.

Below: With Mo on the beach at Pampelonne.

Lychee in bloom.

Rupert by Pierre et
Gilles for the cover of
the *roman reportage
The Hairdressers of
St Tropez*.

The author as supermodel. Linda – Kate – Kristin.

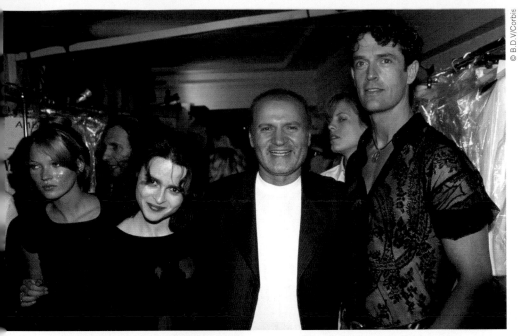

From backstage to front row.
Above, left to right: Kate Moss, Helena Bonham Carter, Gianni Versace and me.

Below: Boy George, me and Trudie Styler.

Helen Mirren observes strangulation by Paul Schrader in *The Comfort of Strangers*.

Overdosing with Maria Aitken in *The Vortex* at the Citizens Theatre.

wealth, he had recently bought a bright yellow Lamborghini and would arrive for work in front of the borstal in a cloud of gravel that often brought shooting to a standstill. Marshall banned him from driving but he continued anyway. One Saturday after work he drove me up to London and the journey was one of those times upon which memory hangs an entire era. I was utterly happy. All of life's strains melted away. 'Crime of the Century' played on the stereo, the hooray's mantra. We sped through country lanes across the cornfields towards the motorway, and into London at a hundred miles an hour.

'You're right, right, bloody well right, got a bloody right to say,' I shouted into the wind and Freddy threw me a withering glance from underneath his tweed cap. I adored him. The sky was pink. The car was yellow. Tail lights and traffic lights had a romantic intensity in the fading light. They drew us like a magnet into the metropolitan flow: Finchley Road, Swiss Cottage, the Central School. 'Fuck you very much!' I screamed as we roared by.

The King's Road was jammed with people and cars and twinkling lights. The parks in the little squares were literally bursting out of their railings. We were starring in a film and driving through Chelsea in a sports car. Things would never be better. This was Freddy's last summer, so it had to be good. He was to die in the same car only nine months later. But that night, and all that summer, we wallowed in our good fortune. We didn't really have to try very hard. We knew our parts inside out. Pat and Meinir had the fridge in the make-up room stocked with drinks. A boy in the art department dealt coke and marijuana, and we all lay in the sun between scenes in our cricket clothes, or if there was time we walked to the village pub, and we dreamt out loud of the future and how famous we would become, and what we were going to do with everyone once we were. We lazily compiled lists of people who were going to be cut dead as Colin Firth strummed his guitar, pretending not to listen. Colin had been cast in the role Kenneth Branagh had played on stage. At first I quite fancied him, until he produced that guitar and began to sing protest songs between scenes. 'There are limits!' said Freddy, when 'Lemon Tree, Very Pretty' began. Colin was visibly pained by our super-ficiality.

It took twenty years for Colin and me to become friends. That long and winding river of show business, with its rapids and its stagnant pools, threw us together again in *The Importance of Being Earnest*. Even though I had done my utmost that he should not be cast at all – I coveted his role for myself, as I wanted to play both brothers *and* Lady Bracknell – time had worked wonders on us both. He was no longer the grim *Guardian* reader in sandals; he no longer took the missionary position on everything. (His parents had been in the business of saving souls, despite their son's image of being an upper-class cad.) And I was perhaps slightly less brash, less nasty, less self-obsessed. So after all that time, I found him to be one of the most delightful actors to work with. We hit it off straightaway and laughed our way through another beautiful English summer. The foundations of our friendship were laid at that pretend school, and so practical jokes and schoolboy pranks were still the order of the day twenty years later. I played one really good one.

As part of my research, I was smoking a lot of pot during *The Importance of Being Earnest*. Strictly for the role, of course, and I was always trying to persuade Frothy, as I now called him, or Collywobbles, that he would find the day less boring, and Oscar's bons mots less laborious on the lips, if he had a puff or two. He always refused, until finally, after a long hot afternoon at the end of the shoot, he came into my trailer just as I had constructed a big wind-me-down joint. We settled down for one of those long waits that inevitably punctuate the filming day. Anna Massey walked past the trailer and came in. She had played my mother in *Another Country*. Now she was Miss Prism. For almost the first time I saw what a laugh it was to be getting older in show business. Our shared experience stretched out behind us. And through the open door of the trailer a beautiful lawn sloped gently towards another country house, another completed film and another crossroads. In the woods on either side, pigeons flapped in the branches and cooed to one another while we chatted and drifted off. I didn't bother to offer Frothy the joint – his abstemiousness was legendary by then – but he suddenly asked for it and paced around the trailer, smoking. He soon became giggly and unusually animated (in other words, camp). There was a knock on the door, and he opened it with a flourish, exhaling a huge gust of smoke and holding the joint up by his face like a character from a Noël Coward play. Harvey Weinstein clambered aboard with a school of executives. Poor Collywobbles was caught in the act. During the brief explosion of chit-chat that ensued, the mutual compliments, the casual discussion about the marketing strategy, the confirmation of dinner next week, we all looked at Frothy, wondering what he would do next. He was determined not to be shown up, and was quite giddy at the same time, so he defiantly took another couple of puffs, as he chatted to a bemused Harvey, before handing the joint to me.

'Here, Rupert. Do you want this?' he said in his coolest voice.

'Actually, no thanks, Colin,' I replied in my most understanding voice. 'I'd love to another time, but I just can't do it while I'm working. I wish I could. I'm so envious that you can get high and still work.'

Colin was like a cartoon character who had just overshot the edge of a cliff. After Harvey left we laughed until our eyes were red from crying and our stomachs hurt.

But that was still all ahead of us. On the last two days of *Another Country* we shot the beginning and the end of the film, scenes of Guy Burgess alone in Moscow at the end of his life. After six hours in make-up I had been turned into a blotched skeleton with a huge forehead and hanging eyes. I wasn't very convinced by myself when I looked into the mirror. You can never disguise the age of an eye.

Suddenly, a strange sprightly man in glasses arrived on the set with a camera. 'My name is Roddy McDowall,' he said. 'May I take some pictures?' I'm not quite sure how he came to be on the set that day – I think he was a friend of the director of sound, Ken Weston – but he tinkered around with his camera, snapping pictures of me wheeling myself down the narrow corridor of my Moscow flat. His glasses had thick lenses, his eyes were magnified through them, and he looked like a thin owl. He chattered to all and sundry as if he knew us all intimately.

Roddy was the Hollywood version of Vernon Dobtcheff and he ran one of the last Hollywood salons in his cottage off Laurel Canyon in LA; knowing him was definitely a key into the forbidden city. Bathed in the flickering candles of Roddy's dinner table shone the whole lifespan of Hollywood. Ancient silent stars and newcomers from Aaron Spelling's TV soaps mingled gratefully with one another, along with all the usual pimps and users, asteroids and dead stars that glitter in the firmament on a clear night in Hollywood. Tinseltown was a 'virtual' community by the beginning of the eighties and suddenly everyone was locked behind electric gates, physically and psychologically. An evening at Roddy's was an oasis in the desert for all those isolated idols of yesteryear. He was Elizabeth Taylor's oldest friend, Bette Davis adored him, and he himself was one of the most talented child actors that ever came out of the lubed desert, having starred in *Lassie* and *How Green is My Valley*. He was profound and moving and beautiful, but although he was still slightly childlike at fifty, that early intense depth had somehow evaporated for his adult career. Maybe it had all been sucked out by the studio and he was a little bit brittle as an actor in his adult years. But he had an extraordinary talent for friendship, and he was genuinely funny. He knew everyone, though he was never a snob, and for anyone who had loved the dream of ancient Hollywood, Roddy was its patron saint, the keeper of its flame. He pioneered the role of the gay best friend. He lived through the whole drama of *Cleopatra* and was close to both the women in Richard Burton's life. He was there when Montgomery Clift crashed his car after dinner at Elizabeth Taylor's: running with Elizabeth down the canyon towards the wreck, standing by as Elizabeth cradled Monty's smashed head in her arms. These images were my dreams. And if all this wasn't enough, according to legend, Roddy was sensationally hung.

But all this I was to discover later. That day on the set of *Another Country* he left me his card, and so began a long friendship. 'Goodbye, dear,' he cooed. 'Call me when you come west.' And then he disappeared.

CHAPTER 18

Dance with a Stranger

In January 1984 I started rehearsing for Webster's *The White Devil* back at the Greenwich Theatre. My ambition knew no bounds, and I had persuaded Philip Prowse, with a good deal of difficulty, to direct a season of plays there, starring myself, and my two best friends, Maria Aitken and a brilliant actress from Glasgow called Johanna Kirby. But no sooner had we set the whole thing up than I wanted to back out.

I was living in Chelsea with Susan Sarandon. We were having a strange, guilty affair. I'd stolen her from one of my best friends, during a night flight from New York to London. Now, suddenly, she was working at the BBC, I was in the theatre at Greenwich, and we were like a frantic pair of newlywed parents: I was the man(ish) but mostly I was our baby. We gave parties in my house in Bywater Street for our bemused mutual friends, and faced criticism with the dignified defiance of Wallis Simpson (me) and the Prince of Wales (Susan). But guilty kisses have their own curious flavour. Our ex always stood between us, and it wasn't long before our affair evaporated into that strange miasma of a friendship built around a forgotten sparkle.

Meanwhile, Richard Gere, Susan's neighbour and best friend in New York, was living round the corner (under the assumed name of

King David) and we often met for dinner. I was only twenty-four and the whole thing went to my head. I became incredibly grand and hired a huge Daimler limousine to take me to the theatre every night. Johanna lived near by, so we travelled there together, hiding on the floor as we went through Deptford. Once Philip came with us. He must have thought I was insane when a car the size of a boat steamed up in front of the house but he looked seriously worried when we suggested that he hide as we went through Deptford. He refused. Sure enough, at a red light, by a street market, a man began to jeer, and made all kinds of unkind insinuations about Philip, who stared icily ahead like royalty, and then suddenly – thwack – a tomato smashed against the window and slid down the car.

At some point during rehearsals for *The White Devil* I was offered the role of David Blakeley in a film titled *Dance with a Stranger*. It was a beautiful script by Shelagh Delaney who had written one of my favourite films, *A Taste of Honey*. This new script was the true story of Ruth Ellis, the last woman to be hanged in England; David Blakeley was the lover she killed. I knew I had to do it, so with my heart in my mouth I went to see Philip one Sunday afternoon in the restaurant underneath his flat to ask him whether I could drop out of the next two plays.

The extraordinary thing about Philip in those days was that he was never ruffled by anything. He took everything in his stride. He never relied on anyone else, and didn't expect anyone else to rely on him. He was sitting at a table with his best friend, a thin queen called Thelma. Thelma always wore white, and Philip never veered away from black. They went back a long way to the days when Philip designed for the Royal Ballet and Thelma had been a choreographer, and they sat with straight backs like a couple of bearded Victorian ladies as they ate their meal and listened.

'Who's playing Ruth Ellis?' asked Philip finally.

'A girl called Miranda Richardson.'

'Not one of those frightful Redgrave girls?'

'No.'

'Well, that's something. Who's directing?'

'Mike Newell.'

'Aha,' said Philip knowingly and began to laugh.

'Well, what do you think?'

'My dear, it sounds too grim for words, but if that's what you want to do . . .' he trailed off and let me hang awkwardly for a moment, surveying my discomfort with ill-concealed pleasure, before launching into a story of how Mike Newell's girlfriend, Bernice, had once tried to kill him by putting broken glass in some avocado dip. And that was the end of that. A great actor called Bob Gwilym replaced me, and sadly I never got the chance to play Konstantin to Johanna's brilliant Nina.

By the time I came across Mike Newell and *Dance with a Stranger* in that May I had become a fully fledged diva in a frosty land where that crazy bird had become extinct. A real diva is a bundle of contradictions. On the one hand she feels beautiful, but on an 'off' day she can be staggered by her own ugliness. This makes her wildly unpredictable. My face was good, but it sat on top of a squeaky skeleton. I had grown too fast, too late. Fifteen inches in seven years and still growing. The result was that I walked with a tremendous stoop and had no arse or arms or chest or shoulders. Luckily I found a pair of queens in the Holloway Road who made intricate body stockings that could turn a stick insect into a Greek god. Barry and his boyfriend made me special underpants with sexy buttocks, padded vests with broad shoulders, and stockings with huge calves and thick knees. I would visit them secretly in the dead of night and come away with huge Harrods bags with arms and legs sticking out.

A real diva is split between utter conviction of her brilliance and secret crashing panic. This only adds to her signature unpredictability. I knew what I could achieve, and actually I was not unrealistic. I was a riddle as an actor. On screen, I had a lot of 'feeling' but I couldn't really act. On stage I could act, but people said I had no depth. Hey-ho. I learnt how well my face worked with the camera, but I wasn't sure how long my life would last under Barry's padding.

The face of Aids grew clearer by the minute: first in newspapers and magazines, then on the street, and finally up close in the terrified eyes of friends. I remember sitting with Ian Charleson in his car one rainy December night around that time. We were part of a large group going from someone's house to a restaurant. We sat in his car waiting for the others to arrive. He had those haunted eyes, but had never mentioned anything was wrong. How could it be? He was starring in movies. Everybody loved him. He was one of my heroes. And yet, as the rain tapped on the roof, he told me how he had received a letter a couple of months before (agonisingly, while his parents had been staying with him) from an ex who had become ill and was dying, and now he was paralysed with fear. So was I.

Mike Newell was as English as Yorkshire pudding. He was caught in the middle of that awkward identity shift from Old Labour to New. Socialism was fine when you earned £200 a week at the BBC, but the idea of 98 per cent tax paled with the Thatcherite sunrise. At the same time, compared to Marek, he was still very old school. It wasn't that he wanted to be called 'sir', but he definitely needed a master/pupil dynamic with his actors. Miranda Richardson had cleverly disguised her ego as an endlessly bubbling spring of neuroses, and she fed them into her part like meat into a grinder. Mike could channel this towards the camera without feeling that the 'special relationship' was compromised. But I was a tornado, a Force Ten twister. I didn't want a guru. As far as I was concerned, I knew what to do with my role; it wasn't that complicated after all. But Mike wanted blood and control. In rehearsals he would claw at his face with his giant hands. 'I want to see the agony,' he said.

'What agony?' I replied. Yes. It was agony for us all that Ruth Ellis was hanged. That I understood; that was our film. But Mike wanted to take a line on the character of David Blakeley that couldn't or shouldn't be shared with the actor. He was confusing my job with his job and me with my role.

Why couldn't he just leave me alone? Soon I was called in for special sessions. It was like school. We would rehearse tiny little three-second sequences, over and over again. Mike wanted proof that 'we were on the same page'.

'But, Mike,' I'd say, 'it's obvious I can play the role.'

'Yes, but you've got to work at it!'

Nothing could be done effortlessly in those days. You had to be seen to be sweating bullets. 'I don't feel like we've fucked,' he said one morning, as my hair was being cut for the film, and he rearranged it with those giant hands in its most unflattering way. Looking back, I'm sure I looked fine, but that day it was as though a black hole opened up in the mirror and everything was being sucked inside. The twister took a taxi straight to Smile, a trendy salon in the King's Road, ripping up anyone who got in the way, and Derek my hairdresser totally restyled my hair. It was an open declaration of war and, of course, the stupidest and most irritating thing I could do (although two years later, working with Julie Andrews, I noticed that she did the same thing. She arrived for the first day of filming with a totally new hairstyle and colour. It must run in the family!)

The next day I showed up for a photo shoot with my new look and Mike went through the roof. 'You look like a fucking GI!' he screamed.

Things got worse when we started shooting. One day we were doing a scene in the countryside. I was driving Miranda in a sports car across a beautiful valley in Oxfordshire. Mike was standing with half the crew on the top of a hill. The road wound down across the fields and up towards the other side. It was a two-mile ride from side to side. We were just about to go. The car was in gear. But Mike lumbered up, leant in and recited the usual creed. He wasn't seeing the pain, he wanted to see the character's flesh crawling; and as he was talking, I ran over his foot.

'Ahhhh!' he bellowed right into my ear, like a bear in a trap. I quickly reversed and ran it over again. Another roar. I had not done it on purpose, but later, as we were being towed across the valley by a truck with the other half of the crew on it, I regaled them with the story. I cruelly mimicked Mike's bearlike howl, at which point the entire crew broke into hysterical laughter. The noise of the truck was really loud, so we had no idea that our voices were crystal clear across the valley to Mike, alone on the hill with the camera. When we got to the end of the scene, he came up to the car, and said, 'I just want to tell you, I have never felt so lonely in my life.'

'Why, Mike?'

'I heard everything.' And he walked away.

Twister was momentarily mortified.

For all the problems during shooting – and I was a cunt – *Dance with a Stranger* was a great film. It was almost entirely lit with fairy lights by Peter Hannan, a brilliant DP. It looked beautiful, and Mike directed with style. Michael Storey wrote one of his best scores. Pat and Meinir made Miranda look incredible as Ruth Ellis, and of course she was mesmerising in the film. I was good too. My first two movies were classics. I should probably have died in a crash if I had been at all serious about my career. However, I didn't die, even though, in the crash of egos that marked my encounter with Mike Newell, he had the last word, and I didn't work again in England for ten years.

I was sitting in my house one afternoon catching up with Simon Callow when the telephone rang. I never answered these days, and we went on chatting. The Pink Pussycat had just closed down and we were lost. (We were obsessed by a pair of blond twins that went there every Thursday night. We would never see them again. They both died from the big disease with the little name.) A static hiss from the answering machine announced an international call – still a relative novelty – and I stopped talking. 'Hello, Rupert,' said a voice we both recognised but couldn't place. 'This is Orson Welles.' Simon froze. Orson was his god. 'I stole your number from a mutual friend. Please forgive me.' Me, forgive Orson? It was beginning to sound suspicious.

'Pick up!' bellowed Simon, but I didn't.

'I have recently seen *Another Country*, one of the best films of the last few years,' continued the voice on the answering machine.

'This is a wind-up,' I groaned.

'I would like to talk to you about a new movie I am preparing.' He left a number in LA, and the line went dead.

I had recently been the victim of a brilliant hoax. I had received a series of letters from a man who said he was dying. He had watched me in the theatre on several occasions and wanted to leave me all his money. His letters were long and detailed. He sent pictures of himself, and his home, a rather lush castle in Germany that caught my imagination. He said he had over £20 million and he wanted to arrange meetings with his lawyers in London to begin making it over to me. I was over the moon and fell for it hook, line and sinker, answering the letters with rather half-hearted protests. Of course, it turned out to be an elaborate game. Whoever played it had managed to get hold of some headed writing paper from a large firm of attorneys and had forged the promised letter of introduction, but when I called the lawyer in question he had never heard of my dear benefactor. To this day I have no idea who conceived this brilliant plan, although for a long time I suspected my own partner in hoaxes, a formidable lady called Min Hogg.

Min was the editor of the magazine *World of Interiors*. At a certain point, both unemployed, we had been inseparable, a lethal pair on the circuit, until we got jobs and drifted off into different worlds. But in our heyday, along with Robert Fox, we spent a good deal of time devoted to some extremely elaborate phone games. Our idea of an enjoyable night at home was to get on the phone to as many rich and famous people whose numbers we knew, and ring them up, pretending to be the Water Board, and ask them to turn on all their cold taps because there was a 'build-up in pressure' under their house, with a risk of explosion. We discovered that people were extremely gullible, and we would give them the numbers of other celebrities to call back when the taps had run dry.

One night the game went horribly wrong. We had called the home of famous society hostess Nona Summers. She was having a party for Jack Nicholson to which we were not invited.

'Do you have any idea how many taps there are in this house?' she piped. The party was in full swing in the background.

'Er, yes, miss,' I sang with a vague leprechaun lilt. 'Let me see now . . .' and I began to count an imaginary list. We were in Robert and Celestia's house, about ten of us, and everyone in the room craned around the phone, silently exploding with mirth. For some stupid reason, instead of giving Lord Snowdon's number, as we usually did for the follow-up phone call, I gave theirs.

A few minutes later the telephone rang and it was Martin, Nona's suave husband. 'Look, we've got all the taps going. Have you got hold of everyone else in the street?'

'Well, actually, sir, we're having a little bit of difficulty with number 29, number 17 and number 34. Maybe you could knock on their doors for us and warn them.'

So Martin went out and woke up the whole of Glebe Place in Chelsea where they lived. This back and forth went on for about three-quarters of an hour. We made them flush all the loos. We made them go over to an ancient lesbian club on the corner called The Gateways and evacuate it in readiness for the Water Board's arrival. By midnight they'd had enough.

'We can't go on flushing loos non-stop,' screamed Nona. 'We pay enormous bills. Who is this? I want to speak to someone in charge!'

I burst out laughing and slammed the phone down. The evening went on. Nobody thought much more about it. I shared a taxi back to Chelsea with Min, and was having a nightcap at her flat in Brompton Square when the phone rang.

'Robert's been arrested,' gasped Celestia between gut-wrenching sobs. 'We were just going to bed, and the doorbell rang. Twelve policemen burst into the house and pinned Robert to the wall. Now he's in prison, but I don't know where. What shall I do?'

Min and I rushed back to Clapham to console her. The mirror in the hall had been knocked sideways in the scuffle. Celestia looked demented in her nightdress. We couldn't help laughing. Finally, their lawyer was woken up. Robert was located in Scotland Yard, and the next morning he was released.

Apparently, Nona Summers was convinced that she was being targeted by the IRA. Either she had spent too much time in the bathroom prior to turning on the taps and had become paranoid or my Irish accent had been chillingly convincing. Either way, in the ensuing panic they evacuated their three hundred guests and called the police. According to legend, a confused Jack Nicholson thought he was going back into the house after the all-clear, but went in the wrong door and ended up dancing the night away with a couple of lesbians at Gateways.

The trouble with being a prankster is that at a certain point one no longer believes anything. It never crossed my mind that the real Orson Welles had telephoned me. Actually he had. But the misunderstanding was soon cleared up, and our people on the ground arranged another teatime for us to talk.

Simon Callow came by specially and listened on the phone in the kitchen.

'Greetings,' said Orson, in the low familiar growl of the Holsten beer commercials. Simon gasped in the kitchen.

We talked for about five minutes. Even down the phone from thousands of miles away, I felt terrified as I talked to him. He was extremely flattering. He had loved *Another Country* and told me that he thought I was one of the best actors he had seen. He was rewriting a script by John Houseman about a famous musical, *The Cradle Will Rock*, which Orson had directed in the early thirties. Orson called Houseman's script 'pompous and long-winded, like John'. I had no idea who John Houseman was. Orson wanted me to play him (Orson) as a young man. I heard Simon gasp again. He wanted me to come out to LA as soon as I could so that we could start talking. Meanwhile he was sending the first twenty pages of the new script that day and would send the rest as and when it was written. I replied in monosyllables. Yes. No. Great. Goodbye.

Simon staggered upstairs from the kitchen and accused me of being 'grand and surly'.

'Si, I was terrified,' I said. 'I couldn't think of anything to say.'

Over the next few weeks the rest of the script dribbled in. It was utterly brilliant. Whereas Houseman's had ploughed unimaginatively into rehearsals of the famous musical, Welles began his story at a matinée of *Dr Faustus*. Under the stage, men in ghostly shafts of light prepared to unleash the stage effects of hell as a young, unseen Orson could be heard above, performing that astounding speech by Marlowe: 'See, see, where Christ's blood streams in the firmament.'

In a stunning sweep from under the stage to high in the flies (which reminded me of the opera scene in *Citizen Kane*), Orson disappeared into hell, as trapdoors sprang open, things flew down from above, smoke engulfed the stage and thunder rolled. The faces of stagehands, each counting quietly to himself, perched in various niches above and below the stage, were the picture of working America. Seconds later, Orson jumped into a waiting ambulance outside the stage door, that sped through the New York traffic, removing his make-up in the back, and climbing quickly into a suit. As the wailing ambulance screeched to a halt outside NBC, a suave unruffled Orson stepped onto the street and went into the building to give a radio recital, before rushing back to Broadway for the evening show.

On every page something extraordinary happened. The dialogue was poetic and funny. The relationship between Orson and his wife was touching, and he managed to make the story of a play into a kind of thriller. Orson had definitely not lost his touch. God only knew how I would manage to play the part, but I would jump over that hurdle later. For now the preliminary contracts were hastily drawn up. Nobody ever moved a muscle in Hollywood without 'something on paper', and soon I was on my way to LA.

CHAPTER 19

The Lubed Desert

It felt like the most important journey of my life. By Cornwall, I was already drunk. I toasted the endless ocean with champagne, red wine and port, and greeted the green fringe of America with a host of exotic liqueurs. Glassy-eyed and reflective, drunker and drunker, yet burning with anticipation, I smoked a thousand cigarettes as the high deserts crept by below, the salt lakes, the snaking dry river beds, the weird isolated farming grids, irrigated green crop circles that looked like signposts for the extraterrestrial community, and mountain ranges like the frozen waves of a primordial ocean, their crests lightly brushed with snow.

It was late afternoon by the time we arrived out of the violet sky into the Los Angeles basin. Miles of shimmering squares unfolded as far as the eye could see on either side, merging into the blur, red and white rivers of headlights and tail lights carved through them. The Hollywood hills – shrouded in a lacy smog – were like the giant spine of some half-buried, billion-year-old dinosaur with their blinking antennae reaching towards the blackness of space. I had never seen so many houses – so many streets – so many cars – as the plane flew low towards the airport. It was beautiful, hard and cold. A feeling of disease, of panic, invaded me, challenging my sense of self. It was a feeling I would never shake.

On the drive into town the vastness of the place hit me again. It was nearly dark. The silhouettes of little oil rigs pumping on the surrounding hills reminded me of Breugel's paintings of hell. Bedraggled palm trees caked in exhaust fumes lined the road, but not a human being in sight. Finally, the Chateau Marmont, nestled against the Hollywood hills on Sunset Boulevard. From a distance it looked like one of King Ludwig's castles in Bavaria, tall and white with pointed slate roofs, balconies with striped awnings and a tower. In those days it was still delightfully seedy. Its hallway was like the set from *Sunset Boulevard*. There was a big baronial fireplace, high gothic arches, and a large, pretty, old Indian rug. Otherwise the furniture was dog-eared and ugly, covered in foam cushions riddled with cigarette burns. There was an old untuned grand piano in the corner, occasionally tinkled by some eager beaver, a newcomer, who would be frowned upon by the nightclub recluses and unsung geniuses that flitted through the hall like ghosts. There were rules in the Chateau, although no one ever told you what they were. The place was a kind of junkie retreat, a backwater. It was watched over by the Marlboro Man, a sixty-foot cut-out of a cowboy with a cigarette that dominated that part of the strip. He was lit up at night, and could be seen through the musty net curtains of your room, like God, always watching, staggeringly beautiful, and as dawn broke over the strip, still lit, he strode towards you, defying his one-dimensional state in that trick light between night and day. His days were numbered, as were those of the cigarette in movies. Indeed, the whole ramshackle shanty of the Sunset Strip was about to be swept away by the tsunami of political correctness that was gathering force to crash over Hollywood.

There was a spectral feeling to the hotel. The guests kept to themselves. Only occasionally did you come across one shuffling from the elevator, unshaven and scratching. There was no dining room and limited room service. The telephonist was a famous Hollywood voice, adding to the hotel's myth as he answered the phone in a low cracked whisper, with just one word, 'Chateau . . .'

The rooms had not changed since the fifties. Mine was a small apartment that looked out over the Marlboro man's groin. Dirty custard walls, shaggy brown carpets, a kitchenette, a sitting room, and a bedroom with a macabre 'walk-in closet'. If one had a tendency towards suicide this was the perfect place. The kitchen had a gas oven that taunted one, and empty cupboards and drawers with a peculiar smell. There was a dining 'nook' with an old table and four chairs, and the bed had a rubber sheet on top of the mattress so that the sheets slid off and strangled one in the night. The bathroom was vaguely Deco with faded green tiles, a thick chipped sink and a plastic shower curtain straight from *Psycho*. It felt as if the last inhabitant had died there. I thought I was miserable then but looking back, the Chateau was the pure essence of Hollywood, its corridors haunted by a thousand forgotten stars, and the walls of its rooms oozing the hopes and fears of everyone from Bette Davis, to James Dean, to John Belushi. Everyone had set up shop in that dusty old motel. Young hopefuls had dreamt there and old has-beens let the dream go. Now the Chateau was part of that dream. It held onto the past, like a lingering mourner at a graveside unwilling to move on.

It rained that first night, pattering on the palm trees outside. Through the musty net curtains Sunset Boulevard glistened and the whole city stretched out beneath me, and the feeling of isolation was almost like a terrible shattering orgasm, an endless shiver down the spine. This was not what I had expected.

The next day, after a sleepless night, I went to meet Orson for lunch at Ma Maison, a famous restaurant. I had read about Ma Maison in Jacqueline Susann novels and had a picture in my mind of plush velvet banquettes where the love machine sat alongside studio heads and Sharon Tate. Therefore I was quite surprised to find myself outside a sort of tent in a crumbling parking lot. Admittedly several Rolls-Royces were parked outside, but it was one of the shabbiest places I have ever seen. Inside, the floors were covered with AstroTurf, the diners sat on cheap white plastic chairs, and there was that thick hot smell of sun through tarpaulin.

The great man was alone at a small table away from the main dining area. It had real chairs around it. He looked like a mogul king and he dwarfed this little corner, as the Marlboro man dwarfed Sunset. He was beautifully turned out, in a grey suit and a shirt done up to the collar. No tie. He smelt vaguely of lemons. His beard was long and perfectly groomed, and he had large hands that charged you with a strange electricity when they shook yours. His eyes were deep and wise and magical. You knew they could turn to fury at the slightest provocation. He was a cobra, a Bond villain and a buddha. I could hardly breathe. I was mesmerised.

On the chair beside him sat two little dogs that growled dangerously as I sat down. With the utmost gentleness he took one in each giant hand and put them under the table.

'My God, you're thin!' he said.

Damn. I knew I should have packed my bottom, and perhaps my Body Map suit had been a mistake? By now I was in a free-falling panic, so no sooner had I sat down than I got up to go to the bathroom. As I pulled back my chair there was a piercing yelp from under the table. Orson's face flinched and his hands briefly made fists. Already he wanted to club me. The two tiny dogs snarled up at me from under the table and as I sat down again one bit deep into my ankle. I didn't dare say anything at first although the pain was excruciating. We began to talk about the movie, or rather Orson talked while I bled. I had nothing in my head. My voice had turned falsetto. I noticed Orson looking at my wrists on the table and very slowly I pulled them up into my jacket. The dog bit me again, and I gasped. Orson looked at me with those terrifying eyes.

'I think your dog has taken a bit of a dislike to me,' I said.

'Mmmm,' he growled, and summoned the head waiter. 'Patrick, Mitzi is such a fan of this young man, more so even than myself, that I'm afraid she has taken a memento from his ankle. Would you bring us Band-Aid and antiseptic?'

That first lunch was terrible, although I would never have admitted it. I could tell that he was disappointed. I was nothing that day. I had no personality. I was totally overwhelmed by him. We left the restaurant and an old junk heap of a car, a weird freak with a ponytail at the wheel, spluttered to a halt outside. Orson got in. The seat was definitely in the recline position and he lay there and waved as the car roared off at a snail's pace, belching exhaust from a pipe that scraped along the road.

Lunch was at Ma Maison every day for the next few months. Sometimes just Orson and me. Sometimes we were joined by 'the prince', a faded Italian crustacean in a polo neck and dyed jet hair. He had heavy shiny eyelids and they blinked through dirty black spectacles.

He smoked through a tortoiseshell cigarette holder, which remained clenched between his aged teeth. I never caught his name. Was it all a dream? I wondered to myself. Certainly Orson was a kind of Don Quixote, and there was no shortage of potential Sancho Panzas. But were we chasing a windmill or was a movie actually going to be made? My American agent, Michael Black, was suspicious.

On lunch three, Orson had a total meltdown. Patrick, the glamorous head waiter, was the son of the famous French actor Jean-Pierre Aumont. Orson always gave him a hundred-dollar bill as a tip. We were lunching with the prince that day and Patrick was settling us into Orson's table.

'Careful when you shake my hand,' said Orson. 'The last time you shook my hand, you nearly broke my finger.'

Patrick laughed good-naturedly, but suddenly Orson exploded with rage. 'Don't laugh at me!' he roared.

We all stopped dead in our tracks. The prince's head sank into his polo neck and Patrick turned a beetroot colour as the huge bear bellowed at him. It was an alarming moment. Orson was a very large man. He moved with difficulty, and rage needs a body to express itself and through which it can escape. Orson had only his face. The rest of him was rigid. Finally he fell back into his chair, the face drained of colour, the huge frame heaving. He was Big Daddy from *Cat on a Hot Tin Roof*. The dogs caught the aroma of violence, baring their teeth and yapping crazily. I drew my legs high up under my chair. I didn't want to start a feeding frenzy with my delicious ankles. Poor Patrick looked as if he was going to faint. He was rooted to the spot, shaking like a leaf.

'Now back off!' Orson growled.

There was a moment's silence. The prince studied the menu as if it were a thing he had never seen before and slowly things returned to, what, normal? In an almost theatrical Italian accent, his head coming back out of his polo neck, he guided our windswept ship into calmer waters. 'I have very interesting con-ver-sation with Lorimars today . . .'

Orson cast Amy Irving as my/his wife, and sometimes she came to lunch. She was pregnant with Max, and strangely so was Virginia at the time of the story. The prince set off for Rome. Orson disappeared for a while. Michael Black kept talking about a thing called 'escrow'. We had to have it.

One day the prince called me from Rome to say that I had to move out of my hotel room.

'Officially, the movie is on hold,' he said. 'Unofficially, we are still shooting.'

'Oh,' I replied uneasily. 'What does that mean, exactly?'

'It means, don't worry. Ciao, bello,' said the prince, and hung up.

Amy and her husband at the time, Steven Spielberg, took Orson to dinner, to try to help salvage the project, but I suspect it had always been a dream for Orson and not a reality. Sometimes I caught him looking at me under those hooded eyes – sombre, puzzled, and pulling away. I was a bird. He was a bear. I wasn't his Orson. Clouds of depression seemed to gather above him as he sat in that converted tent on Melrose. Over lunch he told enchanting stories. A midnight trip to Machu Picchu; Marlene getting a taxi to Paramount to find an old wig to wear for *Touch of Evil* . . . His voice was breathtaking, full of power and emotion with an extraordinary range. One can only imagine what he must have been like in the theatre. It flew through the registers, one moment deep and resonant, and the next higher, thinner, on the breath. Stories were told slowly, deliberately, often ending with a deep sigh.

Things had been quickly patched up with Patrick. He would pull the table back and accompany Orson out into the winter sunshine, lower him into the clapped-out car, and wave him off. The magician disappeared in a cloud of smoke.

On Christmas Day, I called him. 'Any news, Orson?' I said.

'Storm clouds are gathering,' he replied. 'It doesn't look good.' We never spoke again. He died three months later.

CHAPTER 20

The Harris Hollywood House

I couldn't go back to England empty-handed, and so I moved to a bed on the landing of my friend Damian Harris's house on Hollywood Boulevard. It was a rambling tumbledown place, a plantation house from the Deep South plonked in the middle of suburbia. It was made of white clapboard, with a broken weathervane on top that permanently pointed down. Like every house in LA it was made for show, and certainly not to have its doors slammed. The walls were paper-thin and there was something spooky about it, particularly downstairs at the back where there was a swing door between the kitchen and the rest of the house that creaked back and forth without the slightest hint of a draught. I lay there on my landing every morning in a deep depression, unable to get up, watching the comings and goings of the various inhabitants, thanking my lucky stars for Damian. The Harris household was the foundation of my life in Hollywood for years to come.

Damian had married a mutual friend, a beautiful giantess called Annabelle. At about eight o'clock every morning Annabelle flew out of their bedroom dressed for *Flashdance*, thundering down the stairs and out of the house. A moment later her car squealed out of the drive and peace descended for a while. Like most young people in LA, she divided her time between AA meetings, acting classes and aerobics.

When I moved in, one of her friends from AA was staying in the spare room upstairs, and one of her classmates was living on the couch in the breakfast nook off the kitchen. Who was the addict and who was the actor was a game that enthralled me in my leisure hours – i.e., all the time – especially after I found a bong under the actor's bed one morning on a rummage around for a bit of cash; but it was generally agreed that the addict was the girl upstairs. Crystal was an LA punk with a tiny voice and stiletto heels. Her peroxide hair was whipped into a huge cone. Like many of us in that house, she slept a lot, although Annabelle valiantly dragged her out to the morning AA meeting and then to another at night, but she needn't have bothered. Poor Crystal had no intention of submitting to a higher power. She gave us all crabs and then set fire to her room with a blowtorch while secretly doing crack in her bedroom cupboard. Damian, who mostly never seemed to notice who was staying in the house, put his foot down and she left in tears with twenty dollars borrowed from Mel Bordeaux.

Mel had recently graduated from NYU and arrived in LA to help Damian with a script he was writing. I was sent to collect her from the airport. She was standing on the kerb in an old suede jacket and dirty black jeans. She wore wraparound shades that hid her strange pale hooded eyes. When the shades came off she tugged at her long messy hair and looked out from behind it like a forest animal. She was quite chaotic. Tickets and tissues stuck out of every pocket. You could tell at a glance she was fun and trouble. Within five minutes we were old friends. Twenty years later we began to get to know each other. But friendships in Hollywood often go backwards.

In an apartment at the back of the house lived an actor called Eric Stoltz, with his girlfriend Ally Sheedy and their best friend, another actor, John Philbin. These three, like Annabelle, divided their time between AA and acting class, although they were all rather successful actors and didn't seem to know very much about drink or drugs. But then in those days, going to AA could be much better than being represented by one of the big agencies. You were on a fast track right onto a recovering studio executive's lap. All the addicts from the glorious seventies were still on Step 4, and one got the chance to meet and audition for some of the biggest producers and directors in town at the evening meeting. Once one had gone through the preliminaries – Hi, my name is Rupert, I have been shooting up Vim for the last ten years – one could spin any old yarn one wanted, going through the A to Z of emotions as one talked. AA was a talent show, but your award was a cake.

Hollywood Boulevard was a brilliant madhouse that was only quiet between seven and eight at night when all the recovering alcoholics were at a meeting and all the practising ones – Damian, me and Mel – were left briefly in peace for a few quiet drinks. Later, they all came back, with a screeching of brakes and a slamming of doors, with their scene partners from class, and for the rest of the evening the house turned into a sort of theatrical Cineplex. Annabelle would be hobbling around the sitting room on crutches being Vanessa Redgrave in *Julia*, while upstairs Eric and John would be rehearsing something more highbrow like *Waiting for Godot*, and Ally would be in floods of tears on the landing in a monologue of her own invention. At these moments, Damian, Mel and I slipped out of the house and went for dinner.

Annabelle swam ten miles a day in an enormous pool owned by the director Tony Richardson. He lived on the side of the hill above Sunset on an almost vertical street called Kings Road. His house perched on a crag and beneath it was a beautiful jungle of orchids that led down to the pool and a tennis court, which were cupped in the floor of a small canyon, the leftovers of some large estate from ancient times. It was a beautiful pool with a pink cottage at one end, the canyon towering above it. Houses clung precariously to the rocks. The sky seemed to be far away. Noises bounced off the hills: snatches of laughter, music, a car straining up the canyon. In the evenings long shadows quickly engulfed it, dragging everything into the cold Hollywood night, and the cities of the plain below could be seen in the cleavage of two hills twinkling in preparation for another early night. Exotic golden pheasants strutted round a large aviary and Tony's gardener Bob could be heard arguing on the phone from the little pool house.

Inside Tony's house was a vast picture window with a view over the whole city. In front of it that evening four ancient men sat around a small table playing bridge.

'Annabella!' said one.

'Two hearts!' said another.

And they went on playing.

'Who are all those men?' I asked Annabelle as we sat with our legs dangling in the shallow end of the pool.

'Christopher Isherwood, his boyfriend, Don Bachardy, and Gavin Lambert,' she replied carelessly.

'*Inside Daisy Clover* Gavin Lambert?' I asked, aghast.

'Inside what?' She laughed and jumped in.

I watched her swim for a bit and then I crept back through the jungle of orchids to the house to have a peek at the legends inside. They were almost silhouettes now against the huge window. The glimmering backdrop of the city they had adopted sketched their faces with mauve and silver outlines. Why had they come here? They seemed impossibly ancient, tribal elders locked in some pagan ritual, their faces carved with lines. They hardly moved. They stared at each other solemnly. Occasionally in slow motion, someone laid a card on the table, an eyebrow raised slightly, one face turned imperceptibly towards another, a hand reaching for a drink – whisky – through which the setting sun sparkled amber.

Isherwood and Bachardy had matching crew-cuts. Tony had a massive naked cranium to house his enormous brain. It was covered with a few wisps, which in the dusk could have been a mist of ideas rising from his head. Gavin had a majestic comb-over. He was the young girl of the party, slightly coy. I wondered if they'd all had him. ('Good gracious, no!' he said, years later, when we became close friends. 'One has to draw the line somewhere!')

But Tony presided over the group like an eagle. His face was gaunt and his gaze deep and unnerving. His nose was a dangerous beak, and the lower lids of his eyes hung slightly. He was dressed scruffily and he had the strangest voice I have ever heard.

Suddenly Annabelle was behind me, dripping. She sailed into the house. 'Rupert's been watching you all through the kitchen window,' she announced.

'How exciting!' said Christopher. 'Were we interesting?'

'Very,' I mumbled, embarrassed.

Tony and I became great friends. He was fascinating; in that city of conformity his utter indifference to what other people thought set him apart. There was everyone else and there was him. People were afraid of him, and like a semi-tame bird of prey he responded to fear and could be vicious. Getting to know him was no guarantee of safety. He could still be blisteringly scathing and famously reduced everyone at some point or other to quivering jellies. But he was always interested. He was neither gay nor straight, although he had passions for both men and women. His detractors, and there were many, said that he was simply a closeted homosexual. But he was much more complicated than that. He was a genuine outsider and hated the idea of being part of any group. He was particularly horrified by religion; and having discovered that I was Catholic and still went to mass, he loved to needle me about it.

'Baby Jesus is very worried about you at the moment,' he would say solemnly, apropos of nothing.

'Really, Tony? He told me he was having kittens about you!'

'Immaculate kittens?' he'd reply.

His best friend was an inventor called Jeremy Fry, and together they travelled to the furthest reaches of the world. They both owned villages in the hills of southern France. Tony's was called Le Nid de Duc – the owl's nest – and was lost down an impenetrable dirt track in the middle of the forest north of St Tropez. It was a cluster of ruined cottages over a pool that had been made famous by Hockney. It had a strange feverish atmosphere, and people were liable to go off the rails there, encouraged, needless to say, by Tony. He fed on drama.

'You look absolutely miserable today,' he would tell a downtrodden guest at breakfast, and usually by dinnertime that guest would be in floods of tears. It was *Heartbreak House*, and he was Captain Shotover. Huge dinners were cooked by his dutiful daughters at a trestle table under a string of coloured lights. I loved him and them and it, and my heart always jumped as I drove down that track towards Le Nid de Duc. It was an idyllic spot although Tony always seemed anxious to return to Los Angeles.

'LA is simply the best place in the world,' he'd say stubbornly.

It was a long dry winter, that Hollywood winter of 1985, and I never got a job. It was the day of the brat pack, and there wasn't much around for a tall thin English freak. I was offered a vampire movie called *Fright Night* but on the day I was about to sign the contact, I went for lunch with Tony and he persuaded me against it.

'Why would you do something like that?' he asked.

'I thought it could be a good move,' I replied.

'A good move? Oh dear!' he said, and then added, 'Poor Rupsie-poopsie. You're a bit of a floozie, aren't you?'

Soon afterwards, I called up Michael Black and told him to pass on the movie. 'Babe,' he said, 'don't lose any sleep. You know who they got for the role of the vampire killer?'

'No, who?'

'Well, listen to this. They wanted Laurence Olivier. They would have accepted Christopher Plummer. But they got Roddy McDowall!'

Roddy was as good as his word. I called him one afternoon after a particularly awkward lunch with Orson. I had been brought up in that post-war dinner party world where conversation began with a gruesome swapping of names in order to find common ground. ('Did you come across the Cheveleys in Delhi?' 'My dear, I absolutely worship Ronnie Cheveley. Tony, Rupert knows the Cheveleys!') Thus bonds are forged, and insider dealing may begin.

Reduced by sheer terror to my colonial roots, I tried this approach at lunch that day with Hollywood's Genghis Khan. 'Do you know Roddy McDowall?' I asked carelessly.

Orson looked at me with a cruel sneer. 'It depends what you mean by "know",' he said. 'It's a rather charged word.' I giggled like a vicar's wife. 'After all,' he continued, 'the acolytes of Sodom wanted to "know" the angel of the Lord, and they got zapped.'

'Right,' I said, and that was the end of that.

'My dear, you're here,' said Roddy when I called later. 'Can you come to dinner this Friday?'

'I should absolutely love to.' At last I was back on home ground.

I took Mel with me. Roddy's house was a long stone bungalow in a street of creaking eucalyptus trees. It was on the unfashionable side of Laurel Canyon, but then Roddy was famously careful with his money. Actually, it was a pretty street that wound up a small hill. A stream, a rarity in LA, ran across the road in front of his house, just a dribble of water, but it gave the place the feeling of somewhere much further north. Roddy opened the door in a black velvet suit and a white polo neck jersey. Behind him the house was crimson. Pictures of Bette Davis by Hurrell hung on the wall of the loo. Toby jugs with their jolly gargoyle faces stood in rows above the wide stone chimney that crackled with a cheerful fire. It was spring but there was a feeling of Christmas in that house.

Twelve people sat around the crimson lounge. Gregory and Veronique Peck were the staggeringly perfect older couple on a sofa. Facing them in a wing armchair, with her *Cabaret* hair and *Clockwork Orange* eyes, was Liza Minnelli. She was talking animatedly and waving her arms. Gregory and Veronique watched her with surprised smiles fixed to their faces. You knew the first thing they were going to say in the safety of the car on the way home would be, 'Well, what about Liza?' (Life was a cabaret whether you liked it or not when Liza was around.) Luise Rainer, the only woman to win an Oscar twice in a row, was perched like a little old featherless lovebird wrapped in a beautiful black cocktail dress with a pageboy haircut. She had escaped Hollywood and lived in Switzerland with a fabulously wealthy man. She stared into her cocktail as if it was feeding her lines. Mel and I looked at each other across the room. This was it. A couple of frisky queens giggled at a secret joke. Roddy wagged his finger. 'Now, you two!' he laughed. 'Come on everyone. Grub's up!'

I sat between Luise Rainer and Veronique Peck. Candles fluttered. Mel looked at me meaningfully from the other side of the table. We were in heaven. A teacup and saucer stood next to the wineglasses, and modest helpings of nursery food were served. Roddy's culinary sense had not developed much from the studio schoolroom. He held forth at one end of the table and Liza talked about her mother to the two giggly queens at the other end. It was epic. Roddy was a great host, with a sincere curiosity about everyone, and his eyes twinkled at us all from behind his glasses. Later, as we filed into the screening room to watch one of his collection of forgotten movies, Liza grabbed my arm. 'May I talk to Andrew Lloyd Webber about you?' she asked, almost desperately.

'Certainly, I would love you to,' I replied.

'Thanks,' she said, and squeezed me. This was the kind of absurd conversation that flourished in the lubed desert.

A few days later I took Roddy up on his offer to go and 'lie out' by his pool. This time he answered the door in a pair of Speedos, confirming the legend that along with Milton Burrell he was the best-hung man in Hollywood. His garden was astonishing. There was a huge twenty-foot statue from *Planet of the Apes* outside the back door, surrounded by tall waving bamboo, and at the top of the hill, with a spectacular view over the valley and the San Fernando mountains, was the bench from *Lassie*.

Lying by the pool that afternoon I told Roddy all my tales of woe. He listened patiently. He must have heard it all a thousand times before. 'Don't worry, dear,' he soothed. 'One always thinks it's the end and then something always comes up.' And we toasted each other with that strange hideous drink, iced tea.

One morning I was with Mel at the traffic lights on Sunset and La Cienega. We were on our way home from breakfast in some faraway dive where Mel swore Jimi Hendrix wrote 'Are You Experienced'. Mel loved this sort of sightseeing, walking in the footsteps of her tragic Hollywood heroes. She spent days scoping out disaster scenes, the Sharon Tate house, the Ramon Navarro house, the spot where Montgomery Clift crashed his car. Suffering and torture were a must. We didn't like anyone who ended up well. They were cop-outs as far as we were concerned: the Bings and the Bobs. You had to be destroyed by Hollywood to count; that was the whole point, it redeemed you. We fully expected, indeed hoped, to be destroyed ourselves by it and were prepared to throw ourselves into the flames. Mel's patron saint du jour was Frances Farmer, whom Louella Parsons described as 'crashing off a liquor-slicked highway', and to whom Mel bore more than a passing resemblance. Roddy, of course, had known Frances Farmer. ('Utterly deranged, dear. Came at me once with a carving knife.') Mine was Monty, tortured, terrified Princess Tiny Meat, patron saint of all closeted queens.

There was a tumbledown Deco tower on Sunset, now renovated and called The Argyle, where, according to one of his potboiler biographies, Monty was once trapped in a darkened penthouse drinking vodka laced with barbiturates. The building was boarded up, but I had recently discovered a hole through which to squeeze into the basement. You could climb to the top of the tower, past the dingy remnants of apartments, with their peeling wallpaper and damp half-eaten carpets, the odd rotting armchair, and the smell of piss. Now there was only a soiled mattress and some old newspapers in Monty's penthouse. The view over the city was stunning. It was the perfect spot to sit and dream about the freaks, the overdoses and the murders, and, of course, what fabulous tragic turn my own career might take. I wanted to take Mel there, but she was unsure (or just lazy, as far as I was concerned).

'Omigod, Sean Penn is in the next car and he's waving,' she whispered at the lights, and then nudged me hard in the ribs. 'Wave back, asshole.'

He was with a director called James Foley. We volleyed compliments from car to car while the light was red, and swapped numbers before they sped off and we groaned on in my old red-velvet-upholstered rental car. Plans for the Monty tour were put on hold as we raced back to the Harris house to tell everyone about Sean.

The next day he called and asked me to come over to a friend's house for dinner. The place was on Mulholland Drive, the road that winds along the ridge of the Hollywood hills. You can see the valley on one side and Hollywood right down to the ocean on the other. Needless to say, Mel was beside me as we drove up and down it that evening, looking for a ludicrous number like 973. Eventually, we found it, rang the buzzer, and electric gates swung open. A Chinaman in a white coat and gloves answered the door and led us through a large empty house to a kitchen where Warren Beatty, Twiggy and Sean were having coffee and cookies.

Hollywood was amazing. You never knew where you were going to end up. Far from being an impregnable fortress, in those days you could get to know everyone within a couple of weeks. (It was losing them that took for ever.)

Warren handed round cookies. 'These are made by Molly Ringwold's mother,' he said.

'Mmm,' said everyone, except for Twiggy, Hollywood's Eliza Doolittle.

'Gawd. I don't like this one.'

'Then try these,' said Warren, proffering another tin of cookies.

'Oo maid thays?' asked the Twig.

'These are Mrs Fields'.'

'Sally Fields' mother?' I asked, amazed by the notion that everyone's mother baked cookies for Warren.

'Mrs Fields is a brand,' he replied.

Sean had a new girlfriend, though we didn't meet her that night. A couple of days later he called me. 'I told my girlfriend about you and she went really quiet,' he said. 'I'd like you to meet her. Let's go for dinner tomorrow.'

I had met many stars. At seventeen I had sat with David Bowie downstairs at the Embassy Club and been lectured on the mystical potential hidden in the number seven. At eighteen I had dined at La Coupole in Paris with Andy Warhol and Bianca Jagger. I had sniffed poppers with Hardy Amies on the dance floor of Munkberrys. I had done blow with Steve Rubell and Halston at Studio 54. I was spoilt for excitement and I knew what it was to be drunk on fame by association, how it felt to be a part of 'the gang', the cluster of small gems around the large canary diamond, the obligatory whirlwind dancing dangerously about the eye of the storm. It was intoxicating to be around stars. People smiled at you and even if that smile was for someone else, the queen bee nestled in the middle of the banquette, it didn't matter, because you were a part of that queen bee's hive. People talked to you, but really it was a campaign. If it was a good one, or helped you with yours, then you passed it on. Nights under the stars were feeding frenzies of self-interest, and in the mirage of the celebrity world you were who you knew, and who you knew could change your life and wash you up anywhere. Exotic shores. Behind bars. Or just behind the bar.

Yet everything was a pale imitation of the impact Madonna had as she walked from a car across a sidewalk and into a restaurant. Even before she arrived, as I was still sitting there waiting with Sean and Mel, there was a flurry outside. Two people knocked against the window of the restaurant, like leaves in a strong gust of wind that blew open the door, and the Immaculate Conception was among us. She was not yet the material girl, nowhere near the peak of her fame. There was no bodyguard. She had parked the car herself (God help the others). But still there was an energy field around her, like a wave, that swept everyone up as it crashed into the room.

She was tiny and *pulpeuse* with long auburn hair, slightly curled. She sat down. Sean's beautiful forget-me-not eyes watered with adoration. Hers were the palest blue, strangely wide set; any further and she would look insane, or inbred. When they looked in your direction, you froze. In no way was she conventionally beautiful. She was a bit like a Picasso. When she fixed you with her regard, there was a tenderness and warmth that made your skin bump, but when she looked away, it was like sunbathing on a cold day and suddenly a cloud comes. She was raucous but poised, elegant but common. She had the cupid-bow lips of a silent screen star, and it was obvious that she was playing with Sean's cock throughout the meal. She was mesmerising. She oozed sex and demanded a sexual response from everyone. It didn't matter if you were gay. You were swept up all the same. In those early years there was *no* male who would not fuck her.

At some point during the dinner she got up to go to the bathroom. 'Come with me, Sean,' she said. Her voice was high and whiny, like Citizen Kane's wife.

'You'll be okay, baby,' replied Sean, who was clearly going to have his hands full. Madonna was no Elizabeth McGovern (Sean's actress ex).

'No, I'm scared. C'mon, baby.' She stamped her foot in a sexy pastiche of exasperation.

Sean got up. 'I'll be right back,' he said.

Twenty minutes later Mel and I were still eating breadsticks. Mel snapped hers in fury. Madonna had not learnt how to charm the female population. Yet. Time stands still for a superstar. When they eventually returned to the table, neither of them made the vaguest reference to their lengthy absence as they settled back into their cold plates. Mel huffed and puffed through the rest of the meal. Her hair dangled dangerously over her food, but I lost myself in Madonna's attention and by the end of the meal I had fallen in love.

CHAPTER 21

Fred Hughes

'I'm a friend of Andy.'

'I'm meeting Andy and Fred.'

'Fred and Andy told me to come.'

'I live with Fred.'

These were the passwords that from 1965 to 1985 opened all the invisible doors in New York.

Fred lived in a brownstone on Lexington Avenue at 89th Street that Andy had shared with his mother, until she died, at the end of the 1970s, when he moved to 66th Street. The house was built by a famous architect, Stanford White. Inside, the walls were grey and the floors were black. A gloomy light battled through louvred shutters and heavy silk curtains, and Fred's fabulous mélange of art, his federal furniture and tribal woodwork, waited to be seen, shrouded in the endless dusk. A fifteenth-century portrait of a man covered in pearls hung next to a Warhol of the Prince of Wales, watched from the shadows by an African gargoyle with a dumbstruck expression. Trains rattled underneath, and the traffic on Lexington shook the windowpanes and yet there was a tomblike silence in the house that was at first unsettling. But the more one came to know New York, the later the nights, the more dramatic the big breaks and the heartbreaks, the more one appreciated the dawn returns to the silent screamery, creeping up the squeaky staircase and collapsing onto a huge federal bed in the grey shuttered spare room at the top of the house.

Outside, Fred planted wisteria that by the time he died had overcome the entire façade, wrapping it with thick tentacles through which the shuttered windows were barely visible. As multiple sclerosis dragged Fred into the ground, the wisteria pulled the house down around him. A solitary light shone through the foliage covering the front door, and driving down that block of Lexington of a night towards the end of the century it was the only confirmation to all the friends that had deserted him that Fred was still alive.

But in the good old days, when New York was still New York, Fred was Andy's manager, the *éminence grise* behind the Warhol empire. He was a small thin man with tiny wrists and ankles, slicked-back jet-black hair and sensuous lips. Like his master, he was the very essence of his time. No one quite knew exactly where Fred began. He was discovered by Dominique de Menil a fabulously rich lady from Houston, Texas, either because his acute eye for art caught hers, or because his father had been her chauffeur. There were all sorts of theories. What is certain is that he flew into New York on Dominique's magic carpet and was taken up by Diana Vreeland, through whom he met everyone.

Fred was an extraordinary invention, a collage of dress codes and mannerisms, stolen from the wealthy, cut out by a discerning eye and a piercing wit, and stuck onto the relatively blank page of his Houston origins. He wore blazers and breeches and laced bootees. His striped shirts had tiny white collars fixed together with a gold pin and the knots of his ties were tight to the point of strangulation. He wore his watch outside his cuff like Giovanni Agnelli, although if you dared to suggest that such an homage was possible you risked an explosion of wrath. He was Southern, although after a few drinks he affected an alarming English drawl, as unlike the British upper class as Dick Van Dyke's impressions of a cockney chimney sweep. He was obsessed by the Duke of Windsor, but bore more than a passing resemblance to the Duchess. He was extremely funny, and was kind and generous to his friends.

Thus he was a controversial figure in the backstabbing, spot-lit world of the Factory, partly because right up until the day Andy died, the Factory was the unchallenged epicentre of New York, the adaptor through which all the disparate live wires in that extraordinary place were channelled, creating the electric shock that made New York the city of cities. It was also partly because, by the middle of the eighties, Fred's drunken behaviour had become wildly eccentric. He was gripped by frenzy. Actually it wasn't just drunkenness; it was the disease leaving its calling card. His wrath was often unleashed on the English liggers who, like myself, used his home as their New York pied-à-terre: Sabrina and Miranda Guinness, Sarah Giles, Anne Lambton and Natasha Grenfell, to name but a few. Some of these girls rather half-heartedly went out with Fred, but Fred was not essentially a sexual man. His detractors claimed him for a closet queen, but his passions were not really sexual at all. He loved Europe, history, aristocracy and art.

At times he was exasperated by his entourage of penniless English roses. We ran in and out of the house, slamming the front door, monop-olising the phone. Fred had to shout from the bottom of the house every time it rang for us. His good-natured call gradually degraded into a maniacal scream as the old school bell rang again and again on all the antique handsets scattered about the dark house. His maid, a formidable black lady named Hazel, was seventy years old, tall and thin, and wore a wonderful wig under a beret. She didn't have much time for any of Fred's guests and would fill him in on our comings and goings in the afternoon when he came back from the Factory. He sat at the kitchen table in his shirtsleeves and suspenders. The tiny old TV set blared and Hazel stood grimly by the stove making fried chicken wings and trouble.

One such afternoon, when Fred was half seething, half amused – always a dangerous combination, which we wary hoorays knew could lead to internal combustion at any moment – Sabrina Guinness, Natasha Grenfell and I were put on trial at the kitchen table. Fred was our demented judge and Hazel was witness for the prosecution. The case: overflowing ashtrays, too many lights left on, not locking the front door properly. We three accused sat in a row, chain-smoking and look-ing repentant as the phone rang for the thousandth time. Fred's lips twitched involuntarily into an anguished scowl.

'Rupert Everett's residence,' he said, in an English drawl. We glanced nervously at each other. Immediate evacuation was imperative. 'No, I'm afraid he's not in. May I take a message?' Fred's eyes bulged for a moment.

'Would you spell that for me please,' he said with a demonic grin. 'M–A—' he repeated slowly, writing the letters on the yellow legal pad beside him. 'D–O–N–N–A. I'll let him know you called, sir.'

There was a dark moment of silence, as we all braced ourselves for whichever direction the rollercoaster was going to take us. Then Fred jumped from his chair and ran around the room like a laboratory primate, clutching his face with his hands and rubbing them up and down his body. 'Oh my God! I can't believe it!' he screamed, writhing on the floor. 'Madonna called my house!' And his body jerked and shuddered in a parody of orgasm. It was funny and frightening. The pent-up courtroom exploded with laughter. Even Hazel nodded grimly as she laid her chicken wings carefully on a piece of kitchen towel.

Fred and Andy were perfect foils for one another. Andy was dishevelled, still very much a Pittsburgh Warhola trudging home from the foundry. He wore cheap clothes and carried a brown paper bag wherever he went that housed his tape recorder and camera. His wig was studiously plonked wonky and his face underneath was an unrecognisable landscape of pink mounds. His lashless eyes were surprised raisins hidden behind dirty glasses. The only thing that gave one an inkling of the minute observation machine that lay underneath was his cranky half-smile that lit the raisins briefly and was inevitably accompanied by a signature inanity. ('Aww, gee! That's great!')

By his side, Fred was the perfectly groomed attaché, the Southern aristocrat who brought in endless commissions for work, much of which has now been officially discredited. Women adored Fred, but soon his behaviour began to make people weary. He discovered his oncoming MS sometime in the early eighties, when he consulted doctors in Switzerland about the strange sensations he was having in those tiny extremities, but courageously he never told a soul. Soon he began to use a stick. Sometimes on a Saturday night at Nell's the rage would grip him and he would knock the entire contents of a table onto the floor with his stick.

'Fred's off again!' we would say. Everyone turned a blind eye. After all he was a linchpin of a world that didn't know it was crumbling. When Andy died, Fred was in Los Angeles staying at the Chateau Marmont. Who knows what he felt, although any affection between the two men had long since been spread extremely thin.

Not much later, on holiday in Guatemala with Sarah Giles and Tim Hunt (now the chairman of the Warhol Foundation), Fred finally lost control of his muscles while crossing a ditch and fell into an open sewer. He had to be pulled out and dragged, covered in shit, and dunked, screaming abuse, into a water tank in a village bar.

By the time I moved back to New York in 1997 after a twelve-year absence, Fred was bedridden. He had briefly had it all after Andy's death: recognition, wealth and bad health. I went to see him a couple of times. The house was just a giant tree by now, wisteria branches overflowing onto the rest of the block. Not much had changed inside. The trains still rattled underneath. A hospital bed was poised theatrically in a pool of light in the middle of the library off the main hall, which had been repainted a beautiful emerald green. By the bed, pumps moved silently up and down, keeping Fred breathing. He could only just talk. One word per breath. I brought my second novel along to read to him. I forgot that it was largely about death. I sat by the end of the bed, skipping parts that might upset him, as he lay in front of me, his body jerking up and down mechanically under the blankets. Outside, on a chair in the hall sat one of the Russian bodybuilders who looked after him. In the dim half-light, he could have been a new piece of Soviet reality that Fred had found on his travels.

'I'm sorry, Fred, this is really boring. Shall I read something else?' I asked, after a while.

'No,' he said, as the machines contracted his chest into an out breath. 'I – love – it,' he gasped, and a large glistening tear ran slowly down his cheek.

I went back a couple of times, but then I, too, dropped him. I don't remember how exactly. I went to LA, came back. Things weren't going well with my boyfriend. Whatever.

I never finished reading my book to him, and I regret it enormously. He lay there for another four years, alone but for his Russian muscle nurses. One faithful acolyte from the Factory days went to see him, and so did his brother and sister, but otherwise he was more or less abandoned. Nobody could face him. In an agonising slow motion he was stripped of all his faculties. First he went deaf, then blind, all the time aware. He finally died in 2001, the last full stop marking the very end of a time.

CHAPTER 22

New Year's Eve

My friend Lucy Hellmore had married Bryan Ferry. She invited me and Natasha Grenfell, Sabrina's brother Hugo Guinness, and Isabella Delves Broughton (soon to become Isabella Blow) to join them for Christmas in a house near Heron Bay on the island of Barbados.

Bryan might have fallen in love with his frosty upper-class beauty but perhaps he didn't realise that marriage to her was also marriage to her circle of friends. We all decamped to the house from the various parts of the world where we had been 'working' and more or less immediately the tension mounted. Bryan and I had known each other for years, introduced by Nicky Haslam when I was seventeen and fascinating. He had adored me then. Now I was twenty-four and famous, 'desperate', according to his best friend and my ex-lover Antony Price, 'to wrestle the steering wheel out of Bryan's hands and drive the car myself'.

Antony told me this while we were walking down the beach on the morning after my socks had been found on the sitting-room floor and had provided Bryan with the material for his first major meltdown of the trip. The sea gurgled against the white sand. Sunbathers looked at us aghast. Antony was dressed in a green leather aviator suit complete with peaked cap and goggles.

It was subsequently decided, during a summit meeting of the liggers, that to protect us all from expulsion I should move out of the Big Brother house and into the incredibly expensive Sandy Lane Hotel next door. I was utterly broke but there was no alternative.

The next day it was agreed that Natasha should move out as well. She was furious, mostly with me. She felt that if I hadn't come, everything would have been all right. Then Isabella and Hugo delivered a final decree from HQ.

'Bryan doesn't want you to go anywhere he goes,' said Izzy, smoking a large reefer and giggling.

'That's awful,' I said.

'Yuh, I know,' said Izzy, looking at me sombrely with those huge, mad eyes.

'Well, then, I might as well leave,' I said, feeling rather crushed and wondering where I could go at this late stage.

'Yuh, you might as well,' she replied, handing me the joint. And they all burst into fits of laughter.

Whether or not Bryan and Isabella had been joking, that afternoon I was on the plane to LA, taking drunken, maudlin stock of my life as I ploughed back across the freezing desert towards the end of the year. I was miserable. Nothing seemed to be working out. I had no job and no prospects (and, as it turned out, I wasn't to work for another year). I was obviously not the golden marauding star of my secret dreams. My conquest of Tinseltown had all the drama and charisma of a silent fart and now I faced the end of the year alone in a shabby hotel room.

At about nine o'clock that night I was checking into the Chateau – the Harrises were away and Mel was back east. There was a windswept shutdown feeling to the place. I was leaning over the reception desk, wondering what to do with my evening, when I heard a familiar voice behind me.

'What are you doing here?'

It was Michael Roberts, the fashion editor of the *Sunday Times*, the creative genius behind Tina Brown's *Tatler*, the man who pioneered the role of stylist superstar. This was indeed a bit of luck.

'I'm going to Mr Chow's for dinner,' he said. 'Come.'

Tina Chow sat alone in a priceless vintage nightdress (probably Vionnet) at a large round table in the middle of the room. She was staring out to sea, lost in thought. The restaurant was half empty and the diners whispered together, afraid to be overheard. It was a gloomy night of the gloomiest week: that black hole between Christmas and the New Year . . .

This was the beginning of a long low season for Mr Chow and it was to be some years before the place was seriously taken up again, first by the agents from the neighbouring Creative Artists Association for lunch, and then, later still, as a kind of canteen for the hip hop community. But Tina would be gone by then.

That night, an Italian waiter in a starched white apron tapped her gently on the shoulder and she turned round. Something was different. She was imperceptibly dishevelled, which was strange because Tina was always immaculately groomed. I could see Michael screw his eyes up. He was the Sherlock Holmes of fashion, and could solve many a crime by looking at a person's clothes. Why was she wearing vintage couture on a quiet Wednesday night instead of her usual T-shirt and Kenzo pants? Her face was powdered a mauvish white that made her look like a ghost. She jumped up from the table with a little shriek and ran towards us, her bangled arms outstretched, a geisha on the morning after perhaps, but easily the most beautiful woman we knew.

We settled down at a table together, three exhausted people in a lonely town, with a huge collective sigh of relief, and soon we were laughing till the tears ran down our faces, drawing the evening out, afraid to leave. Such is the pleasure of seeing a familiar face on the road to hell.

We had dinner there every night that Christmas of 1984, always the same group: Michael and Tina Chow, Helmut and June Newton, Michael Roberts and me. Michael Roberts was styling for Helmut, and we were all staying at the Chateau.

Michael and Tina Chow were an enigmatic couple, well mannered, considerate, always interested. They never gave you a hint of what was really going on but there is a photo by Helmut, taken in the restaurant, that probably says it all. Michael leers at the camera in a tuxedo from behind the bar, while Tina, in a long Chanel dress, is tied with huge ropes to the front.

On New Year's Eve, I spent the day helping Tina blow up thousands of pale green balloons. We tied little glitter aeroplanes to them on pieces of string and watched them float off towards the ceiling. When we came into the restaurant later that night there was a low bank of little green clouds over the whole room and beneath it flew hundreds of sparkling planes. It was like the Blitz. For that brief season we became a sort of dysfunctional family. Helmut was the father. He fought with Michael, the adopted son. June was mother earth with a shrill streak, her accent straight from the Melbourne Theatre Company, and even when she was being genteel, she had the twinkly eyes of a tomboy-ish younger sister. Though with her bob and a black pearl necklace, she looked like a picture of Anaïs Nin. ('Anaïs Ninja, you mean!' said Michael later.)

Tina was the forlorn household goddess, and I was the wounded faun who had been run over taking a short cut across the freeway. Conversation veered towards the past. Helmut told stories of his life in Berlin as a young man, before the war, of swimming in summer in the lakes outside the city, of assignations for sex on the little islands, of meeting June, of driving with her in a car across Europe, and of an apartment they once had in Paris.

'Haunted!' said June.

'It was not haunted, Juney!' shouted Helmut.

'The previous owner committed suicide in the bathroom, Helmy.' June never backed down, although Helmut could be quite ferocious.

'So what?' said Helmut.

June turned to me with a sigh. 'I had to sit in the little bar downstairs. All day!'

'God, you exaggerate!'

At a certain point just after midnight, as streamers were still falling through the air, the music was blaring and everyone had on their paper crown, I passed Tina on the way back from the bathroom.

'Tina, I'm so depressed,' I said.

'Me too,' she replied flatly, looking up at me through the cloud of balloons and planes, and suddenly tears burst out of her eyes. She held her hand up to her face, perplexed, like a stunned leaking robot about to short-circuit.

'Tina! What's wrong?'

I put my arms around her and her body convulsed against mine. Behind us, the party whistled and blew their horns. I could see our table, ludicrous in their hats. Helmut talked earnestly with Michael Chow. June, always very connected to Tina, looked around. Just one deep sob and Tina pulled away. It was not in her make-up to expose herself and for a second she surveyed me strangely. Then she wiped her eyes and began to laugh.

'I'm sorry, Rupi. I guess it's just that time of year. Come on, let's go back to the table.'

None of us knew, but Tina had Aids. One day we were out shopping in a limo with her children, China and Max, and she was violently ill. We all laughed, thinking that she had drunk too much, but I caught Michael looking out of the window, puzzled. It just wasn't very Tina. Not long afterwards, she retired from the world and very few people ever saw her again.

Seven years later, in another Hollywood incarnation, I was in a health food shop on Melrose. A beautiful teenage girl watched me from behind a trolley laden with goods. She began to follow me around the aisles.

'Are you Rupert?' she asked, finally.

'Yes,' I replied.

'You're a friend of my mother's.'

'Who's your mother?'

The girl looked from side to side as if she was checking that no one was listening. 'Tina Chow,' she said. I felt the blood rush up to my head and tears prick my eyes.

'China?'

'Yes,' she giggled.

'My God, you've grown. How's your mother?'

'She's okay.'

We talked for a few minutes. I was gripped by a wave of emotion. This teenage beauty was shopping for her dying mother; just a second ago she was a little child, whining that her mom had been sick in the car. She gave me a phone number and then disappeared around the corner, waving.

Later, when I called, a man answered. He told me that Tina was busy.

'Will you send her lots of love, and give her my number?' I said.

'I certainly will. I'm sure she sends you love, too,' and the line went dead.

She never called back.

CHAPTER 23

Julie Andrews

One New Year later I was sailing through the night on a yacht belonging to my friends Jan and Jane Wenner towards the island of Mustique in the Caribbean. There was a full moon. Jane, Sabrina, her sister Miranda and I were sitting on the deck. Jan had gone to bed. The sea was quite rough, grey and white in the moonlight. Mustique was a distant mass with a few twinkling lights towards which we ploughed. The wind was strong and hot. It filled our sails and we flew through the water. At midnight we were still far away and fireworks exploded above the island. It was an entrancing end to a desolate year of trailing like a medieval pilgrim around the festival circuit. With little else to do, and not much money to do it with, I went from one grim event to another, spinning all kinds of yarns to explain away the fact that I was never working, a poor player strutting and fretting his hour upon the podium, dropping off my laundry as soon as I checked into the hotel, living on room service and festival dinners, free flights and hot air, before packing up and moving on to the next. From Bratislava to Brisbane, I ligged my way across the planet.

One evening, early in January 1986, I was having a drink at Basil's Bar on Mustique when the telephone behind the bar rang and someone called my name. It was Duncan, my agent from London.

'*There* you are,' he said. 'I thought you were in Sydney. Julie Andrews is making *Duet for One*. They want you for the role of her protégé but you've got to get over here soon.'

I nearly fell off my barstool. Could it be true? All those years pretending Julie was my mother, and now art was finally imitating life, or rather fantasy life, which was better.

I was on the next flight back to London.

Duet for One had originally been a play. It was based on the true story of the cellist Jacqueline du Pré and her battle with multiple sclerosis. For some reason, in the play the character became a violinist but the role was a tour de force. The movie was being made by a freaky couple of producers, a pair of overweight and dishevelled Israelis famous in the eighties: Menahem Golan and Yoram Globus. Their company, Golan Globus, sounded like the name of some kind of shot for hepatitis, but they made hundreds of films a year. And even though their cheapness was legendary, and people turned their noses up at them, they were a famous couple on the Croisette at Cannes, and everyone ended up going to them for a deal at some time or other. Some of their films were good. Some never made it any further than a gaudy full-page ad in the Cannes edition of *Variety*.

Andrei Konchalovsky was one of their stable of directors, a handsome, talented Russian in his fifties who didn't look a day older than thirty. His father had written the Soviet national anthem and had been on intimate terms with Stalin. He and his brother, a concert pianist, led privileged lives in the Soviet Union, or rather out of it, in Andrei's case. He had just completed another film for Gamma Globulin that got quite a lot of attention: *Runaway Train* with Eric Roberts and Jon Voight.

It had been arranged that I was to come back a month early to have violin lessons with Julie. After almost a year of failing to get anywhere in Hollywood, I decided to try the 'method' approach. I borrowed a jacket from Adam Ant and modelled my character on the latest prodigy on the violin scene, a rockabilly called Nigel Kennedy. I developed a quiff and a nasal Bromley twang, wore my costume at home and at work, and never came out of character, even when going to confession at the Holy Redeemer in Cheyne Row. My fake London accent couldn't have been that successful because the priest peeked out from behind the curtain. 'I thought it was you,' he said, before disappearing back inside.

Even though I had in fact studied the violin for years as a child, I lied and told everyone involved in the film that I was an absolute beginner; I had visions of Julie being overcome by how deeply I was embroiled in the character, so much so that I had miraculously mastered the instrument in two lessons.

Rehearsals took place in the Oliver Messel Suite at the Dorchester Hotel. It was all extremely old school. Julie's assistant opened the door, and I sat around tuning up with the violin teacher for about five minutes, waiting for my mother to finally arrive and claim me for her own. Would she recognise me in character?

She came gliding in, wearing a pair of tight beige trousers and a woolly jersey. I could hardly stand up. She hadn't changed since *Mary Poppins*, still looking remarkably young, beautiful and frosty with a kind of wartime no-nonsense cheer.

'Wotcha!' I said.

'Do you normally talk like that?' she asked.

I had to keep reminding myself not to call her my pet secret name that I had invented all those years ago, sitting in the wardrobe in my mother's red tweed skirt.

'No, spit spot. Normally I talk like you,' I wanted to say, but instead I said, 'I'm in character.'

'Ah . . .' she said, disapprovingly, thoroughly unimpressed by the method.

For Julie and me it was one-and-two and three and turn-and-bow and look cheeky and say the line and hope for the best. We were to play the Bach Double Violin Concerto. It was not too hard, and we were going to mime to playback, but it was still pretty difficult to master the bowing and the fingering. We rehearsed every day for two weeks. I was in heaven, even though I had still not managed to conquer Julie. She was a hard nut, and I could tell she didn't approve of my interpretation of the role.

Rehearsals began, and many of the usual suspects were wheeled out. Being in a movie in England was rather like going to a camp prison. The studios all looked a bit like prisons – long cold corridors with shiny, painted brick walls – and inside were the same old criminals, time after time, happy to be home.

Liam Neeson played Julie's cockney lover, Alan Bates played her husband, and Cathryn Harrison the demure secretary. They all knew about my secret obsession and goaded me to tell her. What was I going to say? 'Miss Andrews, I just want to say that because of you I was taken to a child psychologist'?

Julie was extraordinary to watch and her performance was brilliant. There were some moments during the shoot that were hysterically funny but at the same time really uncanny. The most unsettling (for me, at least) was a scene when Julie came back from the hospital. While she was away, a lift had been installed on the staircase because she could no longer walk. She struggled onto it as we all stood around, Alan, Liam, Cathryn, and – for good measure – Max von Sydow, as she rode up the stairs looking sadly down at us all. I thought I was going to explode. It was all getting too weird. In the old days Mary Poppins had effortlessly slid up the shiny oak banister of Cherry Tree Lane and now she was being hoisted up to her deathbed.

But the scene that was most astonishing for me happened towards the end of the shoot, and probably I should have retired immediately after it. No psychiatrist could have hoped for a more perfect resolution to a childhood obsession. It brought a whole new meaning to that funny word 'closure'.

Julie and I were filmed performing the Bach Double Violin Concerto *live* at the Albert Hall. Arriving that morning at dawn, there were posters of the two of us all over the walls of the huge round concert hall. I nearly fainted. As a child I had the record cover of *Mary Poppins* pinned to one side of my bed, and *The Sound of Music* on the other. We had never heard of posters then; but now I was in the poster.

Andrei had filled the Albert Hall for the scene. Queens with Julie obsessions jostled dangerously for seats. There were a couple of full-on scraps in the stalls; tempers were frayed – people had been lining up since dawn. These fans, some of them quite freaky in wigs and flashers' macs, watched me with undisguised hatred from the stalls as we rehearsed. I played them to the hilt, chatting with Julie, sharing jokes, generally acting as if I ruled the roost. One friend of mine, Stewart Grimshaw, looked positively green with envy at the front of the stalls.

After the rehearsals, the scene was to be shot in one long hand-held camera move. In my white tie and tails, I knocked on Julie's dressing room door, deep down in the bowels of the Albert Hall. She answered wearing a beautiful dress.

'Good luck, darling. I love you,' she said. This was better than tripping.

We began the long walk through the sloping backstage corridors up towards the stage. Andrei had told the crowds to chant and so we could hear them pounding on the floors above us. The camera crew were in front of us, walking backwards up the wide curving passage, with their lamps, their squares of polystyrene, their microphones, their total attention trained on our every move. I can't remember what we said but it was one long orgasm. The corridor led right up into the middle of the stage and as Julie and I arrived, the whole audience stood up and screamed. I knew I was living the best moment of my career. We stood there bathing in the applause, the orchestra behind us, the conductor beaming in front. Julie looked at me and winked. We put our violins up to our shoulders. The conductor tapped his stand with his baton. There was that moment of silence, like just before you jump off a high diving board.

Then we played the entire first movement of the concerto.

Actually, the scene was a dream sequence so at a certain point Julie's character began to freak out. Her hand was not working. She stopped playing but I continued with the orchestra smiling maniacally at her. She began to shout, 'Stop! Stop!' But we went on playing. Two nurses in white coats arrived from the wings and forced her into a wheelchair. They pulled her off the stage screaming. It was chilling.

Afterwards, Julie came up to me, and said, 'You've done a great job. I love the way you're playing the role.'

I was ecstatic. Unfortunately, the film got terrible reviews, but it is memorable for Julie's performance (if not mine).

CHAPTER 24

Colombia

I made my Italian debut in a film called *Chronicle of a Death Foretold*. It was shot on location in the small village of Mompos on one of the great South American rivers, the Magdalena. I took a friend with me, a girl called Frances.

There is nothing quite like an Italian film crew at work. The noise, the chaos, the dramatic confrontations. You are permitted to scream at other people on an Italian film, whereas if you ever raise your voice anywhere else in the world on a movie set, it is like a misdemeanour on a driver's licence and takes ten years to delete.

When we got there, they were shooting the arrival of a huge old steamer on the banks of the river. It was 1952. Canoes flew back and forth in the background. Little naked kids jumped into the water. The river was swift, brown and wide, the far bank no more than a thin green line dividing it from the vast creamy sky. The paddles of the steamer ploughed majestically through the water and its horn throbbed and echoed across the sound. Between each take the various screaming matches took up where they had left off. Arms gyrated and hands prayed in that secondary vocabulary of gesture only understood by Latins. The director, the legendary Francesco Rosi, sat calmly in the shade wearing a straw hat, surveying the chaos with a benevolent smile. He was talking to the cinematographer, Pasqualino de Santis – another legend. The two men were a music-hall double act. Rosi, who came from Naples, was a huge sturdy communist with a big nose; Pasqualino was a tiny skeletal diabetic in a sun visor and white shorts. They were both brilliant. Nobody remembers now, of course, but the films of Francesco Rosi are among the greatest to come out of Italy in that extremely fertile period of the sixties and seventies. *Hands over the City*, *Salvatore Giuliano* and *Three Brothers* are just some of his films that were enormously influential around the world, particularly to men like Scorsese, Cimino and Coppola.

In the story, Ornella Muti plays Angela Viccario, whose family agree to marry her to a handsome stranger (me) who has been travelling around the country looking for a wife. On the wedding night he discovers that she is not a virgin, and returns her to her family, who beat her until she provides the name of her deflowerer. To protect someone, her father probably, she says the first name that comes into her head – Santiago Nasar (Anthony Delon). Then her twin brothers set out to avenge their family honour with butcher's knives. All this takes place on the morning the bishop is coming to bless the town, and by breakfast time everyone knows except for Santiago himself that he is about to be killed. Several people try to warn him, but for some reason each attempt fails, though finally his mother (Lucia Bosé) is informed. Thinking her son is inside the house she locks the front door, just as he is being chased towards it. As he bangs on the door the brothers kill him. The whole story is told in a series of flashbacks twenty years later by the legendary actor Gian Maria Volonté who has come back to the town, which has fallen down. Allegedly, it is a true story and without doubt it is the most beautifully crafted film I was ever in although I was wildly miscast.

Ornella Muti was stunningly beautiful. She had one of those weird leech husbands that Italian divas feel naked without and two gorgeous little daughters. She was not haughty like most of the great beauties because she had a pair of the largest ankles that kept her feet firmly on the ground. God had given her two bodies, and that kept her sane. Her eyes were pale green and almond shaped. People dismissed her as an actress, but I thought she was excellent. Her real name was Francesca, but when she was fourteen she chose to be called Ornella. Now she had to live with that doll's name and everything it implied. She was funny, with a touching humility, and we adored each other. She was followed wherever she went by Divo, her own personal photographer, a balding, sleazy-looking man with long hair and an unkempt handlebar moustache, who recorded everything she did.

We stayed in a lovely house on the main street. There was a courtyard with a mango tree in the middle. A tame green bird with a red beak lived in it, and spent the day delicately peeling mangoes. A black boy of quite staggering beauty worked in the house and slept on a hammock in the hallway, and the cook, a little Indian woman, slept on the kitchen floor. When the moon was full, it shone into the courtyard and bathed the tips of the mango leaves, the sleeping parrot and the sprawled body in the hammock in fine silver lines. Coming out of my room, during sleepless nights I could hear cook's little snores from the kitchen, deeper ones from the hammock, and the muffled voice of Frances talking in her sleep to her sister Boom.

'Really, Boom? You can't be serious. Boom? Boom! Where are you?'

I stood in the moonlight with my long shadow, listening to the snores and the whispers and the cries of faraway dogs, and I felt lost from my own life, and, looking back, that was my endless quest. Not acting. Not fame. Not love. Just losing myself.

But I couldn't. In the part of Bayardo San Roman, the very name confronted me with myself, and in scene after scene I was always conscious of trying to throw myself off, like a schoolboy trying to get rid of last term's best friend. Everyone else acted so effortlessly in the film – they were all Latin – but for me every step required supervision. I was anxious and twisted throughout my stay in beautiful Colombia, so that when I rose for the last time before dawn one morning to sail to Cartagena, I left that enchanted house, the red-beaked bird, the beautiful boy, the dusty village street, in a trance of anxiety.

We left at four o'clock in the morning while it was still dark, and we arrived at the coast as night fell at ten o'clock. We took it in turns to lie on the boat's roof and sunbathe. Otherwise we just sat and watched the river. Sometimes you could only see its banks, small jagged lines of jungle, but at other moments they fell away and you were in the middle of huge still lakes covered with floating islands of lilies, and the clouds and the sky were mirrored in the water. As the sun rose, the river shimmered with silver ripples; as the day progressed it turned from brown to beige to grey to white and then to black as the moon came up. Long taxi canoes filled with ladies holding umbrellas flew past us. We stopped for lunch in a small village, a run-down shanty with a suspicious-looking bar and scrawny chickens. Our bodyguards prowled around as if they were in a war movie. They had packed machine-guns with their sandwiches. As we approached Cartagena the traffic intensified and in the mouth of the river rusty old cargo ships were moored for the night. Passing close we could see into the cabins where dirty sailors in tank tops lay on their bunks or played cards, whole universes anchored against the flow.

There was a bar near the port where breakfast was known as *blanco y nero*: a line of coke and a strong cup of coffee. It was open all night, and some of us used to meet there on the way to work in the morning where a crowd of hookers and sailors were in unusually high spirits for the time of day. When I was at lunch there one day with Frances, Francesca and my mother, who had come to visit, some men came in with a baby baboon tied round the waist with string. The string was cutting into its stomach. They wanted to sell it.

'Don't buy it, for God's sake,' warned my ever-practical mother. 'It'll go to the loo everywhere.'

'But we can't just leave it,' said Frances. 'Look, it's bleeding.'

We bought it, and even though Mother is always right, he was the sweetest thing. He was christened Rupi by Francesca's girls and he immediately adopted Frances and me as Daddy and Mummy baboon, clinging to our necks with his little hands and winding his tail around our larynxes. Sometimes he nibbled our ears, which was sweet. At other times he had a lovely long pee down our backs. And if you were lucky he made a dirty protest. If you removed him he screamed like a little baby and held onto your hair with all his might. He reminded me of myself going away to school.

'Don't bore me, darling,' said my mother. 'It wasn't a bit like that.'

He was a tragic little thing. We fed him with a bottle and he stared at us with little black abandoned eyes.

'What are we going to do with him after we leave?' asked Frances, already thinking she was going to have him at home.

'I should have him put down before you go,' said my mother, and she was probably right.

But we didn't. When we left we put him into the vine outside the sitting room. He held onto it and watched us soulfully. It was horrible. We left money and instructions, knowing that the moment we left they would probably be ignored, and a week after we got back to London we received word that he had climbed up the high wall of the courtyard and fallen to his death.

CHAPTER 25

Bob Dylan

Nineteen-eighty-six. I killed my first director. Richard Marquand was making a rock and roll film called *Hearts of Fire* with a script by a famous writer from *Rolling Stone* magazine, Joe Eszterhas. The story was extremely improbable. A young girl works at a tollbooth on the freeway at the entrance to some nameless steel town in the USA. She lives for her idol, an English rocker named James Colt. (Yes. Even the name sends shivers down the spine.) She is picked up one day by an old has-been rocker from the dawn of time. He sees a spark in her and takes her with him on the road in the band he is forming. They arrive in the UK, where they meet the thoroughly obnoxious James Colt, who is already a big fan of the has-been, but becomes a bigger fan of the tollbooth girl; so much so that he offers her a record deal and they go to bed, leaving the has-been to make his own way back to the US. She becomes a star. She splits with the English rocker, but they all get together at the end in a big stadium jamming session, and everyone lives happily ever after.

I suppose I should have known better. But Celestia was casting, and I had an idea to morph my friend John Taylor from Duran Duran into James Colt. So I got some long black hair, some show suits from Antony Price, a fabulous stick-on unibrow and some of the most withering reviews of my life, which to my mind were slightly unjustified, seeing as my take-off of John was really quite good. But it wasn't my time. Sometimes it isn't, and the best thing is to sit still until it goes away. Anyway, *Hearts of Fire* was the full-on, no-survivors crash of my career. We started shooting in September at Shepperton. Pat and Meinir were with me, and my friend Suzanne Bertish was playing my manager.

The tollbooth girl was played by a newcomer named Fiona. She was a mixture of Stevie Nicks and Natasha Richardson. She had a great scratchy voice, long brown hair and a blond, muscle-hunk, music-producer boyfriend called Beau. He was her heavy metal Svengali, and probably should have played my part in the movie.

None of this was of much interest to me. Fiona was sweet, if irritating; Beau was sexy and phobic. Yet even when the poor terrified girl jumped out of the bed during our sex scene, and ran screaming to her dressing room, I was strangely unperturbed.

'She says Rupert lives with a gay guy in LA,' the assistant said, returning from trying to coax her out. If only I did.

Meinir sidled up to the bed, as the producer, the director and the lighting cameraman stood around my naked body, deciding what they could shoot instead. She winked as she opened her little Aladdin's cave of a kit. Inside gleamed a bottle of vodka. Well, if one couldn't get legless after one's leading lady had fled the lovemaking scene, when could one? I settled down on the floor in the corner of the set and drank the whole bottle with the help of hair and make-up; when the powers that be finally decided on the next scene, I could barely walk.

The reason I was there, apart from the pay cheque and the gamble – because you never knew, the movie could have been one of those freak runaway hits; many a wooden clog turned into Cinderella's slipper at the box office – was that the part of the has-been was played by none other than Bob Dylan, my hero.

Bob looked as though someone had sucked all the fluids out of him. He was hunched and crumpled under a wistful afro. His skin was parchment, and the famous nose seemed to stretch his face to breaking point. What was he doing here? He knew he was taking part in a piece of unmitigated rubbish. His hangdog eyes said it all, as Richard the director clambered onto the make-up bus in the morning and regaled him with ideas for the scene, peppered with all the words he thought Bob would appreciate.

'Great idea, man!' he would say, and heartily slap Bob on the back, nearly winding him. Bob listened, as solemnly as a condemned man. He nodded his head and stumbled back to his trailer, where he often fell into a deep sleep from which he could not be woken. Bob lived in a parallel universe. He was with us, but not with us. He didn't go to bed like a normal person. He slept for a few hours and then pottered and then slept again. The twenty-four-hour structure that the rest of us timed our lives by had been left behind years ago, which meant that he might just have gone to bed at the time of his morning call. If so, it would be hard to move him. He would come into the trailer and collapse into the make-up chair, like a wild animal that had been shot with a tranquilliser.

But we all adored him. He was like a pixie, scrunched up, his matchstick legs crossed, tendrils of smoke snaking from his mouth through the afro, like mist rising off the top of a jungle. It was a cold autumn and so he often wore a huge fur-trimmed parka, his head peeking out from the shadowy interior of the hood, his drainpipes and cowboy boots clip-clopping like a puppet's legs underneath. He had beautiful hands, twenty years younger than the rest of his body. Maybe he was there because he needed to keep connecting, and being on a movie set was the easiest place to do it. Getting locked inside a celebrity stronghold, an ivory tower, is the death of creativity, and the unhappy lot of the rich and famous. They lose themselves in the quest for security, but Dylan was the real thing. I think he lived to create. At the same time he was also desperately retiring. On the film set he could interact and somehow keep himself from calcifying.

He never said a bad word about anyone. Actually he never said a word. But he listened and watched and nothing escaped him. On the odd occasions when he did talk, it sounded like a lyric. He spoke just as he sang, and 'Where's the toilet?' sounded as interesting as 'Lay across my big brass bed'. But he had a hard time remembering his lines, and it was touching to be with him during a scene.

It is hard to describe to a civilian the weird pressure of living inside the bubble of a film crew. They sit right there on top of you. Your every move is scrutinised. If you want to have secret thoughts, then they must be really secret, because you are wired for sound and someone is always looking at you through a lens. Once the clapper slams and the director shouts 'Action!', there is a strange electric atmosphere that contracts your chest ever so slightly and shoots adrenalin around your body. If you begin to forget your lines, there is no escape, no moment to collect yourself, and you are liable to be carried off by a wave of panic.

I don't know whether Bob learnt the lines beforehand. Possibly it never occurred to him. They always look so simple there on the clean white page at home. Probably he thought he could wing it once he got onto the set. But actually he just drowned in front of the camera, floundering on the open sea of one short line. This genius, one of the only authentic American heroes, was sitting there in a pool of light like a frying egg, trying to focus his splintering brain on Joe's inane rock-star banter. But it constantly eluded him. The camera boys thrust tape measures at him. The sound boys asked him to speak up. Richard asked for more energy, and there he sat, like a crushed mutt on an operating table or a rabbit frozen in the headlights, and we were all moved. Even the grips and sparks – a hardened lot – were silent. They didn't want him to see them watching him, so they walked about with their heads bowed in respect, like men at a funeral.

'It's that bloody bitch Joan Baez. She stole all his money,' concluded Meinir.

She adored him and always gave him a drink from her portable bar; Jim Beam was his favourite tipple. One day Meinir was walking across the lot at Shepperton when a bottle broke inside her kit and began to leak, leaving an incriminating and odorous trail in her wake. The producer was following behind. Pat and I were behind him. We watched in horror as he bent down and sniffed.

'Meinir, what have you got in your kit?' he asked. Meinir gasped slightly as she observed the stream of whisky dripping from Aladdin's cave. But this girl was quick on her feet.

'I'm washing my brushes. It's alcohol. Must have spilt! Oh dear, I'd better nip back to the truck, hadn't I?' And she beat a retreat before our producer could move on to the next question.

The production moved to Toronto in November to film all the big concert scenes. Winter had set in and it began to snow. We worked in the Maple Leaf Stadium, and played to the sixty thousand fans of some other band who let us shoot for an hour each night. There is nothing more exciting than filming in a real environment; you are acting, but everything else is true. It gives the actor a chance to inhabit his role without even thinking twice, blurring the division between reality and art. We were flanked by platoons of bodyguards. Roadies ran around the stage like mice at our feet. Our trailers were parked at the back of the stadium and anyone who came into them needed a sheaf of passes. The baying crowd literally shook your bones to the marrow. It was like living in a volcano. Suddenly Bob was in his element, unruffled like a duck in a thunderstorm. 'You gotta stand up to them when you get on stage,' he advised, 'otherwise they just wash over you.'

We all piled into his trailer before the show and got incredibly drunk. Bob strummed on his guitar. Assistants came and went. Richard dropped in. By the time we got to the wings we were in extremely high spirits, but Bob was too wobbly to make it up the very steep steps onto the stage. We all held our breath as we watched him trying to do it. Our tiny pixie teetered on the third step before half climbing, half falling backwards to the ground, then steeling himself for a second try. He turned around to see us all laughing and, shrugging his shoulders, beckoned for the girls to go and join him. Pat and Meinir pointed at themselves with question marks written across their faces. Bob nodded. They gingerly crept into the no man's land between the stage and the wings, and he put an arm around each girl's shoulders, and so Pat Hay and Meinir Brock made an entrance with Bob Dylan onto the stage of a gigantic stadium. As the three of them lurched into the limelight, like three drunks leaving a pub, a roar went up from the crowd. I don't think I have ever laughed so much. The girls stood there like shy three-year-olds at a birthday party and then began to shuffle backwards into the shadows where they belonged.

By now Richard was on a short fuse. He had already developed a crippling pain in his left leg that made him limp and forced him to walk with a stick. When he saw Pat and Meinir on stage in front of sixty thousand fans he threw the stick to the ground in fury. It hit the continuity lady in the back. He stormed over to Bob between takes. His face was purple. All his habitual tact and diplomacy evaporated and months of frustration poured out into the deaf ears of our star. Now he may have been crumpled and hunched, but no one raised their voice to Bob Dylan. 'I always have girls take me on to the stage,' he said. And that was the end of that. The girls were called back – they knew the shit was going to hit the fan, but what could they do? – and on take after take they had to push Bob up the stairs and give him a comical final shove onto the stage.

For my entrance, I arrived down a staircase from the back. Searchlights slashed across me, and the crowd went berserk. They were paid to, but I didn't care. I've never been fussy about paying and I got an erection. I began to sing my set to playback. Fans jumped up onto the stage and tried to rape me. I just stood there as roadies beat them to a pulp at my feet and dragged them off. I was nearing orgasm. I finished the first number. 'Good evening, Chicago!' I shouted, and my voice bounced around the arena, as flashlights exploded like stars. I had come a long way since that other live performance in Camberwell. I introduced Bob, he came on and we played a song together. We must have been an odd couple. He was tiny and I was a giant, but I didn't care, even though I had to bend double to sing along with him at his mike. It was the most fun I have ever had filming.

The next morning there was hell to pay. The studio had seen the rushes, and could tell that Bob was having difficulty getting onto the stage. When they heard that his girlfriends were none other than the make-up lady and the hairdresser, they had a meltdown. They threatened to fire the girls, and Bob and I were given headmasterly lectures by Richard and the producer. We reshot the offending scene, and Bob mounted the scaffold alone this time.

In a way Bob reminded me of Andy Warhol. You could never be certain whether he was really vacant or just playing vacant. Like Andy, he had perfected the art of being the still centre of a raging storm. Whether it was a contrivance or not, who knew? Probably not even him, at this stage.

On the last day, we shot a scene in a limo. The car was parked in the dark studio. Bob and I sat inside. A burly grip stood at each corner and bumped the car up and down to simulate movement. Others swept the beams of hand-held lamps across the windows to look like traffic. Someone else ran in with traffic lights, red, yellow and green, and another man stood on a ladder with a hose and made rain. (This is often how car interiors are shot in the movies and it is an eccentric sight: portly men running around a parked car with lamps, being hosed down by another man up a ladder.)

Bob was his usual self in the car. Squeezed into the jump seat were Richard, the camera operator and the soundman. It was fairly crowded. We played the scene over and over. We chatted between takes. We had drinks in the scene and they were constantly refilled – the real thing, needless to say. The props guys who were in charge of administering drinks didn't even ask. Apple juice was for babies. Bob dozed off, sinking into himself like a parrot. We must have been there for a couple of hours. When we finished the first assistant opened the car door. Bob climbed out. He looked around, squinting. 'Where's the hotel?' he said, apparently confused, thinking he had been driven home. Or did he? Either way, the whole set exploded with mirth. Bob shrugged his shoulders and shuffled off into the gloom wrapped in the giant parka.

That night he made a rare exception and came out to dinner in a restaurant. His assistant was a lovely Australian girl who always walked beside him with her hand in front of his face if there was a camera around. She was our bridge to Bob. We toasted and reminisced, knowing that we would probably never see him again. We all longed to say how much we had loved being with him, but of course none of us did. But I think he knew. After the meal we awkwardly hugged, and he shuffled off back to some undisclosed location and that was that.

On the plane trip back to London, Pat and I somehow ended up sitting next to each other for take-off, and we were all given official warnings by the airline when we got off the plane the next morning. Our whole crew was on the flight and we sat around drinking and laughing all night, infuriating the other travellers. We were still at it as the exhausted air hostess glumly announced, 'Doors to manual,' the next morning.

I never saw Bob again. He didn't attend the bloodbath of a première in London. The film brought my career to a standstill, but I wouldn't have missed it for anything. I had played the Maple Leaf Stadium with Bob Dylan, and the Albert Hall with Julie Andrews, all in the same year. Things were never going to be any better. It was time to get out.

As for poor Richard Marquand: a few months later, he was getting out of his car at Heathrow airport, where he was meeting his daughter. He had a massive heart attack and died on the way to the hospital. The movie business is a strange affair, demanding total dedication from its lovers, although it gives none in return. Health, home and humanity often fly out the window during the making of a film. There are no days off for a director. When his strength fails, he often finds himself with only blind ambition as fuel; or passion, if he's lucky (it's less corrosive to the system). Richard was a big handsome Welshman, built like a rugby player. He probably thought he could wing it, but *Hearts of Fire* earned him his worst reviews and cost him his life.

CHAPTER 26

Rock Follies

My rock and roll descent into hell was just beginning. Early the next year, in 1987, I got a record deal, a manager and some more crippling press. My first single shot up to number 115 in the charts. My manager was a man called Simon Napier-Bell, a self-proclaimed legend, who lived in a ground-floor flat in one of those damp gloomy squares north of the Bayswater Road. It was a brilliant mirage. There was a huge entrance hall with a grand old oak staircase that swept upstairs, although around its first corner was a brick wall. The front door would be opened by one of Simon's Asian ingénues, and as you came into the hall, thinking to yourself how successful Simon must be, the man himself walked nonchalantly down the staircase as if he were just coming from another part of the mansion. Actually, as far as I could tell, the flat only consisted of the hall and a small room off it. But it gave a marvellous impression of opulence, and Simon was the unparalleled master of fakery and hype. He was a great salesman, who never listened to a word anyone else said, but steamrollered on with his latest point of view, which might be the complete opposite of the one he was airing yesterday. I thought he was utterly delightful, like a campish sergeant major from one of those entertainment platoons during the war, his 'boys' a gang of Thai twinkies who seemed to come up through a trapdoor from the basement.

After he'd got me a record deal, he told me I needed a publicist and introduced me to Connie Filipello, who was another of Simon's inventions. She had been a telephonist at a record company, and Simon decided on a whim that she should PR his new discovery, Wham. It was one of his hunches that paid off, as she proved to be a demon of a PR. But now she had the challenge of turning my record into a number one hit.

Unfortunately, on the week of the release of my record, both she and Simon disappeared to China on a PR tour with Simon's hairdresser boyfriend, a sweet man from Singapore called Alan Soh, who, according to Connie, had revolutionised hairdressing with his all natural 'chopstick perm', which he was now going to launch upon the Chinese.

'But what about me?' I whined to Connie, to whom Simon had forced me to pay an enormous salary.

'Don't worry, darling, you'll be in the papers every day,' she said.

It all seemed a bit 'Your dinner's in the oven' to me, but, true to her word, I was in the papers every day. The problem was that each article was more blisteringly vile than the last. By the time she and Simon got back from a triumphant trip where Alan Soh had been recognised as a genius, I was on the verge of nervous collapse and my record had slipped from its position in the top two hundred. But after a pep talk from 'Sarge' (Simon), I set off to conquer the rest of the world.

And despite the assassination I received at the hands of the British press, I managed to enjoy myself on the promotional trail, playing festivals across Europe. The usual spoilt suspects would meet at Heathrow on a Saturday morning, us 'artistes' sticking out from the crowds in our funny clothes, bolshy and belligerent, sitting stiffly in the departure lounge, no longer real people, but not quite unreal either. Around them flurried their managers, their record company reps and sometimes, depending on how much they were selling, their PRs. Little girls and queen fans would be kept at arm's length by these enablers, some of whom would lay down their lives to get their artist a cappuccino. Occasionally the flight was delayed and some eager beaver manager would bring out Trivial Pursuit.

Once, somebody asked one of the Spandau Ballet brothers, 'Where's the coccyx?'

'Don't tell me! Off the coast of Cornwall!' was the delightful reply.

My record company had another band doing the rounds at the same time as me. They were called Living in a Box and we travelled everywhere together. We hit it off, sharing dressing rooms at all the festivals, and when we were at San Remo, the boys had agreed to back me during my set so that the record company wouldn't have to pay to bring my band out. In return I played bongos during theirs.

We were sitting backstage before the show, having a good whine, when the Italian producers came into our room.

'Hi, the gangs!' said a tall raven-haired rock chick flanked by two over-caffeinated assistants. 'I am Andrea. This is Salvo. We have some leetle sings to talk you with. Is true Rupit is playing drums?'

'Yes, Andrea. Is true,' I replied, slipping into the vernacular.

'This is great. Absolute wow! So when Leevin in de Bogs is fineesh, Mike Bongiorno, our presenter, is play leetle jokeen wiz ziz.'

'Oh yes?' we said, politely, though none of us understood a word.

'Yeah, toe-tah-lee! Is veree funnee! Ee com an ge you an ee say – in Italian – guess oo eez ziz playing drums? Is good, non?'

'Great,' we all said, nodding, still completely bemused.

'It will be total freek out!'

Unfortunately, somebody had not fixed my bongos onto their stand properly. We all ran onto the stage and the boys went straight into the first number. The crowds went crazy, and I bongoed away, living the dream, until suddenly I felt one of my bongos begin to slip off the stand. These drums were about three feet tall and quite heavy. I managed to hold it against the stand with my leg, but it kept slipping until I couldn't grip it any longer and as the boys went into the second chorus ('I'm living in a box, living in a cardboard box,' etc) it fell to the floor. I lunged at it but the stage was steep and it was already rolling off towards the footlights. I chased after it, my eyes blinded by tears of laughter. Gianni Versace had given me a black silk coat for the show with a matching felt hat, and I looked like a deranged Orthodox Jew chasing a sacred scroll. Just as the bongo was about to fly off into the audience, I grabbed it and staggered with it back to my spot. Breathless and sweaty, I fixed it onto its stand but the song was over.

As the screaming died down, the presenter lumbered onto the stage followed by cameramen, cables and roadies. 'There is a very special guest here tonight, playing with the boys,' he said in Italian. 'I think he is playing drums. Let's go and see!'

I braced myself for my big moment, but instead of coming over to me, the caravan swept past me to the very back of the stage where little Titch sat at the drum kit. Titch didn't understand a word of Italian, and Mike Bongiorno clearly didn't know me from Adam. He was, however, a comedian. When he saw Titch, he screamed like a mad fan. 'Oh my God! Oh my God! Eez it really you?' he said in English, thrusting the mike in Titch's confused face.

'I'm not sure,' said Titch.

Mike looked to the camera with a big laugh. 'I'm not sure?' he mimicked. '*Non è sicuro. Che divino, questo inglese!*'

He clapped Titch on the back and dragged him to the front of the stage. The crowd was quite puzzled by now. Unlike Mike Bongiorno, most of them knew who I was. But Mike was enchanted by his own vaudevillian prowess, looking at Titch and then looking into the camera, eyes like saucers, mouth wide open. 'It can't be true. Yes, it is. Oh my God! It's Rupert Everett!'

Titch understood the words 'Rupert Everett' and started shaking his head, but it was too late. Playback waits for no man and my song began. Titch looked up at me. 'What should I do?' he mouthed, but the rest of us were laughing so much it didn't seem advisable to try to clear up the misunderstanding. All our reps were gesticulating wildly from the wings, but it was too late. I was doomed to play bongos while Titch did a cruel and perceptive impersonation of me, and before we knew it the set was over.

Andrea was right. It was 'total freak out'.

CHAPTER 27

France

A sequence of events had unfolded, a storm, actually, that blew me from a bar stool on Mustique to a violin class at the Dorchester Hotel, where suddenly Bach to playback had rekindled a childhood obsession with music. I was blindly ambitious, too young to be wary, and these elements created hurricane conditions. I had thrown myself like a lemming into *Hearts of Fire*, despite the warnings of friends and detractors.

'Go back to the stage,' they wailed.

'Stop trying to be Tom Cruise,' snapped Philip Prowse.

But the opportunities came, and I grabbed them. With the release of that sorry rock snuff movie, the bad weather intensified. I had always been considered a talentless nob, but now there was proof. Then when my first single came out, the deluge blew everything away. My credibility was shredded, my character was sucked up in the tornado, ripped apart and scattered. And then my acting career hit the doldrums. It was a long squall that only began to die down in August a year later.

My record was coming out in France and Simon Napier-Bell, everlastingly optimistic, another Don Quixote, towed me, by now a leaking vessel with torn sails, into port, or out to dinner as it happened, one creamy Parisian dusk down the banks of the Seine, looking for a restaurant.

In those days Paris still closed down for the whole month of August. Shops were boarded up. Restaurants were closed. White shutters shrouded entire buildings into summer tombs. Inside the only movement was dust playing in slashes of light. Outside the streets were empty. The air was close, smelling of the sticky sap that oozed from the chestnuts and plane trees and stained the pavements around their roots. There was a wonderful silence during August in Paris, and the calls of wood pigeons, the distant murmur of traffic or the odd echo of a *mobilette* straining up some nearby cobbled street, were all a part of it.

We were staying in L'Hôtel, the establishment where Oscar Wilde had died. I had the fatal room. Simon was leaving the next day, and that night at dinner we gently concluded the business between us. The following morning, he left and I did interviews in the basement of the hotel, an icy stone *cave* with that peculiar smell of damp and wine. A chubby young queen came to talk to me, and suggested taking me out that night with his friends.

At about ten o'clock they arrived in a large old American Cadillac driven by a bodybuilder in a tight white T-shirt. A beautiful Asian girl in a white fur coat was spread out on the back seat. Her name was Lychee. On either side sat rare specimens of Parisian youth. I jumped in without a thought.

We went to the Palace, the famous converted music hall that had been opened by Fabrice Emaer nearly ten years ago. I had been there that first night, not knowing then that it was the last shout of the glittering Paris of the seventies. Now we sat in a large booth in the half-empty club. People came and went; a handsome Algerian boy fell into the banquette.

'This is my colleague, Pascal,' said Lychee, before bursting into peals of laughter. She laughed so much that she had to cover her mouth with her hand. Pascal put his arm around me. He had dilated pupils and flared nostrils.

'I want to kiss you, but my boyfriend is coming,' he said.

'Oh. What a shame,' I replied stiffly.

They were a good-looking, fast-moving crowd and they never stopped laughing, drinking, smoking and knocking back pills. A pretty little American girl, Polly, sat down. 'You shouldn't take those,' she said, gesturing towards the drugs. 'They're really bad for you.'

'Honey!' Lychee snapped back. 'Your mother is a dealer.'

Sure enough, a few minutes later a ravaged but handsome Woodstock hippie tottered sideways like a crab across the dance floor towards our banquette.

'This is my mom,' said Polly.

'Oh, hi, I'm Meredith,' said her mother.

Whenever I politely asked anyone what they did, the whole group cracked up, but from what I could gather – I didn't speak much French in those days – one was a graphic designer, two were art students; and there was also a journalist, a policeman and an *attaché de presse*.

'What's that?' I asked Meredith.

'It could be anything,' she said and then collapsed into giggles like all the others.

People weren't like this in London, I remember thinking. Graphic designers were geeks. Dixon of Dock Green was my idea of a policeman, but this one was a sprawling, lithe piece of trouble who stroked himself distractedly while looking at Lychee's breasts. In London everyone was moody and cynical; these kids were having too much fun. But then everything about the evening was also a little 'off'. I was kissed by everyone ('Quick, my boyfriend is not looking') and couldn't help feeling like poor Oscar Wilde, stumbling out of the club as the dawn rose behind the slate roofs, and the overflowing stars wrapped in the summer haze looked like a painting by Van Gogh.

Lychee followed me. We stood outside waiting for a taxi, and she regarded me with a curious half-smile. 'We know each other,' she said, finally. She was unforgettably beautiful leaning against the wall, smoking, but I couldn't place her. We looked at each other for a long moment. Then she laughed. Again her hand went up to cover her mouth and a bell rang. For a second I was back in the Club Sept. Another face and fingers framed in flashing pink neon. Now the hand and the mouth were painted and manicured, and the beautiful woman before me bore little resemblance to . . . 'Kim?'

She laughed again. 'Maybe. You have my number. Call me. Tomorrow I am in my studio all day. I am an artist, you know.'

She blew me a kiss and returned to the unnatural night. Her receding silhouette was just recognisable as the gangly boy dancing by himself at the Club Sept. Both of us had vowed to change everything about ourselves. All our dreams were of escape and although becoming a movie star was not quite as complicated as becoming a woman, we both needed good lighting and tons of make-up.

I got into a taxi and clattered back to the Latin Quarter, as the sky turned to a pale summer blue and another long hot lazy day began in the deserted city. I returned to the room where Oscar died. He must have limped through the same streets, penniless and toothless, after nights spent leering at grooms and footmen in the Moulin Rouge. I shut the curtains and lay on the bed, wondering what the wallpaper had been like that inspired his final recorded witticism. ('Well, one of us had to go . . .')

I made a decision. I was going to move to Paris.

And so two weeks later, I put my house up for sale and left England. I spent the summer in the South of France at Tony Richardson's house outside St Tropez. At the end of September I moved into the Hôtel Lancaster on the rue de Berri, behind the Champs Elysées. I planned on staying a few days but ended up living there for three years. It was a beautiful place, small, discreet, lost in a time warp. There was a marble hall, a dining room – always empty – and a bar with a weird mural of monkeys hanging from vines. The stone staircase was carpeted in blue with gold borders and wound around the lift, which was padded with red morocco leather. The manager was a stooping friend of the arts and gave me the deal of the century. I had a suite of white-panelled rooms on the third floor that looked over the garden. The ceilings were high, the carpets were pale blue and old-fashioned curtains covered in garlands of roses hung over the french windows. A little mouse called Seraphim looked after me. He wore a starched apron under a black and red striped jacket. His office was a small pantry down the hall, which he shared with his colleague, a thieving peroxide witch called Maria Christina. They cooked and ironed and gossiped in an impenetrable Portuguese French, and one could always hear them cackling or hoovering as one left one's room. But when they appeared in public or came across a guest by chance, they adopted a kind of silent-movie pastiche of themselves and shrank against the walls with bowed heads. One day I came into my room to find the two of them poring over my stash of porno magazines, and from then on the ice was broken.

There was a restaurant across the road called Le Val d'Isère, decorated like a Swiss chalet, but nevertheless a traditional brasserie with an oyster stall outside. It was open until two in the morning, which gave our street a sleazy edge over the rest of that stuffy *quartier*; after midnight it became the meeting place for all the pimps and dealers and bent policeman of Paris. The waiters had all spent their careers there, and were a crusty old bunch in white jackets, bent from years of leaning forward. Every day I ate lunch and dinner there; my whole life had shrunk and was contained in that one street. I cut myself off from the outside world and lived in virtual seclusion. The past disappeared and I felt like a ghost.

Being a foreigner is one of the great delights. You are a silent observer. Slowly I learnt French but that first year, at dinner with Lychee and the colleagues, the new 'me' was silent and mysterious. Conversation washed over me and I couldn't have been happier. Lychee was my official spokesperson and I left everything to her. Soon I began to know the colleagues well enough that they no longer tried to translate or to speak slowly. Without words they were romantic and affectionate and so was I. They carried on in their guttural slang across me but put their arms around my shoulder and their hands on my thigh, and that was as much as I really wanted to understand.

On Sunday mornings, after the clubs had closed, they would follow Lychee and me back to the hotel, trooping through the hall into the lift and up to my room to be served hot chocolate and croissants by a breathless Seraphim. Sometimes these parties lasted for days and I would have to take the adjoining room to accommodate the overflow. Then Lychee and I would nod to one another, slip into the lift and go downstairs to the dining room in fur coats and dark glasses to have breakfast. Little by little my grasp of French improved and it occurred to me that Lychee wasn't an artist at all, at least not in the conventional sense, and the colleagues were a band of gypsies, tramps and thieves, living wonderfully wicked lives. They were exotic blooms in a jug of water. They lived fast and faded fast. During the twelve years I spent in Paris, one by one they fell away. They jumped, they overdosed, they got sick or were murdered. But that summer, they were still fresh and shiny. They all thought the train they were on would stop at a convenient station and they could get off. One always does.

*

It was quite hard to get work in France. The French cinema is fiercely Francophile, but I managed to make one film in all the years I lived there. *Tolérance* was written and directed by a brilliant maniac called Pierre-Henri Salfati. He was a Hassidic Jew with all the trimmings: a handsome black beard, dark glasses and a hearty laugh that gradually became more strained as the job progressed. We started filming at the end of the summer of 1987 in Calvados, in north-western France. In September, Pierre-Henri and his whole family moved into a tent and observed a string of Jewish holidays while the rest of us sat twiddling our thumbs in the hotel. My room overlooked the birthplace of the wackiest of Catholic saints, Thérèse of Lisieux, the little flower. She had been one of my favourite saints at school, partly because of her actual physical passion for Christ, and partly because after her death, during the First World War, her ghost was believed to wander through the trenches at night comforting soldiers about to die. She had certainly understood something about trench warfare – at least of the psychological kind, having been incredibly unpopular in her convent at Lisieux. Her career began at the age of twelve in Alençon, opposite our hotel, where for no apparent reason she started to cry and didn't stop for three months. Afterwards, according to legend, she was unrecognisable as herself. She had been touched by God. Or abused. I could see her bedroom window from mine, and I sat there during the long afternoons of Yom Kippur, Rosh Hashanah and Succoth, wondering at the insanity of it all. Thérèse thought she was married to Jesus, and Pierre-Henri was camping out in a tent hung with fruit and vegetables while he was supposed to be making a film.

He had written an amazing story about a period in French history after the revolution, the decadent new 'high society' that replaced the aristocracy, known as Les Incroyables. A family who live in a lovely chateau are given a hermit, their own family saint, called Assuerus (played by me). He is unpacked from his box and let loose in the forest around the castle. The lady of the house, Tolerance, played by a beautiful French actress called Anne Brochet, develops an unhealthy interest in his spiritual powers, and her husband, a gourmet obsessed by cooking, becomes insanely jealous. He ties poor Assuerus to a stake in his vegetable garden and a miracle occurs. Thousands of butterflies gather and giant asparagus grows around him in the garden. Tolerance is convinced that her hermit is a saint.

To prove he is a fraud, the husband, played by the Italian comedian Ugo Tognazzi (famous for *La Cage aux Folles*), shaves and washes the poor hermit, dresses him up in all the foppery of the period and passes him off as a visiting dandy gourmet from England, to disastrous effect. The hermit plays his role to the hilt. He becomes the avenging angel to the little court inside the chateau, and everyone gets their just deserts. The wicked mother-in-law falls in love with him and dies of a heart attack while he is kissing her. Finally he prepares a banquet for the Académie de Gastronomie, of which the husband is president, and for the main course cooks his latest victim – Tolerance. Eventually he is guillotined, but we never know whether he was a saint or a sinner, although when his severed head is lifted from the straw it glows with a saintly aura.

It was a brilliantly eccentric story but would Pierre-Henri have the experience to bring it to the screen? He had made a short film, but otherwise he was a teacher and a religious expert, whatever that means. Filming always began with a delicious lunch. Trestle tables with white paper cloths were set up in the gardens of the beautiful chateau. The chatelaine, a delightful tiny old lady with a little beige wig, hobbled across the unkempt lawn to join us, accompanied by her sexy grandson, Charles Édouard. Lunch on an old-school French film set was an extremely civilised affair. Wine bottles, baguettes and wild flowers decorated the tables. The three-course meal was followed by dripping Camembert and coffee, and slowly the conversation drifted towards work. 'And what are we shooting today?' the chatelaine would excitedly ask as she spread Brie onto a biscuit. Pierre-Henri would look up from peeling an apple and describe the scene. 'Today Rupert is going to climb a tree.'

Lychee and the colleagues came and went, causing a stir wherever they set foot. They bundled noisily out of a taxi in front of the chateau just as we were shooting. They were refused entry to St Thérèse's house and complained at the police station. Terrible arguments would blow up in the local restaurant and Lychee would send the offending colleague home. I had two double beds in my room and there was a steady flow of guests. Sometimes, arriving late from work, I didn't know whom I was sleeping with.

But despite the disturbances, the chateau was a deeply romantic

place of honey-coloured stone, with turrets and steep slate roofs, surrounded by a moat. The lumpy remains of formal gardens stretched out
on all sides towards beautiful woods full of pheasants. An ancient geo-
metric pattern of overgrown avenues carved through them and
sometimes Madame could be seen toddling along one of them with her
little old dog by her side. I think she was on her last financial legs,
which was why we were there, but she cheerfully lived in a tiny corner
of the immense palace, where Lychee and I went often for drinks after
work. She called Lychee 'Mademoiselle' and Lychee called her
'Madame' and their rapport was a film all of its own.

It was, of course, delightful to be on the other side of the colleagues'
lies. Lychee loved weaving her web, her eyes glittering at the beauty of
her fabrications, although sometimes she got tangled up in them. One
day she was a concert pianist; the next day she worked in a bank. Her
fantasy pastime very much depended on her mood, and as with all
ladies of her slightly modified nature, those moods changed with the
wind. I don't know whether anyone believed a word she said, or even
listened. Mostly they just stared at her tits and her arse. All men wanted
to have sex with Lychee in those days, when she was still fresh. It was a
wave you could feel as she walked past. She considered setting herself
up in a little tent in the woods, but luckily she soon tired of the country life, and one day she disappeared without a word back to Paris.

The film, when it was eventually finished, was a disaster at the box
office. This was a shame because it could have been great but Pierre-
Henri needed to be guided. Although extremely talented, he wasn't a
technician, and this is where movies often fell short in that haughty
marriage between French socialism and its *cinéma philosophe*.
Everything was constructed around the *auteur*, resulting in hundreds of
aimless meandering films financed by the state. Some of them were
good – a few were excellent – but most of them were aborted schemes
with potential.

CHAPTER 28

Béatrice

This was also the year of my final heterosexual love tryst. At the Cannes Film Festival, I met Béatrice Dalle and we immediately became inseparable. We were totally unsuited to one another, quite aside from the fact that I was gay, but incompatibility is the agonising driving force behind many dangerous liaisons. We were two strange boats colliding in the night and, mesmerised, we held onto each other as the current gently but firmly moved us along. She was a wild, unpredictable beauty, tinged with the sparkle of madness; the latest in a long tradition of French sirens. Although she was quite scornful about her country, she was as French as Joan of Arc – the suicide bomber version. Her kind of beauty was definitely pre-Botox, much deeper than the cash-and-carry bargains of today. Its origins were the gaslit barmaids of Manet, and the Parisian *demi-monde* between the wars. She was *jolie laide* – pretty and ugly. If you pulled back her hair, her head was the shape of a woodland elf's. Her mouth was large and she outlined it with a brown pencil. She had a gap between her teeth and a mole on her cheek; her brown eyes held yours with a warmth and a purity in their regard that destabilised everyone she looked at. (Unless you happened to be Franco Zeffirelli. 'She looks like a gargoyle,' he said one day when we went to lunch at his house outside Rome.) Her body was as full and ripe as a delicious peach. She was in many ways the negative image of Madonna, the black virgin of France.

Béatrice had a dangerous sidekick, Sophie, who worked for the couturier Azzedine Alaia. Sophie was from the South and quite wild in her protection of her friend, ready to tip a full champagne bucket over the head of anyone who insulted 'Béa'. Both girls dressed identically and smelt deliciously of vanilla. They wore large gold hoops in their ears under their thick jet-black hair and buttoned tight little cardigans around their voluptuous breasts. There was always trouble when they were around; I called them 'the French Resistance'.

Béa was discovered by our mutual agent, Dominique, when he was looking for someone to star in the film *Betty Blue*. She was married to a beautiful boxer called Jeff at the time and was immersed in her role as a *femme au foyer*, or housewife. That was quite a performance already; she loved to look after her man and initially resisted the call to the silver screen. When Dominique phoned to ask her to come and audition, she hung up. After three or four abortive attempts to contact her, the movie people were so intrigued that a car was sent round to her apartment with a begging letter. She got in and went shopping, but passed by the audition on her way home. The director, Jean-Jacques Beineix, hired her immediately.

Although Béatrice had never set out to be an actress, by the time I met her she was not just a star but France's image for the eighties. It was 1986 and the country was floundering in a crisis of identity, unable and unwilling to move towards the twenty-first century. During one scene in *Betty Blue*, Béatrice burnt down a pretty wooden beach house, and that was the startling image of the times: a deranged pyromaniac burning down tradition, accompanied by a wailing nostalgic saxophone. (Gabriel Yared wrote one of the scores of the century.)

'My dear, too ghastly – after she burnt down that lovely beach hut, I left the cinema,' said Philip Prowse, when I told him about her. But whatever Philip thought, *Betty Blue* was a legendary debut. Béatrice shot like a meteor into the firmament and outshone all the other stars. She didn't have the faintest interest in rules and regulations, of which there were many in the genteel world of French cinema. She was not remotely educated, but was extremely clever and dangerously forthright; as her fame gathered momentum, it ran away with her marriage.

The boxer was wildly jealous of the attention she got. But it was too late to turn back the clock and pretty soon the couple were on the rocks. At this delicate point we met.

Back in Paris, she came to see me one morning at the Lancaster. She rummaged about in her bag and extracted a large metal crucifix covered with sculpted flowers. 'Oh, how lovely, Béa,' I exclaimed. 'Where did you get this?'

'I found it with Sophie in the cemetery near my house. It was on a baby's tomb.'

'Thanks,' I gulped. (Years later, worrying that the cross was giving us bad luck, I went with Sophie back to the cemetery and we found the grave. A little *putto* was sitting at the feet of the headstone, with its empty arms outstretched. The cross slid into its hands. It was quite uncanny.)

But Béatrice was always fascinated by bones and graves and death. At her studio in Montmartre, at the top of five flights of stairs with one of those huge windows overlooking the rooftops of Paris, she kept the skull of a priest over her bed.

'Where did you get that?' I asked nervously.

'I found it,' she replied obliquely.

She was a brilliant girlfriend because all she wanted to do was roll you little joints, or sit around perched on you like a bird on a branch, watching the day pass by, eating crème caramels, or lying in bed watching TV. Time stood still; everything else dropped away, and the world outside became a weird blur. I remember once lying in the bath at the hotel, and she was leaning against the sink, smoking, in a pair of dark glasses. She threw her head back and smoke snaked out of her mouth and I wondered whether I was part of some black magic spell.

She didn't want to stay at home after the split-up with her husband, but she didn't want to stay at the Lancaster either, so we briefly moved into the apartment of a mutual friend, Natacha, in the Place des Vosges. Natacha owned a fashionable restaurant in Montparnasse in the building where Verlaine and Rimbaud had lived. One morning an envelope slipped under the front door. Footsteps receded down the staircase and out into the courtyard while Béatrice lay rigid in the bed. She got up. The letter was from her husband. As she read it she collapsed slowly to the floor. This was a movie I wasn't sure I really wanted to be in. I watched her from under the covers. The letter was endless. After she finished it she put her head in her hands. She looked over at me. I pretended to sleep.

Then she got a lighter and set fire to it right there in the middle of the carpet. The flames leapt up, but Béa held the burning missive in her hands with the sang-froid of a *pompier*, entranced as the words that hurt her were consumed and floated into the air. She threw the whole burning pile into the waste-paper basket. It seemed to be getting a little bit out of control even for her, and she tiptoed out of the room. I lay there, fully prepared to hear the front door slam and more receding footsteps. The waste-paper basket crackled ominously. Just as I was about to jump out of bed, she came back with a bottle of Perrier and calmly emptied the contents into the inferno. She waved the smoke away and got back into bed, but a low black cloud settled above us. Jeff's hurt could not be burnt that easily.

I had imagined myself at the centre of a beautiful Technicolor romance but actually I was hanging onto the edge of someone else's *film noir*. I don't think Béatrice knew it then, but she felt alive when there was drama. She loved it when the elements howled around her. I did not.

At dinner a few nights later with Lychee in the Val d'Isère, I told her all the latest details of my terrible love triangle. She had not been the same since I had been going out with Béa. She was thoroughly put out, although she pretended not to be. At dinner she was tight-lipped and uninterested. She may not have fancied me, but she certainly considered me her property. She punctuated my tale with irritating little sighs and puffs.

'And now her husband says he's going to kill himself!'

'*Ah bon*,' said Lychee, deeply bored. She stubbed out her cigarette, smoke snorting from her nose, and looked at me distractedly. I wanted to pull her hair. '*Tu vois*,' she said.

'I see what?'

'You are completely out of your depth.' She had a point.

'I'm going to St Tropez next week.'

'What about Béatrice?'

'She's going to come.'

Another snort from Lychee. '*Oh la la!*' Now she began to laugh.

'Why are you laughing?'

'How are you going to explain Frank and Thomas?'

'There's nothing to explain,' I replied testily.

Lychee was cheering up. 'Honey. You change a lot. I'm scared.'

This was one of her stock phrases. It meant we were out of the woods and she could now have a good laugh about the whole thing. Lychee's tragedy was that she could never be serious for very long.

CHAPTER 29

St Tropez

St Tropez was half an hour's drive from Tony Richardson's house, Le Nid de Duc.

At breakfast in the mornings, sitting at the long table in the garden, in the shade of the plane tree where Tony's ashes were soon to be buried, it was sometimes decided that the party would go to the beach for lunch. Then everyone disappeared to perform their various chores, or lie by the pool, and a wonderful silence fell on that magical hamlet buried in the heart of the forest, broken only by the odd splash of someone diving into the pool, or the car straining up the dirt track towards the village, and of course the surround-sound effect of the creaking, invisible crickets. As the sun got hotter their croaks became more insistent, and the whole forest throbbed and cooked. The air became dangerously still, almost liquid, and as one walked from one's room to the pool, down the little stone steps past a half-ruined house, the various scents of cork, dry earth, jasmine and wild rosemary were like invisible currents in a clear sea.

We piled into cars with straw bags full of towels and books, and painfully bumped our way to the main road three miles away. It was like a ski run by comparison, the old road from La Garde Freinet down to the seaside. It snaked through the forest, under a canopy of scrub oaks and cork trees, the sun shining through their leaves in a million beams. It passed under a village with a ruined castle on a crag. We flew down that road, all the windows open, Tony in his cowboy hat, Natasha at the wheel, Annabelle and me in the back, or Grizelda, Tony's ex, and their daughter Katherine, plus Robert Fox, who was now married to Natasha, crammed in together, all talking at once. Sometimes we stopped off at the port to buy newspapers, but mostly we skirted through secret lanes and dirt tracks known only to the Richardsons, avoiding the summer traffic, to the beach at Pampelonne.

There were a hundred different beach clubs along the three-mile bay. Wattle fences separated them from one another, and every morning the sand was meticulously raked by the lithe, tanned *plagistes* in brightly coloured shorts. Beach mats were arranged in rows, little tables and umbrellas placed beside them. It was the best part of the day. The sky and the sea were white as the morning humidity slowly evaporated. A speedboat buzzed back and forth, pulling a parachute out of the water into the air. It sounded like a faraway bluebottle battling with a windowpane. The workers lunched early, when the beach was pristine and ready. Everything changed as the holiday crowd began to trickle in. The sea turned a deep Mediterranean blue. The silence was eaten by the screams of the Arab *planchistes* in the kitchens, the waiters flying around the restaurants, the clatter of plates, the popping of corks, the holiday hysteria and the din of a thousand outboard motors.

Tony liked a restaurant called the Aqua Club, which was owned by a man called Paul, who often greeted his clientele dressed as the pope, to whom he bore a startling resemblance. Tony's party lay about on their beach mats, reading their books and swimming. Later, they went inside behind the bar to have lunch where they were ideally positioned to observe the passing circus.

The Aqua was a gay beach, and a brilliant array of queens and fag hags flip-flopped in from foreign climes for a late lunch and an afternoon's cruising in the forest of bamboo that waved seductively between the beach and the vineyards behind. Glistening with Ambré Solaire, flat-footed flubsters sat at the bar nursing cocktails with umbrellas on sticks. Like hungry babies, they sucked through long stripy straws and surveyed the beach for a possible dinner companion. Hairy stick insects in thongs marched purposefully up and down the shore.

George, an American lawyer who fell in love with France during the war and never left, entertained effeminate twinkies for lunch at his regular table. Professional youths danced attendance, and when the summer's hit song was played at full blast over the stereo, they whooped and gyrated, grabbing the nearest fairy and whirling her around while the whole restaurant applauded. People danced on the tables, and if it was someone's birthday a cake would be produced by Paul which would then explode in the face of the birthday girl to the general glee of the entire place, who must have seen this stunt a thousand times. France's first air hostess Isolde lay like a beached whale on her mat, regarding herself in a little shell-encrusted mirror, painting on a thick wobbly gash of lipstick before heaving herself up for lunch. Gay agents from LA sat with Joan Collins. Upper-class English queens and the ladies who loved them stopped by Tony's table and dinners were arranged. Not everyone was gay. The infamous model agent Gerard Marie sported his new girlfriend, a young gangly Linda Evangelista, and the French rock star Johnny Halliday arrived on a boat with his entourage.

Paul had two sons, Frankie and Thomas. They were born on the beach and were like a pair of scruffy wild dogs, their hair all matted and salty. Thomas was Cinderella and Frankie the poor ugly sister. They had spent their childhood being adored and ogled by all the aforementioned queens and they had become ruthless teases, but I adored them both. That first year in St Tropez, the one before I met Béatrice, I hardly left their side all summer. To begin with, I was entranced by the beach. The only holidays I had ever been on were to Scotland, stalking or fishing, and you couldn't wear a thong and flip-flops or carry a clutch on the hill. During the day I swam to a raft out in the ocean and lay there for hours. It rose and fell on the swell, and the water gurgled underneath. Other people lay there but on the raft no one talked. At the weekends I helped Thomas in the bar. As dusk fell and the last giggle flew out to sea on the breeze, the beach was reclaimed by the kids who worked there. They picked their way slowly through the debris, putting away the mats and umbrellas. At nights we went out in Thomas's beat-up car and sat around in one of the little villages, at Gassin on the ramparts, or Ramatuelle at the bar L'Ormeau, or on the port at St Tropez. Later we crashed Le Bal, the little discotheque over the car park. I felt as if I had fallen off the face of the earth. The boys lived in a tiny whitewashed hut at the edge of the beach. As I returned there at dawn, after a night at Le Bal, the sky streaked with pink and the waves crashing right up to the door, my escape from reality seemed complete.

That first summer, Tony had lent me Le Nid de Duc until the end of September. Then I went back to the Lancaster for the winter, but the following spring of 1987, I dropped by on my way to the festival at Cannes. When the film *Tolerance* finally looked as if it was going to happen, I took a little roly-poly dialogue coach with me to the coast, and we stayed for six weeks in a boarding house at St Tropez owned by an old spinster, Madame Fournier. Each morning we set out for the beach on a scooter, the dialogue coach on the back with her scarves blowing in the wind, clutching the script in one hand and the talent with the other, and we rehearsed together at the Aqua Club, sitting on a banquette staring out to sea. We never moved. Our lunch was brought and cleared; our progress was observed by the entire beach. Queens borrowed the script at night so that they could have a better grasp of what was going on. Thomas and Frank would flop onto the banquette, dripping from the sea. Sometimes we would perform scenes to a selected audience of the flubby and the thonged. They all listened attentively for errors in my French and wagged jewelled fingers at any mistakes. I grew a beard; my hair was long and dirty, and slowly I turned into the hermit.

When Béatrice arrived she was naturally nonplussed to find herself more or less living on a gay beach, but she put her best foot forward and made the most of it. She was not the seaside type. There was no question that she was going to jump into a bathing suit. It was simply not her style, particularly since we were stalked by paparazzi who hid in the dunes behind the Aqua. Yet Béa had a natural talent to be at ease wherever she was, listening to us on the banquette during our rehearsals, chatting with Frank and Thomas at the bar or with Gerard and Linda at their table. Everybody worshipped her. Thomas wanted her, and Frank wanted to be her, and sometimes we stayed with them in the tiny cabin by the water. Watching her gossip away as if she had known everyone all her life, all of us sitting in bed in our underwear, passing around joints as the waves crashed outside, I knew that I would never find another girl as good as Béa. She was perfect. When she was with you, she was with you. It didn't matter what you did, she went along. She had faith, and you could do no wrong: until the moment when she decided that enough was enough. Then that attention would be switched off, like an electric light, and the situation would be plunged into a darkness that could never be relit. It had happened to her husband. It would happen to me. No one left Béa. But that was for later. For now she left to be a weather forecaster in the Dordogne and I left to be a hermit in Calvados. We were the French show business couple du jour.

Then Béa thought she was pregnant. Endless telephone calls late into the night between Alençon and Bordeaux brought things to a head. What would we do if she were? The dice were rolling on our future. I spent my days in the forest, hiding in the high branches as the autumn leaves fell around me, while Pierre-Henri screamed through a megaphone from a scaffolding tower near by, all the while wondering just how it would be. Béa, baby and me. Sometimes I felt deep waves of joy. At other times I wanted to throw myself out of the tree. At night I stared out the window at St Thérèse's bedroom, wishing for a sign. And then one night Béa called and said in a quiet voice that she wasn't pregnant after all. We were both silent.

'I'm really sad,' I said finally, and I was. A door had just closed.

'*Moi aussi*,' she replied. And somehow, that was it.

CHAPTER 30

The Vortex

The following March, in 1988, I was back in the West End in a play by Noël Coward, *The Vortex*. The story was about a young man who went to Paris and came back a junkie. Philip directed the play in Glasgow first of all. It was an unqualified success. Maria Aitken played the mother, and the rest of the cast was a group of Glasgow regulars. Uncle Derek played a mad pianist. Fidelis Morgan (who had been a brilliant André in the Proust play ten years before) played a neurotic soprano. Anne Lambton was a jaded society leech and her gay husband, Pawnie, was played by Tristram Jellinek. My love interest was a lovely Spanish girl, Yolanda Vasquez, and I was Nicky the concert pianist. Apart from Maria, we had all started our careers at Glasgow and were as thrilled as St Trinian's schoolgirls to be with each other, back in line at Rose's canteen. Philip turned fifty during rehearsals. Maria and I stayed in his flat on Sauchiehall Street, over a hairdresser's called Forgotten Dreams, and Hob Nob the coffee shop. Joe McKenna and I used to hang out in these establishments all those years ago when I first went to Glasgow in the hope of bumping into Philip. We would sit there for hours, looking out over the street, dreaming of starring one day at the theatre. Finally, it had all come true.

On Hogmanay the whole cast came round. At midnight we opened all the windows to let the spirits out, and then we launched ourselves upon the city for 'first footing'. Tall people bring good luck and I was kissed by the whole of Bennets, the gay disco. In retrospect, and even then, it was one of the best times. Philip was relaxed. The cast adored one another. We took the work seriously but we were there to have fun, and that was the unique thing about the Citizens.

But the transfer to the West End tore several friendships apart, including mine with Philip. Maria had been a sweet, docile gang member while we had been up in Glasgow; as soon as we came into the West End, she transformed into a terrible head girl figure, and she took Philip along with her. Under the new regime, what had once been a living thing on a Glasgow stage turned quickly into a dead body on the West End slab, drained of its blood and filled with theatrical formalde-hyde to sustain its waxy lifeless form through eight open-coffined funerals a week.

The only thing that cheered us up was Fred, the stage door man, who had been at the Garrick Theatre for thirty-five years. He was very tall, slightly backward and had a bit of a shake. He shuffled about at a snail's pace and couldn't master the new (fifteen-year-old) switchboard, so if there was a phone call he would creep downstairs to your room and knock on the door, but by the time he had got back upstairs to put you through, the person had long ago hung up. He lived in the house where he was born, in north London, and he had a lovely quavery voice. He called us all 'Mr' and 'Miss', and he gave scarabs that he had bought in the British Museum to his favourites in the cast. He had seen some comings and goings, but was possibly unprepared for some of the fireworks that took place while we were there.

One night Fidelis threw a fire extinguisher at the company manager and had to be restrained by Anne Lambton. There was a terrible tussle on the stairs. The girls were a magnificent sight, dressed only in hats, earrings, bras, tights and high heels; Fidelis was screaming as Anne tried to pull her back into the safety of their dressing room. Maria emerged from the bowels of the earth, like Matron, except she was dressed for Act Three in a torn tangerine negligee with a mascara-streaked face. She stormed up the stairs. 'This has got to stop,' she commanded.

'Shut up, you old cunt,' screamed Fid, as she grabbed the fire extin-guisher from the wall and threw it down the stairs, spurting foam.

'Miss Morgan. Miss Morgan. Telephone call at the stage door,' sang the querulous voice of Fred over the tannoy.

'I'm not fucking available,' screamed Fid as Anne dragged her kicking into the dressing room and slammed the door. Fidelis's muffled screams could still be heard as we fixed our smiles back into place and made our way to the stage.

When we decided to do the show in the West End, I told Philip and Maria that I would be taking some time off, and at Easter I decided to take a little holiday, so on the Friday night after the show I presented the company manager with my doctor's note saying that I had a relaxed throat.

As she took it, an actor called Nickolas Grace came into my dressing room. We had a drink. Sean Mathias came by to pick me up. We were going to a club called Troll. When Maria was informed of my relaxed throat, Nickolas was by this time in her room, sipping pink champagne.

'Where is he?' snarled Maria.

'He's gone home to bed,' repeated the company manager bravely.

'Nonsense!' said Nickolas Grace. 'He's gone to Heaven with Sean Mathias.'

Maria jumped into her car and went straight to Heaven to find me. She scoured every corner of the club but actually I was in Troll. Then she sped over to Earl's Court to the Coleherne, of all places, and poked around there. Finally she gave up, but the next morning she called my mother.

'He said he was ill, but actually he was in a gay club all night,' she ranted.

'I don't think you'll find that's true, Maria,' replied my dear old mum stiffly. (As you may recall, there was already bad blood between our two families.)

By this point I was relaxing my throat at the Lancaster in Paris, having a marvellous reunion with Lychee and the colleagues, and came back fully refreshed for the performance on Monday evening. Maria and I hardly spoke again, and there were still three months to go.

During the most intense scene of the play I spoke very quietly, and people who were used to the trilling gargoyles of yesteryear could not or would not hear. Indeed, sometimes members of the audience shouted up at me, 'Speak up, Nicky!'

Even one of Noël Coward's only surviving girlfriends, a doddery old actress who came to the first night, accosted me with a message from beyond the grave. 'Noël came into the auditorium during the second act,' she croaked.

'Really, how fascinating,' I oiled.

She stared over my shoulder for a second as if the master himself was perched there, and then grasped my hand. 'You must speak up, dear. You really must.' And she turned around and left.

It was after my trip to Paris that the 'pubic hair scandal' erupted. I was deeply hung-over from a Tuesday night at the Fridge in Brixton, when I opened a really irritating letter from Lorraine and Peter Landau, a couple in Northwood. They complained about the audibility of my performance in rather pompous terms. I replied to the letter saying that I was 'so sorry for the audibility problem and would they please accept my heartfelt apologies'. I then cut a clump of my pubic hair from my groin and sellotaped it to the letter. 'And these few pubic hairs, in the hope that they may make up for any inconvenience. Ever yours, Trudie Trumpeter.'

Needless to say, they were furious and sent the letter to the *Evening Standard*. I was asked for a statement, which I gave through Duncan, my agent.

'Rupert gets between five hundred and a thousand letters a week, and as you know some fans do ask for some rather strange things. I spoke to Rupert this morning but he doesn't recollect having any requests for pubic hair from Northwood.'

The story made the cover of *The Stage* and *Television Today*.

And then one night Laurence Olivier died. Without warning, at the curtain call, Maria stepped forward in her peach negligee and all that running mascara, and motioned for silence. 'Ladies and gentlemen,' she said, the head girl addressing the school assembly. 'Tonight Laurence Olivier died.'

It could have been a very dramatic moment, except that a man in the stalls said to his friend, 'Who's he?' I could already feel my stomach tense as a fit of giggles began to tingle deep inside my pelvis. I looked down at the floor. I knew that if I caught either Anne's or Fidelis's eyes, the game would be up. All of us knew that we would never work again if we started laughing on the night Larry popped his clogs.

'We will now observe a three-minute silence,' continued Maria.

Three minutes? After one, I was aware that Anne's body was shaking like a spin-dryer next to me. I glanced up and she glanced at me, a frightening eye outlined in thick black with a red dot on the inside overflowing with tears. Soon I was shaking, too. I tried to concentrate on Larry in *Rebecca*, Larry and Vivien, Larry in *The Betsy*, anything, but it was no good. We both tried looking up at the spotlights. Sometimes they could stun one. Tears were streaming down our faces but we were just about under control when a lady in the audience said, 'Ahh, those two must have been really fond of him.' That our mirth had been mistaken for grief had never occurred to us, and I'm afraid we began to howl with laughter. The audience watched us with deep sympathy. Maria stared ahead with a pained expression, and mercifully the three minutes came to an end as the lights faded dramatically in the entire theatre to pitch black. Anne and I were crying so much we couldn't find our way off the stage, so that when the lights came back up we were still there, arms outstretched, banging into the furniture, wailing like Russian women around a grave.

Looking back, I was a terrible monster. Poor Maria was simply trying to do her job. I was far too grand to attempt anything so mundane and that was my problem. Trying was beneath me, so I manipulated everyone I could and enjoyed the state of siege much more than the performance.

If going into the dusty gloom of the theatre every day felt like live incarceration in some giant tomb, then outside that endlessly shaking edifice was an explosion of life and colour. The wet spring turned into a beautiful summer. House music filled the airwaves. Gyms had appeared all over the city. I made friends with an ex-ballet dancer turned trainer, Hugh Craig (Huge Crack to his inner circle), and together we started renovations on my skeletal frame (twenty years later, I am still a work in progress – Rome wasn't rebuilt in a day).

In the aftershock of Aids, our collective gay aura was a question mark. Everywhere we went there was never more than six degrees of separation between us and some recent death, but we couldn't spend the rest of our lives worrying. We either had it or we didn't, and most of us weren't going to find out. So that season, at the Fridge in Brixton, or Kinky Galinky's, or Troll, rushing on ecstasy, dancing to the summer hits ('Brothers, Sisters, Take Us to the Promised Land'), the tension and uncertainty of the last few years evaporated and there was a kind of strange camaraderie, an honour among thieves that coloured every kiss. With the gyms came a new silhouette. The Pet Shop Boys were the pied pipers who led the new muscle-bound queer (gay was not a good word that year) from the back room to the ballroom. This new identity attached itself to the prevailing winds of upward mobility and soon people were talking about the pink pound. In the lull between Thatcherism and New Labour, you could still play Monopoly with London property. Some queens who rented a sandwich shop on Old Compton Street soon owned the whole block, and that year Soho was claimed by the queens. There was a restless unruly feeling in the city. It was the second summer of love and the ecstasy generation were like woodland elves that appeared out of the blue at vast raves in the countryside or on the commons of London. The police were always two steps behind, arriving just when it was too late. I moved into a small hotel in Soho, a converted seventeenth-century house near the square, and gave myself up to the pleasures of the West End.

Across the road from the theatre lived a couple called Baillie Walsh and John Maybury. We had been introduced a couple of years before by a mutual monster, Fiona Russell Powell, but had kept each other at arm's length. Now Baillie and I became great friends, and soon I was going over the road every night after the show, fascinated by the dangerous set of designers, *discaires* and dealers who sat on the floor tearing the world to shreds. Smoke from a thousand cigarettes curled around them in the shards of light from a motionless glitter ball. Baillie and John were both extremely handsome, and lay across each other in sequinned T-shirts on the floor. Sometimes the girls from Bananarama were falling down the staircase as I arrived; or clambering up the steps in two-foot heels, with only a slit for his mouth in a latex body suit, Leigh Bowery would appear from the gloom of the passage like a gay Darth Vader. There was a girl who called herself Princess Julia, with a voice like Eliza Doolittle, a DJ by the name of Tallulah, and a pair of gay carpenters called Alan and Fritz. Everyone seemed to have fairground names: Greek Andy, Gary the Cleaner, Space Princess. I was a newcomer in this crowd, and possibly too successful in the wrong way, so I kept my head down, hoping that no one would notice my name winking at them in red neon through the octagonal turret window of the sitting room from the other side of the road. I invited John, Baillie and Alan to the play, and they were suitably underwhelmed. They thought theatre was old hat. They were right. But that night at dinner we discovered one thing in common: we had all gone out with Antony Price.

Between the matinée and the evening show on the last day of the run, I gave a party on the roof of the theatre. Philip didn't come, and neither did Maria; but my mother did, and so did Fred the doorman. It was a beautiful afternoon. The view was sad and nostalgic, like a scene from *Mary Poppins*: roofs and towers and flags under the white summer sky. I stood with Fred, looking out over Trafalgar Square. He gave me a farewell scarab.

'Oh, Mr Everett,' he said. 'You know, I haven't been up here since Mr Novello was in *King's Rhapsody.*'

The next morning I left for Paris. But *The Vortex* wasn't yet over for me, unfortunately. A director called Robert Allan Ackerman restaged it with Philip's original sets and designs at the Doolittle Theater in Los Angeles a year later. Suzanne Bertish, my great friend who had played my manager in *Hearts of Fire*, took over Anne Lambton's part and Stephanie Beacham, of *Dynasty* fame, played Maria's role.

CHAPTER 31

Los Angeles

There are places you do plays, and places you don't. You know you are down and out when you are in a play in LA. But I was out of work and broke, and Suzanne persuaded me that I would get a great job if I went, and so in December 1989 I left for LA with a puppy I had bought in France and moved into a little cottage off Laurel Canyon that was owned by a director from England. It was a sweet house in a maze of winding roads that clung to the crumbling side of the canyon. By the end of our street, the hill had become too steep to develop, and after the last house, a brown clapboard bungalow on stilts, the asphalt became a sandy track, which in its turn was quickly reclaimed by nature: swaying desert grass, wild rosemary and tall flowering cacti. Coyote packs howled at night and came down to our street to eat the garbage, and any small dogs or cats they could find. There was a small oval pool in the shape of a Xanax, and the house was shrouded in a freezing shadow from lunchtime onwards; in the basement lived a curious spinster called Alicia.

Rehearsals were in the converted morgue where Marilyn had been taken after her death. She had the right idea. The only way to go into that place was feet first. It was the third time I had rehearsed this play and I began to hate it. Rehearsals were like those dreams of trying to run when your legs won't move. Ackerman had a strange hushed manner and directed like a gynaecologist locating polyps. Everyone adored him and thought he was a genius. I liked him too, but could only imagine what Philip would have said. The stage manager was a huge prison warden of a girl with a Bay City Rollers hairstyle.

During the dress rehearsal Stephanie Beacham arrived for her first entrance sporting a huge carrot-coloured bouffant upon which perched – like the Sydney Opera House – a 'discreet and chic little hat', as designed by Philip. It looked absurd. 'I'll fight you for this!' she warned, peering into the gloomy auditorium. I buried my head in my hands. This was going to be a long slow death . . .

But the reviews were good. The production was okay. An extraordinary crowd of mediums and dressers to silent-movie stars collected every night to see the show. Stephanie was deaf in one ear so if you said your line from the wrong angle she acted as though nothing had happened. There were some amusing star wars as Suzanne found her feet. First she declared war on the prison warden, goading her in the wings before the show, but she never got very far. The poor girl just pursed her lips and turned a beetroot colour. 'That is very inappropriate,' was as much of a retort she could muster, after some venomous aside from Suzanne as she breezed onto the stage. Suzanne needed blood to get through. How well I understood her. She needed someone who could at least lob the ball back over the net. She didn't have to look very far.

Stephanie was by turns very starry and very vulnerable. Sometimes she was deaf and sometimes she could hear a pin drop in the back of the stalls. She had just left the *Dynasty* spin-off, *The Colbys*, that bubbling marsh of old-school swamp bitches who took no prisoners and ate people whole, and so she was probably spoiling for bit of fisticuffs herself. She and Suzanne had met their match and, after an initial spell as best friends, fell upon one another as only best friends can. Suzanne had all the ammunition. Act Three of the play begins with a bitter confrontation in which Suzanne's character tries to ram some sense into Stephanie's character. Suzanne played it to the hilt. 'Pull yourself together, Florence. You are spoilt and unreasonable,' she would scream. It was exciting theatre. One night she was so tough that as the curtain came down, Stephanie collapsed howling on the floor. Then the curtain flew up again and the applause revived her. She bravely staggered to her feet, smiled wanly and the public adored her. The exhausted curtain call is one of the oldest crowd pleasers. Then she crumpled again and stumbled wailing to her dressing room.

That was the only fun. The run went on for ten weeks and, needless to say, I didn't have another job. Movie folk had to be drugged senseless to get them to the theatre in LA.

At dinner one night after the show with Tony Richardson and Candy Bergen, both expressed enormous curiosity about Madonna and asked whether I could arrange a meeting. Tony had seen her in a David Mamet play in New York and had loved her. I was an inexperienced host, but I invited them all to dinner at my house. Alicia from downstairs was going to cook.

It was one of the most disastrous nights on record.

Before dinner we lit the fire in the sitting room. Then a sudden freak storm began to howl around the house, the upstairs terrace collapsed into the garden and the wind blew the smoke from the fire back down the chimney into the room. By the time Tony and Candy arrived you could hardly see. Finally Madonna appeared with Alek Keshishian and they both ignored Tony and Candy. Actually, to be fair, they could hardly see each other at this point in the smoke-filled room. But there was no chemistry, as we say in Hollywood. Madonna was approaching the dizzy pinnacle of fame, and at those heights you don't bother to disguise your feelings. If she was bored, she let you know. Manners were something she had discarded at base camp. She didn't seem comfortable with the older generation, just as she didn't seem to like the countryside. She knew how everyone her own age reacted to her. And she knew the laws of the asphalt jungle. The older generation were looking at her from another angle and that scared her. Added to this Mo, my puppy, already a sex maniac, took one look at the material girl and was entranced. He started to lick her, sniffing her crotch and nipping at her dress before pinning her into a chair and humping her leg, leaving weird secretions on her stockings. This she didn't mind so much. Any form of sexual adulation was an affirmation to the material girl and she looked down with a mixture of horror and delight at Mo's lolloping tongue as he pounded away at her.

Finally we sat down to dinner. I wished the ground would swallow me up and vowed never to entertain again. (I haven't.) Alicia served up some undercooked vegetables and bloody chicken legs. It was freezing cold, because we had to open all the doors to let the smoke out. During a lull in the sticky conversation, the remainder of the upstairs terrace came crashing down into the garden. Madonna and Alek were only interested in each other. They were in the middle of their triumphant collaboration, *Truth or Dare*, and after dinner they huddled in a corner talking to Harvey Weinstein on their cellphones, making high-flying Hollywood plans. The party was over before nine o'clock; the post-mortem went on until two.

I saw a lot of Tony during that trip, and we hatched a plan to do a world tour of *Hamlet* and *The Cherry Orchard* with Vanessa Redgrave. Calls were made all over the world, from the Odéon in Paris, to the Opera House in Sydney. Robert Fox was roped in; Tony set his mind to it, and so did we, although at the same time I think we all knew it was a dream. Unfortunately, Tony's health was fading. He never talked about it, although sometimes he would carelessly say he had been to the hospital, at the same time challenging one with that sunken pale-eyed gaze not to enquire further. His neck had shrunk and his head with its giant brain looked more than ever as if it had recently stepped off a spacecraft. His hands were covered in blue marks, which he valiantly covered with make-up. Such was his control over his friends that we were mesmerised into dumb acquiescence. He wanted to go on as if nothing was happening. He had no time for self-pity or the pity of others; nor was he hindered by fear. At dinner in Spago's one night during that hideous holiday season, somebody was going around the tables with a video camera asking people what they were hoping for in the New Year.

'Death,' said Tony bluntly. He got it.

On Christmas Day I drove out to Malibu to Herb Ritts' house where Madonna, her sexy boyfriend Tony Ward, and a famous beauty, now dead, Anthony Daniels, were playing Truth or Dare. Madonna made me snog her boyfriend, which I must say was the highlight of a wrist-slitting Christmas. Herb's house was beautiful, unlived in and looked out over that mournful sea. After lunch, we watched a video of Pasolini's *Salò* (otherwise known as *The 120 Days of Sodom*). At about six o'clock we all got into our cars and drove back in the dark to

Hollywood. I felt that numb exhaustion one has at the end of one's best friend's funeral.

Antony Price came to stay with me; meanwhile, Baillie and John, Alan and Fritz were camped out on the other side of the canyon at Paul Fortune's house (Baillie was making a Massive Attack video). Paul threw a party on New Year's Eve, but I left before midnight, and went home and sat quietly with Mo. Together we watched random fireworks explode across the canyon. Their pops sounded like gunshots as they ricocheted across the hills.

The best thing in LA is the walking. With Mo at my side, I discovered the trails that threaded through the Hollywood hills all the way down to the sea. Right in the middle of those vast godless suburbs were hidden valleys of giant eucalyptus trees. Tiny paths overgrown with wild flowers cut into the side of the hill and zigzagged past the rusting shells of cars that had shot off Mulholland Drive long ago and now hung in the clutches of nature. At the bottom of the gulley we lay on the ground and watched the trees sway and creak over our heads. The only other noise was the trickle of a stream and the faraway murmur of a car passing on the road high above. The anguish of making it or not making it was replaced by the simple fact of being a young man with his dog in an enchanted wood, and the endless quest to be someone more than one was briefly evaporated in the heavy scent of eucalyptus and rosemary and skunk.

But the peace I found there was short-lived. Driving to work at the Doolittle Theater one evening, Madonna's 'Justify My Love' was playing on the radio. It was the perfect song for that sleazy strip of old Hollywood where the Doolittle's marquee winked sadly at a disinterested world. Hookers in hot pants and halter necks looked vulnerable in the orange glare of the street lights, standing in stilettos on the name of some forgotten star. Car after car after car drove by; their heads turned with each one, with a promising glance glued to their faces. These were the little seeds of desire from which the vast heads on the billboards blossomed. Ambition was the currency in Hollywood although it was justified as love: love for the craft of cocksucking. The song ended and the DJ chimed in with some very disturbing news.

'This is coast one-oh-one and you're listening to X. Now, if you play that last track backwards, apparently there is a message to Satan. Just listen to this.'

A weird noise groaned over the radio as the track babbled backwards and then a deep voice said, 'I. Love. You. Satan.'

My blood went cold. This was it. Madonna was Satan. I had been sent to kill her. It all made sense. My fascination with her . . . *Salò* . . . everything! 'Some of you will be chosen . . .' I could hear the abbey bells ringing. But then the feeling subsided. My bigoted Catholic superstitions receded back into the deep sludge, but I was quite shocked by my reaction. I only had to be two or three degrees more bitter and neurotic, and there could have been an explosion. And I suddenly saw Madonna in a different light. Her life was full of people who could turn at any minute. How dangerous it was to tickle the world's fantasy. And how vulnerable you were at the dizzy summit . . .

That night, I embarked upon my third novel. I called it *Guilt Without Sex: A Jewish Bestseller*, a title I borrowed from Michael Black. The story took place in 2020 when actors, like drummers, had to be able to programme performance. A failed programmer finds religion and falls in love and hate with a beautiful transgender superstar. I never got very far with the book, but I told Madonna about it a little later.

'Don't you think it would make a great film?' I said.

'No,' she replied.

'Oh. Okay,' I said, as casual as could be. Now I wanted to kill her again.

CHAPTER 32

Windy Ridge

In November 1987, just before my West End sojourn in *The Vortex*, I bought Windy Ridge. A fatal mistake. It was a half-finished tip up a steep track above the beach at Pampelonne, outside St Tropez, owned by a couple in the throes of divorce; he lived in one part and she lived in the garage. It was a large rambling place, three unfinished houses around a yard, no central heating, just naked wires sticking from the walls. But despite all this, it looked over a beautiful vineyard on one side and the pine woods down to the sea on the other, and beyond you could see the lighthouse at Cap Cammerat. I had hardly any money left, and it was expensive, but I bought it and, with the help of my father, managed to raise an 85 per cent mortgage. It would become my prison.

I moved into my new home one cold afternoon in December. I put a mattress on the floor in the little house at the bottom – Bâtiment 3, it was called on the plan of my new sprawling estate – and spent one of the most agonised nights of my life. How could I have got myself into this mess? The house was huge and horrible. My mortgage compelled me to earn a great deal of money, and yet my career was going into the early stages of rigor mortis. That first Christmas I celebrated with Thomas and Frankie, shivering in bed while eating oysters as we tried to make a fire with damp logs that steamed in the hearth but never caught fire. In the New Year I found a rather surly couple, Monsieur and Madame Petit, to come and live in the house, along with their son Pascal, while I was away.

Monsieur was a builder. Madame was a lazy housewife with a quivering chin, in the hot flush of life and brilliant at emotional blackmail. They took one look at me and knew they were on to a winner. They moved into Bâtiment 1 (aka the garage) the week before I left for London and seven months in *The Vortex*. I was so relieved that I had managed to get the house inhabited, and even more relieved to be getting out, that I just left with some vague instructions to them to start rebuilding the house.

When I returned in September, they had built themselves a luxury home out of the garages. It was beautiful. Monsieur Petit could certainly build, I thought to myself, as I curled up on my foam mattress in Bâtiment 3. Now the Petit family had been there longer than me. I tried to wrestle the reins from them, but they controlled me like a puppet. He half-heartedly began work on the big house, knocking down the whole interior, while I spent the days at the beach, tiptoeing home after dark past the warm glow of their luxury pad to the naked light bulb hanging from the ceiling in Bâtiment 3. The summer ended, and the bars were boarded up. The weather cooled, and the sea turned into a grey metal sheet. The inhabitants of the surrounding villages snuggled down for the winter to count their money. It was desolate and beautiful, and I realised that I had completely cut myself off from the rest of the world. I had spent every last penny on this fantasy and couldn't escape.

Madame Petit brought me a tray every night and I sat alone in front of a little electric fire. As I lay in the dark, the beam from the lighthouse grazed across my bed and the east wind howled and banged against the shutters.

I decided to get a dog. Someone gave me the number of an English breeder near Paris called Felicity Leith Ross. She was terribly grand and sounded tipsy when I talked to her.

'We're just delivering a litter now. Aren't we, Susie?' she slurred.
'Who's Susie?'
'My lovely prize-winning black bitch.'

It was more like applying for adoption, getting a labrador puppy out of this woman, but finally a deal was struck and I was summoned in February to collect my bundle of joy.

There was a bent taxi driver in Paris who was often at the taxi stand on the rue de Berri. He haunted Lychee and me. I hailed him one day, we talked until he dropped me off and that was that. A few days later I got into another taxi and there he was again. I thought nothing of it, but when it happened a third time, I realised that he was keeping tabs on me. Not only me, as it happened, but Lychee as well. I was about to freak out but then I remembered how taxis were so hard to come by in Paris, and so I tried to be encouraging. The driver, whose name was Denis, was very handy. He had a network of spies all over the city. At one time he had been a *flic*. He knew if I had been out and if I'd come home alone. It was through Denis I discovered that Lychee worked in the Bois. He was obsessed by her and tried to collect her every night after work, but Lychee hated him. If we came across him together she turned into a dangerous Vietcong gutter person, shouting and kicking his car while I smiled helplessly, hoping he would still pick me up.

One afternoon in February 1989, I drove with him to a little village an hour or so outside Paris to collect my dog. I had chosen a little male. Felicity said he was 'a really good chap because he always says thank you after his tea'. Propaganda, I thought, as she presented me with the puppy and I presented her with a large cheque, but actually it was true. I christened him Moïse. He had a dumpy body, tiny paws with little jet nails, a salmon-pink tongue inside razor teeth, sweet-smelling breath, raisin-black eyes and triangular ears. His tail was a squiggle that stood up in the air and vibrated with joy. But as soon as we got into the car everything changed. He clawed at the window as the kennels disappeared for the last time and, when he realised he couldn't escape, he hid on the floor and howled all the way to Paris.

That evening we took the night train to St Raphaël, and he still hadn't forgiven me for abducting him from his family. He sat obstinately in the corner of the *wagon-lit* as we clattered slowly out of Paris, and I lay on the bed. We stared solemnly at each other for about half an hour, but he was scared of the tunnels and the flashing lights and soon he began to edge closer to the bed. I picked him up and laid him on my chest. He breathed in through his little black nose and then gave a

Ready to wear with Rossy de Palma.

Swamp bitches in Tennessee Williams' *Milk Train* and Paris Fashion Week.

© Getty Images

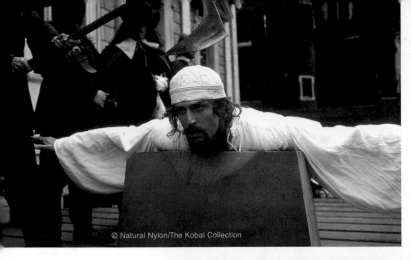

My royal family album.

Charles I

Charles II

Prince Charming

George IV

Reinvention with Julia Roberts in *My Best Friend's Wedding*.

My career in villains.

Right: *Inspector Gadget*

Middle: *Dellamorte Dellamore*

Bottom: *Dunston Checks In*

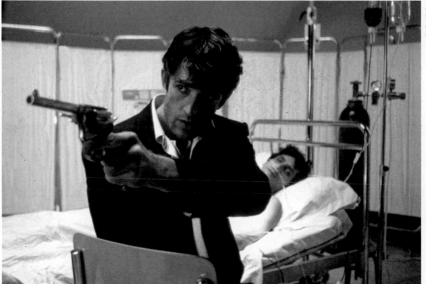

With Joan Collins.

Christopher Walken.

Jade Jagger.

Heaven on earth: co-starring with the Madonna.

Pretending to take direction from John Schlesinger.

Left: Ebony and Ivory.

Below: Muscling in on the success of *Shakespeare in Love* with (left to right) Geoffrey Rush, Gwyneth Paltrow and Ben Affleck.

Unconditional Love. One of my best films – never released.

heartbreaking sigh. His tail wagged one last time in defiance and he fell asleep. I woke up later as we were thundering across France and he was looking at me. He stretched himself towards my face and pounced on my nose, and the tail wagged again as for the first time I felt the force of those razor-sharp teeth.

So Mo and I settled down together in Bâtiment 3. I put a plank between his sleeping quarters outside the bathroom and mine, but he barked all night and shat everywhere he could. Then it occurred to me that there was very little difference between the passage with his mat and the room with my mattress, so I made the fatal mistake of removing the frontier and he galloped around the room in victory before jumping on top of me and going to sleep.

In France at that time there was a thing called the *minitel*, which was like a computer, connected to your telephone. There was a screen and a keyboard and you could cruise online, so in the evenings I would make contact with people all over the region, then Mo and I would set out in the car with our map, to villages in the Alpes Maritimes, or to some suburb of Marseilles, only to find that the young Olympic athlete who had written so disarmingly about his sexual agility was in fact a roly-poly baker who would be hard pushed to touch his toes, let alone anything else. Then Mo and I would look at each other and sigh before starting the long journey back home. Mo sat on the passenger seat and watched me curiously with his raisin eyes. Sometimes I braked too hard and he would fly into the dashboard, but he was a good-natured dog and climbed back into his place. He loved the car and when he was big enough to see through the windscreen, he concentrated on the road, or leant against the window so that his ear fluttered in the wind. Whenever I left for a trip without him and the bags came out, he disappeared. I would look for him to say goodbye, but he would already be sitting in the passenger seat. Staring ahead, very still so that no one would notice he was there.

'Come on, Mo. You're not coming,' I'd say, and he would climb out with his tail between his legs and shuffle off towards the house. I don't think the Petit family were very kind to him when I went away and left him in their charge, because right up until his death if I said the two words, 'Monsieur Petit', Mo's hackles would go up and he would start to bark.

Driving back from Toulon one day we saw an old gypsy caravan in a field with a For Sale sign beside it. I parked the car and went to have a look. It stood under an umbrella pine and was covered in needles but underneath it was painted pale blue and white; a little chimney with a dunce's cap grew out of the roof. A tyre was flat and it leant tragically to one side. There was no one about, and the door was open. Inside was a little kitchen, with wooden cupboards, a sitting room and a bedroom at the end. It was falling to pieces but I had to have it. A week later it limped up the steep driveway and became an annexe for the overflow of guests during the summer.

There was a little nightclub that stayed open during the winter months in St Tropez. Le Pigeonnier was an old round cellar, danger-ously crowded in the summer, but out of season there were never more than ten people dancing under its lonely glitter ball. The waiter was an extraordinary freak called Bruno, a tiny Inca pixie with hair down to his waist, a shrill cackle of a laugh and pretty green eyes. He was twenty years old, with an entourage of school friends who had all followed him from the northern town of Mulhouse to the fleshpots of the Côte d'Azur. They were sweet and every weekend Duchesse (a boy who looked like Charles I), Catherine, Pascal and I danced all night in the little club, served with free drinks by Bruno.

The Aqua Club was open for lunch during the winter weekends, and all the regulars sat around the fire in the *salle d'hiver*. My particular friends were George the lawyer, his boyfriend Alain, and Jacques Monthelier, who reminded me of an elderly badger. I loved their old-school gay banter and tales of post-war life in Paris. George had met Alain in the Piscine Déligny, the houseboat swimming pool on the River Seine, when Alain was only seventeen. They both met Jacques in a club called Le Pimms in the sixties. I was entranced by the longevity of their relationships. In my world no one knew anyone for more than five minutes.

But none of this was sufficient to keep my anxiety at bay. Whichever way I looked at it, I was stuck. I was broke. I was unemployed. I lived in a huge ugly shell on a desolate beach. Eventually, in utter desperation, I began to attend the eight-thirty morning mass in the hilltop village of Ramatuelle. Maybe God would get me a job.

The church had large double doors that were always open. The first day that I went, I was surprised to see Jacques shuffling in. I waved but he made no sign of recognition, even when he took the collection. His neighbour was a buxom peasant woman called Madame Amiel. She was the other regular at mass. She was also the village gossip. She raised her arms in supplication as the sacrament was revealed by the little old padre and proclaimed in that marvellous Provençal accent, better suited to barter for fish in the port, 'O Christ, prends pitié . . .'

Soon Jacques and I had breakfast together on a daily basis in the Bar de l'Ormeau after church. He was a fossilised old queen of seventy-nine. He came from Lille and his family made taps. Under his hopeless leadership the tap business had gone bust in the sixties. He had retired early and brought his sick mother down to Ramatuelle where he nursed her until she died. Now he was old and bored, horrified and entranced by the world that swept into the tiny village during the summer months. Like me, he was stuck in his little house in the fortifications of Ramatuelle. He was diabetic, and smelt musty and unwashed, but had a wry sense of humour and a twinkle in his eyes. We became very fond of one another.

Everything went wild during the summer at Windy Ridge. The house was full of people. One of my best friends from London was a designer called Tom Bell. We had decided to leave England together. Now he lived in Madrid and came every summer to stay in the caravan. Bruno and his clique lived downstairs in the big house, which little by little was being rebuilt, and Mo and I lived on in Bâtiment 3 with whoever we were having an affair with at the time. We rarely sat down less than twenty to dinner, and developed a dangerous reputation in the bars and clubs of St Tropez, where our unpaid bills and jilted lovers waited for us accusingly when we arrived en masse in the town. All my friends from London came to stay and the summers were crazy whirlpools of arrivals and departures, ones I had no means of supporting and, finally, in the February of 1990 the electricity was cut off. On the way up the hill to morning mass, my car, my faithful Renault 25, burst into flames on the side of the road. I couldn't pay the mortgage. Nor could I sell the house. I'd knocked most of it down. It was only a shell. I was well and truly stuck . . . And then Carol Levi, my Italian agent, called. Did I want to go to Russia for fourteen months to make a miniseries based on Mikhail Sholokhov's novel, And Quiet Flows the Don?

The Richardsons were in France for Easter that year, so I went up to Le Nid de Duc to break the news to Tony that I was leaving for Russia. I told him I had no choice, which was true; I didn't. He listened as I asked whether we could postpone the *Hamlet* tour for a year and just looked at me. We both knew there wouldn't be a next year for him. It was a terrible betrayal. His face closed up in front of me. He became icily polite, then got up and walked inside. Even though we all met for lunch on a freezing Easter Day down at the Aqua, Tony never talked to me again.

I never saw Jacques again either. The day I was leaving for Moscow, we said goodbye after mass, and I watched him through the rear-view mirror, waving as I drove away. One morning not long after, his car broke down and he disappeared while he was walking back to the village. Madame Amiel told the police that he frequented a macabre band of young *pédés* and a half-hearted search ensued. His body was found six months later, sitting against a tree, decomposing and half eaten by foxes.

CHAPTER 33

Russia

Aeroflot was my first taste of Soviet Russia. A big girl with thick ankles and that Soviet make-up that seems to stand out from the face directed me with a stiff smile into my seat in first class. 'You will sit, please, and wash face,' she said, handing over an evil-smelling hand towel the colour and texture of a spring roll.

'Could I have a drink?'

'You will have vodka? No! This is for later.'

It was July. I wouldn't be back for a whole year. I definitely needed a drink.

Throughout the flight I could hear Mo down in the hold. He barked across France, Germany and Poland, and was still barking – hoarse now – when he appeared through the flaps of the conveyor belt in the weird sepia-toned baggage claim at Moscow airport. When he saw me he barked even harder. He was furious. This was his first flight.

A small unshaven Italian man called Gianni greeted me and guided me through customs. There was a dead feeling in communist Russia. It banged into you as you stepped off the plane. Men in uniforms with blunt dull faces, tiny and cruel under enormous hats, went through my belongings item by item, endlessly examining a bottle of soy sauce, or a bag of rice. (I had brought a trunk of provisions.) Others stood in groups watching with glassy lobotomised eyes. Stocky babushkas in headscarves swept mops back and forth, grim and mechanical. Where were the thick-necked heads thrown back in laughter, exposing gleaming Slavic molars? They had turned to stone and were standing on plinths high above the streets of Moscow in the amazing statuary of the Soviet Reality movement.

Outside a huge old limousine stood by the kerb. A man with frizzy hair, Dame Edna glasses and bellbottom jeans was at the wheel, and a stocky girl with short red hair and a round face stepped towards me and firmly shook my hand. She was what they call in Russia a 'Hello Goodbye girl', which in those days meant a KGB operative.

'I am Jana. I will be your interpreter,' she said and we all climbed into the back of the car, a Chaika or, as Jana translated, a Seagull, which used to belong to Brezhnev. A small spotlight was fixed in the door that bathed your face in a ghoulish light. If it had been embarrassing driving through Deptford in a limo on the way to Greenwich all those years ago, then this felt really weird, because the traffic, a million identical Ladas belching towards the city, more or less stopped when they saw us coming, such was their response to authority and its various props. This car was one of them, and we swept along the fast lane as the little tin boxes cowered at the edges of the road. Even the policemen with their whistles waved us on. No one seemed to care that a car like this hadn't been seen for twenty-five years. Time stood still in Soviet Russia. But not in the good way.

Miles and miles of crumbling tower blocks surrounded the city and the production had put me up in a French hotel in one of these suburbs. It was allegedly one of the only decent places in town. I was deposited there with my dog, my trunks, and an envelope of dollars, and left to my own devices until the next morning.

That evening I felt like a ghost. I took Mo for a walk. It was warm as we threaded through the muddy labyrinth of high-rises around the hotel. Everything was falling to pieces. A porch hung precariously over a front door. Windowpanes were held together by tape and newspaper. Under the trees in the little parks, broken people sat on broken benches, and children screamed on ancient climbing frames that looked like strange installations. Pollen floated in the air, which had a metallic taste. Old men twisted by arthritis and alcohol sat hunched over chessboards wearing army hats from the Second World War, while sturdy women in shabby mackintoshes walked dogs.

It was overwhelming. Back in the hotel I felt completely lost. I couldn't phone from my room. There was no restaurant. Mo looked at me with grave eyes. 'You've really done it this time,' his gaze said. I went to the coffee shop downstairs, ate a sandwich and washed it down with vodka and a tranquilliser.

The next morning Dame Edna and my KGB agent came to collect me and we went to the studio, Mosfilm, which was built by Stalin from plans his spies had stolen from Twentieth Century Fox. At the entrance an aggressive female labourer operated a barrier. She looked at the piece of paper we gave her for twenty minutes, then telephoned using a huge red receiver that looked like a child's toy. It was exhausting, but this was communism. It had hit them over the head and now it hit me over the head. One had to slow down or die trying. On several occasions over the next year this freak refused point-blank to let me on the lot. Once I grabbed her by her anorak and we had a furious tussle but she was the stronger man, of course, and flung me to the ground.

Inside, the crumbling studios were caked with years of mud and dust. Pipes with big rusting taps grew out of the ground, like living things, and ran along walls and up over the street before diving back into the earth. The huge sliding doors to the sound stages were open. Inside was a kind of mill with giant saws, stacks of wooden planks, carpenter's benches and incredible machines, with pistons and hammers. God knows what they did. People stood around in dirty brown coats, toothless, blotchy and backward looking. The men had moustaches and so did many of the women.

We walked through the sound stage, the biggest in the East, an indoor football field. On it a sloping hill had been constructed with two thatched cottages divided by a fence. A cyclorama surrounded the whole space, studded with fairy lights to make stars.

Upstairs, off a long corridor, was the office of Sergei Bondarchuk, twice People's Artist of the Soviet Union; friend of Stalin; Director General of Mosfilm. He sat behind a large desk with his palms flat on the table in a pose of absolute power. At any minute you felt he might ring a bell and you would be frogmarched to Siberia. He had a shock of thick snowy hair and a handsome moustache. He wore thick glasses over hooded murderous eyes. He was old but vigorous. Communism had been kind to him. We shook hands and then he kissed me on both cheeks. I giggled. Pleasantries were exchanged in several languages through Jana and another interpreter, an Italian girl called Leila who had the voice of a cartoon mouse. It was like being at a meeting at the United Nations. Sergei had waited thirty years to realise this dream. Now that he had seen me, he said, he was sure that everything was going to be all right. When I walked in, he saw the character.

'You and Grigor are two peas in a pod,' he pronounced, and I giggled again.

It should be pointed out, at this stage, that I was vastly unsuited to the part in which I had been cast. *Quiet Flows the Don* is the story of a Cossack, Grigor, the toughest, bravest Cossack of them all. It is a beautiful book, mostly true, about the tragic life of a family torn apart by world war and revolution. The poor Don Cossacks were dragged one way and then another in the messy birth of communism. Strangely, the book was sanctioned by Stalin, even though its hero was a tragic victim of his system. The result was that the character of Grigor became a symbol for Russians; he was a man who stuck to his guns and lost everything. Even seventy years later, in 1990, every car still had his picture and that of his love, Aksinia, on the dashboard for good luck. He meant far more than Robin Hood to the English; more than any folk hero we have. He was a religious figure. He was Soviet reality.

The fact of the matter was that everyone from Richard Gere right down to me at the bottom of the list had turned the movie down. No one wanted to go to Russia for a year. Neither did I, now that I had got there. As Sergei droned on and Jana translated into terrifyingly literal English, I wondered how I was going to make it through. But there was no escape. I had to face it. At the end of the interview, Sergei took me down the long corridor to the hair and make-up department where he handed me over to the Italians to turn me into the part. 'One last thing,' he said. 'Don't shave your armpits.'

Cheeky. What did he know?

Maria Thérèse Corridone was a legendary hairdresser in the world of cinema. She began with Visconti and ended up with Bondarchuk. In a couple of hours she artfully turned my short hair into a long shaggy Cossack quiff made of extensions, dust, pomade and artful backcombing. Her cousin, the make-up man, stuck moustaches, sideburns and stubble onto my face. The adhesive and the itchiness, the mortician's wax and the scattered facial hairs, were enough to drive one totally insane; to repeat the torture for six days a week for the next fourteen months hardly bore thinking about, and my eyes brimmed with tears. I slipped into my bodystocking – thank God for that – and tried on my Cossack costume. Everything was fine until I put on the hat. My neck was so long, my shoulders were like a bottle and the silhouette stubbornly remained British. We put in giant shoulder extensions, and then I began to look the part.

If a sissy like Victor Mature could do it, so could I.

I knew enough about my job by now to construct what character I could. I had to take everything down to a minimum. Do nothing. Everything I had was wrong. It was going to be a very old-fashioned performance, and I would need help from all departments to pull it off, but by the end of the morning I was quite inspired by the prospect. I loved the Marlene Dietrich School of acting.

Soon afterwards, Bruno arrived with seventeen Barbie dolls and half the kitchen from Windy Ridge. The next night I asked the director, his wife and the producer to dinner in my suite. We all came directly from work. As I walked in, I noticed a Barbie in full evening dress swinging from the chandelier in the hall. I eased the party as quickly as I could into the sitting room, hoping they wouldn't look up, but then Sergei wanted to use the loo. I opened the door for him. Sitting on the toilet paper in a bikini was another Barbie. Horrified, I threw it into the waste-paper basket where it lay with its legs in the air, before taking Mrs B into the sitting room where three more Barbies were having cocktails on the sofa. I nearly screamed, and ran into the kitchen, grabbing the dolls as I went.

'Bruno! What the fuck are you thinking, leaving Barbies all over the place? I'm meant to be a fucking Cossack, not a schoolgirl!'

'Relax!' said Bruno, with a high-pitched shriek. 'I'll tell him they're mine.'

The next morning Tom arrived from the South of France with more food, and he and Bruno set about looking for an apartment, while I left in the limo to start shooting the First World War in a field twenty miles outside Moscow.

Sergei was famous for his battle scenes. For his masterpiece, *War and Peace*, the whole army had been put at his disposal. Now entire tank regiments arrived at the location every morning. On the first day I had to get on my horse with a sabre at my side and a gun over my shoulder, and charge with 2000 other riders towards the enemy trenches. It was extremely dangerous and would never have been allowed anywhere but in Italy or Russia. If I fell I would undoubtedly be killed.

It was then I had an epiphany. Thanks to my upbringing, so much of which I resented, I was a fairly good rider, and in the minutes before the first take (no rehearsal, by the way), just as a soldier going into battle reflects on all the things dear to him in life, I thought of Netty and Crisp, of hunting and cleaning tack, with a new fierce gratitude. They were going to save my life.

Sergei shouted, 'Action!' through a megaphone from the top of a huge crane. Three thousand of us began to trot across the summer fields. The brigadier rode ahead, screaming instructions from beneath his waxed moustache. First we presented our sabres. I drew mine with a flourish but unfortunately it was a dummy sword and stopped right under the handle.

'Cut! Cut! Cut!' shouted Sergei through the megaphone. I made a mental note to kill the props man later. Meanwhile they brought me a proper sword, as my colleagues sniggered and made rude jokes in Russian, and we started again. We trotted. We presented arms. We charged. As I galloped across that field I have never been so afraid in my whole life. Explosions were detonated all around us. One horse was actually blown up and no one warned us about a trench that we had to jump over at the end of the charge. People fell into it but I sailed over with a technique that June Osbourne from the Braintree Pony Club gymkhana would have been proud of.

The boys from the army were incredible. Here, finally, were the laughing beauties of Soviet Reality. We couldn't understand a word the other was saying and the KGB were not very helpful. Jana thoroughly disapproved of any contact, and translated anything the boys said with a pained expression as if their comments were beneath contempt. I fired her on the spot. (Needless to say, she stayed on the film, and we became good friends. On the last day of shooting, in an old schoolyard in the middle of the steppe, she came up to me and said that because of me she had become a lesbian.

One morning I was driving to work with Dame Edna, and on the road towards our field we passed hundreds of trucks containing all my army colleagues going in the opposite direction. By the time we got to the trenches there was not a Russian in sight. The Italians gesticulated wildly over walkie-talkies. It was a mystery. No sign of Sergei. We waited for an hour. Two hours. We lay in the sun listening to the rooks in the nearby forest, complaining about the organisation, laughing about the crazy things that had already happened, and then Gianni arrived from Moscow. 'There's been a coup. Everyone should return to the hotel and await further instructions.'

Our regiments had been called back to defend the White House. Yeltsin had deposed Gorbachev in a military coup. Communism was dead. We drove back to Moscow, and I collected Bruno, Tom and Mo, and we went to explore the city centre. Barricades had been erected everywhere, but thanks to the official nature of our car we were waved through and arrived at the White House just before lunch. All our army friends were standing in their tanks. 'Grigor!' they shouted. We clambered on board and toasted the new Russia with the boys, who seemed to have an endless supply of vodka. Dame Edna took our pictures, and then we went for tea at the gay coffee shop behind the Bolshoi where Tom got lucky and stayed out after the curfew.

The coup went on for four or five days. It was strange to be in the place the whole of the world was watching, and we sat around Mosfilm, kind of hoping for civil war so that the project would be abandoned and we could all go back to our comfortable homes. Fuck bankruptcy, I thought. Anything rather than this. But the coup ended peacefully and we were back in the field within a week. Meanwhile Tom and Bruno had found a pair of flats and we moved into the centre of town.

Smolenskaya was a large boulevard that ran all the way from the Ministry of (dis)Information to the river and Gorky Park on the other side. Dilapidated eighteenth-century villas stood beside large Soviet apartment blocks and the ministry, which was one of Stalin's fantasy towers, its gothic spires, topped with hammers and sickles, dominating the skyline. When the sun set, it turned into a jagged black crag and its shadow swamped the street. Our new flat was in a typical apartment building. There was an archway into a large interior courtyard, and four different blocks backed onto it. Hidden among the trees in the middle was another tumbling remnant of pre-revolution Moscow that someone had forgotten to knock down.

We lived up four flights of stone stairs past front doors of black upholstered leather, like the entrances to kinky fetish clubs. We hardly ever met anyone on the staircase. Muscovites kept to themselves, but nonetheless one always had a feeling of being watched. During the first week our neighbour burnt to death in his bed. At about four o'clock in the morning I was woken by the howling of sirens and footsteps running up the stairs. I opened the front door. The hallway was filled with smoke. Firemen emerged from next door with the charred body of the neighbour and carried him downstairs. In the morning the door was shut as if nothing had happened. It might have been a dream but outside the front door was a burnt mattress, a standard lamp with its singed shade, an armchair, and various books and magazines. They were never moved. Autumn leaves made a pretty blanket for the mattress. Then the snow came, and icicles formed on the lampshade. In spring the whole sad mess was revealed again. The burnt patch was black and boggy, and in summer weeds and thistles were happily growing where once a poor drunk had snored.

I settled in at Mosfilm. We were one of those lugubrious international productions, a film about Russians in English where only two from a cast of hundreds could speak it. F. Murray Abraham played my father. The cinematographer thought I was useless but was enraptured by F, although to my mind his performance was more *Fiddler on the Roof* than *Quiet Flows the Don*. A frosty French girl called Delphine Forest played the sexpot Aksinia. When I had to throw her into the snow and ravage her, she screamed, and when we kissed her face puckered up like a child taking its medicine. The other actors were brilliant Russians who were taught their English text phonetically by poor long-suffering Leila. They made little or no sense. Their accents seemed almost vaudevillian and pretty soon I was speaking the same incomprehensible patois. But nobody seemed to notice. It is virtually impossible to act in a foreign language, though the Russians got on with it. They needed to eat.

Sergei was on a rollercoaster. First communism had fallen, and then he discovered that his beloved Grigor was being played by a *goluboi*. His world had crashed. But he was philosophical. He was still working.

His wife and daughter were in the film, and he soldiered on with only the occasional blistering outburst, mostly directed at the women, thank God, but otherwise he was quite a laugh.

The Italian crew lived at the Intourist Hotel. The most beautiful hookers in the world were in Moscow that year, to be had for nothing, and some of the Italians had two or three under permanent contract. They rushed back to their harems after work, and were spent by the time they got to the studio in the morning. Being gay provided less opportunity. Gays were still criminals in Russia. If you dared to be one, you were a total outcast, and all the boys we saw in the coffee shop at the Bolshoi seemed to be shrieking pickpockets. It didn't look like much fun. There was the toilet at the Kremlin and the Centralna bathhouse, where midgets and amputees hovered in the steamy shadows brandishing birch twigs. I was taken there once by a Russian priest and given a severe whipping. Then Father handed me the twigs.

'Now you!' he said and bent over.

I was celibate for the whole year.

Gangs of Turks posing as queers hung out in the little park in front of the Bolshoi, as Bruno found to his cost one drunken night. Mid-embrace, his lover's friends leapt out from behind trees and stole all his clothes, leaving him in his underpants in minus ten degrees, jumping up and down while trying to hitch a ride home.

It was a tough city, but soon I was in love with it. The resilience of the people, physically and emotionally, made our whiny life feel desperately shallow. That sudden change between tears and laughter that eludes Western actors playing Chekhov was the secret of their charm. Life was a tragicomedy. You didn't know whether to laugh or cry when the rouble began its terrible skydive. When we arrived there were thirty to the dollar; by the time we left there were three hundred. The people met this challenge with a proud stoicism and dignity, even when it came to selling their bodies to the Italian crew. They were used to suffering. Babushkas sat on freezing street corners selling everything they had. Every car was a taxi, and you paid what you wanted. The only food for sale was for dollars. In the Russian shops the shelves were empty. In the hard-currency supermarkets, where you met the smoothies from the diplomatic corps with laden trolleys, everything was available, but a loaf of bread cost a month's wages.

At weekends I took Mo for walks in Gorky Park and we became wrapped up in the drama of the changing seasons. The summer ended and the trees turned red and gold. The first gusts of winter, blowing at Moscow from the southern steppe, stripped everything bare. Mo chased whirlpools of leaves. One day the white pregnant sky suddenly turned into snow. As the winter set in, holes were made in the ice on the ponds, and nude men and women stood around chatting in minus twenty degrees before jumping into the freezing water, still chatting, their talking heads sticking out of the snow. One man managed to do this and sustain a massive erection.

My Russian entourage included a new interpreter, Tania Bubenkova, a beautiful blonde who was endlessly shocked by us. She lived in a tiny room with her daughter on the outskirts of the city, and she loved America. We nicknamed her Malibuvitch. I had a chauffeur called Valodir (soon to be known as Car-Valodir), and my own Cossack, also called Valodir (or Horse-Valodir), who had been in the circus. He was incredibly strong and sexy, and taught me how to jump on a horse like a Cossack, which was very difficult, though it became much easier when I secretly hid a mini-trampoline under some leaves next to my horse.

There were two long-haired boys in the crew, Igor and Ilya. Igor was a beauty, and he knew it; Ilya, on the other hand, looked like a hag stirring a cauldron. They were best friends and lived in an amazing squat with several other kids in an abandoned nuclear fallout shelter, with a coffee table made out of an old bronze of Stalin's head. They knew where to get grass, or *anacha*, and we used to sit in the maze of bridges high up over the stage, smoking and watching the Italian-Russian battle for supremacy below.

I was definitely on the Russian side, although I adored some of the Italians. The producers paid the Russians next to nothing and gave them different food from us. ('They prefer it,' they said.) As the rouble tumbled, the Italians made no effort to help the floundering crew. Soon, giggly on *anacha* and blurry on the endless swigs of vodka proffered by my friends on the Russian crew, I turned into the tipsy Vanessa Redgrave of the set and led the crew on a disastrous strike.

When the snow began to fall Moscow was an enchanted place. The river froze. The Kremlin looked like an iced cake and the snow fluttered silently past our windows day and night. As we filmed the winter scenes of the First World War, there was a strange silence in the snow, but it made you feel sick and drowsy.

One morning at about 3 a.m. the telephone rang. It was the Richardson family calling from LA to say that Tony had died. I spoke to everyone: Natasha, Joely, Katherine, Grizelda, Vanessa, and Robert. They were having a party and were exuberant and grief-stricken at the same time. I put the phone down and Mo came in. Tony used to call him Movies. 'Come here, Movies,' I said and we sat watching the snow fall outside the window.

It was deep winter by the time we arrived on location in Vioshky, a village in the middle of the steppe, on the banks of the River Don. Rows of coloured doll's houses with thick white icing lined the street. Their twinkly lights splashed the snow gold, through delicate window frames that looked as if they were made from paper doilies. There were no cars, just carts and horses, and the odd motorbike with a sidecar.

Dina, our new landlady, welcomed us into her cottage. She was a large lady with conical breasts, similar in build to the dangerous-looking boiler next to the kitchen table that shuddered into gear every fifteen minutes and smelt of paraffin. The hut was like a sauna. The bathroom was in a kind of potting shed. The hot water steamed majestically from the tap but the water in the loo was frozen solid. There was no noise. The dogs were too cold to bark. Snow fluttered endlessly past the windows. Later on, when the winter gales swept across the steppe, the whole house groaned.

Tradition compelled Dina to hold a wake every month for her recently dead mother. So every fourth Saturday I arrived back from work – by now I never removed my costume – to find a little group of tiny drunk babushkas sitting in the house. These ladies, peasants in the old tradition, were twisted by osteoporosis. Some had nails for teeth. Their knuckles and fingers were tree stumps. (No one over fifty in Vioshky could walk upright.) One night three ladies were so drunk they couldn't move. Dina tried to pull them up, but they swatted her off, and finally she shrugged her shoulders and left. A cloud of vodka and condensed breath hung over these shelled reptiles, passed out in a row on the sofa, and we all went to bed. In the morning they were gone.

The Russian crew lived aboard a rusty old destroyer that sat lopsided in a backwater off the River Don. It was a strange place inhabited by ex-cons and bearded ladies. If ever there was an end of the line, this was it. It was far away from town, hidden by trees, and all the cabins leant to one side. You felt drunk just being there. Our crew held tremendous parties every Saturday night and I began to drink as heavily as they did. There seemed to be no alternative to their feverish, drunken exuberance. Some of them dropped cigarette ash into the vodka, and this drove one into a hellish dimension, where suddenly it seemed perfectly normal to chuck a table through a window and start punching everyone while one was dancing. A bloody nose felt like orgasm. The ex-cons and bearded ladies joined in, bathing in the sophistication of their glittering Muscovite guests.

When the spring of 1991 came, the crew commandeered an old ambulance and would pick us up on our day off to take us for picnics on the steppe. We lay under the blossoming apple trees and ate shashlik prepared by Mama Zoya from the art department. Sometimes one of the Russians would get so drunk that the others would have to tie him up and throw him into the back of the ambulance. On the drive home, Mama Zoya would give a masterclass in Chekhov, laughing and crying with the bumps in the road as she held onto her legs. She had a dislocated hip.

There was a Cossack restaurant out in the middle of nowhere. A band played and elaborate fights broke out. Chairs were crashed over heads. Hefty women pulled red-faced men from one another's throats while the rest of us went on dancing. I had my thirty-second birthday party there at the end of May. I danced with all the local ladies, and when, exhausted, I declined an invitation to foxtrot with one delightful matron, she smashed a plate over my head. Apparently it was a compliment. She felt she knew me well enough. I *was* Grigor to these people by now. They would come to Dina's hut to ask advice about problems they were having and expect me to solve them. On Easter Day there was literally a line around the block of men coming to pay their respects and ask advice.

If I was the adults' hero, then Bruno was the pin-up of the under-tens. He was neither boy nor man, and became their mascot. They waited for him outside the house on their bikes in the morning and followed him wherever he went. They provided him with valuable scoops about vegetables and meat once the spring arrived, and they would knock at the windows at 6 a.m. on a Saturday morning if there were tomatoes in the market, or come by in the afternoon if someone was killing their pig.

With spring the streets of Vioshky turned into tunnels of apple blossom. Horse-Valodir and I rode for miles, leaving early in the morning and coming home after dark. The steppe was endless. The only noise was the wind and the cries of birds high above. We explored ruined villages, uninhabited since the revolution.

In one such tumbledown place we found one of the biggest queens I have ever met. He called himself the cultural attaché. How he had learnt to be so camp was a mystery, because he had no apparent references. He lisped and shimmied and made Marilyn kiss poses, while Valodir shook his head in disbelief. Then he ran into his home and brought out half a pie as a present which we ate while he cavorted before us. When we left he walked alongside singing Cossack songs. After a while, without a word, he turned around and the singing disappeared into the wind.

Goodbye was goodbye. There was little chance that any of us would ever see each other again. In the final embraces on the windy steppe – I was leaving straight from work – it was as if a whole lifetime had passed, and we had grown old together. Our hair was matted with sand. We all had liverish rings around our bloodshot eyes. Italians and Russians were finally united by exhaustion. Bondarchuk pointed at a kestrel hovering high above in the sky, and Tania translated his final thoughts. It had been a bumpy ride. I fought him in public, and he had never really forgiven me. I was not Grigor and could never be. He forgave me for that. And he saw the affection between me and the Russian crew, between me and his daughter, and after all we were just two men standing together on the vast Russian steppe in a chaotic world. 'This kestrel will guide you home,' he said. 'Finally I have met an English gentleman. Very dangerous,' and he kissed me on both cheeks.

There had been five deaths and four weddings during the making of the film, and quite a few girls had become lesbians. The man who operated the wind machine, an old aeroplane propeller, was decapitated by it one morning outside Moscow. We watched his head fly across the sky and land in the snow, which turned crimson around it. The chief electrician from Rome had a heart attack outside the Intourist Hotel and died on the way to hospital. The drunken driver of our cherry picker, the large crane used to floodlight the night, had crashed into a young couple with their baby, and killed them all. Car-Valodir was run over after the film wrapped. Such was the price of a film that was never shown. The footage ended up in a bank vault in Naples, and many of us own a part of it since the producer, a Neapolitan builder, still owes us money. Tania came to the South of France for the summer, but I never saw anyone else ever again.

The experience killed Bondarchuk but it brought me back to life.

CHAPTER 34

Ready to Wear

A year or so later I was back in Paris.

Robert Altman was making *Prêt à Porter*, a comedy exposé about the world of fashion. I hustled a meeting with him in Paris and I explained that I'd been a model and there was no excuse for me not to be in the film, so that I would either have to give up acting or move to a different city if I didn't get a role.

He regarded me for a moment. 'I can see you're in quite a predicament,' he said. 'The problem is I already have too many actors. Let me think about this.' And he shuffled to another room, leaving me with Scotty, his browbeaten producer.

'I had no idea how pushy you were,' she said sweetly.

'Desperation!' I said.

Fortunately, I got a part playing the son of a fashion designer; Mummy was Anouk Aimée. 'You are very old to be my son,' she said testily when we met at the initial get-together. She turned to Sonia Rykiel, sitting next to her, as if I wasn't there. 'It's ridiculous, isn't it?' Sonia nodded sagely, like Dougal from *The Magic Roundabout*.

Everyone was in the movie: Sophia Loren, Marcello Mastroianni, Julia Roberts, Tim Robbins, Richard E. Grant, Lauren Bacall, Rossy de Palma and Kim Basinger. We were shooting the movie during

Fashion Week in Paris, at the actual shows, mingling with the real people we were portraying. Unfortunately for Bob, the venue for most of the shows had just been moved to the extremely ugly Carrousel du Louvre, a vast underground concrete complex underneath the Palace.

As the film crystallised it had all the ingredients for disaster. First of all, unbeknown to us all, Bob was recovering from heart surgery. Added to this, he chose Sonia Rykiel to be his oracle. They had met sometime before, at one of her shows; Bob had been enchanted by it all, the sexiness, the absurd posturing, and the seed of a movie was planted in his mind. Fifteen years later, he thought to look no further than poor Sonia to guide him through a world that had become much more complicated in the interim, and that she was no longer in the thick of. This is not a criticism of Sonia as a designer; Yves Saint Laurent would have been an equally disastrous choice, if Bob had wanted a real insight into just what the fashion world had become.

His next fatal mistake was to use his son to design the film. He simply wasn't capable and, since the story was largely about style, the fact that the final product had the look of a Jackie Collins miniseries was the petard by which Bob was eventually hoisted.

Inside the exotic squawking jungle of fashion, a thick silence fell as Bob entered the forest with his camera. Anna Wintour stared icily from her front-row perch, her enormous black glasses reflecting Bob's tungsten like the blind eyes of some underground rodent in a nature documentary. André Léon Talley sat in a high branch chattering, 'It's new, it's fresh, it's evocative, it's clean, it's Lagerfeld,' before staring open-mouthed into the camera. These were the people Bob should have pursued. Anna held the magic wand that controlled the destinies of all the players who strutted and fretted their fifteen minutes upon the stage, and Sonia Rykiel wasn't one of them. Suzy Menkes watched Tracey Ullman pretending to be her, like a clever fish unfooled by a garish piece of bait. She went on typing as usual. On the lower rungs of the evolutionary ladder, buyers and stylists chattered like monkeys screeching and throwing bananas.

The fashion press clenched, and the designers shrank, leaving only the supermodels, always open for business, to shimmy back and forth on jungle twine from fitting to show to after-party, repeating their impromptu entrances with unusual bonhomie if they had swung too fast in front of Bob's camera.

And then the actors . . . What a funny bunch we were. We each had little tents backstage, like stalls in some trade fair, and we sat there in our costumes waiting to be called onto the set. Groups sat around chatting. Once Kim Basinger was telling a story to a few of us sitting at her feet. Richard E. Grant interrupted. She held a hand out like a traffic cop. 'I'm talking,' she said, and went on. I could see righteous indignation bubbling up under Richard's heavily powdered face, but he got his own back on camera, when Kim, who played a Southern fashion journalist, was interviewing him. In two-foot heels and a wide-brimmed hat made for him by Vivienne Westwood he was on a roll, in one of his funniest performances. When Kim asked him a question, he put out his hand. 'I'm talking,' he said and looked at her with a twinkle.

We never knew when the camera was going to be upon us. We all worked hard preparing improvisations, huddling in groups, writing notes, rehearsing little asides. (I recently found a scrap of paper covered with mad spidery ideas and the following bits of dialogue: 'Bitch. You copied my collection.' 'You're being paranoid. I never copy. Everyone knows that!' 'Hell-oo! Roman sandals! I did Roman sandals for spring couture!' 'Those sandals came from the fall collection *two years ago*. Look in the archives.')

Danny Aiello had a different idea of improvisation. He simply ran through the A to Z of reaction as soon as the camera came near him. One time he would laugh hysterically. (Me: 'Interesting what he's done with hemlines this season, non?' Danny: 'Hahaha-hahahahahahahahahahahaha.') The next time he would be snoring and wake with a jolt. He was very good at all these states but it was deeply frustrating for the actors who had to play alongside him. The only people he had time for were Sophia and Marcello. He would sit in their tent acting Italian, talking about pasta, reminiscing about places he had been in his childhood, as they listened politely.

I pointed this out to Betty Bacall and she fixed me with those piercing blue eyes. 'You are the wickedest woman in Paris,' she replied.

One day we were shooting a scene in a huge long room. The whole cast were at one end, enjoying some fashion show after-party, when Sophia arrived at the other end, saw Marcello for the first time in twenty years and fainted. 'When she faints,' said Bob as we set up the shot, 'I want you all to run down to that end of the room and surround her. Remember, she is a *very* important woman.'

As we stood around waiting for action, Richard E. Grant, Tracey Ullman and I made a bet that Danny would arrive first at Sophia's side. Bob shouted 'Action!' and we all rushed towards Sophia, like some mad end-of-term egg and spoon race. She collapsed gracefully on the floor and we all crowded around her. Danny Aiello barged through the group, shouting, 'Let me through. Let me through. I'm a doctor.'

This was a new one. I nudged Betty, and Richard began to laugh.

'Stand back. Let me give her mouth to mouth,' said the ingenious Danny, effectively removing us all from the scene.

'You want to kill her?' I asked politely.

'Cut!' shouted Bob. 'Fantastic!'

We all began the long walk back to first positions, giggling like schoolgirls, when Danny lumbered up to me. 'You gonna say that?' he asked, threateningly.

'Yes, Danny. I thought it was rather funny, didn't you?'

He stopped me roughly. 'No, I don't think it's fucking funny,' he said, like an Italian cop in a cheap movie. All eyes were upon us. An electric silence fell as assistants got ready to pull us apart. Bob was watching from the other end of the room, thrilled. This was the meat and gravy to him.

'Listen, Danny, I'm sick of your Italian macho act,' I said, showing off wildly. I'd never had such a captive A-list audience.

'I'm not Italian!' he screamed. 'I'm Jewish! Is that a problem for you?'

'It's not a problem for me, but do Sophia and Marcello know?'

He looked like he might head-butt me. He was fiercely intercepted by Betty Bacall. 'Go away, you bully,' she commanded, coming between us.

'Fucking liberals!' screamed Danny. 'I'm sick of all you fucking liberals!'

Altman is a brilliant filmmaker. He sets up a scene in the most exciting way for the actors. Three or four different conversations take place at the same time. Bob shoots on long lenses from all four corners of the room and the effect can be dazzling. Actors adore working for him, because he keeps us on our toes. We don't have time to take a nap, because we are constantly plotting what we can do in the back of the scene to steal the focus. Being 'in character' at a Paris fashion party where half my real-life friends were gathered was the most fun I have ever had at work. Acting merged with reality. Sadly, *Prêt-à-Porter* just misses being a great film. Bob was the perfect man for the job, but the whole circus just got bigger and bigger, and he ended up being swept away.

I was sitting on a staircase during a break, feeling tortured and needy, when Bob walked past me, looking like the Kentucky Fried Chicken man. 'How are you doing, Rupert?'

'I feel terrible, Bob.'

'Me too,' he said, and ran off before I could go on.

I sold my house in the South of France and moved into an apartment near the Place de Clichy in Paris. *Prêt-à-Porter* came out, and I became the face of Yves Saint Laurent's Opium for Men. I saw myself pass by on buses, in the metro, and in South American airports. All those years after Saint Laurent danced with Nureyev at the Club Sept, I was finally by his side for a moment, surrounded by paparazzi, holding his hand as I was introduced by aides as his latest face. By then, Saint Laurent's love of Proust had turned him into one of that tome's characters. Vacant and disorientated, with a faraway smile and thick glasses, he could have been one of those duchesses kept alive by paraffin injections at one of Madame Verdurin's afternoons. Soon he would sell his name, and be just a body, a vague hologram wandering around the souk of Tangier, where all men who lose their names end up.

Once best friends with Karl Lagerfeld, the two men mysteriously fell out. (The faces of the inner circle still become rigid upon enquiry as to the reason why.) Karl lived in a palace in St Germain, chubby and alone, mourning the loss of his one great love, Jacques de Bascher, from beneath the mink coverlets of his tiny Empire sleigh bed. Jacques' precious body, never once possessed by Karl, but possibly by Yves, was now the unlikely bedfellow of the Carnation Queen herself, Karl's mother. Side by side they lie in the stone vault beneath the family chapel in the Loire waiting for the day that Karl squeezes in between them. (He is so thin now, he will probably be able to slip through the cracks!)

Claude Montana was equally isolated, avoided by all his old friends.

Only his sister Jacqueline remained loyal. Sometimes I would see them dining together outside the Restaurant Voltaire. Claude had physically shrunk in the aftermath of the scandal concerning his wife's death. Wallis, his muse and model, best friend and wife, was found one morning crumpled like a rag doll in the courtyard beneath their apartment. How did she fall? This was the question that no one dared ask. Now, caked in foundation – a colour not used since the silent movies – his hair frozen into a majestic translucent wave, humour still in his eyes, he too was a shuffling relic from *la grande époque*.

George the lawyer was hit over the head in New York and developed Parkinson's. He sat in a chair and stared out the window of the apartment where he had lived since the war, looking at the Eiffel Tower and the grey rooftops from which, in the last moments before his mind froze, he had tried to jump.

I had affairs with a volleyball player, an actor and a hooker. My best friend was an English boy called Jerry Stafford, who lived near by and together we went to the tea dance at the Palace on Sundays. Alone I prowled like the Baron de Charlus through the necklace of dark rooms and dungeons that hung around the graceful centre of Paris. Everyone who was anyone seemed to be there, hiding in the shadows.

The lady who ran Saint Laurent, Ariel, looked after me like a prince. I was clothed in crushed velvet, fed at high tables and paid a good deal of money. Jean-Baptiste Mondino took the pictures for the Opium ads; unfortunately during the second campaign he photographed me on an upholstered leather sofa with chalk-white make-up, and the picture looked like a zombie emerging from an open coffin. I lost the job. But until then, I went all over the world with Ariel for four years, and we became close friends. Living in Paris and working for Saint Laurent opened doors that had previously remained closed.

In the January of 1996, ten years after moving to France, and two years after moving from St Tropez to Paris, I got my second job in French, playing Algernon in *The Importance of Being Earnest* at the Palais de Chaillot, France's National Theatre. The play was an enormous success. My picture by Pierre et Gilles was on all the Morris columns. (Morris columns are wide round green pillars with posters on them for plays and films, made famous by Proust.)

It had snowed that Christmas, and on New Year's Eve, Lychee went to the Bois as usual. She never returned. A few days later her distraught mother and I went to the police and for one month we waited for news. Mo and I walked through the snow to the theatre every night in a strange dream. It is a weird feeling, waiting for someone to show up. You become a sort of ghost yourself. Life goes on, but every corner reminds you of their absence, and there is a constant flutter in your stomach.

As we reached the theatre, Mo would gallop ahead down the five flights of stairs to visit various friends around the enormous underground maze. There was a whole world inside that theatre, and we both loved it. The applause washed over me every night, and as I bowed I could feel the dark mass of the Bois near by. Somewhere inside lay Lychee under a snowy blanket. But each day brought no news. Paris never looked more beautiful. A clairvoyant said that Lychee was being held hostage, and someone else said they had seen her in Marrakesh. She was a thread that wove through many different lives, and all sorts of people called to ask for news. It was Pacrète, another lady of the night, who finally told me that the old hookers in the Bois had seen her being bundled into a car by two men in the dead of night on New Year's Eve. Finally her body was found in a ditch inside the walls of the great park of Versailles, naked but for her white fur coat. Sophie and I went to identify the body. A weird man with a ponytail pulled her out of a drawer. She was frozen and her head was cracked like a nut.

Lychee is buried in the same row as Oscar Wilde in the cemetery of Père Lachaise. Buddhist nuns sang chants at the funeral while her poor mother screamed silently. Her friends stood around in the freezing February morning, and then we all went to a bar outside the walls of the cemetery. Nightclub recluses, opium addicts, society sex maniacs and me. It was the last time we would ever see each other. Lychee had been our point of contact. Now that she was gone, there was nothing much to say and we drifted from the bar like seedheads blown from a dandelion.

CHAPTER 35

Miami

On my way to the press junket for *Prêt-à-Porter* in New York I decided to take a holiday in Miami. People had been raving about South Beach for at least a couple of years. As far as I could tell from their rather exaggerated descriptions it was just a place where old Jews competed for deckchairs with drag queens. I was determined to hate the place. But several hours into the flight I woke to find myself flying over the Caribbean towards Miami. The sea was a deep blue, iced with little waves. Soon it became shallow and pale. Scrubby flat islands barely rose out of it. Waves broke on reefs like lace on a glass table and between us and all this was a pale blue sky tinged with pink as a big red sun went down behind thousands of cotton wool clouds, round and puffy, stretching into the far distance. Suddenly America at dusk was upon us, flat and endless. First the beach where people as big as dots played in the surf, and then mainland Miami spread out in a giant urban sprawl, grid after grid, before finally giving way to the vast swamps of Florida over which we circled. As we touched down, lights were already twinkling in the vast suburb and the clouds turned into long dark fingers on a white sky.

Miami International has always been one of my favourite airports. I first came across it as a teenager on those faraway trips to John Jermyn's boat or to the Harris house on Paradise Island. It was the first port of call before catching the Shanks seaplane to Nassau Harbour. As the doors of the plane open the wet scented Florida air rushes into the cabin. It smells of sun cream, air-conditioning and tropical drinks. A light glow breaks out on the brows of the passengers like a golden shower from heaven, an instant feeling of health, and that glorious bucket and spade anticipation of a seaside holiday. Inside the terminal, the smell of damp carpet is the eau de toilette that will follow you around Florida. Rivers of delicious-smelling green fitted carpet guide the traveller past gates to destinations that have only been dreamt of or read about in the pages of Graham Greene and Ian Fleming. Port-au-Prince. Port-of-Spain. Caracas. Montevideo. São Paolo. Miami International is a traveller's sweet shop and seeing the names of all these places made my heart miss a beat. I wanted to know them all.

The first brush with exiled Cuba is at the airport. They have their fingers in every pie and the best ones (*empanadas*) are sold in La Carretta, my favourite airport restaurant. There you will notice that even if you are first, while there is a Cuban standing in the line, you will not be served. The unaccustomed traveller can taste racism and an authentic *café con leche* in the same gulp, and should get used to both. You will always be a gringo in Miami. Little did I know that I would be playing some of the most dramatic scenes of my career at its counter.

I had booked my flight a day early by mistake, and my hotel was full, so I decided to stay for one night in the airport hotel, located right in the middle of the terminal. It is one of the seediest places I have ever been, but nevertheless possessed a special glamour of its own. I got into a shiny stainless-steel elevator from the departure lounge. A pair of Gideons were lurking politely by the door.

'Are you ready for some good news?' one of them said.

'Not really,' I replied and the doors closed.

Upstairs on the twentieth floor was a barely lit restaurant with a panoramic view of the airport. South American cut-throats huddled around tables. The Gideons arrived and joined a hearty group of Bible black belts. They pointed at me, whispered and the whole group fell about laughing. Planes roared through the sky in the background, their tail lights blinking. The effect was magical, lonely and very American. After a 'gourmet buffet' I wandered around the airport like a lost soul in purgatory. At one gate was a line for a midnight flight to Asunción. At another people flooded in from Fort Worth. There were shrieks of reunion and waves of regret as travellers crashed in on the tide and were sucked out on the undertow. I spent a sleepless night on a foam mattress as a couple bonked in the room next door, but after a delicious break- fast at La Carretta I left for the beach in a clunking old taxi with red velvet interiors.

The Raleigh Hotel was located on Collins Avenue and 17th Street. It stood in a row of run-down Art Deco towers on a buckled road. It was a sleazy neighbourhood of fleapits and rest homes, and on the porches of these peeling establishments with their romantic but misleading names – Surfcomber, The South Seas, Coral Reef – were rows of metal chairs upon which the old people sat listlessly watching the traffic bump along Collins. Nothing had changed on South Beach for years. You only went there to die. It was cheap, very Jewish and the weather was good. But things were changing.

Fashion had arrived in the mid-eighties, attracted by the light, the beach and the crumbling Art Deco painted in garish colours, and soon there was a restaurant – the Strand – and a couple of hotels. Queens with Aids began to migrate south. President Reagan had not so much as mentioned the word Aids during his eight-year presidency and the queen had become a pariah. You gathered up your children in your arms when one went past. They cashed in their life insurances and came to Miami to die; if not with dignity, at least with a tan. And so they began to trickle in, and with them came an entourage of club freaks and drag queens that were sick of New York and entranced by the dan- gerous Cubans recently released from Fidel's prisons who roamed the streets south of 5th. They were gorgeous Latino panthers, a far cry from the bejewelled bitches that sashay through Lincoln Road today. You didn't know whether they were going to fuck you or shoot you, and so by the beginning of the nineties a scene had been born that was to transform the beach in fifteen tiny years from a clapped-out dinosaurs' graveyard into the physical manifestation of the whole grab-it world of Baby Doc Bush's America.

For the time being I was well hooked up at the Raleigh. My friend Robert Forrest, Joyce to his intimate circle, had made my reservation, and so I was met on arrival by the owner Kenny Zirilli and his silver-haired lieutenant Jay Coyle. They were an incongruous pair. Kenny looked like a homeless person. His skin was dark and parched as though he had been sleeping rough for a couple of years. His eyes were possessed, two glowing coals sunk into a gaunt face. He shuffled around, speaking in a voice that was barely understandable, and rather sweetly offered me a line of coke as I was checking in. So this was how they did things in Miami. I was surprised but the bumptious receptionist just rolled his eyes and said, 'Kenny!' Jay stepped forward and smoothed things over, laughing like an old drunken sailor, and with impeccable manners diverted Kenny's attention while I was taken up to my room.

Jay met me in the foyer later. 'Don't worry about Kenny,' he said. 'He's quite crazy.'

The garden at the Raleigh was beautiful, and Jay doubled as head gardener. It was dominated by a large ornate pool shaped like a barrel with a waterfall at one end, and surrounded by palm trees with branches like fans. The tips of their fronds were burnt by the salty wind and they rustled seductively. At the end of the pool was a round custard-coloured pool bar that could have been a set for the musical *Anything Goes*. Inside it stood a lazy Latin boy leafing through a magazine and chatting idly to an old crustacean perched on a stool. Unbeknown to me, I was going to spend the next eight years with this character. (The boy, not the crustacean.) Meanwhile, Jay and I walked over the dunes and onto the beach. It was dusk and the moon was rising over the sea. Large cargo ships with pretty lights moved across the horizon, like spaceships circling a planet. The wide beach stretched as far as the eye could see in both directions. People jogged and biked along it. Kites flew in the air. Dogs careered towards the ocean. Ugly weather-beaten condominiums stood in blank rows facing the beach just like the post-cards. It was the last stand of a crumbling old America that we Europeans adored.

I fell in love with the Raleigh, its intrigues and eccentrics. It was hopelessly disorganised and the staff were completely anarchic, but it was a strangely classless place and the room-service waiter who brought you a snack before your disco nap could easily be meeting you later in Twist (bar), to take you to Warsaw (club). But then Kenny was no ordinary boss. They were constantly hiding the strongbox with the petty cash from his midnight raids, and were always trying to cajole him away from the foyer where he liked to lie on the red leather couch in a pair of shorts and provide a hysterical running commentary on all his guests.

These were the days when all the movie stars and fashion models stayed at the Raleigh. They had to. There was almost nowhere else. They could be found complaining at all hours to the albino queen with the great ass on reception. She didn't much care, and nodded sympathetically before getting back on the phone to organise her night. When bills arrived all hell could break loose, but the Raleigh was full of glamour. Mickey Rourke lived in the penthouse with a pair of chihuahuas. Anna Nicole Smith paraded naked through the foyer. She had a Finnish boyfriend, a model called Bieren. They fought all the time, and when she finally dumped him she wrote, 'Fuck you Bieren,' in lipstick on the mirror of their room before leaving for the airport. A girl called Suzy took it down and kept it. Kate Moss and Johnny Depp were there in the prime of their affair, little identical budgies grooming each other on a high perch. I once came out of my room to find Klaus von Bülow stalking down the barely lit corridor. Even Anna Wintour made the mistake of coming one weekend. She looked puzzled on Friday and was furious by Sunday afternoon.

People came and went throughout the night. You might come back at four in the morning to find Kenny in his shorts making out with some unsavoury gangster in the foyer, while in the background Mickey Rourke sat at a table in the dining room surrounded by gangsters in a cloud of smoke. Kenny was a genius, the Miami version of Basil Fawlty. He was famous up and down the beach. On a recent trip to Cuba he had bought a big black Cadillac, and the second time I stayed there, I was checking in with the albino (Junior) as Kenny screeched to a halt in the Cadillac at the front of the hotel. He jumped out, ran through the lobby and disappeared into the men's toilet. Everyone froze for a polite moment, then went on with what they were doing. But ten seconds later, with a wailing of police sirens and a flashing of lights, three armed cops ran into the building and followed Kenny into the loo.

The manager, a flat-footed queen named Mario, poked her head through the door from the office like a headmistress. 'What is all this ruckus?' she asked sternly.

'Kenny's gone to the bathroom with three cops,' said Junior flatly.

'Three?' said Mario, before turning to me. 'Oh hello, dear. Good trip?'

There was no time to reply because now Kenny was being dragged from the bathroom by the three cops with his trousers around his ankles. He was kicking and screaming but still found time to play host for a moment. 'Hi, Rupert. Everything okay? Anything you need, just let me know.'

Kenny had a resident Cuban decorator called Albert, a small middle-aged queen with a little tummy and a mischievous face. He had black hair and black-framed glasses but was otherwise swathed in white linen. He would scour the vast second-hand warehouses that abounded in Miami, through all the stained couches upon which the ancient had recently croaked, and find cheap furniture for the hotel that he could sell to Kenny at inflated prices. He was the type of plotting maniacal queen that could only have come from Cuba. Mercifully, they don't make them like Albert any more. He ripped off everyone, but was hysterically funny and, as he remarked himself, he occasionally 'came through'. Over the years he became one of my best friends, and it was through him that I finally got a grasp on Cuba.

His family, the Rosells, left Havana in a hurry in 1959. According to legend, there was an old bell-rope with an ornate handle in the hallway of the house that the little Albert snatched as he was being spirited away. Now it sat on a table by his bed, the only thing left from a life of excess in Batista's dictatorship. You could never be entirely sure if Albert, or any Cuban, for that matter, was telling the truth. The Cubans in exile have turned the past into a colourful mirage. To start with, even a Cuban taxi driver owned a sugar plantation, according to them. I remember early on in my Miami experience some queen who wore monogrammed velvet slippers told me he came from a noble background. Finding him frankly rather common, I later asked Albert whether this was true. He shrieked, 'It means there was a doctor in the family. Maybe.'

Albert was the apple of his mother's eye. Her name was Sylvia and he milked her as regularly as a dairy cow. When I met him he lived in a white on white on white apartment on Collins Avenue. Over the years of endless evictions and scandals this apartment was identically reproduced in a variety of different locales, so that walking around South

Beach today, it is almost impossible to forget Albert because every-where you look, he lived. On weekends he conducted a sort of virtual open house, sitting on his white couch, doing 'bumps' of coke off a key, drinking neat vodka with ice, and going through his rolodex monitoring his world as they migrated through the night from bar to club to after hours. He rarely went out himself, but he received until such time as one of the parking attendants of his acquaintance arrived. Then the phones would be switched off and for twenty dollars Albert would get parked.

His would be the first phone call in the train wreck of a morning after. 'Girl, I heard you took a left turn with a negro from Santo Domingo.' And you had to smile as you looked in the tangle of sheets, for sure enough there seemed to be a gentleman of Dominican extrac-tion passed out on the other side of the bed. News travelled fast on South Beach.

The lazy Latin at the pool bar was called Martin, and pretty soon I had joined the old crustacean to sit through the humid afternoons, chatting about this and that and hearing all the gossip of the hotel. Martin had a funny turn of phrase, a curious vocabulary, and spoke in a kind of mumble that was impossible to understand at first. The crus-tacean and I listened entranced to improbable stories from Martin's early life and his eventual emigration to America. He was born on the banks of the River Plate in Juan La Casa, a village in Uruguay. He was an only child, raised in the worshipful clutches of two pairs of grand-parents and a mother. His father, Juan Daniel, left for the States when Martin was a small boy. According to Martin, his great-grandmother, a certain Frau Schenk, had arrived in Montevideo from Germany, smug-gled in a barrel.

'When exactly was this?' I carefully asked. The crustacean and I were thinking the same thing, but Martin couldn't remember. Instead he told us how his grandmother, Frau Schenk's daughter Yolanda, broke her jaw opening her mouth too wide one day while singing in the choir.

Martin and his mother came to Miami when he was thirteen and never returned. All the grandparents waved goodbye at the airport and they didn't see each other again for years. Little Martin went to school. His parents split up, and mother and son moved to a small studio next

to a pair of queers whom Martin spied upon through a crack between
the apartments. He scraped through school and made it into that bastion of further education, the University of Miami. I was fascinated to
learn about fraternities and what one had to go through to get into
one. Apparently you had to eat sachets of mustard, mayonnaise and
ketchup, before jumping off a high bridge into the bay. Then you got
a big brother, and after that a little brother.

'Next stop you're a mason,' I said.

'Yeah, or a waiter,' he replied gloomily. You never quite knew
whether Martin was being clever or not.

Something clicked in my head, and as I sat listening, or half listening (to another story about the grandmother whose toes were sliced off
in a moving elevator), an image began to develop like a photograph in
a dark room, grainy and undefined at first, but quickly gathering form
in the ghostly red light. It was of me and Martin together, and by the
time he was describing the grandmother putting her toes into an envelope and hobbling over to the doctor's in the vain hope that they could
be sewn on, it was there, in focus, a picture of us together that was so
real that, as far as I was concerned, there was no room for question.

The first hurdle was Martin's very good-looking boyfriend, Gonzalo.
One night the three of us went out in a group, which unfortunately
included Albert, to Salvation, a famous club on the beach. I made my
first unlikely move and started getting off with Gonzalo. We were all
hopelessly drunk, and for some reason I thought it was a genius plan.
Albert danced past me with a look of horror on his face. Later I heard
him talking on the phone from a stall in the men's bathroom. 'Girl,
she's blind as a bat. She pounced on the wrong one.'

Martin was furious, dragged Gonzalo into a corner, and didn't talk to
me for three days. Obviously it hadn't quite worked. Or had it? Because
now I noticed a wounded look in his eyes when I went down to the
pool.

I left, and it was coming up for Christmas by the time I came back.
Miami was a galaxy of fairy lights. On the drive from the airport entire
houses were swathed in flashing bulbs and blow-up Santas complete
with reindeer landing on the roof. A Christmas tree was a different
thing in a hot country. It glimmered with a new intensity and the tinsel
waved about in the tropical breeze. At the airport the check-in girls

wore sad lopsided red hats and snapped, 'Happy holidays,' as they took your tickets. It was no longer PC to say Christmas. You might be trampling on someone else's dreams. The Haitian taxi driver's radio was one long sales pitch that would have given Jesus a sacred heart attack had he come down from heaven over Christmas. But I was only coming from LA and my reindeer was my black dog Mo.

He was to be my secret weapon. Anyone who has a dog will tell you. They are brilliant cruising tools and Mo broke whatever ice there was between Martin and me. He liked Martin straightaway. Actually they had a lot in common, even though Martin was to nearly kill poor Mo later on (albeit by mistake). Mo's relationship with Kenny was more complicated. On his first day at the Raleigh he jumped into the pool as Kenny was shuffling by. 'Will someone get that fucking dog out of my pool!' Kenny screamed. But Mo wouldn't get out so Kenny barred him from the garden.

Gonzalo was away doing a modelling job and so one night Martin and I went out. Thankfully, this time Albert didn't come. The next morning as the sun rose over the sea, bleary-eyed, dehydrated and wasted, we collected Mo and took him out on the beach. We walked in silence. The water lapped encouragingly against the sand. Seagulls squealed. Mo looked at us expectantly. This was a crucial step. One false move, and it could all go wrong. Finally we got back to the hotel and Martin said, 'I've got to be at work in four hours.'

I replied, as though it had only just occurred to me: 'You might as well stay here then.' We sat looking at the rising sun for what seemed like an eternity as the question hung in the air.

Finally Martin said, 'Okay. I'll meet you up there in ten minutes.'

The next day I woke to hear the door quietly close. I stumbled from the bed to the window. It was a beautiful morning. Martin emerged below from the fire exit and walked with a spring – or was that projection? – over to the pool bar and started work. I got back into bed. Mo was looking at me solemnly. He sighed and rolled over with a huff.

CHAPTER 36

My Best Friend's Wedding

When my agent sent me the script for *My Best Friend's Wedding*, I thought I had finally arrived at the end of the road. Actors can leaf through a script faster than a gang of termites can get through a wall. All you have to do is keep an eye out for your name to come up in the first shuffle through. Then back to the top to get a little taste of the material. First few pages; last few pages; a spot check somewhere in the middle, and then your character's first entrance. How does the writer see him? George, a middle-aged gay man, sits at a table with a flute of champagne. Gag.

Well, maybe he has some sparkly dialogue. Negative. Three lines and then completely ignored as the star launches into a set piece with a pastry chef.

'Is this what it's come to, Carla?' I said to my agent that night on the phone from London.

'Honey, it's a great opportunity. This is a Julia Roberts movie. And P. J. Hogan is directing. It's a big studio picture.'

'But there's no part. He has three lines.'

'But you're great casting for it.'

'Why? Because I'm gay? Just being gay doesn't necessarily mean I should do this part. I've been the lead in some great films, Carla. I've never played a two-line part. It's the end of the road.'

'Just take the meeting.'

At the time, April 1996, I was playing an extraterrestrial disguised as a New Zealand journalist at the Hampstead Theatre Club in London. The play, *Some Sunny Day*, was by my friend Martin Sherman. It was an eccentric story about a household of misfits in Cairo during the Second World War when the Germans were about to take the city. It was a curious script that would have been better suited to film. The director, Roger Mitchell, asked Uri Geller to come and talk to us about spoon bending etc, because there was a scene in the play where I had to throw an extraterrestrial fit and all the spoons in the house bent and the clocks went backwards. Uri was a strange man, as thin as a rake, but very amenable. He bent spoons for us and totally cured my bad knee. We invited him to the first night, and after the show, which in my opinion was pretty cranky, he came backstage.

'I worked on all the critics during the interval,' he said. 'The reviews are going to be sensational.' And they were. One unbridled rave after another. Nobody could believe it.

At the end of the show, everybody has fled the city, leaving me on my own for a last moment on earth before returning to my planet. I bid a regretful goodbye to the follies of man as bombs explode and plaster falls from the ceiling. Then I hide behind a cupboard as a big green balloon, the real me, floats jerkily across the stage on wires in a ghostly follow spot and out through an open window. It was an underwhelming moment at the best of times, although once the balloon got caught on the windowsill and popped. 'Oh dear, Mummy!' piped a child's voice from the stalls. 'Now he'll never get back to his spaceship.'

Too right! I was miles away from home and just as luck would have it P. J. Hogan was in the audience that night. Afterwards, at dinner, he sat like a pinched nun on the other side of the table. He was one of those people who couldn't lie, but at the same time was too timid to reveal what he really thought. Clearly he had hated the play, but couldn't bring himself to say so. We did, on the other hand, talk fairly bluntly about the character of George in the film; and PJ said he was in the middle of rewriting it. Dinner ended, and we both called our agents in LA to say how boring we each thought the other was.

But the next morning he called and asked me to come and meet him for breakfast in his hotel. I went along, and he showed me a scene he had written during the night. It was the famous sequence where George sings 'Say a Little Prayer'. It was a brilliant piece of writing. Foolproof. No actor could fail. I became very enthusiastic.

But still PJ was reticent. He went back to LA. He couldn't decide and asked me to test. I did. Then he wanted me to test again and I said no. You can't persuade people in show business. They either see you or they don't. I have rarely got a film I tested for. There was silence for a week or so. Carla and my manager Marc did a magnificent job because it is one thing to persuade a reticent director to use your client, but quite another if you must persuade your reticent client that he wants to be used by the director at the same time.

Finally they got me the part. And for a little while I was De Niro to PJ's Scorsese.

The shoot of *My Best Friend's Wedding* was one of those enchanted times for me, where the prevailing winds were in my favour. They blew me along and everything fell into place around me. On a whim I decided to move to New York and found a pretty little house in the West Village. It was hidden down an alleyway in the gardens behind three streets. Leaving there one morning for Chicago, who should I see coming out of the next-door house but Joc McKenna from dressing room D at the Aldwych. We had not talked for over ten years. After being fired from the theatre he had become a pop singer and then a fashion stylist. One of his early shoots was with me for the *Tatler* magazine in 1985. The day began pleasantly enough but none of the clothes fitted and soon the two of us had a blazing row. The magazine published a picture of me with some snot on my nose. War was declared, and we hadn't spoken since. Seeing him now, I shrank back into my alleyway. I wasn't quite ready to make up. Now he was the world's most successful stylist, a different animal in a simple white shirt and black jeans from the child star dancing with his tin lunch box down the Aldwych twenty years before. As he disappeared around the corner, I made a dash for the car and left for the summer in the Windy City.

The heat was unbearable that summer of 1997. Downtown Chicago was a dramatic fortress of mirrored towers clustered together on the shore of Lake Michigan, appearing out of the haze of the lake like a modern Emerald City as the plane banked towards the airport. That vast expanse of water shimmered in the heat and millions of little silver fish lay dead on the shore. The crew (and me) stayed in the Marriott Residence Inn, a weird new kind of American hotel with absolutely *no* character. Complimentary coffee, creamer and sweetener were laid on a table in reception, and strangely shaped travellers lumbered past with paper cups full of this watery concoction to the elevator where we all looked jaundiced in the neon glare. The hotel was a stump in the forest of skyscrapers, constantly in shadow, but for odd splashes of light reflected by the mirrored towers. The street was airless. The tarmac was melting and smelt delicious. Every squeaking brake bounced dramatically off the walls of our glass canyon, an uncanny melody accompanied by the drone of a million air-conditioners and the hum of North Wacker Drive.

PJ was as good as his word and the part of George had grown into a scene-stealer on every page. On the first day we shot a scene in a taxi between Julia, Dermot Mulroney and myself, in which Julia pretended to Dermot that I was her fiancé. The next day the powers that be at Sony called PJ. They were ecstatic. It was clear that Julia and I had a strange on-screen chemistry. Just as in real life you click with someone for no apparent reason, similarly on screen sometimes a vivid relationship effortlessly materialises. It can't be bought, and there's no technique to get to it, but when it happens work becomes a party and already you are a better actor. Dialogue trips off the tongue. Eye contact is charged with a strange glitter. It feels so great not to be straining for once that you fall a little in love with that other person, and the film turns into a delightful mountain of virgin powder snow across which the two of you slalom, looking beautiful and radiant, and everything feels like the first time.

Julia was beautiful and tinged with madness, that obligatory ingredient for a legendary star. Most of the time she was a calm, practical earth mother, curled up on a director's chair in a Marilyn cardigan with her knitting needles and a bag of wool. But sometimes she would rear up like an untamed filly, with flared nostrils and rolling eyes, at some invisible lasso. She had a vein on her forehead that occasionally stood out. That was a sign not to make any fast moves. She could buck you, or kick out. She would have been perfect as Nicole Diver in *Tender is the Night,* that funny, beautiful, capable thoroughbred, suddenly prone to screaming breakdowns in the bathroom.

Sometimes on a Friday night at the end of work, she would give me a ride back to New York on the Sony jet. Then I witnessed the whole machine grind into action, the grandeur of Hollywood in transporting its livestock from A to B. With a cocktail in a cut glass, wearing a towelling robe, she would hop barefoot with wet hair from the trailer to the car. The only baggage was the key to her apartment and her newly acquired gay confidant. Chatting intensely on subjects that a girl could only discuss with a man who was not nursing a hidden erection, we huddled in the back of the limo and sipped our drinks as we sped through the suburbs towards the private airport. Gates opened as if by magic and we drove towards a huge jet in the middle of an empty airfield. A carpet stretched across that brief yard of the real world; she tiptoed across it and jumped on board. The doors were shut and the jet moved simultaneously. We sat on the large double bed with drinks and delicious snacks served by sympathetic girls in uniform, and time flew. America passed by. It seemed impossibly far away now. We lay back for touchdown. Standing by the open door of another car was a bodyguard with a large bouquet of flowers in his arms. Before getting out at her place, she put on a pair of grandmother's slippers to bridge the only gap that Hollywood could not control – the sidewalk between the car and her front door. A star never really had to touch the ground.

The Mistresses of the Universe often end up with their trainers, and Julia was going out with hers, a man called Patrick. I was fascinated by these powerful women. Instead of being the escorts of presidents, they ended up marrying their hairdressers. They were the fairy princesses trapped inside ivory towers. They only met co-stars and staff.

Like Madonna, Julia smelt vaguely of sweat, which I thought was very sexy. There is a male quality to the female superstar. There has to be. If a girl is going to survive in Hollywood on that journey from the broken eggshell to the sea, she must develop special 'people skills'. Flocks of executive seagulls will try to take her and drop her onto the rocks. The casting couch is *not* the solution for a young hopeful. She must learn to fuck them before they fuck her if she is to survive, so she becomes a kind of she-man, a beautiful woman with invisible balls. In her personal relationships, after sex with a man, she quite possibly fights the desire to eat him. For him, all of the hims, the smell of a superstar is a strange and powerful reminder, attractive and terrifying, of who is wearing the trousers. It marks him as her territory.

And this film was her territory. But there was another embryonic super-star taking her first tentative steps across the beach to the sea. Cameron Diaz was the antithesis of Julia. She was gangly and exuberant, a tomboy with gazelle's legs, and good in high heels, which Julia wasn't. She loved greasy burgers, didn't care that they made her spotty, and she wiped her hands on her jeans after she ate. She went out with Matt Dillon.

'Why can't Cameron relax around me?' asked Julia one day. Actually Julia couldn't relax around Cameron. It requires a strong nerve for a superstar to take a part where she loses the guy to a younger girl. It meant that Julia was no longer an ingénue. Already she was listed as Hollywood's thirty-third most powerful person. She had survived the crash of *Mary Reilly*. *My Best Friend's Wedding* was her comeback film. Suddenly here was this gorgeous kitten whom everybody loved, who talked about 'window treatments' instead of curtains, so natural as to seem unnatural. It must have been unnerving.

Cameron came of age before our very eyes. From the brilliant scene in the karaoke bar to the confrontation in a station toilet, she staked a claim for Julia's crown. She might not have known she was doing it, but Julia did.

But nothing matters when the job is well done. If the girls didn't hit it off, so what? The scenes between them were charged with the dan-gerous energy that money can't buy, when art flirts with life. Julia was never better. She couldn't afford to be anything else. She put everything into her performance, and in my opinion it was a yardstick for roman-tic comedy that no one has surpassed. Her perfect timing and flawless beauty were offset by a vulnerability that was really touching and turned the film into something deeper than the usual tinny sitcoms served up by the studios.

Martin left Miami and moved into my house in the West Village, and that summer was the best time of the sketchy years we spent together. Life was all coloured lights. Drunk on success, in love with everything, on weekends with Martin and Mo I discovered New York. It was unrecognisable as the city I had known before. Now it was safe, corpo-rate and middle class. The danger had evaporated. Your heart no longer lived in your mouth and 'Native New Yorker' was no longer the song.

Now it was Junior Vasquez and the DJ culture. A world of remixes and remakes. Trashy old TV series were suddenly art and movie stars had turned their wily eyes to advertising. The only hookers left on 42nd Street were Minnie and Mickey Mouse.

But I loved it more than before.

On Sunday night the car would arrive, I would jump in and the reverse journey would take me back to Julia's front door and on to the Marriott Residence Inn, dropping her off at the Four Seasons on the way.

Sometimes I went for dinner with PJ and Cameron, or Dermot and his wife Catherine, but otherwise it was also quite a lonely summer. I hardly worked but I had to stay in Chicago in case it rained, when one of my new scenes would be squeezed into the schedule. So I sat around the Marriott Residence Inn, watching the comings and goings and dreaming of my meteoric rise to stardom during the long blistering afternoons. There was only one problem. My character ducked out halfway through the movie. I had to find a way to muscle in on the end.

In a bittersweet finale Julia loses Dermot to Cameron and in the first cut of the film she finishes up dancing at the wedding party with a blobby frat boy and the movie ends. But when the studio looked at the 'scores' from the test screenings, the results were unanimous. Middle America wanted their sweetheart to end up with 'the gay guy'. Why? Because he was funny.

PJ wrote a new ending and we shot it on the Sony lot at Easter the following year. My prayers had been answered. George was all set to score.

There is nothing like the head-trip when Hollywood's giant eye turns its attention on you. When the movie hit $100 million at the box office I was summoned to meet the heads of all the studios on a kind of *Evita* victory tour. Being a complete slut, I loved these meetings. Walking through the hive of offices to the queen bee's headquarters was an intoxicating catwalk, bathed in the surreptitious glances of interns and assistants, flanked by agent and manager, and greeted at the end by glossy powerful men in starched white shirts and ties. Sitting down in an office, graciously accepting coffee and compliments, while being sized up, measured and compared, was enormous fun. I had two ideas. I wanted to make a gay James Bond story, and a comedy with Julia about a pair of superstars who were married but he was gay. I sold them both.

CHAPTER 37

Sea Crest Apartments

Just after the 1997 shoot of *My Best Friend's Wedding*, Albert found me an apartment in a crumbling old building on Ocean Drive and 2nd Street called Sea Crest. It was just one room, with a tiny bathroom, but it was right on the water. A crippled palm tree grew sideways in the garden. Next to it lay an old catamaran half submerged in the sand and a path led through the dunes onto the beach. My neighbour was a German chef called Michael, and above lived a boy who played a piano late at night. The previous tenant had died in my apartment, from Aids, and people would come by and suddenly go white. 'Oh my God,' they'd say. 'This is where John Jacobus lived.'

There was a strange trace of him about the place, and over the years I felt I came to know him through a collage of gossip and legend. In his heyday he had owned the famous Torpedo Club, but he had a date with the grim reaper and first his puggish face and exceptional body were splattered, as if by a paintbrush, with small black dots: Kaposi's sarcoma. More and more they clung to him like barnacles on the bottom of a boat, so that by the time he died he was so disfigured that the Latinos who hung around the bodega on Collins called him the Elephant Man. The apartment had been his travelling companion, witness to his terrible loneliness and fear on the road to death, and there was definitely a strange atmosphere there. Mo felt it, and sometimes in the night I would wake and see him looking intently in the air, his eyes a liquid black, ears slightly raised and his shiny nose flexing in silent dialogue.

For all that, it was an enchanted place. Lying in bed with the windows open, between Martin and Mo, were some of the happiest times of my life. It was like being on a raft on the high seas. The breeze swept through the apartment, sometimes wailing, sometimes just flapping the blinds, carrying on it the crash of the waves, the benediction of John Jacobus, and all the mystery of death and love.

There was one other dog at Sea Crest, a Doberman called Midnight who was very ancient and could hardly walk. Her owner Cathy and I would chat as Mo watched Midnight wobble across the yard and shakily squat, like Marie Antoinette on the way to the tumbril. On the night she died everyone helped to bury her under the palm tree. In those days I never locked my door. Our neighbourhood was a community.

I rediscovered housework; I could clean that place from top to toe in forty-five minutes. Mo had never seen me clean before and was initially confused. He would stand in the doorway to our room and bark as I scurried around with my mop. But soon he accustomed himself to my new role and lay on the porch, baking himself in the sun so that the tips of his coat turned bronze. As Michael, our neighbour, came back from the store and began to cook, he would look up and sniff, before lumbering off to help with the preparations.

Next door was a fleapit hotel, the Villa Luisa. Luisa Pigg was a tiny old lady with a penchant for sailor hats and naval regalia. She ran a brothel in the early days, and she made her own cheese out of milk and vinegar in a bit of muslin. She pretended to be Italian and spent the mornings sitting in front of her hotel with crones from the neighbourhood, legs and arms akimbo.

'Tutto bene,' she said each morning as Mo and I passed by.

'Tutto bene, Luisa.'

Then she shrugged her shoulders. 'E cosi!' That seemed to be the extent of her Italian.

Across the road was the famous Century Hotel, owned by two lunatic queens, David and Willy. They were known as 'the Germans', even though Willy was in fact Austrian and David was English. The Century was the other hotel, along with the Raleigh, in the renaissance of South Beach, a celebrity halfway house with a more hardcore crowd, such as Thierry Mugler, Claude Montana, Kristen McMenemy, Janice Dickinson, and a famous New York furrier called Larissa, who looked like a mixture of Cruella de Vil and Coco Chanel. It was a low-key, lazy sort of place, even more disorganised than the Raleigh. The whole staff disappeared in the afternoon for a longish nap, or a spot of sunbathing, which could be awkward if you were in a hurry to check out and catch a plane.

They had a beach club on the other side of the road with a beautiful garden (now Starbucks) where they threw extravagant full-moon parties. Returning from a late-night walk with Mo across the park on Ocean Drive, under a huge Florida moon sailing through the sky, we would sit under the trees and watch unobserved as three hundred freaks in fancy dress were squeezed inside the white wicker fence of Willy and David's magic garden. They were this year's bright young things, a frenetic party set caught between two wars. Lit by flaming torches, Cleopatra (Larissa) chatted with Nero (Mugler) and a Cuban hairdresser (Oribe). The real Linda Evangelista gave tips to a drag version of herself. Sometimes Luisa would make a rare appearance in a rubber dress and dance round and round like a spinning witch. The laughter and music could still be heard back at Sea Crest as I slipped into something a bit more comfortable and left my disgruntled dog to join the party.

When they finally sold the Century to property developer Bobby Stretcher, the death knell began to toll for all of us south of 5th, and the quiet hot days on that crack house street were drawing to a close. Ingrid Casares (Madonna's friend) and Chris Paciello (also Madonna's friend until he went to prison charged with murder) opened a snippy A-list restaurant, Joia, that served inedible food. Suddenly the neighbourhood was a traffic jam of limousines carrying Puff Daddy, Donald Trump, Madonna, and J. Lo into our midst. The new glossy world had arrived, and one by one the huge towers of South Point grew up, much like the Kaposis on John Jacobus's body. They had new names for the tech crowd and the Botox runners who were moving into Miami. No more Surfcomber, South Seas or Coral Reef. The new Miami Beach was christened with more 'powerful' names like Continuum, Portofino, Murano, The Icon.

But the most powerful word of all was Versace. Gianni Versace's arrival on South Beach in 1991 was a turning point for Miami, as was his death on the steps of his mansion in July 1997. As Andy's death had been for New York a few years earlier, Gianni's murder marked the end of an era.

The Versace man had become the image of South Beach, a brilliant cartoon version of something one could glimpse on a good day through the telescope in the observation tower that sat atop the Versace mansion on Ocean Drive. That telescope had once been trained upon the firmament. Now it was focused on the earthbound stars of the Twelfth Street Beach, unemployed Latino hunks with a feminine streak who stretched out on colourful towels in the afternoon sun. Their legs were shaved and their bodies glistened with sacrificial oil. Occasionally they looked up, out to the sea from whence they came (possibly on a raft), all thick necks, little ears and flat heads, to check whether they were being noticed. Little did they know! These men were aware of themselves in a new way that was totally outside the conventions of masculinity. Gianni translated this into silk shirts made from ladies' scarves over necklaces heavy with charms and crosses, as if to save the wearer from himself. He squeezed muscular thighs into low-cut white jeans several sizes too small, and he dressed his doll in dangerous metal-tipped boots. The angle of their cuban heels forced the wearer into a room crutch first, and his buttocks followed in a mouth-watering clench. It was an original vision, not stolen, not a reaction, and even though the people who should have worn it didn't, and many who shouldn't did (Elton John and David Furnish lounging on a couch behind a velvet rope), nobody seemed to mind. It was converted into virtual reality by a plethora of top photographers and beautiful models on the crumbling streets of South Beach, where those silk shirts fluttered across the body like the clothes on Greek statues that Gianni loved so much.

Gianni had presided over South Beach like a household god in his mausoleum. He was given free rein by the city and allowed to tear down a listed Deco building next to his house. 'Art Deco. So *démodé!*' he said.

But each year Deco Drive got rowdier and cheaper around the Versace mansion. First, rows of high trees were planted, and then a secondary interior wall was built to shield the family from the crashing waves of progress. There was a feeling that the outside world was a bit too close for comfort. When Gianni bought the house, after all, Deco Drive was still a sleepy row of rest homes. The only noise you heard at night was from the odd ambulance that came to rush some ancient to intensive care. Now the house was the sore thumb on a strip of cheap flashing bars on eternal happy hour.

In those early days, dinners would be large affairs in the dining room made of seashells. Then we all wore our Versace finery, and the flickering dream became a brief reality. Gianni was polished and lively at the head of the table. Antonio was the perfect consort at the other end. The room, the china, the linen, the stars, the staff, and of course, the young men, were all the Versace ideal. Those meals were hysterical romps that would stretch out until we all jumped into limousines and danced together in The Warsaw until dawn. Later, when Gianni had met everyone and they all looked like the same person over and over again, he got bored and begged off after dinner, waving us off into the night. Later still, those dinners were shorter and ended abruptly, like an evening in Hollywood when you are just thinking of having a second cup of coffee and suddenly everyone has got up to leave.

Once, a few months before he died, I walked over to the house for a quiet evening, just the three of us. It was a holiday weekend, and America was out on Deco Drive. But as the thick oak door clunked shut behind me, the real world receded into a muffled thud and the sound of the fountain in the courtyard tickled the senses into the Versace bubble. The table was set on the terrace in front of the beautiful pool. Mo headed straight for it and jumped in with a splash, casting an amazing shadow through the water onto the glittering face of the mosaic Medusa beneath.

'*Ma, guarda!*' said Gianni, distractedly.

That night screams and broken bottles, demonic laughter and screeching brakes, accompanied a polite conversation that bordered on the macabre. Gianni was there but not there in the candlelight, visibly bored in black, an orthodox priest drained from an exorcism. Antonio, by now a polished diplomat, the Cardinal Richelieu of the house of Versace, guided us through a dinner-party conversation that could have been lifted from a post-war drawing room comedy.

It was incredible how Gianni had changed since the first time I met him at the Versace headquarters in Via Gesù all those years ago. Then, he was a timid humble dreamer with a shock of frizzy black hair and a gentle reedy voice that only spoke Italian with the very slightest Calabrian lilt. Such was his ability to concentrate that within a year he had learnt a fluent flexible English, and was already a different man. But fifteen years of power and accolade would turn a nun into a frenzied dictator, and by now Gianni had a reputation for flinging girls from the catwalk during rehearsals and screaming at all and sundry. Ironically, cancer found its way into his throat. Trying to find a point of contact with him, sitting at dinner all those years later, I remembered out loud a September long ago when he and I had met at the Edinburgh Festival. He was returning from a solitary trip around Scotland and had called out of the blue. We had dinner together and I remembered him talking about his trip in a sweet faltering English.

For a moment the recollection brought life to his eyes. 'What a beautiful place is Skye, and Eigg . . .' he said and described to a surprised Antonio his adventures round the Western Isles. The image of him alone on deck, wrapped in a cashmere sweater, eating a solitary meal in some island port, or ploughing through a slate-coloured ocean towards a craggy green rock surrounded by screaming seagulls, made us all laugh and then fall silent. The gulf between then and now was huge and poignant. Hip hop suddenly blared from a passing car. Gianni got up from his chair.

'Call me old-fashioned, but give me beauty,' he said, laughing, and then went upstairs.

CHAPTER 38

The Hollywood Year

That summer of 1998 I had it all. One hot dusk early in July found me looking out of my new bedroom window at the whole of Hollywood. Well, to be precise, the valley. I had rented a sprawling estate in the Hollywood hills. It was a dusty, run-down wooden 'ranch house' owned by a family of Christian Scientists called the Cheathams. Bob Cheatham had built it with his bare hands. You could tell. And Mrs Cheatham was the neighbour from *Rosemary's Baby*. She was a tiny little thing with a penchant for purple. She could creep up to the house undetected and would appear without warning at our kitchen door in her striped sun visor bearing little gifts – a pot of honey, or a plate of home-made cookies. Under her sun visor, blue eyes the size of saucers blazed out at you.

At first, we were disturbed by these sudden apparitions. She seemed to be mysteriously intuitive concerning medication because whenever one was about to gobble an antibiotic or take a swig of Nyquil before going out to work, the sun visor would miraculously pop up from behind the privet hedge by the kitchen window. She was actually very nice but like many Christians she was 'firm', to say the least; and the house was extremely expensive for what it was. Fergie, the Duchess of York, had rented it before us and had rather aptly told an exasperated Mrs Cheatham that it was like the seven dwarves' cottage. 'Can you imagine?' retorted Mrs Cheatham. 'Bob built this house with his *bare hands*. And who's she? Not Snow White, I'm sure.'

But for all Bob's hard work, it was a rambling and makeshift rest home for daddy-long-legs, and it smelt of a hundred tenants and their shattered dreams. There was a stable door into the kitchen and Mrs Cheatham would lean on the lower half and drop her little gifts on the counter, often accompanied by leaflets and books by Mrs Mary Baker Eddy, who invented Christian Science.

'What are you taking there, you rascal?' she would say.

'Er, it's called Night Nurse, Mrs Cheatham.'

'It won't do you any good, you know. It's all in there.' And she would tap her sun visor, before scampering off. During the course of my year in Hollywood I grew to love this woman; not least because much later, after a visit from the material girl, she popped up from behind her hedge saying, 'She's a curious little thing, that Madonna.' It became our code name; as in, 'The curious little thing on line one.'

Anyway, the great thing about the house was the garden and the view. The house was cut into the side of the mountain and the lawn rolled right to the edge of a sort of cliff where an incongruous wrought-iron gazebo was dangerously perched. In hot weather there would be tiny growls from the earth below, miniquakes, our planet's groans at the weight of Hollywood sitting on its face, and the gazebo would shudder and jangle suddenly, as if for no reason.

The whole valley spread out beneath it for miles and miles. On one side you could see Warner Brothers Studios and the airport at Burbank, where full-sized jumbos looked like little ice-lollies taking off into the sky. On the far right was the Forest Lawn Cemetery, and beyond that the Disney lot where I was currently employed making the $100 million mess, *Inspector Gadget*. Through the beautiful poisonous haze, grid after grid of strangely named streets engulfed these landmarks, and freeways cut across them that looked like lava flows at night. Above it all in the distance stood the San Bernardino mountains; everything looked close enough to touch except it wasn't – the mountains were thirty miles away, a visual reminder that we were living in a land of illusion.

As another day ended, the street lights below silently twinkled and shimmered into life. My garden was a hive of activity, reflecting every facet of my latest incarnation. Martin, my hyperallergic Uruguayan boyfriend, was shambling across the lawn, just back from work, shedding his shirt and tie and dropping them on the grass as he went. (Who is going to pick them up? I muttered to myself as I inhaled deeply on a giant spliff; me, I suppose.) Mo gambolled along at his feet. Underneath the plane tree sat the obligatory family that often comes with a Latin American liaison. Martin's grandparents were Keela and Oswald, a sweet old couple who had moved to Uruguay from Europe. They were visiting for a month. Their daughter, Martin's mother, Juana – just a couple of years older than me – was married to the only other gringo in the family, Richard. They were playing cards under the tree and chatted softly in Spanish. As their pride and joy arrived they raised their arms as one in cooing adoration. This man could do no wrong, and I must admit he cut a fine figure as he let himself be drawn into the collective embrace. On the other side of the garden, Larry, my psychotic gay chef, was laying the table for dinner in the gazebo. Jay, the silver-haired man from the Raleigh Hotel with the laugh like a sailor, my immaculately brought-up (Yale-educated) lady-in-waiting, was pruning roses with Mrs Cheatham, and my best friend and resident writing partner Mel was stomping about downstairs in her signature clogs hunting for cigarettes. It was, as usual, that time of the month, so tonight was going to be bumpy.

This was my world. It was all too good to be true. I sat upstairs, king/queen of all I surveyed. The weed was making me giggly. Thank God for British Sterling, my new Rasta dealer-writer-friend from Jamaica. He made nightly rounds of the hills in his souped-up Lincoln. The weed was strong. I was already feeling weightless and prone to hysteria when a large straw hat entered the garden below. All I could see underneath was a little pair of feet. It was John Schlesinger. Mel came clonking out of the house, red and puffy . She looked as if someone had been holding her under water for too long and had then put her in a tumble-dryer with a pair of trainers. The hat turned and two arms came out to greet her. I tensed to see whether she was going to continue being as moody as she had been all day, but luckily Mel had a smiling public face, like most of the great monsters, and tonight was going to be no exception. After all, Madonna was coming to dinner.

'Hi, John,' she tinkled. 'Have you settled into your new house okay?'

'It's really quite ghastly,' sang John in his famous falsetto. 'But it'll *do* dear. Where is Princess Flat Feet?'

'Up here, John,' I shouted, and the hat looked up.

John Schlesinger was back in Hollywood: the mischievous blue eyes, the perfectly groomed beard, the little stomach, the enormous hands. ('You know what they say, dear?') Fergie might have been forgiven, had she arrived at this moment, for thinking she was still in the seven dwarves' cottage. John, Mel and I settled down with drinks served by Larry, who was brewing up for a meltdown.

'Where's M?'

'Late.' As usual.

'Who on earth are all those people?'

'Martin's family.'

'My dear, it's all very Tennessee Williams. They look as if they might lock you up in a cupboard at any minute. How long are they staying?'

'A month.'

'Goodness! Are they having dinner?'

'No, they're going out to the Beverly Center.'

'Good, because we must have a serious discussion. I had that cunt Sherry Lansing on the phone no sooner than I had arrived.'

Backtrack. The week after the release of *My Best Friend's Wedding*, I was in the car with my new agent, Nick Styne, on my *Evita* tour of victory around the studios when Sherry Lansing called. She had a film named *The Next Best Thing*. It was a sickly script about a nasty humourless woman and her flubby gay best friend. She (the woman – not Sherry) was such a bitch that no man could tolerate her and, needy cow that she was, she didn't feel complete without a baby. Enter the flubby queen. Everybody's favourite person. Funny, supportive, great dress sense, everything a man was not. He was ideal, he could break into a show tune at any given moment and also – an added plus for the studio – he was that rarity in the homosexual community, an NPB (a non-practising bugger). He gave up the awkward subject of sex years ago when all his friends died. His solution to every one of life's little problems was to go out and buy ready-made whipped cream and spray it into his friends' mouths.

These two highly revolting people decided by page twenty-three to go ahead and have a baby. At which point came one of the most distasteful montages I have ever read. It started with Him and Her giggling in bed as he tried to mount her. He was wearing a caveman outfit. They collapsed in peals of laughter and after a couple more futile and unlikely tries they ended up in hospital, unfortunately not with anything serious wrong. This time he was jerking off over a gay porno magazine into a little paper cup (talk about the glamour of cinema!). She was in the stirrups on the other side of a screen and by the end of the montage she had been upped by a turkey baster, and an egg was cracked by a flubby gay sperm. I turned it down flat. But it kept coming back, like a boomerang.

Sherry Lansing said that if I agreed to take the part she would greenlight the movie. Now this is a big deal for an actor. You know that you are getting somewhere when a studio head says they will green light a movie for you: it immediately gives the script a golden aura; and you, too. What was bad about it becomes something that can be fixed as all your people (agents, managers and lawyers) get on the phone to make the most of the moment. Hopefully by teatime, the news will have spread around the town and they will be able to haul in a shoal of other offers by the end of play. And so, slowly but surely, what was once something that you would *never* do, first becomes the thing you're using to get something else, and then suddenly it's what you *are* doing. *Next week.*

At the outset all the cards were mine and I could approve the casting. Elaine, my New York agent, called me one day saying, 'What if Madonna played the other part?' I was ecstatic. I adored Madonna. Sherry was less enthusiastic, citing the kiss-of-death theory about Madonna in the movies. Elaine, the pushiest agent in the firmament, said that in this case Madonna would be so perfect for the role that the old rules would no longer apply. She could be pretty persuasive; eventually, Sherry said, if that's what we wanted, then she'd go with it.

Enter Tom Rosenberg. Handsome. Late forties. Mood swinger. His company, Lakeshore, was making the movie under the Paramount umbrella. He was a very charming man but you could tell at a glance that he could turn. Big time. He had a reputation of being a fairly tricky customer, but actually he was more like one of the old studio heads from the golden years. He ran his company his way. He didn't much care what anyone else thought, and it was hard to change his mind about things. At the time he didn't know a great deal about cinema, but he knew what he liked. The problem was, as far as I was concerned, his ideas were very different from mine. However, he was a great businessman and a fabulous manipulator. Pretty soon I thought I had him around my little finger, but actually he had me round his. His expert foreplay lulled me into a false sense of security.

The first thing I did was to persuade him and his partner that Mel and I should rewrite the script. Our way. That is to say, with two or three major changes. My character would be a real gay man with a real gay life, not some token queen with his weird whipped-cream parallels. He would not be a decorator, and she would get pregnant because the two of them had sex. We wanted the movie to be a slice of life, and to take place in LA where stories like *The Next Best Thing* were already happening.

In Hollywood, pitching is an art in itself. Part of the classic formula is to say something like, 'You know what? It's *The Matrix* meets *Mary Poppins*,' at which point everyone says, 'Oh, I get it!' So we said, 'It's *Shampoo* meets *Sunday Bloody Sunday*' – and as if by magic, Duncan, my English agent, called me up and said that John Schlesinger (who had actually made *Sunday Bloody Sunday*) had heard about the film and was interested in taking part.

'But Duncan,' I said. 'He's seventy years old!'

'Yes, but his eye is still very much on the ball.'

'On balls, you mean!'

'No, but seriously, Rup . . .'

John had directed some of the movies that had most turned my head in life: *Sunday Bloody Sunday*, *The Day of the Locust* and *Midnight Cowboy* were some of my favourite films (quite aside from the fact that we'd been friends for twenty years, and I was very fond of him). But directors are like actors; and a great director is a reflection of his time. John's best films described their times perfectly, they were his view of the world; but would he be able to cut a real slice of life out of Silver Lake in the late 1990s?

Unfortunately all the directors we approached had turned the movie down. I discussed all this with Tom and said that if we got the right actors, the right cameraman and the right production designer, we could recreate a classic Schlesinger look and tone to the film. We could guide John.

The strange thing was, Tom said yes to everything I asked, even offering me the role of executive producer, which I accepted with drunken alacrity. Producer, writer *and* star all at once! I couldn't believe my luck.

Without delay Mel and I were dispatched to London to meet John, where we came across our first hurdle. John loved the script as it was. And when we started telling him our ideas he very cunningly fell into a deep sleep. Mel and I looked at each other, not knowing whether to stop pitching – we were now getting quite good at it, and rather enjoyed the sound of our own voices – but the trouble was, we were about to get the giggles as John's head sank deeper and deeper into his shirt. There was a big sweetie bowl in the middle of the table and I began to rummage around in it noisily, saying something inane like, 'I'm sure I saw another liquorice allsort in here . . .'

It did the trick, and he woke up with a little start. Mel smoothly went on as if nothing had happened, but we laughed all the way home.

Fast forward. So much for the green light: it had taken two years to plough through our deals. Now it was July, and John was finally here to work with us on the script and go into pre-production. It was going to be a bumpy ride.

Back in the garden of the seven dwarves' cottage, after about an hour the sun went down and the curious little thing appeared through the sliding doors. She was a brunette.

'My dear,' said John under his breath. 'She looks like a vampire!'

Madonna stalked towards us across the lawn, in her black embroidered cargo pants. This woman was breathtaking and tonight she was in her prime. The original material girl, with her puppy fat and boot-boy legs squeezed into a tutu, was a vague whispering wind around this new alabaster goddess with her swimmer's shoulders and tiny waist. Just like America, everything about Madonna had changed, and what hadn't had been carefully wrapped in psychological clingfilm and locked inside an interior fridge. Sometimes, in moments of stress, Madonna had power cuts and the old whiny barmaid came screaming out of the defrosting cold room. Which was good: I loved Holiday Madge, too. But either way, when she gave you her attention, it was 100 per cent. And it was mesmerising. She was famously late (except for work) but never apologised or explained.

Dinner was a riot. John was at his very best. At one point Madonna asked him what his favourite pick-up line was and he replied, 'My face seats three, and it's leaving in ten minutes. Be on it!'

Mel had written the sex scene. I thought it was brilliant. And tonight we had to pitch it to John and Madonna. It went like this: Madonna comes round to my house. It's the 4th of July. Everybody is at some party except us. It is very hot. We make margaritas in my blender and get really shitfaced by the pool. The day wears on in a moody *Shampoo* meets *Sunday Bloody Sunday* montage of a baking hot day in an LA canyon. Silence is broken by the faraway noise of a car. I jump in the pool *à la Bigger Splash*. Madonna sleeps in the sun. The hot desert wind rustles in the palms; there is the odd snatch of conversation from a nearby house. By now we have passed out in the baking sun. I open my eyes. Look at the sleeping icon. She's on her front, dribbling a bit. I adore this woman. I ask her to rub some sun cream on my back. Topless, in shades and bikini bottom (some chance, but we put it in anyway because you never know with M), she sits on my bum and rubs the sun cream into my shoulders and then my lower back. At a certain point I start to laugh.

'Why are you laughing?' she whines. I don't answer. She asks again. She gets off me to fetch her drink, and I turn over. I've been sleeping and drinking and lying on my front. I have a massive hard-on under my Speedos. Madonna screams and throws the rest of her drink over it. Laugh laugh laugh. Realising her glass is now empty, she reaches for the blender and the by now lukewarm remnants of the margarita.

'Fuck. There's none left,' she says.

I make a pond in my stomach by tensing my abs. 'Here's some,' I say.

She laughs and swoops down to lick my tummy. 'Waiter, I think there's some Factor 15 in my margarita.' Her face is a sticky drunken mess. She swoops down again. And the camera pans up to me. Laughing.

'Waiter,' I say. ' I think there's a cock in my friend's mouth.'

And we cut straight to a shot of Madonna riding me. Charging on me actually. It's the drunk-fuck-that-should-never-have-happened of a lifetime. Later we have passed out again and are dribbling in the dusk as suddenly a 4th of July firework display explodes in the hills above and the noise bounces around the canyon.

Larry appeared out of the gloom carrying a flaming candelabra, which he put on the table. John and Madonna looked thrilling in its guttering light. Mel nudged me under the table. They listened silently. John leant his head on his huge hands. Madonna leant back in her chair, lithe and coiled. Sometimes they laughed. Sometimes M wrote notes. (Later, in the deteriorating relationship between her and John, John turned to me, purple with rage, and shouted, 'If only she'd stop writing those fucking notes . . .') I loved her black hair. Her eyes shone with Manson girl intent. When I said, with schoolboy relish, 'And now you ride me for all you're worth,' she threw her head back with her little shriek: 'Dream on, Muriel!'

We made it to the end of the pitch as Larry slammed down the pudding (he was in another rage by now, because Mel had been smoking his cigarettes). John said, 'Let's have a moment to think about it, shall we?' We were silent for what seemed an eternity. The gazebo shook a bit. The freeway flowed silently below, a jam of tail lights. Martin and the family could be heard coming back from the Beverly Center.

'Well?' I said, finally.

'One thing right now!' declared Madonna, looking straight at us. 'I'm not fucking on camera!' Mel and I sagged, although caring interested smiles were glued into place.

'John?' I said.

'My dear, I told you in London. I prefer the original.'

Dinner ended. Mel and I arranged to go over to Madonna's house the next morning at ten to 'observe' a yoga session. We were all stuck for a career idea for her character and she wanted to be a yoga instructor.

'Well, all I can say is not with that hair, dear,' John said at the front door, on his way out. 'It'll be like the Addams family. It really will.'

'Crisis meeting in my room in ten minutes. Bring two hundred dollars,' said Mel as we shut the door. We locked ourselves in and spent the night tearing the evening to shreds, while at the same time trying to come up with an alternative means of fertilising Madonna. By 3 a.m. we were vague shapes in a thick smog of cigarettes, going over it all for the zillionth time, but as British Sterling pointed out, this was about as much fun as we would ever have.

'You got Madonna. You got Joel Slenger an' you got British Sterling. What more could you all want?' reasoned Sterling.

'A good idea?'

At 5 a.m. we were back at the gazebo, bleary-eyed, as the sun rose over the mountains and the street lights jerked and cut out across block after block in the valley below. Stubs from a million cigarettes lay on the table. We could hardly speak. Suddenly I remembered our morning appointment. By the time we had to present ourselves in Las Villas, where M lived, for the yoga class, we had hardly slept.

We just about managed to make sense as Madonna and her instructor began wrapping their ankles behind their heads. Ludicrously, we had both brought little notepads and sat there studiously like two junkie secretaries. But I'm afraid by the time Madonna came to the pièce de résistance where she balanced on one fingernail in a cloud of prana breath, both Mel and I were fast asleep. John's sleeping sickness must have been catching.

Work on *Inspector Gadget* was continuing at a snail's pace. Each evening we worked late and so the next morning would start later and end later. By Friday we would be going in to work at teatime and finishing at four in the morning. In the Hollywood food chain, the director was the poor browbeaten victim of the producer and the studio. He exuded exhaustion. Behind the scenes lurked a panel of executives, each with their own theory and agenda. A string of writers had written version after version, each adding to our scripts on a different-coloured paper, each one losing the plot a little bit more, so that by the end, or rather the beginning, they had managed between them to render the thing utterly meaningless. This is the lunacy of the studio system. But it could have been a lot worse. I was playing Doctor Claw, the evil inventor; I had a cat called Sniffy; and we shot on a huge sound stage that housed my dungeon laboratory. It was fully equipped with its own electric shock treatment machine, and even an emergency room. But we were a helmless ship and the browbeaten director was never given his day. He was squeezed like an orange from morning to night by our benign, unflappable producer who really should have given us all a break and directed the movie himself. I based my character on Gore Vidal. He should have been Dr Claw. Lines like, 'I'm afraid I'm going to have to torture you now!' would have sounded good coming from him. I was a pale burlesque.

It was my first time on the Disney lot and I spent many of my free hours searching the endless sound stages for the secret door to the underworld refrigerator where, legend had it, Uncle Walt lay undead. A very unreliable source at a Hollywood dinner party had described to me a thick metal door with giant handles that led into a kind of nuclear fallout shelter where Walt was taken on his deathbed. My imagination was on fire. Could Walt have been smuggled out of hospital in the dead of night and been met at the studio gates by Goofy and Snow White with a hypodermic? Was he trundled down Mickey Mouse Avenue on a gurney by the seven dwarves? And then, did he disappear in a cloud of dry ice like a disco queen mourned by studio bigwigs and top animators? And does he lie somewhere down there still, like Snow White herself, in a glass coffin of ice, ready and waiting for science to catch up? These were my dreams during the endless hours on the sound stage floor. I crept onto all the stages and shuffled around the outer edges with a little torch, behind the huge cycloramas of pink clouds at dusk or Manhattan skylines at night. But I never had any luck. If there was a secret door, Michael Eisner had probably very sensibly bricked it up by now.

My co-star in *Inspector Gadget*, Matthew Broderick, was a great mimic and kept us all laughing through the interminably long hot days, but the real discovery for me was the mafia of grumpy make-up ladies and hairdressers who ruled the set with a rod of iron from the make-up trailer. They had all been in the business for years; they earned fortunes, lived in palaces and went from movie to movie like the witches in *Macbeth*. They were the ones who had the real dialogue with the other great on-set movie mafia, the teamsters. The teamsters are the oddest group of movie folk. They are uniformly huge, living on Diet Coke and jelly doughnuts. They park the trailers, pump out the shit, make the hairdryers work and collect the artistes. These two groups could seriously fuck up a movie if you got on their wrong side. They were the men.

Christina Smith was the chief of the make-up trailer. She had a little tinkly voice that belied her authority, and had been born in Scotland. You could easily imagine her with a bun in a hairnet behind a lace curtain on a Glaswegian close. I had met her before when I was making *Dunston Checks In* at Fox, after she was brought on to that picture as a last desperate measure. We had a dangerous legend in the house who was famous for keeping a set waiting for days on end as she applied and reapplied her make-up. Nothing could get her out of the chair, no amount of threatening. But Chris Smith was a legend, too. Instead of guns and grenades her secret weapons included a miraculous eye bag cream that would make a haemorrhoid duck, a paraffin-and-wax bath for ageing hands (unbelievable) and her famous individually laid eyelashes, invented for Liza Minnelli. She used all these weapons to great effect as she stormed the trailer of that impossible but most fabulous of divas, Faye Dunaway (or Done Fadeaway, as she was known in certain circles). The word in the commissary was that the studio was on to poor Faye and she had a stipulation in her contract that she couldn't spend more than two hours in the make-up chair; but she'd met her Waterloo in Christina. To everyone's surprise she was ready on set while our lovely star, an orang-utan named Sammy, was still under the hairdryer.

'Chris Smith knows where all the bodies are buried,' someone once told me, but she didn't know where Uncle Walt was. Barbara Lorenz was my favourite. She did hair and, along with Susie Germaine, whose father was Marilyn's hairdresser, they marketed a line of extremely expensive hair products called something like Lights, Camera, Action. Their hairspray was called Final Checks, their volumiser, Curtain Call. You could forget your wig if they were working on your film, because they were constantly disappearing to trade fairs and talking on the phone to their stockbrokers, but they were really fun. We used to pretend that I was the spokesman for their brand and make commercials on my Super 8. 'I am Rupert Everett and this is my Curtain Call.'

But they didn't like it when you made jokes about any of *their* Hollywood legends. I remember that one day I came into the make-up trailer with an amazing tape of a drunken Judy Garland, talking about a planned comeback with Liza at the Palladium. Broderick was in the chair, and I couldn't wait to play it – it was very camp, and I knew he'd like it – but soon you could cut the atmosphere with a knife. Christina had shrunk to half her size and was sitting in her place like a recently unearthed mummy. The others all looked aghast and stared at me reproachfully. Pretty soon I got the message and took the tape off.

There was always something going on in the make-up trailer in the hot afternoons when nothing else was happening. The manicurist would come in; Christina would set up her paraffin machine to do everyone's hands if she was in a good mood, and when my mother and aunt arrived from England they both got a total make-over.

I met them at the airport. On the deluge of travellers that poured through the sliding door, every shape, size and colour, sailed my mother and her sister in their headscarves and smart coats. My mother was a little dishevelled with a deathly hue and looked as if she were going to be sick at any moment. She hated leaving home and was normally violently ill as soon as she set foot on a plane. I watched them manoeuvre their way through the crowd. In a rare reversal of roles, my aunt was in charge. She was ploughing a path through the sea of colliding trolleys, tacking this way and that as if they were still sailing through the Norfolk creeks onto the North Sea on board the *Wayfarer*.

Theirs was a delicate mission. Now was the time for my mother to officially recognise the fact that I had turned out the wrong way and was married to a man. Poor old thing. From the cradle onwards, through all the ups and downs of school, adolescence, teenage rebellion, surely every mother dreams of that first trip after the wedding bells when she visits her son and his buxom young wife from a lovely family? All the plans she has made over those years, of how she will while away the afternoons with the darling girl, filling her in about their naughty boy's favourite recipes, shopping together for maternity clothes! At the best of times, the dream is a mirage, but this flight back to reality was going to be a crash landing. (Martin was not much interested in anyone's favourite dish, let alone getting cosy with his in-laws, although I once overheard him invite them to go with him to a spinning class.) My mother was on uncharted ground, and my heart went out to her. But Aunt K was the perfect companion: she knew what a delicate job lay ahead and she was prepared. Apart from anything else, she had long withstood the endless family jibes at her weekend boyfriends who quite clearly played for the other team.

'There you are!' she said now, kissing me lightly on both cheeks. 'I'm afraid your mother has been rather sick during the flight.'

Even though I had recently put on several pounds, my mum said, as always, 'You look terribly thin, darling. Are you eating? Thanks for shaving.'

'I did shave!'

But everything went off very smoothly. The great thing about my mother was that she had been impeccably brought up in the Edwardian style, and nothing was going to unsettle her. She absolutely put her best foot forward and walked into our nest of plotting maniacal queers with the same eager attention she would have given to a garden party at Buckingham Palace. Everybody in our house loved the sisters, particularly Larry the cook. Pretty soon they were out shopping together every day and at least my mother taught *him* my favourite dishes. She went gardening with Mrs Cheatham, who adored her until my mother suggested that the rent was too high. In no time she had settled in and started to do what all mums do once they get their foot inside the door – take over. She secretly negotiated with Larry on their trips to the supermarket that his wages were too high. When we gave dinner parties I would sometimes arrive late from the studio, to find my mother in charge, in front of a huge log fire, receiving John Schlesinger and Helena Bonham Carter, both of whom she adored.

'I think Hollywood rather suits me!' she said.

But like her sister, she had taken an instant dislike to Mel. 'She's a terrible sponge!' Aunt K proclaimed.

One night I went to see my mother in her room. She was sitting in her bed rubbing in hand cream, in a ritual that I recognised from my very earliest memories (even the pink plastic tube was the same brand). 'We think Martin's *awfully* nice,' she said in a stage whisper.

'No need to whisper. He's miles away.'

'Can't understand everything he says. Can you?'

'No.'

'But that can be a plus sometimes. American *is* funny, isn't it? "You guys" this and "you guys" that,' said my mum dreamily as she rubbed Ponds cold cream into her face.

'It's different.'

'Now, we're coming to the studio tomorrow. Christina is going to do my hands, and Barbara might do K's roots. Its all been great fun, but I must say I'm glad your father's not here. He's much better off driving across China.' My father was on a trip with my brother in a rally car across Asia. My mother settled back into her bed. 'Are you happy, darling?' she asked.

'What's happiness?' I replied like Prince Charles.

'John Schlesinger says that you're much more easygoing now. He's an awfully nice man. We must have him to stay when he's back. There!' She settled down into her bed. 'I'm absolutely whacked. Goodnight, darling. If I'm awake at half past four I shall come down and have a cup of coffee with you. What fun!'

They were very popular on the set, where everyone made an enormous fuss of them, and I must say that while they were there I felt a strange feeling of wholeness. I was being accepted on my own terms. Americans love family, and from my pool of tungsten light in the middle of the huge dark sound stage I could watch my old mother and her stoic sister graze through the shadows from group to group, chatting, laughing, pointing at me. God knows what they were saying but our crew was very affectionate to them.

As a parting present, they gave Martin a cashmere sweater that he valiantly put on, despite the fact that he was hyperallergic to wool. Within half an hour he was purple and oozing snot and almost passed out at the table. 'Rather a waste of a good jersey,' said my mother as we pulled it off him. 'I think I'll give it to your father instead. Goodness, what muscles!'

We all gathered outside the house the day they left. Mrs Cheatham came running down her little goat path, swathed in deepest purple. 'You must come back very soon,' she said, passing bibles and biscuits into my mother's arms, having forgiven her over the rent discussion.

'Oh dear,' said my mum. 'It's just like school all over again, but this time it's *me* leaving.' She got into the car and suddenly there we were again: the same image but everything had been reversed. Tears glittered in her eyes.

Aunt K gave me a knowing wink. 'Thank you again, Ru,' she said. 'We've had a wonderful time.'

'When shall we see you?' said my mother, putting on her brave face. 'You're going to Uruguay for Christmas, aren't you?'

'Yes, I think so. But I'll come over to visit you in January.'

'Well, we'll pretend that's half-term. I'll send your love to your father.' And off they drove.

Inspector Gadget wrapped and bad things began to happen. Madonna left for New York to plan her tour, and Mel nearly killed John Schlesinger.

We had been having a script meeting one afternoon; by the time it had finished, John's driver had gone away to run some errands so Mel offered to take him home. She came back an hour later in floods of tears. We could hardly get a word out of her but finally, through her sobs, a terrible tale began to unfold.

When she and John had arrived at his front gate, it turned out that Michael, his boyfriend, had gone out, and John couldn't get the gate open. Mel said, 'Don't worry, John. I'll drive the car right up to the gate and you can get on the bonnet and climb over.' The gate was about five feet high. What was she thinking? John was seventy years old with a heart condition and a big straw hat. But he was jaunty and reckless. The universe froze in horror as Mel and he suddenly became the worst possible combination. John clambered onto the bonnet. 'Then what happened?' I asked, but the question produced renewed floods of tears. Finally, punctuated by moans and heaves and hands through the hair, Mel said, 'I just thought he'd swing one leg over the gate, then the other and lower himself down.' But what actually happened was that John somehow managed to end up standing with both feet on the gate and then jumped like a wild thing, a crazy bird crashing onto the concrete below. He fractured both ankles and lay there screaming in agony while Mel stood speechless on the other side. She called 911 and eventually an ambulance arrived to take John to the emergency room. It was the beginning of the end for him, and for our film *The Next Best Thing*.

CHAPTER 39

Goodbye, Roddy

One night the phone rang. It was Roddy McDowall. 'I just wanted you to know I'm afraid I'm on the way out,' he said. 'I have cancer and they've given me three months to live.' He was very calm, very matter of fact.

'But Roddy,' I blundered. 'What about our film? You have to be in our film!'

'Not this season, dear,' he replied. 'Come over and see me. Bring Mel.' And he hung up.

We drove over Laurel Canyon towards the valley with heavy hearts; both of us loved Roddy. We were early so we went to a nearby restaurant and had something to eat. It was here that the crafty Mel let on that she had been suffering from writer's block and had not written a thing.

'But Mel, why didn't you tell me?' I asked, aghast.

'I was scared you'd scream at me. And anyway, I thought it would pass.'

'But we're meant to deliver the script next week.'

'I know.' And she began to heave with sobs. But it didn't seem to matter much all of a sudden.

We walked into Roddy's house. He was sitting in his red drawing room in a pool of light from the reading lamp by his side, busy writing farewell cards; impeccably mannered till the end.

With Donatella.

In Oscar Wilde with

Cate Blanchett and
Minnie Driver

Julianne Moore

Reese Witherspoon

In the trailer with
Colin Firth,
Anna Massey and
Reese Witherspoon.

Rehearsing with Frothy.

Acting with Judi
Dench and Reese
Witherspoon.

Dangerous Lesbians. Discussing the script with Josée and Catherine.

An intimate scene by the fire.

Letting our characters in. With Sharon Stone in Malta.

Letting them out again in Moscow.

With Julie Andrews, Jennifer Saunders, Antonio Banderas and John Cleese
at the *Shrek 2* premiere.

On the couch with Emily Watson in *Separate Lies*.

INNOCENT

PLOTTING

MANIACAL

© Jerome Prebois/Les Liaisons Dangereuses/Corbis

QUEEN

The Four Ages of Me

Me and Mo during our heyday in Place Blanche.

'Hello, dears,' he said, looking up at us from his work. He was stoned on morphine and looked tiny, though his eyes were huge through his glasses. We sat down and began to chat about this and that. His voice was delicate and disembodied; sometimes he would stop what he was saying and stare for a long moment before collecting himself and pushing on. There was a strange stillness in him, perched on the edge of some faraway abyss. He was neither here nor there, and the room around him, which had always been filled with people and smoke and gossip, had somehow turned in on itself and seemed to be watching. The grandfather clock in the hall kept time with a slow ponderous thud. The rosy-faced Toby jugs on the mantelpiece had turned into gargoyles of frozen jollity. Outside, the huge statue he had rescued from *Planet of the Apes* stared mournfully into the house. A little further up the hill, doubtless out of sight now for ever, was the bench from *Lassie*.

It was difficult to imagine the life going out of this man, because he had been so full of it. It was as if just minutes ago he was sailing through the house, immaculate in a black velvet suit and a jungle-red polo neck, the perfect host administering to his friends, the assorted heartbreakers of the twentieth century – Mae West, Bette Davis, Elizabeth Taylor and other less luminary characters like Mel and me. He mixed the A list with the B list and was equally attentive to all. I had spent some of the most memorable of my Hollywood nights there. But it would all soon be done, a link broken between people who would never hear about each other any more. One would never again be able to say, 'Please remember me to Louise Brooks.'

After about half an hour he said, 'Now you really are going to have to excuse me. I must have my rest.' And we left. That was it. The end. Simple and straightforward, like Roddy.

I gave him a hug, and he said, 'You're angels for coming by. Keep in touch.' He died the following week.

After the funeral (which I was not invited to) Elizabeth Taylor gave a party. I went with Greg Gorman, the photographer. Her home was a modest affair, just a small ranch house tucked away in the far reaches of Bel Air. The garden was full of white flowers; the house was full of Impressionist paintings. A Van Gogh hung next to a portrait of Elizabeth from *Raintree County*, which stared haughtily at a Degas across the room. All the familiar faces from Roddy's dinner table were there, standing round the pool and saying their last goodbyes, to each other as much as to him: Gregory Peck, John Waters, Sybil Burton (Richard's first wife), John Schlesinger, Bruce Weber and Paul Rubens (Pee Wee Herman) among others. For a long while there was no sign of Elizabeth. She was notoriously late, even for her own parties. Sometimes she never showed at all. But when all the guests were assembled, the last of the living legends hobbled down the stairs with silver hair and a kaftan from under which peeked a comfy pair of bedroom slippers. The famous diamond was on her hand, and a galaxy of rocks hung round her neck and clung to her ears like glittering squids. Her lower lip hung slightly and she walked with some difficulty to a podium by the pool and made a beautiful speech.

'I hope you're all having a good time,' she said. 'I can't, because I've been a naughty girl.'

She knew Roddy as well as anyone. The had met, after all, during the filming of *Lassie*. Both were far away from home, two of the biggest child stars of their time; one could only imagine the enormous bond that was forged between them as they acted together and were educated together in those bizarre schoolrooms set up by the Hollywood studios. As they sat on that old bench waiting for shots to be lined up, they must have watched a lot of plotting from the studio monsters and swamp bitches around them, and grown canny together. It was that quality, the old head on young shoulders, that was so mesmerising. It all meant such a lot. These people were the symbols I adored, everything I loved about my job, and Roddy's death felt like the beginning of the end.

As Elizabeth finished her speech a piper could be heard playing a lonely air from the end of the garden. Everyone turned as he walked, fully kilted, up to the pool. We all stood frozen with our glasses in our hands as he passed among us, around the pool, like the grim reaper, into the house and out the front door. It was a chilling moment and nobody moved a muscle, straining to hear the last lamenting wail evaporate into the low distant hum of Los Angeles. Elizabeth had certainly learnt about scoring. The party picked up again, but Roddy was definitely gone with the piper. However, the grim reaper would be coming back for another couple of laps; some others in the room were not going to be there 'next season' either, among them Gregory Peck and John Schlesinger.

*

One hot afternoon, John and I ventured out to explore east LA for possible locations for the movie. The screenplay had originally been set in
San Francisco, but we felt that city was too head-on for the story, and
successfully managed to persuade Tom Rosenberg that LA would be
better suited. But would we be able to pull the movie away from the
streets of West Hollywood and the lush estates of Beverly Hills? Despite
LA being such an extraordinary city, film often seems to place it somewhere between Rodeo Drive and the Sunset Strip.

As we drove eastwards that afternoon on Sunset, the opulent oasis of
West Hollywood – the world's first gay city – soon evaporated into the
sleazy desert scrub of old Hollywood, with its Roosevelt Hotel, Chinese
Theater, sex shops, waxworks and Scientology centre. Pock-marked
hookers looked glumly into the windows of our car. 'Goodness!'
exclaimed John as a toothless girl in a pink miniskirt waved from a bus
stop. 'There's *Pretty Woman!*'

Sunset stuck close to the hills until Las Villas, the original commune
from the beginning of time. Above us was the famous sign and below the
down-at-heel mansions of the silent stars. 'My dear, this is where those
terrible leather queen set dressers lived that I told you about,' said John,
as we were passing a dilapidated bungalow on a ridge with Greek
columns either side of the front door. 'I wonder if they're still alive?'

We pulled up and rang the doorbell. A thin woman with a beak
answered. 'Omigod, the gay guy from that movie!' she screamed. This
was my only identity now.

We politely enquired about the set dressers and she let us in to look
around. The house smelt of cats. There was an incredible view from the
lounge over the skyscrapers of downtown LA. 'Of course, they weren't
there in my day,' said John, gesturing towards the towers.

The lady was horrified. 'Not there?' she said.

John ignored her, looking around the room. 'My dear, what didn't go
on in here!' he whispered.

We sat down on a squeaky leather couch, had iced tea and chatted to
the beaky lady. It is strange, but no one can remember anything in LA.
Life stands still. There are no seasons to remind you that time is in fact
passing and, as far as the beaky lady was concerned, if Downtown was
there now, then it must always have been. Five years is a life, the next
street is another world. The beaky lady knew her house and the way to

work, but little else. She got the place from an old man who had moved to Seattle, and beyond that she knew nothing. 'Anyway, what's a sex dresser?' she asked.

'Set dressers, dear!' snapped John. 'Although they were sex dressers, too, in their way.'

We chuckled on the way out. 'Seattle, with all that rain? Doesn't sound like our friends!' said John as we got into the car.

'Say hi to Julia!' waved the lady.

Now Sunset felt more like herself and swung like a meandering grey river into Silver Lake, Echo Park and Elysian Fields. There was a collapsed romantic feeling down here. Spindly palms rustled with rats. Huge ominous cracks ran across the streets. The big quake felt close in Echo Park. It was always ten degrees hotter, and the heat shimmered over the streets mixed with exhaust that never blew away. One day the crack would open and the whole area would slide into hell. This was where I wanted to shoot our movie.

We drove past the old house of Tex Ritter, the cowboy star from the thirties. It was an apartment building now, perched on the edge of a crumbling hill, and another possible location. 'Too quaint, dear, don't you think?' said John.

Then we went to the apartment building John had used in *The Day of the Locust*. That film (which I loved) began looking through an arch into a pretty grass yard with a little fountain surrounded by white bungalow apartments, where all the protagonists of the story lived. Passing through the same arch thirty-five years later, behind the man who made the film, was another movie. Time had taken its toll on the location and its director. The place was a run-down crack den with broken windows and aluminium foil blinds. An old Mexican lady watched us through a slit in the door. John stood in the middle of the garden, lost in recollection. In his hat, white shirt and stick, he looked as if he had stepped out of another time, the golden age, when refugees in suits and ties braved the California sun and showed us America through the coloured lens of a sad European eye.

At Echo Park there were three enormous hills. A wide concrete boulevard climbed them – the American way, straight up. Spindly clapboard houses with scorched lawns and dingy palm trees clung to their sides. It felt like being on a rollercoaster, straining to the top and racing over the other side. On the brow of the second hill we got out of the car. The city stretched as far as the eye could see in all directions, mile after mile of rolling suburb, barely visible in the smog. In the setting sun it looked like a vast ocean of frozen waves.

'Oh yes, my dear!' said John, bathed in the magic LA dusk. He looked tired and vulnerable as he wiped his forehead with a big spotted handkerchief. 'I hope we're not biting off more than we can chew.'

It was the understatement of the year.

I had known John since I was seventeen, when he came into a shop where I was working, because 'everyone was talking about you, my dear'. He tried on a pair of shoes, and I was rather cheeky. ('Our feet are too tiny, aren't they?' I'd said. 'We don't carry shoes for such delicate pixie paws.') From then on, we were friends, and John was always someone I looked up to. But that afternoon, standing on the brow of that steep hill in Elysian Fields, was really the last day of our friendship. It was downhill from then on.

Of course, I didn't realise this at the time. I was riding on the crest of the wave. I was making a big studio movie. I was the star, the producer and the writer. At the most dizzying heights, Tom even suggested that we fire John and that I direct the movie. One by one I was stripped of these titles.

Mel and I delivered a script in which there was a scene between my character and another man in bed. We considered it an essential element, but Tom went berserk, and in a flurry of phone calls between him, Madonna and me, various conversations were repeated that shouldn't have been, resulting in my being fired as the producer and the writer.

'He can act in the film if he wants,' Tom told Elaine my agent.

He was very clever: he could outmanoeuvre anyone; however, he didn't understand the nature of what he was trying to achieve. He wanted to cash in on the 'gay best friend syndrome' without alienating the female audience. He wanted them to leave the theatre thinking that I 'was the greatest fucking dad'. Fair enough. But this was not a dancing and singing story. It was a story with a serious and contentious issue that was actually happening in the world: gay parenting. It was the year 2000. Surely Hollywood could meet this subject head-on? But we were back to square one with the token fag syndrome, the inference being that a real practising homo could not make a proper father.

I should probably have walked away at that point. Tom certainly gave me the opportunity, but we had gone too far, and anyway I was actually quite enjoying myself. The whole thing was like an out-of-body experience. By now, I could feel the downward pull, like a drowning man, although it was pleasant. Plus, the strangest thing was that through all these ups and downs I really liked Tom. He was a very charming man.

A well-known writer did a rewrite. It was terrible. We all refused to take part in it. Eventually, during an all-day meeting in Madonna's apartment in New York, we hammered out a compromise. The film went in to pre-production, and I went back to Europe, leaving poor John in the clutches of Tom and Paramount. I should have stayed with him. He hired all the wrong people.

'I wish you were here, dear,' he said in a faraway voice on a crackly line one night while I was in London making *An Ideal Husband*.

Unusually, the opening sequence of the film was shot on the first day, and if I hadn't realised it before, I knew then and there that we were aboard a sinking ship. Mel and I had written a glamorous credit sequence in which I am installing a brand-new garden in front of a beautiful deep Southern mansion in Beverly Hills. As the credits roll, a muddy hill morphs into a pristine lawn flanked by palm trees, like the time-release picture of a blooming flower. Borders and flower beds appear. A stream is turned on. At the end of the sequence, dusk is falling and a little old lady comes out of the house to inspect the work as sprinklers are magically activated. On the day itself, one tired old palm tree was dropped by a crane into a manky lawn in front of a clapped-out house. The stage was unfortunately set.

Mel had been fired as well and she moved out of our house after months of guerrilla warfare with my boyfriend. Then, in a magisterial about turn, she managed to claw her way back into Tom's favour. He rehired her to continue work on the script on the strict understanding that we could not speak. We weren't speaking anyway, but it was another brilliant stroke on the part of Tom. He divided and ruled us. Madonna and the costume designer were at loggerheads, and the cinematographer was trying to take over. On the second day, I was rehearsing fainting at Madonna's feet as John stood above me watching through a viewfinder, and I knocked him over. He fell like a giant red-wood with a terrible scream and lay in agony on the floor of the set, before being taken to hospital with a chipped coccyx.

Benjamin Bratt, Julia Roberts's boyfriend, was playing Madonna's love interest. In a scene where he had to drop her home after their first date, Madonna rather sensibly drank a cocktail before the kissing scene. It worked; the curious little thing only needed one drink to become demure and giggly. It raced through that macrobioticised frame to great effect, and after two drinks she began to improvise. I was watching on the monitor and she was right on track. But things had already turned sour between her and John, and he was furious.

'Will someone pour a bucket of water over that slit!' he screamed from behind the monitor. Tom nudged me, delighted.

At about the same time, somebody began a website called Lourdes' Diary where details of the day's events on our set were described in minute detail. It was really funny. Madonna accused me of being the leak. I wasn't, actually. But everyone became suspicious of everyone else, as the diary kept on coming, and we all raced home at night to guiltily read what Uncle John and Uncle Rupy had done to poor Mommy that day. Personally I always suspected Old Mother Childers, John's boyfriend since the dawn of time.

The film cranked along, however. My bedroom scene had been reinstated in the script, but John chose me a fifty-year-old boyfriend. He had reached that age when anyone under sixty seemed young. I was furious. If I was going to have a boyfriend in a movie, one thing was for sure: he was going to be young and cute. 'But, dear, not everyone is like you and obsessed with dangerous Latinos,' shrieked John.

'Yes they are!' I screamed back. 'And anyway, they don't have to be Latino. Just *young* and sexy!'

'You said you didn't want anyone cute.'

'No, John! I said I didn't want anyone *that* cute.'

I won, eventually, but only after pleading with Tom and Paramount.

One day, her Nibs and I were filming some shot. We got to the end of the scene but no one said, 'Cut.' We improvised for a moment, and then there was a loud snore. John was asleep behind the monitor. There was an awkward silence. Nobody moved. Somebody nudged him gently and he said, 'Action,' as if nothing had happened and we all lurched into the scene again like a spin-dryer. It was funny and sad at the same time because John had turned into the creaky old Latin teacher at school. It wouldn't be long before people began to balance books on doors as he came in and put whoopee cushions under his chair.

He had bitten off more than he could chew.

By now he and Madonna were at war. He pushed her too hard and didn't realise when she was being good. Mel, in her new role as Mata Hari (she was born to spy), was caught in the middle, endlessly reworking the tiredest scene of the movie, when Madonna meets Ben. I sometimes saw her slinking around the periphery of the set like a rat, looking right and left before darting into Madonna's or John's trailer. The production designer and John wanted to shoot the scene in L'Orangerie, a stuffy old-school restaurant in Hollywood. This was the last straw. It was symptomatic of the total disaster in the tone and design of the film. We were looking like a miniseries, added to which Mel came up with a scene of startling banality.

The wind was beginning to change and a very weird thing happened. I was approached about taking part in a certain film that shall remain nameless. Suffice to say it achieved a great deal of success when it came out. The director came to see me on the set. Here was exactly the opportunity I was looking for. It was about a man who fell in love with a woman who had a child. A top shark agent, who I shall just call Major Lady, wanted the movie for his client. In a meeting with the producers, he went armed with a copy of the paperback upon which the film was based. On the cover was a little boy standing between the legs of a man.

'If Rupert does the movie, you won't be able to have a poster like that,' said Major Lady, a gay father himself. I found out because an intern in the office was so disgusted that he called my agent and told him. He was fired and I lost the job. Major Lady is a great agent. Things were not going to be as easy as I thought.

My birthday came, and I got more presents than I have ever received. The whole house was full of them. Complete strangers sent me gifts: huge baskets wrapped in Cellophane containing a jar of honey, some pâté and a lot of polystyrene balls. I had a birthday cake on the set, and Madonna gave a party for me and Ingrid Casares, whose birthday it was too. Martin left halfway through to go to a circuit party.

On the last day of the shoot, we filmed the final scene of the movie. We were back on that hill in Elysian Fields, but everything had changed. It felt as if a hundred years had passed. John looked exhausted. We sat together in the shade as the crew set up the shot. We tried to chat, but it didn't really work. He thought I'd betrayed him, and probably I had.

'We really fucked up, didn't we?' said Madonna later in the scene (one of her best).

Another understatement. We wrapped and the film went briefly into remission.

CHAPTER 40

Unconditional Love

The only other film that I 'green-lit' was *Unconditional Love*. After that it would be all red lights. The shoot was in Chicago so I gave up the house in the Hollywood hills and moved a reluctant and sulky Martin back to New York where the only hard-on seemed to be the rigor mortis of our relationship.

Pat and Meinir had fallen out, and Meinir became a chat-show hostess in Wales. I had to reshuffle my entourage, which now included my new *über*assistant Jay, and Jamie, a scally with an aquiline nose and solemn blue eyes who became my hair hag. Together we marched the last leg of my Hollywood year. With them at my side, like Dolly Levi I returned to Chicago in September 1999.

P. J. Hogan and his wife Jocelyn had written a brilliant script for *Unconditional Love*. It was a highly improbable story of three freaks who track down a serial killer in the maze of underground streets and railway tracks that lie beneath the Windy City. It was one of the best movies I have ever done, but remains unreleased to this day.

Back then, however, the stage was still set for a momentous second coming. PJ was the hottest director of comedy, and I was his muse. Or at least I thought I was. His latest discovery, who would upstage us all, was a little person called Meredith Eaton.

'Can't you say dwarf?' I asked her casually, during one of the first long cold nights in the bowels of the city.

'No,' snapped Merrylegs. She was also a Long Island Jewish princess, and she didn't mess around. 'It's derogatory. You wouldn't like to be called fag.'

'Yes, I would, actually,' I said. 'Anything rather than "gay" or "little".'

'Okay, faggot,' she said. 'Let's get a coffee.' And she clambered off her chair. We wandered towards the craft service table that stood like a mirage in that grimy underworld, with its toaster, its jelly doughnuts and its diet sodas.

Merrylegs was a genius, and if I thought it was complicated being gay in show business, she made me think again. Her entourage included her stand-in, Lila, and her boyfriend Michael, who did her stunts, which was a bit weird. She wore a red plastic mackintosh with a hood in the movie, like the little person from *Don't Look Now*, and Michael was identically dressed, with a tiny Clara Bow wig and red gumboots. The three of them sat in a row on director's chairs in their red coats like targets at a fairground shooting range.

We began filming in October. The wind howled off the frozen lake, and Lakeshore Drive was majestic under a blanket of snow. Mo was ecstatic. I lived with him and Jay on the top floor of a hotel off North Wacker Drive. Tom Rosenberg was from Chicago and he looked after us, even to the point of giving me the number of the Chief of Police in case I got into a scrape. (He was momentarily ashen-faced when I said I'd called him asking whether there were any cute gay cops.)

Chicago was a far cry from that summer inferno of just four years ago. Everything was different. This time Kathy Bates was the leading lady. Every night she stepped from her trailer on North Wacker in a floor-length mink coat and marched grimly with her team to a hole in the sidewalk through which she disappeared. My trailer was behind hers, so I would often follow her as the snow swirled around while this flotilla of ladies sailed towards a piss-stained stairway and descended into the bowels of the earth.

It was a dripping and desolate world under the Windy City, and soon the temperature plummeted to minus ten. The homeless huddled in dark corners watching. I sat on a director's chair in a pool of tungsten wearing a suit made of blue sequins. Night after night we all sat there in a silent face-off, the hopelessly poor and the hopefully rich (after this movie), although when I pointed this out to PJ, he swung round on me from inside his hood with a vicious gleam in his eye. 'You're the only person here making any money, and tomorrow you're going on holiday for three weeks!'

PJ was a different animal on *Unconditional Love*. He looked like an elf on the run in his parka with its fur hood. He was under a lot of pressure from the studio and needed his wife Jocelyn to be around at all times. She was Susan Strasberg to his Marilyn. Kathy and he didn't really get along. PJ was a pernickety director, one of those men who can do thirty takes on one shot, which actors hate. After three takes I could tell that all Kathy really wanted to do, as he came over and huddled too close, whispering more last-minute instructions, was to tear off one of his limbs and eat it. One day we would find her standing there guiltily with his feet sticking out of her mouth.

But I loved him. Of all the directors I have worked with, PJ was the one with whom I clicked. He was mischievous, funny and loved crew gossip even more than I did. There is nothing else to do on a movie set but watch the comings and goings of the crew. There is always some mind-boggling scoop waiting to be unearthed. Gangs form; vendettas and sanctions are enforced; embassies are closed and wars declared. Between PJ and Newline the war was time. We were not keeping remotely to schedule.

The studio very cleverly sent an executive in a wheelchair to whip PJ into shape. He was an enigmatic man with huge biceps, who could accelerate from zero to sixty in a matter of seconds. He was nicknamed Ironsides and was a ball breaker, but no match for PJ who could be as slippery as an eel when he wanted to be.

My trailer became a kind of on-set nightclub. We covered the lights with coloured gels. We put up extravagant Christmas decorations. People dropped by for mulled wine made by Eileen the genius wardrobe assistant and Suzanne the set photographer. Both these fabulous women had been on *My Best Friend's Wedding*. We had a special set of stairs made by the props guys for the little girls when they passed by. Mo sat in the trailer until bedtime and we all had a wonderful time.

At weekends I flew in private planes to different destinations in America to either receive an award or give one. Giving an award is one of the most depressing pastimes known to man. You stand in the wings with another publicity starved celebrity in borrowed jewels. You breeze onto the set to one or other of your famous theme tunes. You josh together at the podium, ploughing through lame banter, looking glassy-eyed, like a somnambulist, as you try to keep up with the teleprompter.

'And the nominations are . . .' you sing.

'And the winner is . . .' tweets your companion.

Then you act surprised and thrilled as a third celebrity bounds to the podium and grabs the award as you stand gracefully back, smiling beatifically with gleaming bleached teeth while someone else thanks a God they wouldn't recognise if he came up to them at an audition and said, 'I'll see *you* at the pearly gates.' Then you all sweep off stage and give interviews in the VIP area about vulnerability and becoming a better person (than everyone else), flogging your latest product in between the lies. Your PR stands beside you, listening to every word. They are the nannies of the stars and wag their fingers if you go too far and say something you actually think. After a bit of this you are bundled into the limo and back to the discreet airfield to make that private connection to the movie set you are presently ter-rorising.

The job of maintaining a profile in Hollywood is much more drain-ing and demanding than making a film, and it is done at a thousand and one award shows, premières and the magic red carpets that lead to them. If you know how to schmooze at a podium you will probably get picked up for a TV series. These endless backpatting ceremonies, and the publication and obsession with box office receipts, have stripped cinema of most of its remaining mystique.

I suggested to Paramount that they invite journalists from all the gay contact magazines around the US for a weekend in Miami to present *The Next Best Thing*. If the twenty million gays and lesbians came out to see the film, I would be made, and the gay culture might move into the mainstream of Hollywood. Paramount was enthusiastic but when the journalists got there they were less so. While they couldn't believe they had finally been invited into the world of movie junkets, it was clear that they found the picture tame and lame. They wanted

Madonna to be as stunning as her greatest hits. Being good was not enough. Actually it was bad.

Back in Chicago, I had a Christmas party in my trailer and the suspension broke. It had been snowing heavily, and Kathy, Merrylegs and I had spent the last three nights suspended by our legs over Chicago's freezing river. 'I really love PJ,' lied Kathy, sitting under the Christmas tree, 'but he can be a little irritating. You always seem so cheery. How do you do it?'

'Marijuana. Two hits before each set-up,' I counselled.

So for Christmas, I gave her a see-through negligee, high-heeled slippers and a huge joint. She put the clothes on but did not smoke the joint and the party began. Within half an hour there must have been fifty people in the trailer. Suzanne and Eileen kept the mulled wine flowing. PJ gave me a glass ball with St Paul's Cathedral inside. When you shook it, seagulls flew prettily around the dome, and it sang, 'Feed the birds.' The stunt co-ordinator was my arch-enemy. He was always busting me for drinking on set, and tonight I had to hang again, so he was furious. He was a huge man and, as he came on board to close down the party, the trailer collapsed on one side, and everyone screamed.

The next day Jamie and I went to Miami on a private plane provided by Tom Rosenberg. As we were living the dream, the millennium approached; what I didn't know was that I was about to crash.

CHAPTER 41

Donatella's New Year's Eve Party

The Versace house remained empty after Gianni's murder until New Year's Eve 1999, when Donatella made a new entrance in the alleyway at the back and put a sign on the front door with an arrow directing visitors around the corner. That night, she gave the last party of the old century. She left the next day.

What a feeling of impending doom there was that night. Were the computers going to jam? Was the world going to stop? The TV jumped from Bethlehem to Belgrade and crowds around the world leered dangerously at each other across a billion screens, like too many panting dogs straining at the leash to get into the dog park. Any second now there would be a giant scuffle.

On the way to the Versace house, I bumped into Luisa on Ocean Drive with a piece of tinsel around her sailor's hat. She was drunk.

'*Tutto bene?*' she asked.

'*Tutto bene, Luisa,*' I replied. '*Bon anniversaire!*' And she disappeared waving into the crowd.

The walls of the Versace house could no longer hold the outside world at bay. The noise from Ocean Drive was like the storming of the Bastille, exhilarating and terrifying at the same time. I found Donatella sitting alone on a couch in the garden, wearing a silver dress, wrapped up in a thousand memories.

'I'm so depressed,' she said simply.

'Me too,' I replied, but mine was cosmetic by comparison.

Donatella was clouded by tragedy that night. It curled around her in wisps and tendrils, obliterating her from time to time. Suddenly she was there for a moment, visible through its icy receding fingers, laughing at a piece of gossip, but otherwise it was always pulling her in deeper. It was touching to see her brace herself and greet the throng of guests that swept into the house, wave after wave, a polished swaying Botoxed crowd baying for pleasure. She moved among them with the politeness and precision of a hardened sleepwalker. Luckily for her, and unluckily, people generally reacted to the way she looked and searched no further. To them she was the brash party diva. People didn't see the depth or the sadness, though sometimes she offered it, humbly and with dignity, in a conversation, but it was always overlooked. She had built an image for herself that had become a prison. Nobody could see through the peroxide wall. Then she huffed smoke like a dragon, rolled her eyes in frustration and came back to the couch to sit down. Soon, however, she was back up on the burning deck, one hand in an endless rotation pushing her hair behind her back, the other, manicured, heavily bejewelled, clutching a pink diamanté lighter and a pack of Marlboro reds. Special packs had been made for these cigarettes in the atelier back in Milan, and 'Smoking Kills' was replaced by the letters DV in a gothic scrawl. The tragic cloud could not extinguish that peculiar humour, very Italian, and it broke through the mist that night after Jennifer Lopez made her entrance.

Dessert was being served. A cluster of divas, some of them stars, others not, sat around Donatella at a corner table in the courtyard. The party moved fast around us, the table was a rock, and waves of *fruits de mer* crashed against it, swelling our numbers from eight to twelve, and then to sixteen. Chairs peeled off in all directions in a swastika for intimate asides over cigarettes and crossed legs, but the undertow on this particular stretch of bitch was strong and soon, they had been swept back out to sea by the acid tongue of Madonna's brother Christopher Ciccone, the glum monosyllabic reply of Guy Ritchie, or the polite but firm dismissal of Gwyneth Paltrow. Madonna smiled graciously to all and sundry, secure in the knowledge that someone else would do the dirty work, and give any unwanted jellyfish 'the old heave-ho'.

But Ingrid Casares, Madonna's mouthpiece and Miami's mistress of ceremonies, kept the flow coming, watching her saint all the while, but at the same time ignoring the warning signals from the galaxy around her. She had a job to do, after all, but the table wanted to keep to itself, because with us that night, hanging in the air, were the thousand ghosts and skeletons that come with the holly and the mistletoe: our fears and hopes, and these were company enough. A lot of wires were crossed around that table, and some strained connections were going to be cut loose as the old century rang out. Others were being forged right there; locks were being hammered into chains, as the minute hand approached the extraordinary hour. Perhaps the table had one thing, one aim, in common. Nobody, Guy, Madonna, Gwyneth or Donatella, was *ever* coming back to Miami.

Unbeknown to most of us, Guy and Madonna were having a baby. Strangely enough, so was Ingrid. Guy's body curved around his rock princess in acquiescence though his face was a sheer contractual addendum that night. It said: whatever else, never Miami. The impact of this was dawning on poor Ingrid, who had moved Madonna to Miami in the first place, but she held on doggedly to the fraying lasso around Madonna's neck. For the time being it could stay there, but nothing was going to be the same again in the house of the immaculate deception. Gwyneth had been flirting with Guy Oseary, the child prodigy who ran Madonna's record company, but that liaison was another thin strand that Gwyneth cut with the brisk cheer of a dignitary opening a new wing of a hospital. 'I name this ship . . . Over.' It had snapped before the party even began. Actually, she was thick as thieves with Christopher, and after midnight the two of them danced like whirling dervishes until they wound up slumped and feverish on Donatella's garden couch.

And this was the night that marked the beginning of the end for Christopher and Madonna. They had been inseparable through a trippy childhood in a huge family with a wicked stepmother, and she had taken him with her to the material world, where Christopher had provided a solid raft in the shark-infested waters. And for anyone who came into contact with Madonna, to know her at all you had to know him. The one was incomprehensible without the other. He was her dark side and she was his. People reeled in horror at the mention of his name, because he had a blunt aggressive manner, and he often looked as though he was laughing at you, particularly when he was drunk, but underneath he was a vulnerable funny friend in the old tradition. Once you were friends – you were friends. But Guy and Chris were from different planets, and in a way the one's success relied on the other not being there. Also Guy was not particularly comfortable with queens, and so, as the relationship between him and Madonna quickly deepened, it was a last call for a lot of the disco bunnies and club-mix queens that made up the fabric of Madonna's mantle. It was a surprise, because Madonna came out of the womb blowing a disco whistle, but a whole aspect of her life was about to be hit by the delete button.

The Next Best Thing hung over the table that night as well. 'American Pie' played endlessly on South Beach that Christmas like the first chilling breeze before the hurricane to come. For me, hearing myself chanting away behind Madonna, later that night at Twist, or later still, in a weird remix by Junior Vasquez, it was about as exciting as life could get. The movie was coming out in two months' time and we knew it could make or break us both.

And so, shortly before midnight, Jennifer Lopez swept into the courtyard on the arm of Benny Medina, her new manager. Donatella got up and walked over to greet her while Gwyneth and Madonna gave two snorts of derision and noisily left the room. The men and Ingrid were momentarily flummoxed but followed suit, leaving me and my hairdresser Jamie alone at the table. It could have been a moment from *The Women*. A thousand pairs of eyes swivelled between the two groups of divas, one caravan threading its way grandly towards the garden and the disco lights, the other moving slowly towards the table through a sea of upturned adoring faces. As the last member of the M team left, Donatella arrived with the J team, only to find Jamie and me alone at the huge table.

'Where is everyone?' asked Donatella, startled.

'We don't know,' Jamie and I replied hopelessly.

Jennifer had given a rather startling interview a few weeks earlier, one of her best, as a matter of fact, where she had regally dished all and sundry, saying, among other things, that Madonna couldn't sing and that Gwyneth couldn't act. This broke an unwritten Hollywood law. Think it but never say it. Jennifer was still learning the ropes. (She learnt fast. When Iraq kicked in, somebody asked her what she thought of the war and she replied, 'I leave all *that* sort of thing to Ben [Affleck].' Jennifer was no Dixie chick.) I say, let's have more catfights. The public love it because they finally get a feeling of the diva involved, a glimpse of the snarly side of her character; and certainly, everyone there at the party that night adored the drama. They were visibly shaking with the thrill of it, and so were the girls in question. They were like ducks during a rainstorm, preening, stretching their wings, shaking themselves and quacking. Jennifer sat with Benny, holding a beatific smile in place for longer than a porno star keeps an erection. Gwyneth and Madonna huddled around Donatella's garden couch like bullies from the upper sixth. Guy and Guy were puzzled but played along. Ingrid was like a cartoon cat, caught in a ravine between two cliffs. Jamie and I locked ourselves into a bathroom with Donatella, a bodyguard at the door, and informed the rest of the world what was going on outside. We popped out briefly for midnight and then went back to the bunker like war journalists to phone in the latest explosion.

The next day Madonna had a barbecue at her beautiful house on the bay. It was the last time anyone would see it. She sold it two months later. It was a beautiful white mansion, built in the twenties and had been decorated by Christopher. It stood in front of a huge expanse of sea and sky and had a strange, uninhabited feeling. You wouldn't know she lived there; there was nothing personal within it. A little freshwater creek ran through the bottom of the garden and that day the sky was off-white, so was the bay and so were we. Everything merged into one. Far away on the horizon, Miami Beach was a thin line dividing the elements upon which the new towers of South Point were like little jagged blips on a fading cardiogram.

Everyone was exhausted. Especially Mo, who nearly drowned in Madonna's pool. Luckily Lola was watching and we hauled him out. I thought he'd had a heart attack because he staggered out of the water and collapsed in a puddle on the terrace. I became quietly frantic. Elsa, an eccentric Cuban, came and sat by us. Mo couldn't move. He lay there looking at me from the corners of his eyes. We fed him bread and milk. Finally he got better and staggered to his feet.

Everyone who was anyone left the next day. Madonna and Donatella sold their houses. Jamie and I flew back to a freezing Chicago where we were filming, leaving Mo with Jay. With the coming of the millen-nium, *la belle époque* was officially over. Hardly has a star been seen on South Beach since. Now it was open season for everyone else.

The première of *The Next Best Thing* was the breathless summit of my Hollywood year. Paramount flew me and my friend Baillie from London on Concorde, and for a brief dazzling moment I was on every-body's mind. The trailers were on the TV; 'American Pie' was on the airwaves; my airbrushed face stared petulantly from the magazine stands. My relationship with Madonna intrigued America, and for a few seconds on the street the world froze and I walked on by.

At the première, which was orchestrated with a military precision by Madonna and her field marshal the formidable Liz Rosenberg, our cars pulled up simultaneously at the kerb; the crowds screamed our names as we stepped out into the firing squad of paparazzi, like con-demned men with smiles glued to our faces. Guy and Madonna walked ahead. I kept one pace behind, like the Duke of Edinburgh. We made our way down the long red carpet as the dark holes of a thousand cam-eras dilated in scrutiny, looking us up and down while I said what I loved about her and she said what she loved about me. Stunned by the flashlights and faces – among them, Salman Rushdie and Cilla, of all people – we were swept along by the current, wide eyed and wired, guided by the invisible hands of 'our people' towards this journalist or that studio executive, until we eventually arrived at our seats in the the-atre, where various members of my life waved from different corners of the stalls. Julia and Ben appeared out of an explosion of flashlights, looking glossy and unruffled.

'Hi, I'm Julia,' said Julia, with a huge smile.

'I know who you are,' said Madonna icily.

It was the only good moment of the evening.

The movie opened across America on Friday. At eight o'clock on Saturday morning Baillie and I arrived in the Concorde lounge at JFK. The first person we saw was Robbie Williams. 'Oops,' he said and dis-appeared to the loo.

'What's wrong with Robbie?' I asked Baillie, as we meandered through the lounge.

On a table were the morning papers. 'Madonna Lays An Egg' was written in huge letters across the cover of the *New York Post*. 'Rupert's

Mediocre Thing' said another. 'Next Best Thing is a Stinker.' I nearly fainted. It was a catastrophe. Baillie and I rummaged through the papers as the dowagers and tech billionaires watched us with amused distracted smiles from their comfy leather couches. At a certain point we began to laugh.

'Oh, no! Look at this one. Actually maybe you shouldn't,' said Baillie. I grabbed the paper: 'Rupert Everett's performance has all the energy of a pet rock.'

'That's why I said oops,' said Robbie returning from the loo.

I have never read such bad reviews in my life.

But a film has a *Picture of Dorian Gray* quality to it. Even though its image is 'locked down', the perception of that image ebbs and flows with the years. Sometimes a movie coins the catchphrase of the day but it looks hollow and contrived a year later, and ends its flickering life as a campy classic to be watched, stoned, with a bunch of queens who chant every line. Sometimes it sinks without trace in the initial race, torn to shreds by the vultures in the know, only to re-emerge years later on cable TV with a strange resonance and a new meaning that was unintended or overlooked by its creators. Thus Doris Day and Rock Hudson, the 'It' couple of their day, end by revealing the hypocrisy of their age. Their relationship seems hopelessly fake in an America of suppression and segregation, whereas Nick and Nora in *The Thin Man* series are strangely fresh and true. But what is true? *Mommie Dearest* killed Faye Dunaway, but was Faye as bad as all that? Or was she too brilliant? What made James Dean live on and then suddenly die? They were forced to close his tribute museum this year due to lack of interest. These are questions we in the business ask our shrinks every week.

The Next Best Thing is not a great film. Its tone and delivery are unremarkable. It blew my new career out of the water and turned my pubic hair white overnight. But over the years it has had a strange life. Maybe it was painted in blood. Certainly it was a snapshot that sucked up many souls. The vitriol engendered by Madonna's performance says as much about the resentment felt by a world of neurotic fans for its household gods as it does about her thespian skills. Acres of acting have been cheaper than hers and have yet been awarded Oscars and crowns. It all depends on how the liquor is hitting you. My mum watched the film at a screening and she felt as if she was in a muddled dream of her own life. She was heaving with sobs after twenty minutes and nearly had to be carried out at the end, she was so upset.

In Cambodia three years later, a country largely beyond the clutches of Hollywood but not of Maverick Records, I walked into a bar and *The Next Best Thing* was playing on a TV above a pool table. Madonna was looking sadly at her breasts in a mirror, holding them in her hands. 'Nineteen-eighty-nine,' she said, before letting them flop down. 'Nineteen-ninety-nine.' It was the best scene in the movie.

Kids with billiard cues in their hands stood motionless before Madonna, intrigued and challenged. Now our film was shocking and avant garde, winking at me across the smoky room. Who knew that a chance moment in a bar at Phnom Penh would be one of the high points of my career. Me watching them watching her watch herself was as good as it ever got.

CHAPTER 42

Charity Begins as Far Away as Possible

By the summer of 2000 the whole storm had passed by. I was in London on my way to Rome where I had rented a flat for the month of July. It was the beginning of a nomadic wander around the world that still hasn't ended.

One morning the phone rang. It was my legendary PR, Connie Filipello. 'Good morning, my sweetest little angel,' she sang down the line.

Alarm bells rang. This was the Connie strategy for starting a bumpy conversation.

'Hello,' I replied cautiously. 'This is very early for you.'

'I just wanted to catch you, my little sugar plum fairy, before you left for Rome.'

'Oh, right. Well, I'm leaving in a couple of hours.'

'Hughie and I loved having dinner with you the other night.'

'I loved it too, darling. I thought you were looking magnificent,' I said, hoping to deflect the conversation on to one of our favourite topics – our faces (all four of them). There was the slightest pause. She wasn't biting. I braced myself.

'Darling, I was wondering, do you think you're becoming a tiny bit selfish?'

'Selfish? What a funny question. You know me, Poops, the selfish shellfish.'

'Yes, I do.' She chuckled knowingly. 'I want to organise a little trip. May I?'

'What kind of trip?'

'Just a little trip to Ethiopia, darling.'

'Why, do I have something coming out there?' I was still half asleep.

'Not exactly, darling. I have organised for you to go with Oxfam to help them make a little film about famine. I'm sending Marina with you, and she can write about it in the *Sunday Times*. I think it's important, darling, honestly, or I wouldn't ask.'

Marina was in the same Buddhist chapter as Connie. She was the daughter of the last king of Romania, and was part of Connie's stable of reliable journalists. I liked her very much. We had met several times, in various different places, and she had written some great articles.

It was the summer that Concorde blew up. I was living in a beautiful apartment behind the Piazza del Popolo in Rome. It was an unbearably hot July, and the afternoon before I left we had all the shutters closed to keep out the heat. In the dark Jay turned on the TV only to find our favourite means of transport had burst into flames and crashed outside Paris. It was an eerie exclamation mark for the new millennium, a *Hindenburg* for today. It went down again and again on channel after channel until we could take no more. Mo was particularly upset, although he hid it well. French Concorde was the only plane in the world that took dogs on board. Back in the hold, thought he with a deep sigh and a sideways glance.

I was conducting a rather prickly romance with a Roman boy, and after an unsatisfactory farewell dinner in the restaurant downstairs, where I had hoped that the dramatic nature of my impending departure to the dark continent would wring some profound declaration from his haughty patrician mouth (no such luck), he walked me to the taxi rank on the north side of the piazza. I was driven through the midnight city to the airport. No need to ask which gate once I got inside. Crowds of giantesses in printed turbans with beautiful slender necks made the announcement and hung around the gate with their equally huge men in coloured kaftans.

The next morning I arrived in Addis Ababa where I was met by

Marina and a girl from Oxfam. It was pouring with rain. The sides of the roads were caked with mud and rubbish, and people picked their way along them. Plastic bags hung on every twig like beached jellyfish. I was taken to the Oxfam office, a ground-floor flat in a house on the edge of town. Rain dripped into a bucket like a metronome as a man in a khaki outfit gave a talk and pointed at a map with a ruler. It felt like being back at school. He was a romantic-looking fellow, with kind eyes, although he didn't seem to be quite sure where everything was. That night we all had dinner and were joined by another group just in from the bush where they had been inoculating babies. News was swapped, conditions were berated, bygone disasters were discussed with fondness. Some people had not seen each other since 'the flood in Eritrea'. One girl mistook me for someone else and asked me whether I had seen Penny since the earthquake. A photographer called Brian arrived, with a handlebar moustache and droopy eyes. No one had seen him since the Susan Sarandon trip to Zambia. The guys were the stars living in the trenches, trekking into town with a backpack full of dirty clothes. The girls were the fans. They came here from the Banbury Road in Oxford every few months with provisions or a celebrity or a TV crew, or all three. Each campaign sounded like the name of a play and if I closed my eyes I might have been sitting among a group of actors. ('Brina has just got back from *Hedda Gabler* in Leeds' became 'Brian had a great success with *Mosquito Nets* in Uganda.')

The next morning we flew north to a flat desert. More plastic bags clung to dead trees. Blue and white, they flapped in the endless wind, beautiful and hideous at the same time. The Oxfam compound was like a scout camp surrounded by a high wattle fence. Inside, huts stood in rows with a latrine at the end wrapped in a sheet of bright blue bin liner. The loo roll hung on a piece of string and waved in the breeze. A trowel was stuck into a pyramid of fresh earth beside the ominous hole. Over a wall there was a kitchen hut and a large trestle table around which we ate. It was quite extraordinary. I was feeling less selfish by the minute but couldn't help wondering how Connie would have managed.

The first afternoon we drove out to the feeding station. Thousands of little egg-shaped tents made out of wood and plastic stretched far into the distance. The whole nomadic world had ground to a halt and now hundreds of thousands of people were glued to the feeding stations. A culture was being killed but this was the price for a sort of survival. Long lines of women waited for rations. The men did nothing. Groups of them sat about while the women and children seemed to be endlessly moving, looking for anything that could be eaten or made into a hut. As they moved across the horizon, slowly with extraordinary poise, their colourful robes flew behind them in the wind, hugging their skin and bone into pitiful silhouettes against the baking white sky.

Seeing all this, at first my brain froze. It was impossible to take in and there wasn't any time because now my job began. The TV crew and Brian the photographer were going to walk with me to the feeding station to meet a woman who had just arrived, and accompany her back to her hut. It was an excruciating experience. The woman's husband was dead. She had walked a hundred miles to get to the feeding station. On the journey, one of her children had died. The other was a little, barely breathing bundle of bones in a sling around her neck. She recounted all this, through an interpreter, in a listless voice, with vacant dilated eyes. There was no emotion. Hunger had taken all her energy. There was none left for the superfluous. When we got to her tent, she and I went in, followed by Brian. The plastic roof bathed the hut in a ghostly green light. She looked like a Martian in it. Everything she had was there: a blanket, a wooden bowl and a baby. Brian started taking pictures.

'Move her over a bit,' he said. The camera clicked. The woman looked down. 'Tell her to lift her face. I can't get a picture if she's looking down.'

Obviously it had to be done. The photo op is all. The world only responds when they see the living proof in pictures, at which point it is often too late, but I was amazed and horrified by the photographer, by the whole world around this tragic scene, myself included. At one point we were talking to a little child. He started to have a kind of fit and passed out. One of the girls from the Banbury Road became slightly hysterical. Her anguish stood out among the silent nomads and her more experienced colleagues, who laid the boy down in silence on his side. She paced back and forth, turned grey and generally looked as though she too was about to have a fit. She was on her own. Western emotionalism had no place here. Our paranoid fear of death was ludicrous to these people; they had no energy for terror. Everything they had was given to survival.

We marched on through the wind. We talked too much and our eyes were on stalks, so our throats were parched and our eyes were blood-shot . . . We met village elders. We met kids. We watched little babies with huge stomachs being weighed. Everything was on camera. The nomads watched us silently, hardly moving. We must have looked like freaks. I certainly felt like one.

The next morning, after a fairly sleepless night, I went to the big table for breakfast at about seven o'clock. Brian arrived and suggested we walk around the town before breakfast and do some pictures. For some reason I remembered a conversation I had had with Madonna a couple of months earlier. I was complaining about having to do some-thing or other. She looked at me like an alien who observes an earthling while she's sucking out his database.

'Why can't you learn to say no, Rupert?' I could suddenly hear her saying.

'No, no, no,' I said firmly. 'We've got the whole day ahead, haven't we?'

Brian looked at me for a moment and then disappeared. I sat down and had a cup of coffee. Five minutes later Marina appeared. 'Brian's leaving the trip!' she announced dramatically.

'Why?' I asked.

'He says no one has ever talked to him so rudely as you just did.'

'What? I just said I didn't want to do pictures before breakfast. That's not very rude.'

'Will you come and apologise? Maybe you can convince him to stay,' she pleaded.

'Okay,' I said and we went to the other side of the complex where Brian was sitting surrounded by the girls from the Banbury Road. You would have thought his whole family had been killed in a car crash.

I was beginning to feel angry. This was ridiculous. But we needed pictures. There was no point without them so I oiled up to Brian and his entourage, who were looking daggers at me. Soon he was huffing and puffing and saying that maybe he could stay after all, and we got on with the job. Later Marina and the girls from Oxfam told me that I was the second most difficult celebrity they had ever had.

'Who was the first?' I couldn't help asking.

'Ooh, we couldn't say. It wouldn't be right,' they said. 'How would you like it if we went around saying—'

'Saying I was the second most difficult celebrity? I should be honoured.'

I was a lost cause.

It was a disastrous trip, confirming what I'd always suspected. Maybe I just wasn't cut out for charity work. They all drove me mad with their piousness, and they couldn't stand me. Soon I was hardly on speaking terms with the comrades from Oxfam. But we ended up in Nairobi, anyway, where as it happens my brother lived.

My parents, seizing the first opportunity in decades for a family reunion, flew out to join us. Pretty soon I found myself trapped between them with their friends from the frenetic colonial cocktail crowd and my new charity family, who stared at me accusingly over steaming mugs of tea at the Oxfam headquarters.

One morning we were going on a trip into Kibera, the huge slum in the centre of Nairobi. My mother asked whether she could come. Surrounded by police with machine-guns (quite unnecessary), we picked our way through open sewers and throngs of half-naked kids. The slum stretched for miles on either side in waves of plastic roofs. The railway track to Mombasa ploughed through the middle. Trains shrieked through and the plastic bags that littered the huge siding flew madly around in their wake.

'I'm afraid these espadrilles were not made for this terrain, darling. Would you mind if I went back to the house?' said my mother after about fifteen minutes. Typical. She hogged the whole police escort and hightailed it back to the army base at the edge of the slum, while we went on alone to meet the Revd Anne Owiti.

Anne looked like one of the Mamas and the Papas, in a bright kaftan over a full body. She was very imposing, with a heavy brow and the bewildered regard of someone who is about to bludgeon you with a sledgehammer, but she had the voice of a little girl. I liked her immediately. She marched us around a school where orphans of every age sat at tiny desks. When we came into a classroom they all stood up and sang a little song. 'We-lcome, we-elcome. Welcome to our community.'

After a while I felt like Deborah Kerr in *The King and I*, and only the glum long faces of Marina, Brian and the Banbury Road mob stopped me from breaking into a rousing chorus of 'Getting to Know You'.

Later, in a dark room with windows onto the seething street, we met a woman of about thirty-five and her son, a boy of sixteen. She had Aids. Her eighteen-year-old daughter had Aids. Her sixteen-year-old son had Aids, and her fourteen-year-old daughter had it too. She was being re-educated so that she could sell charcoal on the side of the road, but now she was very sick. Her sixteen-year-old was with her. He was beautiful with a shaved head and a long graceful neck. He had been raped when he was twelve (in Africa the witch doctors promise cures to people who have sex with a virgin) and had developed full-blown Aids the previous year, although you wouldn't have known it that day. Mother and son were silhouettes, almost ghosts in the dull light from the dirty window. It was utterly quiet in the room. The two spoke softly to Anne and she translated their stories in her girlish voice, like a medium passing on messages from the dead. There was a strange presence in the room, and the screams and shouts from outside in the street seemed to come from another world. Here, if anywhere, was God; for there was an awe-inspiring beauty in the quiet dignity of these two souls sharing their terrifying secrets and expecting nothing in return.

Next, Anne took us to a room where a sick boy was having treatment. His legs were covered in cracking lumps. A lady rubbed Vaseline on them. That was all they had. The boy watched us solemnly and was too shy to answer questions. Next door was a small room with an earth floor and a table with a pair of stirrups tied to it where Anne and her girl-friends delivered babies for women who were HIV positive and had been turned away from the local hospitals. At the back of the house was the medicine cabinet for the whole compound. It contained no more than a couple of boxes of tetracycline. Anne watched me closely as she opened the door, talking all the time. She was mesmerising me and I had to look away. Next to the cupboard was a window. I looked out. The house must have been at the edge of the slum because on the other side was the closely mown green of an exclusive golf course. A little red flag waved happily in the breeze. Three men practised their swings and laughed.

If Connie had meant for me to *seem* less selfish, to give a saintly hue to my public persona, she couldn't have failed more dismally. Marina's article ran in the *Sunday Times* with the heading 'Rupert Says "Let Them Eat Cake."' Like poor Marie Antoinette before me, I had been wildly misquoted.

I escaped from Africa and did my best to forget I had ever been there. Back in the Hollywood stream, even the most successful star has the impression that imminent death could be just around the corner. Was the last job career-icide? Should I have butt implants? Are my tits pointing in the right direction? Do I have enough hair? Should I do a stack of steroids? It was taking all the attention I had to ride the rapids of blind ambition and I pushed the African experience to the back of my mind. But once you've seen, there is no way back. You may be in New York at the top of the tallest tower looking out over the world's most exciting city, but now you know that in the same moment the other is happening, and no matter how much you try to confine this 'other' to some dark gurgling recess of the brain, it lies there waiting for you to stop thinking, because that is its chance to escape.

Drifting away during a dreary meeting, or posing in front of a camera, it would literally flood out, and I'd be back in that darkened room in Kibera with the lady who learnt how to sell charcoal and the boy who was raped at the age of twelve. Their murmurs and Anne Owiti's childish sing-song voice would cut through the instructions of a photographer like invisible spirits during a seance.

'Ye-as, Rupert. Wha' dey are saying is da' dey need help very bad. Ve-ree bad!'

'Can you give us a smile, Rupert? Thaat's right. Now. One. Two. Three. Chins up, and flashing.'

I lived in denial for a year. Then one day at the beginning of 2001, I woke up and wrote a letter to all the richest people I knew. Without that much effort I raised a considerable amount of money. Some people sent me a lot. (Madonna, Elton John and George Michael were the most generous.)

Suddenly a whole world opened up and I was on that ropy old bridge called charity that spanned the gulf between the Third World and ours, with all its merchants and fortune-tellers, its saints and its sinners, that flitted back and forth selling their wares. I took part in debates at inter-

national Aids conferences. I listened to an archbishop peddling abstinence, and a witch doctor who prescribed rape. Interestingly, both
men had HIV. I was invited by a revolutionary student group in
Washington to speak about my experiences. I accepted, even though
the only one I really had was of First World indifference and sloth, my
own self-obsession and that curious sensation that constipates action. I
was too busy drowning in my own life to act. Knowing nothing, I lob-
bied Congress with a brilliant preacher activist. We spent fifteen
minutes with a babe in a miniskirt who worked for Senator McCain.
Her voice was so high, it could only be heard by bats. 'As you know,' she
squealed, 'this isn't really the senator's area, but I'll be sure to let him
know about your concerns. Have a great day, now.' While we were
there over a hundred people died horribly in Africa.

I met three sisters from Lusaka who ran a magazine that brilliantly
combined gossip and Aids awareness. With them I trekked into the
Zambian bush and saw exactly how the other half lived. The men did
nothing. The women did everything. They got up with the first streaks
of dawn. They walked for miles to get water and firewood, with babies
on their backs and worked all day, while their husbands sat around.

I met a brilliant doctor from America who lived in a hut in the
mountains of Haiti. I watched child prostitutes at work in the grave-
yards of Port-au-Prince and felt the tremors of civil unrest like a grating
fault line across the country. Eventually, I became involved with a G8
invention – The Global Fund to fight for Tuberculosis, Aids and
Malaria – and then the full horror of our two faced relationship with
the Third World slowly dawned. The Global Fund was a good idea, a
partner without ideology for any grass-roots group with a good business
plan, but it was deeply underfunded and in the end seemed to be little
more than a net curtain for us all, the gun runners and trade terrorists
of the G8, to hide behind. It was desperately ineffective mostly because
it was being systematically destroyed from within. First by Bush who
had his own kitty for Aids, the PEPFAR – a carrot he was dangling to
attract the neo-Christian voter in America. Together they could 'save'
Africa, even if it meant losing a few million lives in the process. The
Christian soldiers offered medication in return for abstinence because,
according to them, Jesus would never wear a condom. The Republican
Congress cut funding to the Global Fund and discredited it whenever

they could. Desperate to score, they threw money indiscriminately around Africa, to the point that in one country they managed to create inflation.

And so the images stubbornly stay the same. The shrunken woman writhing on the mud floor of a hut. The dead boy lying by the side of a busy road. The child prostitute racked by a hacking cough. And, ironically, wandering through it all, the embedded celebrity, the image of the West, ineffective and self-absorbed, out of his depth and impotent.

CHAPTER 43

Goodbye, Albert, Goodbye, Mo

On September 10, 2001, at about the same time as Mohamed Atta was drawing money from an ATM in Portland, Albert and his sidekick Reuben, a penniless Dominican rogue whom Albert used as a slave, were scoring an eight-ball of coke in Hialeah before going to see Albert's parents in Coral Gables. His mother Sylvia, an incredibly active woman, had not been well and was more or less living in bed. This latest twist of old age had driven her slightly mad. The two 'boys' stayed for a couple of hours, flitting back and forth to the bathroom, before driving back to the beach.

At about five o'clock the next morning, Albert had a massive heart attack. He was rushed to Mount Sinai hospital where they were unable to operate because he was too high. Instead they pumped him full of something that left him in a very curious state. The family were called. As they arrived at the emergency room, two planes crashed into the World Trade Center and things came to a standstill in the world. In the hospital people crowded around TV screens and watched in horror as America seemed to crumble to the ground with the two towers. Delirious in his recumbent position, flying about on a gurney, Albert couldn't figure out what was going on. All he could see were the taut faces of his trolley dollies. In the corridors between the emergency room and intensive care, large groups stood horrified around TV screens. As they flashed past, Albert thought he saw two burning candles on the screen.

His best friend, the long-suffering Myrtha, rushed to the hospital as soon as she heard the news, but by this time Albert was locked in a furious hallucination and accused her of going behind the bed to take coke. Everywhere he saw cocaine. He thought the crowds around the TV screens were coke huddles. He told his bewildered father that he needed to get laid and then he'd feel better. He tried to call a dealer on his cellphone and soon was in such a state he needed to be re-sedated. By this time his family and friends were thoroughly distraught. Even as the tranquilliser took hold, he ploughed on in his mirage cocaine orgy.

'You're doing it again,' he snapped at Myrtha, as the needle went in.

'We're not doing coke, Albert!' sobbed Myrtha, reduced by now to tears.

'It's hardly appropriate,' said Albert in a sing-song voice, as his eyelids fluttered like butterflies.

'Fuck you,' said Myrtha under her breath.

'Oh! Go, girl,' yawned Albert and passed out.

They prepared him for a quadruple bypass, shaved and painted his body, then dressed him in green. The anaesthesiologist came to check up on him once more before the operation. Albert clutched his arm. 'Are my family outside?' he asked.

'Yes, your mom and dad, your brother, and your two friends,' replied the doctor.

'Christ,' groaned Albert. 'Do we have to go past them on the way to the theatre?'

'Yes. They want to see you before you go in.'

'Okay. Just make sure that I'm out cold before we go?'

The anaesthesiologist laughed despite himself, and Albert didn't have to worry. He was rigid with anaesthetic by the time he sailed by. The operation was much more complicated than anyone had imagined. His arteries were rotten and they had to use pig veins to rewire his calcified heart.

The next day the whole of America was in shock. As Albert drifted back, on a blanket of anaesthesia, barely able to breathe – he had been sawn right through, like a magic trick – he had nothing to do but watch

TV. On the screen, the post-9/11 world was crystallising. 'It's not about healthcare,' screamed a fat man with piggy eyes. 'It's not about unemployment. It's about homeland security.' It felt like a dream. Late at night, in that drugged trance somewhere between coma and consciousness, he surfed a thousand channels, with just enough strength to work the remote control, and in the darkness watched America begin to bay for retribution.

Albert was not much of a one for introspection – no Cuban male is – but there are times when even the most cunning of escapologists is forced upon himself, and when President Bush came on the TV and said, 'You're either with us or with the terrorists,' Albert had an epiphany. His whole life slid out in front of him on the hospital bed, a completed jigsaw with one missing piece. Certainly he had been a terrorist all his life, to his family and friends. Even though technically he was still alive, as he watched the new America slither out of its chrysalis, he knew that there were no accidents and that, to all intents and purposes, he had gone down with the Trade Towers. He was never going to be one of 'us'. Death was the missing piece and he held it in his hand calmly, enjoying the view of the whole jigsaw for a moment. The grim reaper could wait for a while, but Albert was not afraid.

On the other hand, the strain had been too much for poor Sylvia. A couple of days after 9/11 she collapsed and was rushed to the same hospital where she died a week later. No one told Albert that his darling mother was on the floor above fighting for her life. They were afraid he would have another heart attack.

I was back in Miami by the time Albert finally left the hospital. He had lost everything: his health, his mother, his apartment. (He had been evicted.) His world was unrecognisable. With nowhere to go, he was obliged to move into his parents' house in Coral Gables. For nine months father and son lived together in a brief enchanted coda to the tempestuous *telenovela* of the last few years. Theobaldo was ninety-three, Albert was fifty-four. The one was an old-school, redneck sugar planter, a tough grim man who still plotted Fidel's overthrow every Friday at a club in Hialeah, not particularly a friend to the friends of Dorothy; the other was a lying, cheating, dissolute queen; but they lived in a kind of harmony that was funny and touching. They were the Cuban 'odd couple'. Theobaldo flirted with his nurse. Albert dabbled with the odd boatperson and redecorated the house in a thousand shades of white. They took naps together in the hot afternoons, and in the evenings they reminisced about Sylvia and life in Cuba. They had both adored little Sylvia and couldn't think how to live without her. In their shared grief they forgot the past and attended to one another with an affection and care that reminded me of the end of *King Lear*.

'Cordelia is a bit of a stretch,' said Albert to me thoughtfully.

'Oh, queen! I had no idea you knew *King Lear*.'

'I didn't come from Cuba on a raft, girlfriend. And who said anything about the end?'

For a while, Albert valiantly abstained from drink, cigarettes and drugs. But one thing he never had was willpower. So it was not much of a surprise, three months later, to find him perched on the end of a couch at some party in a penthouse on the bay, holding forth with a joint in one hand and a vodka in the other.

'Just weekends, queen!' he said. 'And don't even go there.'

So I didn't.

A couple of days later he offered to take me to the airport. He looked drawn and grey in the car. 'I'm a bit worried, Albert,' I ventured. 'I heard you were doing coke again. If you are, that would be really mad.'

'I would never do that. Are you crazy? You think I have a death wish?'

'Maybe,' I replied evenly.

'Who told you?' he snapped.

'You know me. I never reveal my sources.'

'It was Myrtha, wasn't it? Anyway, it's not true.'

Of course it was, and one day soon after, Albert fitted the last piece of the jigsaw in its place with a small bump. In the afternoon he began to feel cold. He got into bed and turned a ghostly white. He couldn't feel his arms, then his legs. His body was shutting down. Old Theobaldo was distraught. They called the ambulance, but he died in his father's arms before it arrived.

Theobaldo died a month later. They had all gone within a year. But Miami is like that. The tide turns and whole worlds have been swept away.

I often wonder what happened to the bell handle that lay by Albert's bed. It was such an odd thing to have taken out of Cuba, as he was being spirited away all those years ago; that his last glance should have ended on that, the discreet symbol of slavery. Did he turn it one last time before tearing it out of the wall after its tinkling ring echoed through the deserted house? Perhaps the servants had already left to join the revolution, who knows . . . All the hands that grasped it are dead. But strangely, Albert lives on and the little bell rings in my head all over South Beach, whenever I look up and find myself at one of his numerous front doors; just an echo, because Albert too has gone to join the revolution.

In the summer of 2001, Mo was bitten by a mosquito in St Moritz. We all noticed him walking squiggly as we came back from lunch through the beautiful run-down garden of the old Hotel Kurhaus where I had holidayed with my friend Rifat Ozbek for the last five summers. While everyone else headed for Ibiza, Rifat, Mo and I took to the hills. Every year, we vowed never to return, yet somehow we always did. Normally it rained and the clouds curled into your bedroom window, but there was a heatwave that summer. Day after day, the sun beat down and the mountain air smelt sweet and crisp, of grass and pine and cows; and we all said it felt like the end of the world. In the afternoons, a man played an upright piano under a giant fir tree and all the old ladies from the hotel sat in the shade, chatting. One had just celebrated her 102nd birthday. It was the last summer. The hotel was a hangover from bygone days and was closing down. It had been bought by a swanky chain, and none of the families who came there – the grand-parents escaping the summer heat of Italy, accompanied by grim, dutiful grandchildren – would be coming again. The piano sounded jangly in the vastness of the Engadine valley, playing show tunes from the distant past, and Mo collapsed beside it. Soon he was surrounded by caring octogenarians, and we all laughed later, imagining them from Mo's point of view, peering down, ankles overflowing out of shoes, legs knobbly with varicose veins, and sensible panties beneath the fluttering print skirts.

Later the vet told us he had developed a crashing type of anaemia so Jay took him back to New York, where he was put on steroids that made him as fat as a pig. I followed a week later. Soon it was getting harder for him to walk so we bought an old-fashioned pram. He and Jay could be spotted walking up Fifth Avenue to 28th Street, so that Mo could have his acupuncture from Doctor Zang.

One beautiful September morning, Mo and I were on the corner of Varrick and 7th Avenue when my cellphone rang and Jay said, 'Look at the World Trade Center!' Looking up is one of the great sensations in New York. There is mayhem all around you, but up there is silence and space and the tips of the high towers commune with the heavens like eyelashes brushing against a lover's cheek, and in that glance from the street to the skyscraper lies the whole American Dream.

There was a hole in the North Tower like a tear. Were they making a movie? Then there was a bang like Concorde breaking the speed of sound. You felt it slightly in your body and your ears popped. The second plane crashed into the South Tower. The barrel-shaped dog stood on four tiny legs, his head suddenly alert through all the new folds of extra flesh, and we watched in speechless wonder as glass and metal began to fall from the towers in glittering shards that caught the sun. They were like two fireworks about to go off. People stood in the streets, looking up. Cars stopped and passengers got out. Some people still scurried about their day until somebody nudged them, and they too looked up and froze. I never saw so many vacant faces. The wailing was for later. For now it was like the end of the world in a movie when the spaceships hover over Manhattan. Hollywood had out-tricked us, and at first it wasn't possible to take it all in. Everything one saw that day was lifted from a movie. Every cop. Every scream. Every plummeting body. And of course, the ultimate special effect: the two towers consuming themselves and crashing to the ground. We'd seen it all before in count-less movies, and movies were all we had left in that September of 2001. They were real. Actual life was swept under the carpet and ignored. One half expected to see Bruce Willis appearing out of the rubble holding the movie's unconscious babe in his arms. Then someone would shout 'Cut' and we could move on.

So it took a while for the reality to kick in. But it did, in waves that nearly knocked one over with the terrible impact. Then the screaming began. It was only later, when that hard angry city turned for once into a fountain of compassion, that one was foolish enough to believe that the day's events could be the kernel for a quantum leap towards world peace. Anyone would help you that day. Absolutely anyone. It wasn't just a disco song, a Motown myth. Love was finally in the air. Maybe we could *stop* in its name. But the powers that be wanted to go on with the movie version, and the rest is history.

Mo had seen it all. He had witnessed the fall of the Berlin Wall, the coup in Moscow and the end of communism, and now the destruction of the World Trade Center. He had visibly had enough of life. Soon he and Jay rented a car and took to the Dixie trail one last time: destination, Miami.

I returned there from a trip to Europe and Jay met me at the airport. 'Things aren't very good with Mo,' he said.

When I got back to Sea Crest, Mo could hardly get up to say hello. The steroids had caused a reaction in his coat, and huge, crusty lumps had erupted through his fur. His breathing was short, his forehead had grown into a permanent frown, and his eyes had all but disappeared inside the rolls of flesh, though they were still lively and darted back and forth. He panted a lot, his great pink tongue lolling onto the tiles, but nothing much else moved. He lay on the porch in the breeze, his nose occasionally sniffing, slightly suspicious of all the attention. Dogs are amazing examples in sickness. They are at ease in the process of letting go. In the evening, Michael, Jay and I sat watching him, and Cathy, the lady who owned Midnight, the old dog buried under the palm tree, came by with some bone-shaped biscuits she had made. We sat there chatting quietly, drinking beers, stroking Mo, but keeping our distance – a sick animal likes its space. We laughed, remembering how Mo had always cold-shouldered Midnight, and Cathy wiped a little tear from her eye. Nobody said what each of us knew and at about ten o'clock everyone left. Jay was staying with Luisa next door and was leaving for New York the next morning. I wanted everyone out of the way. The next step was for Mo and me alone.

I lay all night next to him on the porch, listening to his pathetic breaths and the rustle of the lopsided palm tree in the yard, remembering out loud all the things we had done together. He listened carefully, considerately. Occasionally I would say something and he would sigh loudly. Then his little eyes would swivel towards me guiltily.

Once he had got lost in South Beach, and Albert had driven around all night in his car trying to find him. I came home distraught at about three in the morning, only to find Mo asleep on his back on my bed and the door shut. To this day I have no idea how he got back home, but we all laughed afterwards about Albert's valiant attempt to find him. 'See, queen, I finally came through!' he'd said, and the phrase stuck. It was official. Albert could come through.

Finally I started to weep, but Mo lifted his head and looked at me disapprovingly. Then he went to sleep. The sky turned mauve, then white, and the sun came up. We had a sweet Cuban taxi driver, José, who used to take us up to the vet on 118th Street on the bay. I called him, and Mo and I took the last walk down the alley between Sea Crest and Villa Luisa. I think he knew he was never coming back because as we eventually got to the street, he stopped and wouldn't move forward. He turned round as if he was waiting for someone, sniffed a bit, looked towards Villa Luisa and then towards South Point, and afterwards up to me, as if to say, 'Let's go.' We hauled him into the back of the cab.

On the journey he sat in the back seat, slumped against the door with his head leaning on the window. One ear blew valiantly in the wind and he looked out calmly as we crossed over the causeway and into the city.

And so our relationship began and ended in a taxi. I had collected him in a Parisian cab eleven years ago one misty February morning. He had squealed and whined as we pulled away from the kennels that day and lay sulking on the floor of the taxi. Now all these years later we were back in another cab on another journey into the unknown.

At the vet's, my heart pumped fast. I took him into the surgery and the vet, a gentle man of about sixty, confirmed what I already knew, and swiftly the arrangements were made. The male nurse picked Mo up to take him into the next room to be fitted with a drip. That was the only moment I regret, because as he was being carried away, Mo looked at me with sheer terror in his eyes. It was my mother and me on the first day of school all over again. ('I'll say goodbye now, and we'll go while you're having your drip fitted.')

They came back a few minutes later and Mo had a needle attached to his leg. The nurse put him on the table. The vet told me to hold him close. I was about to ask a few questions, stall the procedure for a couple of minutes at least, but they had been through this thousands of times, and the two men moved in a swift ballet. One arm reached out to another. A syringe was passed from hand to hand. 'Hold his head.' The vet nodded at the nurse. The solution was in. Mo looked at me. I held him tight in my arms. He grunted into a last snore, and the tension of life went out of his body. The vet checked his heart with a stethoscope. And that was it.

'We'll leave you alone for a bit,' he said and left the room.

Mo's coat seemed to have changed colour already. A little bit of his pink tongue was sticking out of his mouth. He was still frowning, but he was gone. It's a strange and extraordinary thing, life with an animal. When one comes into your life, it is so young, so full of energy, and you are old by comparison. You take the role of the father. But between then and his death there is a turning of the tables. Soon you become brothers. As he gets older, you become younger, so that by the end he is a grandfather and you are a thoughtless child. In denial of his great age, you force him to do things, to keep going, and he looks at you with the eyes of an elder, sitting in the shade of the village oak. 'Come on, Mo!' you say, and he sighs and lumbers to his tired paws. He's your grandfather but he still obeys instructions.

Mo had seen me through a dangerous time. Without him I should have disappeared into the Parisian night. He got me up in the mornings. He gave me something else to think about apart from myself. And in him I found the ideal companion. Now he was letting me go. The next step was to be mine alone.

Outside in the sunshine José was waiting. He didn't say anything. I got into the cab and we drove back to South Beach. There were some hairs on the seat where Mo had been.

CHAPTER 44

Talk to Me and Then Move In and Out Real Slow

It was a freezing winter in Montreal. It was 2002. I was making *A Different Loyalty* with Sharon Stone. Destined, unfortunately, for a première on a shelf at Blockbuster, it was the last falling star from the firework explosion that happens to an acting career when a Hollywood triumph is scored. I had been offered the part in the wake of *My Best Friend's Wedding* and my agent, Nick Styne, kept his petite pink nail-bitten fingers on it as it rode the rapids through various incarnations over a three-year period. Finally the film was being made, not in Moscow, London or Beirut, where it was set, but in Montreal, where there's a tax break that was imperative to our constantly shrinking budget. This budget loaded the cards against us from the start, and the Blockbuster première was written between the lines of all the initial contracts. But at a certain point, show business is a game of chance, cowboy country; you must grab the reins, hurl your lasso at the passing cash cow and hope for the best. (Or as Philip Prowse loved to say, 'Faint heart never fucked a pig.')

So there we were in Montreal: Sharon was the leading lady, and Marek Kanievska, who had directed me in *Another Country* sixteen years earlier, had come back from a new career in windsurfing to direct the movie, madder than ever before. I had crossed paths with Sharon on numerous occasions, but she was always wrapped up in the protective arms of her attentive husband Phil Bronstein. We kissed and chatted, raised our eyebrows (in the days when one still could) as her husband seethed beside her, and we each kept moving. The first time was on the stairs at the Hôtel du Cap in the South of France. She was radiant in a jewelled dress; he looked like a sexy pug from a downtown gym in the seventies.

Many of the girls from the old school end up at some point with a bruiser. Initially they love the feeling of protection and exclusivity. The intense power they have achieved at the studio has left them completely isolated, hard as nails and yet vulnerable as twigs, deliciously snappable. They cry out to be wrapped in love and taken home. The man in question is usually decent, simple and well hung. His emotional plumbing is straightforward (for the time being) and he responds to this intense stellar fragility by erecting an electric fence around his goddess that they both adore, and for a time life is one long, first-act love montage. He feels ten feet tall. She feels cosy and petite. Sex is a constantly exploding volcano. But at a certain point the novelty wears off. She feels trapped behind the fence. Her girlfriends are vetoed; she can't bat an eyelid at a passing waiter, and she must flirt to keep her engine tuned. So suddenly, one day, without warning, the wind changes and her hard side comes out. He has never seen it before, although he has been warned. But nothing prepares him for the star's first big 'turn'. It is an earth-shattering hurricane and he reacts as only a wounded macho can. The electric fence is hastily built up into a high-security jail, at which point the whole universe usually comes crashing down around them both.

Soon Phil was eaten by a dragon and Sharon had a stroke. By the time A *Different Loyalty* came along, the marriage was over. But for the time being, we winked at each other across crowded rooms and hugged in the corridors of power. Our moment would come. Then one night at the Golden Globes, she told me she was making the sequel to *Basic Instinct* and had suggested to David Cronenberg (the director then attached to the project) that I should play the male lead. I went to meet him the next day, feeling pretty excited because he was a director I really admired. We got along well and he left the lunch to call MGM, the studio making the picture, to inform them that he had found his actor. At which point all hell broke loose. The head of the studio told my horrified agent during a conference call that to all intents and purposes a homosexual was a pervert in the eyes of America and the world would never accept me in the role and therefore MGM would never hire me. My team was horrified on my behalf and went briefly into battle; and in further conversations, the studio enlarged its argument and even exhumed some dismal turncoat fag from the marketing department who whined in agreement at everything that was said. There was no budging them. More phone calls; cries of 'unacceptable' bounced from LA into outer space and back to wherever I was; and it was about to turn into a nasty scrap. The agencies love drama. Up to a point. After a week of swearing allegiance to the client on lines one, two and three, during the relative calm of the weekend they weighed up the pros and cons for themselves. The agency is also a performer and must consider its career. Obviously MGM versus Rupert was a no-brainer and so by Monday morning the whole saga had blown over without a trace. And I do mean without a trace, because when I called people to get their side of the story (researching for this book) no one could remember the incident at all. So much for friendship; as thin and durable as the cardboard walls of the film set. When the movie ends, the friendship is struck. The company is the only connection that really counts in the handling business.

Sharon, on the other hand, never gives up. One Sunday morning, two weekends later, I was in Miami staggering home after a twenty-hour binge in a string of clubs. It was about noon and the phone rang; Sharon was calling from San Francisco. 'Honey,' she said. 'I can't believe what's happening. I'm with my pastor and we agree that we should stop the film and sue the studio. I've put in a call to SAG. What do you think?'

Well, I must say that apart from forgetting all about it until Sharon called, it had crossed my mind that my role in life was to become the Olivia de Havilland of my generation. De Havilland had fought the studios in court after being put on suspension for refusing a role in a film. She won her case, but seldom worked again. My civil rights had been fucked with, and it was not for the first time. Countless studio executives had voiced similar sentiments, but they'd had the sense to phrase them in more delicate, unidentifiable terms ('We're not making *that* kind of a movie.') As Sharon filled me in on the last week, sparing no detail of her latest conversation with the studio, I lay back on my bed, my head spinning. I searched for a cigarette, had a shot of vodka and a couple of Tylenol and, suddenly, for the first time in my entire career, I felt totally overwhelmed and began to cry.

'Oh, honey, don't cry!' said Sharon.

'I'm sorry,' I sobbed. 'I've been out all night and I'm just overtired.'

'I know, honey. It's just so unfair.'

'Yes,' I whimpered.

'Well, you get some sleep. I'm going to talk about this some more with my pastor.' (Who was this pastor? I remember thinking. Rasputin, hopefully.) 'And then you tell me what to do. We can close the movie down if that's what you want.'

All I wanted at that point was a Xanax. After I put the phone down I called my friend Albert on the other line and went over to his house where the party still raged, and forgot about the whole thing. But I always remembered Sharon's sweetness that morning on the phone.

Anyway, we finally got to work together on A *Different Loyalty*, which was based on the true story of the notorious English spy, Kim Philby, and his third wife, an American, Eleanor Brewer. They met in Beirut in the late fifties, fell in love and got married. A few years later he went out to the shops one day and never came back. Suddenly, the whole world turned upside down for the poor woman as she discovered that her husband was not the man she thought he was. In fact, he was one of the most wanted spies in the world. He disappeared for months before resurfacing in Russia. She went there to see him, in an attempt to discover what, exactly, their relationship had meant, if anything, but she hated Russia and tried to organise with the British that Philby be spirited back to England. He had become a dangerous drunk by this stage and was already having an affair with the wife of another famous spy-in-exile, Donald Maclean. At first, Philby agreed to her plan, but then backed out at the last moment. She went back to America and died.

It was a great story, adapted from a book by her, a good part of which was sheer wishful thinking. The truth of the matter was that the two of them were probably just a pair of nasty deluded drunks, who both deserved what they got. However, the screenwriter took her side, turning the story into a big romantic thriller, and it had the makings of a good film. But it needed a rewrite. The dialogue was flat and overwritten. For some reason, Sharon insisted on changing the names from the real characters to new, invented ones. She chose Sally, which was the name of our neighbour's old fat golden retriever when I was a child, and every time I uttered it the image of Sally lumbering across the garden never failed to invade the acting space. But there was no arguing with Sharon, so Sally she was. Equally problematic was the fact that the story took place in New York, London, Beirut and Moscow, and faking them was going to be difficult.

All of this, however, paled into insignificance when, at dinner with Sharon early in the rehearsal period, I realised something that had hitherto escaped me. She was utterly unhinged.

'Honey,' she said in the middle of the first course, after the initial pleasantries had been eaten. 'Have you let your character in yet?'

'What do you mean, Shaz?' I replied slightly wearily. I always find that when another actor wants to discuss character, it usually means that they want to discuss *your* character, specifically what *you* need to do so that they can play their character the way they want.

'How many dead people have you played?'

'Tons. I only ever play dead people,' I said gloomily.

'So you know. Have you let him in?' She spoke quietly and looked at me with a burning intensity. She had never looked better, even if she insisted on cutting her own hair with her nail scissors. She was a great beauty and her eyes were hypnotic. I was swept in by their drama, even if I didn't know what the fuck she was talking about.

'Sort of,' I said, feeling my way.

'Sure. I felt that. Man, she came into me last night. She's right there.' She banged her chest with her fist, then opened her fingers and grabbed one of her breasts, shaking it with passion. A man at the next table nearly fell off his chair.

'You mean Mrs Philby? Dead Mrs Philby? Even though she's now called Sally?'

'Oh yeah! What's in a name! She is in such pain. I'm trying to live with her but she's gonna take over. I can feel it. Once they take over . . .'

She whistled and shook her head. All eyes were upon us. I felt as if we were in a play. I cleared my throat to deliver my next line.

'No, he hasn't come into me yet, thank God, and frankly I hope he doesn't. He was a ghastly old lush, wasn't he?' I had more practical problems I wanted to discuss. 'Shaz, I'm much more concerned about the dialogue. We've got to do something.'

She ignored me. 'The first time was on *Casino*.' Now she was speaking so softly that I could hardly hear and had to crane forward. So did everyone at the next table. Always speak as quietly as possible. It draws the listener in and makes you look riveting as well as beautiful to the onlooking fans. Because, make no mistake: Sharon's career was a 24/7 affair. She didn't have to be on a sound stage to be filming. The world was her camera and her alarm clock was the clapperboard. She was aware of how she looked from every pair of eyes in the room and she gave a bit of close-up to all of them. It was legendary stuff and I adored it.

'Marty left the mad scene for last,' she continued. 'You remember, when she has that total meltdown?'

'How could I forget? It was brilliant.'

'Well, she came inside me while I was in the trailer before the scene.'

'Not very safe! We call that barebacking.' I giggled awkwardly. I was never comfortable when things got metaphysical.

Sharon gave me a withering glare. 'I was, like, completely possessed. She was right there. I *was her*. Bobby could tell straightaway. He said to Marty, "How much film do you have?" And Marty said, "We got a full mag!"'

'God!' I interjected, rather hopelessly. This was turning into one of those conversations one had with a homeless person.

'"So just keep rolling," Bobby told him. "Trust me." He knew. Bobby knew. And when Marty said, "Action," I blacked out. I have no recollection. She took over. At the end of the scene I was on the ground. I couldn't move and Marty said, "Don't touch her. Leave her for a few minutes."'

'That's incredible!' I gasped.

The thing was, if you watched that film, Sharon's performance was possessed. It was on a level that few actors achieve, so it was difficult to know what to think. Maybe she was invaded by the dead. Either way, I was hopelessly out of my depth. (All I knew was that no one ever said, 'Leave her there,' after I finished a scene. More likely, 'Get her out of here!')

'There was a pinkish mist over me,' she continued. 'Everyone saw it. And it's happened again. This could be the last time we speak, you and I.'

This girl was stark raving mad. 'You've got to be careful though,' I said, wondering just what surprises were in store. 'You don't want to have another stroke.'

The filming began. I never found myself, but mercifully neither did Kim Philby, although one night I had a terrible nightmare where I was staggering around a dark room, knocking everything over. I told Sharon about it the next day. 'He's coming in!' she said.

I was scared of her, rather as a dog is scared of a changeable master, and nothing connected. In the middle of the shoot, I had a two-week hiatus. On the day before I left, we filmed the big love scene. Sharon at work was different from Sharon on a thousand staircases. She expected total control. She marched onto the stage, late, offering no reason. Although I knew the reason. She had DFS – Done Fadeaway Syndrome – a disease pioneered by the patron saint of lateness (white, that is), Faye Dunaway. Sharon was Faye's heiress, in a direct Tinseltown lineage from Joan Crawford. They were three of the most electric stars.

Many actresses were late because they were, in fact, terrified to come out of the trailer. Either they would do their make-up over and over again, ripping off individually laid lashes, rubbing cream all over an intricately adjusted face, sobbing into a Kleenex as they wiped themselves, watched by the ashen-faced hair and make-up team before beginning all over again; or they would just sit on the phone, organising business in their bra and panties, while toying with the young assistant directors who were posted outside the trailer doors and instructed to knock every five minutes. But the knocks never changed anything. In fact they often exacerbated a diva's lateness.

The fact of the matter was that these women were such perfectionists that over the years they developed a neurotic terror of doing their job. It is not easy to grow older in front of a camera. It sees everything and responds best to flawless skin and innocent eyes. Every tiny line throws a shadow. The lady who didn't think twice about staying out all night at the bubbling source of her career, now arrives at a quarter to six each morning from a sleepless night in chinstraps, wondering who she is, to confront a face in the glare of the trailer mirror with jaundiced eyes that she and her cohorts must slap and pull and glue and colour into place before she squeezes herself into Wonderbras and corsets and cleverly coloured costumes to become the assertive beautiful star that effortlessly happened to drop by. It is the journey from ingénue to engineer, and the clock is always on. The set was a male world, and few of the men, except the queers, had much sympathy or understanding of how it felt to be a woman in her forties. All they knew is that they didn't want to shag her or go into overtime.

Luckily for Sharon, she was still perfect. There was no squeezing or pulling. Her skin glowed. She was too intelligent to have taken to the bottle, and she enjoyed the trip of her own brain more than any chemical stimulant. But still something stopped her from coming out of the trailer, although eventually she stalked onto the set followed by a caravan of hair and make-up, assistant, nanny and child, looking amazing in a raven wig. Her blue eyes danced dangerously under arched brows. Everyone got up as she came in, putting down their magazines and coffees.

'Gather round,' she ordered.

'Okay, anyone who doesn't need to be here, get out now.' This was normally a line that the director said, but Marek had just returned from a visit to the children's bedroom set that had been finished that day on the next-door stage. Instead of a tasteful colonial nursery from the sixties, the Canadian designer had made the room look like a KMart Christmas commercial with a giant pink dinosaur on top of a Formica cupboard. Marek was now talking intensely with the producer. He was exhausted and just looked up blearily as Sharon strode about the set taking control. 'Have you got a full mag?' she asked the camera operator. He shook his head. 'Then get one. We want to just shoot on this one. Don't we, Marek?'

'Yes, Sharon,' said Marek meekly, but with that English twist of anarchy, as he got up and walked towards her. I loved watching the power-play on a film set. Marek had given his to Sharon. So had I. We had laid our paltry weapons at her feet weeks ago. And all the others who complained behind her back were putty in her presence. She had an unquenchable energy. You didn't have to be a clairvoyant to see the lightning rods crackle from her fingertips. She was exhilarating and dangerous. The unnecessary people grudgingly slunk into the dark corners of the stage to begin a slow grandmother's footsteps back to the action while Sharon stepped out of her white towelling dressing gown and stalked over to the bed, totally naked. Her body was extraordinary. Beautiful hips, wide shoulders, a flat stomach, shapely breasts and gazelle legs, all wrapped in porcelain skin; powdered and highlighted, waxed and perfumed. Sharon knew it was worth the wait. This was the money and you could feel the surge of energy engulf the set. This was why we liked the job.

Several hours later, we were lying naked on a bed in a pool of light from a forest of lamps. I was on top of Sharon, lying between her legs. We both smoked a cigarette, while Sharon's hairdresser rubbed ice cubes on her nipples and Pat covered up a few spots on my bum. There was a friendly, uncomplicated atmosphere on the set, and we all chatted together as if it were the most natural thing in the world for two people to be frozen in flagrante surrounded by a camera crew. Someone measured the distance between the camera and Sharon's pussy with a tape measure. The operator practised zooming in on it with his camera. Sharon watched lazily, leaning back so that the camera could get right in. We both knew how to do sex and the scene had been fairly effortless. After icing Sharon's nipples, the hairdresser blow-dried them with his hairdryer. Everyone laughed and the conversation turned to sex. All the girls complained about men, and the men sniggered proudly at each new story. Bursts of laughter echoed around the stage. Sharon and I were on glittering form.

'You know what I say when I'm fucking a guy?' said Sharon after the laughter had died down.

'What?' replied the whole set, like the chorus of a musical.

'Rupert!' shouted Marek from behind the monitor. 'Could you take your position, please?'

I gave my cigarette to Pat and clambered on top of Sharon as she went on with her story.

'I say, "*Stop*. Look at me."'

I looked at her.

'Now. Talk to me.'

'Talk to you?' I asked, incredulous.

'Communicate,' she said.

'While we're fucking?!'

'And now . . . go in and out *real* slow.'

'Oh my God, now I know why I'm gay.'

'Okay, let's shoot this please,' shouted Marek. Now our faces were very close, ready to embrace. Our eyes sparkled with manufactured love.

'Hon,' said Sharon, looking at me adoringly, 'I can turn a gay man straight in five minutes!'

'Two bells!' shouted an assistant. Our lips were nearly touching, half smiles. Our groins locked.

'How long does it take you to turn a straight man gay?' I whispered.

'Silence on the set!' shouted another.

'About ten seconds in some cases,' murmured Sharon.

'And . . . action!' said Marek, and in and out we went. *Real slow*.

CHAPTER 45

Haitian Hiatus

Real life stops at the huge closed doors of the sound stage and I was living in a delightful pool of light, in a cardboard universe of spies and lovers, treachery and idealism. The film set is a strange compelling hothouse of period costumes, clocks set at peculiar times, newspapers from long ago. And often when you leave this vivid mirage the real world feels like an abstract fantasy – a film, in fact. But nothing prepared me for the total eclipse that took place when I left A *Different Loyalty* for my Haitian hiatus.

On my charity travels I had met an Idaho Indian queen who worked for the Kennedy Foundation. We hit it off at a student conference and he invited me to come to see one of the stars of the Third World health wars, a doctor called Paul Farmer.

Hollywood couldn't have been further from Haiti, although Miami was only an hour away from Port-au-Prince. Here the First and Third Worlds rubbed shoulders, divided by a thin stretch of water upon which floated tax-free islands, millionaires' yachts and communist Cuba. Strangely, in this corner of the world, the Cold War still raged. It felt like the film I had just left behind. Added to this, everyone has a writer who turns their youthful head. For me it was Graham Greene. Suddenly he was implied in everything I did. Kim Philby was the essence of Greene – the two men were friends – and so was Haiti. Stepping off the plane in Port-au-Prince that day in March was like walking into the freshly written pages of *The Comedians*.

I half expected to see Sharon waiting inside the airport surrounded by lights. The chaos, the heat, the noise, the breeze from the overhead fans: all felt like intricate details of a marvellous film. There was a sexy smell of sweat on the customs official as he looked me up and down. I felt like a spy, but he stamped my passport anyway. Announcements in Creole echoed from a clapped-out loudspeaker, and a creaky conveyor belt groaned into action. It sounded like a tractor. Big fat mamas got up and hauled bigger fatter suitcases, held together with a string and a prayer. A group from the Virginia chapter of the Salvation Army gathered around their bossy leader, straight from the pages of Graham Greene or Tennessee Williams. They were off to spread the good news.

Maybe because travel of any sort – either coming or going – in a place like this was such an event, the atmosphere was charged with a certain hysteria. It was as if the whole feverish crowd was stuck in this broken-down airport, like ghosts trapped in a moment between this world and the next, waiting to be released by a medium with a foreign visa.

The Oloffson Hotel was at the bottom of the Kenscoff mountain in Petionville, a suburb of Port-au-Prince. At some point in Haiti's murky history, the ruling rich lived there in large gabled houses with beautiful gardens. Now these houses had rotted and begun the long slide down the hill, their high walls decorated with broken bottles. The roads were steep, and over the years the rich had retreated higher and higher up the mountain towards the last remaining acres of rainforest at the top, leaving Pétionville to be swallowed up by the endless concrete shanty of Port-au-Prince.

It must have been a magic mountain, Kenscoff, because a storm lived on top of it. Caught in a constant clash of sea air and mountain wind, a microclimate rained on the city like a cartoon cloud pours down on a depressed or angry character. Even if you didn't believe in Voodoo or zombies or hell, you thought again after a couple of nights at the Oloffson.

The hotel was falling to pieces and had hardly ever been cleaned, but for the fan of Graham Greene every moment spent in it sent shivers down the spine. The John Barrymore suite was unchanged from the room in which Mr Brown's mother died at the beginning of *The Comedians*. It was a rambling three-room apartment with high white walls and creaky wooden floors, and your own individual terrace with a view over the whole city and the port. There was a huge old four-poster bed in the corner, shrouded in musty mosquito netting. I lay on it that first night, literally tingling with ecstasy, as the endless rain beat down on the corrugated-iron roof. At some point it stopped as suddenly as it began, and screams, shouts and the odd gunshot drifted up from the city below.

The first clue that something was about to happen at the Oloffson was when the hotel's matriarch grandmother made an appearance around noon, in her pink nightgown and gauge-four rollers in her hair. By mid-afternoon the normally tranquil terrace began to fill up with dusty Peace Corps volunteers who had trekked in from behind God's back, their disco outfits in their rucksacks. Drum sets, bongos and shack-shacks began to appear out of cupboards and drawers. Eight-foot-long, oboe-shaped horn instruments wailed plaintively as the band set up in the cavernous hotel lobby, which seemed to have been hewn out of the cliff edge to which the hotel was glued.

Thursday nights were famous at the Oloffson. It was when Richard (the hotel's owner) performed with his voodoo band Ram, and the Port-au-Prince 'in' crowd, the hillside bourgeoisie, danced, drank and cruised until dawn. There was no point in going to bed because the floor literally shook with the noise of the party below. They were all fiercely anti the present Aristide administration and the place simmered with discussion, observed by undercover CIA operatives. 'Ram night' started out pretty harmlessly around nine. The urban expats began to trickle down the mountain, with local beauties on their arms. It would appear that 'foreign affairs' were what the charity, NGO and diplomatic worlds were all about. '*Quelle surprise!*' said the Idaho Indian, as the head of an aid foundation swished in with a very young bit of trade.

'Ayee!' screamed the NGO queen. 'Look what the cat dragged in! You're going to be here for my farewell party. I'm taking over in Asia next week.'

'*Quelle tristesse*. That won't be nearly so much fun!' replied the first.

'Of course, I'm real cut up to be leaving Marcel, but what can you do? My wife was beginning to ask questions, so it's probably for the best.'

He squeezed his date's thigh and the boy looked down, embarrassed.

The American ambassador, a small neat man named Dean Curran, was the central character in Port-au-Prince. When he arrived that night at about eleven o'clock, flanked by his secret service entourage with their thick necks and earpieces, there was a positive frisson around the room. He held all the power on that sorry isle.

By midnight, the place was rocking, and the sissy rum-cocos from the zombie-like hotel waiters had been replaced by shots and bottles concealed up the locals' sleeves and under their skirts. Everyone was past caring, with the noble exception of the coiffed grandma who was left guarding the ancient cash register like a toothless poodle with cataracts. A voodoo belly dancer began to gyrate in front of me. She sprayed magical toilet freshener onto my wrists and massaged 'oil of poulet' into my temples. 'For sex!' she said, dragging me to my feet and onto the dance floor. She nodded her head gravely before shoving her hand down my trousers.

As the night ploughed on, clothes came off, bodies shone with sweat and the room heaved as one. Drums and horns reached a fever pitch, driving harder and harder, the dance floor turned into a giant voodoo rave. In a huddle of glistening youth swayed the ambassador. The NGO queen twirled round and round the wretched Marcel in a kind of trance. Maybe it was just the toilet freshener kicking in, but the whole writhing mass seemed to be on the move, transporting itself back to the dark continent.

Paul Farmer met us outside his clinic in the arid mountains of the central plateau four hours down a dirt track posing as the highway. He was a bit like the flying nun, with an unruly shock of black hair, wearing a white coat that flapped behind him as he swooped around. He had an astonishing energy, an effortless attention and curiosity, and he segued from laughter and idle chatter to serious concern over a patient in a nanosecond. He was worldly and other-worldly. He had a stethoscope around his neck and his hands played with it as we talked, as if they couldn't wait to get back to work. He was an amazing character, half nutty professor, half explorer, and an uncomplicated compassion flowed from him that lit up his surroundings. He was different from everyone else. He wasn't acting. He didn't put on a charity face. He was himself. He had a great sense of humour, and it was lovely to watch him in action as he made his rounds of the clinic. In one of his new TB decompression rooms sat a little girl on a bed. Her hair was braided. Paul held her hand and told her in Creole that she couldn't go back home for Easter. The girl listened in silence, then she gasped and tears poured from her eyes. For several minutes Paul sat with her, not speaking, as she wept. Finally she looked up and smiled at him through her tear-smudged face. He looked back at her with such tenderness that it quite took my breath away.

People walked for days to get to his clinic, and sometimes it was mayhem. When Paul arrived the whole place erupted. People grabbed at him, held onto his clothes as though just by touching him they would be cured. He was unfazed by this constant feverish attention. Actually, he was a kind of saint.

Later he took us to his house, which was up a steep overgrown path at the edge of the village. We ran to catch up as he disappeared over the brow of a hill, talking all the while, coat-tails billowing in the wind. His home was really no more than a hut. He had built a little Japanese pond and a tiny garden. He rummaged around and produced bottles of lethal Haitian beer, and we sat there chatting while the sun went down. Soon he was called back to the clinic for an emergency. We braced ourselves for the drive back to Port-au-Prince and said goodbye. He cut an incredibly romantic figure, waving through the back window of our van. Courageous, compassionate, brilliant and funny: he had it all. But he was a very vocal supporter of Aristide as well, and this put him in a lot of danger. 'Paul should be careful,' someone growled threateningly at the Oloffson that night.

Sunday lunch was at the American Embassy. We were shown through the house and out onto a huge lawn. In the middle distance the Mambo Ambo was holding court by his summerhouse. Two beautiful retrievers jumped in and out of the pool. Port-au-Prince shimmered like a vague dream beneath us, or a forgotten saucepan on a burning hob. A table was set underneath a huge tree. Cut glass gleamed on a starched cloth. As we waded across the lawn, all those pleasant noises from the other world bled in: the murmur of polite conversation, the clatter of cutlery, the uncorking of bottles, laughter thrown into the wind. The gurgle and giggle track of Western largesse. Pretty soon I had drunk a few glasses of wine and found myself talking to an ultra-chic voodoo woman dressed in couture with a huge pair of dark glasses. She was unfathomable behind those shades. She had milk-white skin, but on close inspection she was black. Even more extraordinarily, she had seen me perform on stage in Paris. In fact she was the Minister of Culture here in cloud cuckoo land, although she looked like a Left Bank junkie from the seventies. When I expressed surprise that she was a minister, someone next to me giggled, 'Well, they'd been through everyone else. She was the last choice.' It was water off a duck's back to my new friend, who leant towards me con-spiratorially and told me the one true thing of the trip. 'You don't need to believe anything anyone says here. We are all so jealous, you see.'

She caught the eye of the Mambo Ambo. For a second his piercing blue peepers bore deep into the black holes of the Minister of Culture's shades. Maybe she was talking too much. She looked defiantly back at him and said with a hint of a sneer, 'You should have seen the ambas-sador this morning with the President. I was there. It was quite something.'

Apparently there had been a set-to between the Ambo and the ex-priest that morning about the new Chief of Police, and feelings were running high. But all was forgotten as lunch cross-faded through course after course, and the sinking sun threw long shadows from the huge tree across the lawn towards the house.

I didn't meet Aristide, but we had an audience with his wife. Inside the White House, one was suddenly back in the First World, frisked by muscle-bound mercenaries with machine-guns, and escorted across marble floors past gracious french windows. All the rumours ringing in my head, the smears of the hillside bourgeoisie – that Aristide beat his wife, that he was a devil worshipper – were confounded by Madame Aristide, who was more like an account manager at the Bank of America than a voodoo muse. She was polite, detached and tense. We were served coffee by a butler, and it was hard to join this new piece of the puzzle with the rest of Haiti. The corridors of power seemed to have nothing in common with the cracked mountains, the hungry faces, or the child prostitutes hiding in the graveyard.

Maybe they never do.

Our trip was over before it began. Suddenly we were back in the time-locked airport, this time on a magic carpet provided by Madame

Aristide. We floated through the chaos to a diplomatic room where a government official did all our paperwork. Then we wandered through the airport, bought some T-shirts, had a few coffees. We were exhausted, listless. We had hardly slept but still it seemed like a mad dream. Two porters wanted to know about the war in Iraq. They were upset. They said it was bad. Their concern made you want to cry. Why should they care? Nobody cared about them.

The plane climbed through the ever-threatening clouds and burst free into the bright blue Caribbean sunshine, escaping Haiti's clutches. Goodbye to the Aristides, to the hillside bourgeoisie, the foreign diplomats, and Paul saving the poor in the mountains. The ten-day deadline was about to expire. Would the Chief of Police survive? Who would occupy the presidential palace next week? Would the Aristides make it until the next election? Would there *be* a next election? One thing felt sure: the Ollofson would remain, suspended in limbo, fighting off the rain, its pretty whitewashed balconies glimmering at night through the trees like something you read about in a novel long ago, a stage set for sad goodbyes. Its indispensable terrace would continue to play host to intrigue and subterfuge. Maybe one day the termites or the rain might get the better of it and it would simply crumble against the cliff to which it clung and slide slowly into oblivion.

> *Quelle est cette île triste et noire – c'est Cythère,*
> *Nous dit-on un pays fameux dans les chansons,*
> *Eldorado banal de tous les vieux garçons.*
> *Regardez, après tout, c'est une pauvre terre.*

CHAPTER 46

Viva la Diva

I stopped off in London on my way to Moscow to join Sharon and Marek for the end of A *Different Loyalty*, where I went to Channel 4 and the BBC and countless other establishments, trying to interest them all in a documentary about Haiti, but no one took the bait.

Why Haiti? What was so interesting about it? I tried to explain that the whole country seemed to be teetering on the edge of a precipice, that America was trying to dislodge its democracy, that nothing much had changed since Graham Greene's time. Perhaps I was overzealous about the Greene connection but I was stumped when one television executive said, 'Who's Graham Greene?'

I got nowhere, though nine months later Haiti hit the news as the whole country exploded into chaos after a dangerous coup. Aristide was forced into exile at the hands of American marines. Paul Farmer's valuable jeeps, which had enabled him to treat patients far afield, were commandeered by the rebels who could be seen on the TV, driving about in them and shooting at the crowds. It was too late to go back. Things were too dangerous and anyway all my contacts had flown. The Mambo Ambo had been reposted, and it looked as though Paul Farmer was moving his operations to Rwanda.

Moscow had completely changed when we arrived. There was a

huge seven-floor shopping centre under Red Square, and the old babushkas who had sat with such frosty Soviet dignity on street corners in the old days, just thirteen years ago, selling their pickles and making ends meet, had now turned into deranged beggar women. They hung around the entrance to this huge underground mall, begging frantically, grabbing your clothes and shrieking for mercy. There was no place for them in Putin's Russia. Five-star hotels had sprung up all over the town. There were restaurants and fast cars, and the rich tore through the traffic in convoys of motorbikes with flashing lights and sirens, ignoring red lights and pedestrians.

We had no permits to shoot in Red Square, and Marek particularly wanted a shot of me walking past Lenin's tomb, so early one morning five of us snuck out and hid behind an archway until there was nobody about. When the coast was clear we all jumped out and filmed for a couple of minutes while the soldier's back was turned. It was such fun to work this way, and we were all thoroughly invigorated by the time we got to the Lenin Library, where Sharon and I were to play a scene in which I explained to her why I had betrayed my country and her. We shot it with this incredible building behind us. The two of us walked slowly through the library, as the camera tracked along beside us, and I gave a speech of interminable length and pomposity. The night before, Marek and I had decided to cut it.

When we rehearsed the scene with Sharon, who, needless to say, had a photographic memory, I did a revised version of the endless explanation.

'What happened to the part when you explain to me why you became a communist?' she asked.

'We cut it. It goes on for too long and it's too simplistic,' I replied. Alarm bells.

Sharon's head swivelled around and she looked at me very close, like an alien surveying an earthling. 'But my character needs to hear that, or else she doesn't know why she's here.' To say that her regard was becoming steely would perhaps be an understatement.

'The important thing for the audience is to keep awake,' I replied tersely. Sharon was brilliant but it never crossed her mind that a film she was in could be boring.

Marek joined the discussion. 'Sharon, it's just that from an English perspective, it feels too obvious for him to talk like that, and apart from the fact that the speech is really long, he's telling us things we already know.'

'I don't give a fuck. It has to stay in,' commanded Sharon.

The problem was that I hadn't learnt it. There were two pages of dialogue, but rather than collapse into an all-out scuffle on the last day, I went to my little deckchair and learnt that speech in twelve minutes. My brain cells had a fit but on the first take I got it in one and actually the scene wasn't too bad. Sharon was probably right. But in the end the entire film was so tedious that it was just another dull scene of no special merit.

Finally, we shot the last scene of the movie. Our two characters stood on a bridge. My people (KGB) on one side, Sharon's (MI5) on the other. It was supposed to be the dramatic high point of the movie but we had only three hours to shoot it. Marek screamed 'Action!' through the megaphone. We walked slowly towards each other across the river, stopping in the middle, searching each other's face for the last time. I tried to imagine Rachmaninov in the background, but all I could hear was some grips and sparks from under the bridge, complaining about the catering. I said my lines. I told Sharon that I wasn't coming with her back to the West and we said goodbye for the last time. Sharon was brilliant in the scene but I was curiously empty. I felt as though I was watching everything from a long way off. There was Sharon against a Soviet high-rise and a slate sky with thousands of miles of Russia on either side, and I felt dead. I folded my old school scarf around her neck. My hands seemed to be someone else's. We stared at each other for a long moment. Sharon tried to articulate something but couldn't. I remember thinking, who *is* this woman? before she turned and walked back over the bridge, stealing the brilliant Sally Bowles wave from the end of *Cabaret*. I watched her go, devoid of expression, and then went home to release our budgie into the freezing Moscow winter.

'He finally came in,' said Sharon as she returned over the bridge.

It was a beautiful spring day. It was strange and sad but also exhilarating being Kim Philby all those years later in the new capitalist Russia, walking through the Lenin Library with Sharon Stone on my arm, the ring of Haiti in my ears and the wails of displaced babushkas

from the street below. It was strange and sad and exhilarating to be finishing another film with Marek. Twenty years separated our two spy
films: the first one had established us both, and changed our lives; the
second was unfortunately an ember. My acted deathliness in Moscow
at the age of twenty-two was somehow more convincing than the weird
feeling of emptiness I felt on the bridge and in the Lenin Library all
those years afterwards.

That evening we met in the make-up room at the hotel and took off
our disguises in front of makeshift mirrors in rooms that had been commandeered for the film. Everyone was packing up. It felt like the last
day of school. People ran down corridors with bottles of vodka. We all
got drunk. Post-mortems began, and all the petty grievances and
grudges of the past three months evaporated. Sharon took off her raven
wig, I shaved my head, and we looked at each other in the mirror. We
were back. The possession was over. The ghosts of Kim and Sally disappeared into the white night. Sharon was like Regan at the end of *The
Exorcist*. She was worn out, slumped in a chair, wearing a tank top.
She'd had a bit of a go with the nail scissors, and a great chunk of hair
had been cut from the middle of her head during some late-night meltdown, but she looked beautiful.

'Basically, hon,' she explained, summing up the experience after
several vodkas drunk straight up, 'we've both been around for twenty
years. That's eight lives in dog time. So, fuck 'em. They're not getting
rid of us that easily.'

Viva la diva.

CHAPTER 47

Dangerous Lesbians

My French agent Dominique represented an extraordinary lady director, Josée Dayan. She specialised in what Oscar Wilde might have called, had he lived today, the 'three-volume *telenovela* of revolting sentimentality'.

She had made everything from *The Count of Monte Cristo* to *Napoleon and Josephine*. Her reputation swept ahead of her in the looks and laughs and raised eyebrows that were produced whenever her name was mentioned. She was an eccentric ball breaker. Now she had her sights set on *Dangerous Liaisons* and wanted me to play Valmont. I met her for coffee one sticky afternoon in Paris with Dominique. A smallish Algerian woman in her mid-fifties with short curly grey hair, she dressed from head to toe in black leather. Her only concession to femininity was a lacy bra covered in blue bows that looked like breast-feeding butterflies peeking through her open white shirt. Her *dame de compagnie* was a tall thin lady swathed in cashmere, with long white hair and those perfect two-faced manners that are peculiar to the French bourgeoisie.

During the meeting, Josée petted me as though I were a thoroughbred up for auction. She took my head in her hand and yanked it towards her. '*Quelle tête, dis donc!*' she said to Dominique. Would she check my teeth next?

At one of those agency seances, round-table meetings of pimps and packagers that happen across the show business world every Monday morning, Dominique and Josée managed to summon up the greatest French star of them all to play Madame de Merteuil: Catherine Deneuve. On day one it was clear that this was going to be no ordinary film. Josée stormed around the set like the captain of a pirate ship, but when Catherine arrived she turned into a gallant suitor, a young swash-buckling mariner. Her eyes sparkled as Catherine materialised on the set dressed to disastrous effect by Jean-Paul Gaultier. The telefilm was set in 1963, an unfortunate period for hips, and at times Catherine looked like the Romanian housekeeper of some dentist's wife from Dijon. The two women sparred together in a formal old-school French while the rest of us stood around waiting for instructions. Deneuve played Josée with icy precision, letting her in one moment before freez-ing her out the next, and Josée loved it. They called each other *vous* and *madame*, and no one else got a look in.

Added to this the cinematographer was another woman, Caroline, who looked like Charles I painted by Munch. She was small and thin with long red hair over a drained face. She also wore a leather jacket, but Caroline was no lesbian, although she seemed to be in the perma-nent throes of a shattering nervous breakdown, so maybe she was. (Joke.) She never slept. She fought all the time with Josée while we men trudged on with our jobs in silence, broken slaves, and she would collapse on the set with her head in her hands, gathering what strength she had left, before bouncing back up to stare madly at a lamp through her light meter.

Nastassja Kinski played the young wife. She was one of the few actresses around who had not succumbed to the knife and was ravish-ing, if unhinged. She had a tiny voice. It was almost as if she had stopped dead in her tracks at the age of eight, but she had been on a film set all her life, so she knew how to dig her heels in when she wanted. Another fragile rock. She was a great actress, however, and her performance shone in *Dangerous Lesbians* (as I'd soon renamed the production). It was, in fact, the most unusual affair. Film is traditionally a male thing, with men in charge as the director, the producer and the lighting cameraman. There may be a cinema diva, a Sharon or a Cher, and there may be a 'power female' executive steaming about with castration on her mind, but in general the movie set is a great comfortable place for men.

Dangerous Lesbians was like *Alice Through the Looking-Glass*. Women ruled the stage with rods of iron and we men were their mute slaves. We learnt fast that it didn't do to fight back. These ladies were longing for a full-on scrap. The whole universal war of the sexes concentrated briefly on our set and possessed us daily in gripping tirades and marvellous dressings down. The crew listened with bowed heads, hardly daring to move in case the storm moved from one unhappy spark to another. It was brilliant to watch these speechless men being well and truly pussy-whipped, and I wasn't the only one to enjoy the spectacle. The Romanian housekeeper watched with the flicker of a smile from a shadowy corner of the stage, far away from the lamps, identifiable only by the thin line of smoke from her More cigarette, billowing up into the darkness from a manicured hand like a jungle fire seen from the sky.

In one of my first scenes I had to drive Deneuve in a speedboat around the Gulf of St Tropez. It was May, but still felt like winter. I had not been back there since my *roman-à-clef, The Hairdressers of St Tropez*, had been published ten years before. It had not been very well received by the burghers and I usually refused invitations that took me anywhere near the beach of Pampelonne, for fear of a squabble. I was the Truman Capote of the Côte d'Azur, but no one was able to turn their backs on me that morning when I arrived triumphant at the Place des Lices, with Catherine by my side, for the first day of principal photography. The port was a throng of fans, held back by the local police. I spotted many familiar faces as we clambered on board an old speedboat. Catherine was sporting an elaborate beehive under a little chiffon scarf. Her make-up lady handed her a hamper of goodies with which to check herself between takes. We were left with a walkie-talkie and made for the open sea as the crew crowded onto another, larger boat that was docked beside us. The sun shone, but there was a strong wind. Out at sea it was quite rough. We flew down huge waves and strained up the other side.

'Oh, *dis donc!*' said Catherine, grasping the rails.

The other boat was one of those ancient steel tanks that looked like a minesweeper from the war. Josée and Caroline stood in the stern next to the camera wearing waders and full wet-weather cover. Someone had strapped them into harnesses and they stood there, legs akimbo, leaning into the frothy sea. Josée had a megaphone (fatal) and Caroline looked at the sun through her meter. They were in their element. I had to follow behind at exactly the right distance for the focus of the camera, which was more or less impossible considering the swell. Josée shouted 'Action!' through the megaphone, and Catherine and I played the scene. It was quite difficult to act and drive and pretend it was a hot summer afternoon at the same time, but we managed to get through the first take without bumping into the back of the camera boat. As the boat turned around to go back to the 'first position', Catherine delved into her hamper and produced a round mirror with a battery light. She clicked it on and gazed approvingly at herself from various angles, checking the beehive for wind damage, and then applied eyeshadow and lipstick, lighting a More at the same time, all of this ingeniously co-ordinated as we plunged through the choppy waters and she drew a perfect line around her lips.

Josée was shouting into her megaphone but nobody could hear, so I was unprepared when the other boat turned sharply to the left, and we ploughed into their wake. To my horror, I watched a huge wave explode over our bows. It climbed into the air and seemed to hover over the boat. I looked over at Catherine. She was preoccupied with the end of a comb in the interior of her beehive, looking intently into her mirror with a cigarette miraculously burning in the corner of her mouth. I tried to speak but no words would come out. I looked back up as the wave crashed down in an agonising slow motion all over the leading lady. Catherine's mirror exploded and cracked. The beehive collapsed, and the cigarette hung comically from her lips. There was a moment of silence. Then Catherine threw back her head and laughed, while I giggled nervously as I tried to do the nautical equivalent of tiptoeing back to the dock. There, she stood in a puddle and was dried with all the available hairdryers.

We subsequently moved from the South of France to Paris. The crew felt drained. Working for Josée was like being bent in an endless wind. She never stopped until one day the French Fascist Party scored an enormous success in the first round of the national elections, at which point she was briefly dumbstruck. A quarter of the vote went to

Jean-Marie Le Pen and his National Front Party. The whole of France was in shock, although it seemed to hit our ladies hard in particular. As far as I was concerned it had always been perfectly clear that France had a very right-wing mindset. You just had to take a walk to the Goutte d'Or and Barbes, a stone's throw from the crumbling ninth arrondissement where I used to live, to find a completely isolated world of immigrants and refugees. And those *quartiers* were only the outskirts to the surrounding ghettos of Paris, which were desolate worlds of broken-down sky-rises and dreams. They bore no relationship to the sandblasted wedding cake that Paris had become under the socialists. The French didn't like these people and now they had put their cards on the table, but Josée was particularly appalled. She was a socialist at home and Pol Pot at work.

The Sunday after the elections, we were shooting in an old Haussmann building somewhere near the Étoile. The set was one of those huge rambling apartments with double doors leading from room to room, and high windows looking over the trees onto a wide honey-coloured street. Nowadays these apartments are mostly offices, but this one was still in private hands. It belonged to a retired colonel and felt musty and neglected, the perfect home for Nastassja in the film. That day in a devastatingly cruel scene I broke her spirit, as I walked through those rooms, sneering at them as I passed, savouring the detailed description of each of my deceptions, until I heard her collapse on the floor of the hall, weeping. The old parquet squeaked as the boys with the camera crept round the place in front of me, coiling electric leads, holding polystyrene boards and moving furniture back into place from their wake. Everyone always looked forward to doing a scene like this because it required a great deal of precision and concentration so that the camera wouldn't be spotted through one of the many mirrors, or a sound man was not caught darting behind a pair of curtains. There was no room for improvised movement. The crew and the actor became one body. Everyone else hid in corridors and behind curtains because the whole apartment was in the shot. Josée was locked inside a cupboard with her monitor, and her tirade became muffled and comic. At the end of the third take, I was standing over Nastassja in silence, surveying the results of my cruelty, when a window blew open in the sitting room. A strange noise bounced in from outside. It sounded like a riot or a goal being scored in a faraway stadium. Josée yelled 'Cut!' and everyone came out from where they were hiding and rushed over to the windows.

Outside, the street was deserted, but in the distance the roar pulsed through the air towards us in waves. It was the demonstration against the National Front. Hundreds of thousands of people were moving through a nearby boulevard. As I stood in the window with Nastassja and Catherine, dressed for 1963, for a moment life seemed to be as a scene from a film.

'Oh Christ,' breathed Catherine, hugging herself, as the roar intensified. Had something gone wrong? Had the demonstration turned violent as some had predicted? Was this the beginning of revolution? Everyone in the room was silent. For a moment no one moved, and then the spell was broken. Invisible fingers snapped and we went on with the day.

CHAPTER 48

Travels with My Father

In middle age, time begins to shrink. Days, months and years seem shorter. People who once appeared impossibly old are suddenly contemporaries with much more energy than oneself. The rebellion of youth gives way, exhausted, to the certainty of genes, and little by little one begins the long limp home. The gulfs we build between families and enemies and lovers begin to evaporate.

My father was old now but he was still restless. So one day at the end of 2004, I found myself in the airport of São Paulo where he'd asked me to meet him. He was coming from London, I from New York. He was eighty-three and wanted to go on a trip down the Rio Negro, the black river that flows into the Amazon at Manaus. We had arranged to meet at the Varig desk, and of all the images I will take to my grave of my dad, this will always be the sweetest. I could see him a mile off, although he couldn't see me. As I walked towards him, I thought no cinema designer would ever be able to recreate his look. My dad was wearing his dark City suit; it was slightly crumpled and, it must be said, had seen better days. He was sitting legs akimbo with his hands leaning on his old brolly. His thin long calves tapered into incongruous lime-green socks. The *Financial Times* was tucked under his arm. His shirt was pink and a scarf was tied around his neck. He wore his favourite frayed straw hat and he sat there, an old soldier at attention, ready for trouble if it came. Twenty years ago he would have been appalled at how he was turned out. He'd let it all go a bit, and it suited him enormously. I stopped for a moment and watched him. An exotic Amazon with delicious hips swayed by and his head turned slowly as she passed, looking up slightly as she disappeared into the crowd as if he were sniffing the wind.

'Oh, there you are,' he said. 'Well done. I've been chatting up the girl from Varig so we should get moving.'

He was, as usual, hell-bent on travelling economy, so I had to literally squeeze him into his seat, and I rode to Manaus with my knees up by my chin. A rather cute surfer boy with his computer sat next to my dad and promptly fell asleep on his shoulder. My dad shrugged and giggled slightly but the boy slept on all the way to Manaus and my father looked straight ahead, taking care not to wake him.

That evening in Manaus my dad was calling the shots. He had a lead to a 'rather good bistro in the port area', so we got into a taxi. I stopped trying to take control and just sat back and watched. I loved the way he talked to foreigners, enunciating ev-e-ry syll-a-ble. 'Could you take us via the Opera House to this address?' The driver took the piece of paper my father had in his hand, looked up, faintly surprised, and regarded us strangely. But my dad stared him out with a nod and a grunt, and soon we began to weave through a half-lit and incredibly dangerous-looking part of town into the very depths of docklands. My dad was totally unperturbed.

Finally we arrived at a kind of fish and chip shop in a shanty area by the river. The huge prow of a tanker loomed above us in the background, and the scene only missed sailors smoking their pipes around an old barrel with an accordion. My father marched into the restaurant, which was pretty empty. There were a few dirty tables with plastic chairs around them. A TV blared football on the wall over the bar, and there was a pool table with a huge rip through the baize in the corner.

'A table for two, please,' he said, and pretty soon we were seated and eating some thickly battered fish with rice and beans. A group of four leggy Amazons with peroxide-blonde hair arrived and sat at a table near by. I got the picture. We were in a hooker bar! My dad feigned oblivion and went on eating his fish. 'Rather good, this!' he mentioned as another group of girls arrived, this time with black hair. My dad looked up briefly as they settled down at the table next to ours. 'I much prefer it when they don't fiddle with the colour too much, don't you?'

'I don't know. Depends if they colour all over,' I ventured cautiously.

'Oh, almost certainly, I would think.'

By this time the girls at the next table had begun to vibe us heavily and whisper to each other, giggling and pointing. 'That girl has a really splendid figure!' said my dad of an Amazon beauty near by, at which point, in the bat of a long jungle eyelash, the entire group was at our table. My father could hardly control his mirth. They were all over us, kissing and shaking hands, and absolutely gorgeous into the bargain. The bargain?

'Daddy, would you like me to arrange something with some of the girls?' I gingerly suggested.

'Oh, no,' he replied, still bubbling over with suppressed laughter. 'I'm much too revolting now. I stopped all that kind of thing years ago. I wouldn't say no to another of those delicious drinks, though.'

Unfortunately, the girls had other plans, and after we had drunk endless *caperinhas* together, my dad and I asked the waiter for a taxi. We got up, saying goodbye to our new friends, but up they got too. Outside, we got into our taxi and they all bundled into one behind. Thinking nothing of it, we waved goodbye and settled down for the twenty-minute drive back into the jungle where our hotel was. However, when we arrived, to our horror the other taxi screeched to a halt behind us and out piled 'les girls' (all five of them).

'Oh, dear,' said my dad, hotfooting it up the stairs. 'I think I'll leave this one to you.'

So with the help of the doorman I explained to the girls that there must have been a misunderstanding. After some negotiation I put them back in their taxi and waved them off to the docks. It was quite a night.

Anyone who thinks of travelling on one of the big Brazilian rivers should know that the Rio Negro, being black, does not harbour a thriving mosquito community like the brown Amazon. My dad and I travelled unscathed for nearly a week up this amazing river. Every day we sat on the top deck as the jungle slowly drifted by, talking about our family, our childhoods, the other passengers, and age. It was sitting heavily upon us both. Old age for my dad was hard and middle age for me was confusing. My dad reminded me of a line from Oscar Wilde in a play I had done in Glasgow. 'What was it? Oh, yes. "The tragedy of old age is not that one is old but that one is young." Hit the nail on the head. Now, if I could just get this bloody back right . . .' He trailed off. If I could just get this bloody life right, I thought.

Unfortunately, our trip was all steps: ladders between the decks of our pleasure boat, which I would literally have to piggyback him up. Stepping from a floating dock into a canoe is something one does without thinking until one day the body says no. Every evening at dusk we would be taken out in canoes to motor around the little creeks and tributaries of the huge river but my dad wouldn't go. 'I'll only hold you all up,' he said. 'I've got plenty of reading. Don't worry about me.'

And so as we chugged off into the thick jungle, the American teacher's wife from Orange County said, 'Look, your father's waving!' I turned and saw his waving silhouette on the boat against the setting sun. Behind them, the vast shimmering river. I waved back as I disappeared into the jungle, and thought of all the goodbyes over the years we had had. I could tell that he was sad. He was used to being independent. He loved the adventure of travel. Just last year he had crossed the Khyber pass on a pony, but our trip was telling him to quieten down a bit.

At sunset the pink dolphins would come, performing synchronised leaps from the water; at night we would moor on the edge of the jungle and settle into our cabins with large glasses of whisky that my dad magically produced out of his luggage, and listen to the nightly deluge. When the rain stopped, the captain shone a huge spotlight across the forest in front of us and then snapped it off again. Miraculously a million different-coloured fairy lights appeared, darting about through the trees. They lit up the whole forest. It was one of the most magical sights I have ever seen: my father and me in a picture by Pierre et Gilles.

It was hard to sleep in the stuffy little cabins so in the middle of the night, I would still be up, smoking joints while leaning against the railings of the boat, the dripping jungle foliage close enough to touch, mulling it over. No father–son relationship is entirely easy, after all, and my father and I had had more than our fair share of trouble, but the weird thing was that in the end it came to nothing. There we still were: an old man snoring gently in his cabin and a son unable to sleep on the deck. Both still resolutely chugging upstream in that beat-up pleasure boat; both waiting for the 'click' when we would turn around and give in to the strong black current of the river and just let ourselves be part of the flow on the cruise home. I could watch him sleeping through the porthole of his cabin, still dressed. The light by his bed threw his face into tomblike shadow; both hands lay on his chest; feet crossed, mouth slightly open; the fan blowing beside his bed so that his hair stood up and waved in the breeze. Like a knight of the Round Table, I thought. My father and me. Still going after all these years.

CHAPTER 49

The Old Ladies of the Woods

One afternoon last summer in Paris I went to the Bois to see if I could find the old ladies of the night, those amazing human ashtrays I mentioned before. My friend Lychee's murder remained unsolved (although I thought I knew who did it) and the old girls had seen her on the night she disappeared. It took more than an hour to find the clearing in the woods where they used to sit. In the old days their transistor radio and cackles could be heard from far away. Now only pigeons rustled in the trees. They were not there. Sitting alone on their tree stump was a tiny old lady in a mackintosh and a Bette Davis wig. She reminded me of Maria St Just. It was hard to tell if she was one of them or just a civilian. Soon she got up and walked into the woods. I waited for a while as dusk fell but no one came. They were probably all dead. I sat on the stump and thought about Maria St Just and all the old girls I knew.

I was staying with Natasha in her flat in Ormonde Gate when her sister called telling us to come immediately to their mother's house in Gerald Road. Upstairs, the shrunken body of Maria was sitting on the chair in her bedroom. The window was open and the curtains blew gently in the cold breeze. She looked like a little sparrow in death, a different creature from the woman who made us all cry as children. The girls stood at the door to the room, unwilling to go in.

She became ill the day her husband Peter died. Within weeks of his funeral her fingers were knobbly and swollen and her body began to turn in on itself with arthritis. It was as though a spell had been put on her. Little by little, she became unable to move and soon this eccentric woman took her beloved dogs for walks in the car, driving slowly with them sitting beside her around the tumbledown Wilbury estate, holding forth in an odd patois of Russian and English on her favourite subject: her two lazy daughters.

Maria and I became great friends.

'Roopie doo, you can come to dinner with Tennessee if you're not too pushy,' she would say, and I would sit breathless as the poor little lump sat speechless on Quaaludes around Maria's dining-room table. I met Franco Zeffirelli at Maria's, and Gore Vidal. She always came with 'Peterkins' or with a queen friend to see shows I was in and take me out for dinner afterwards. She was the only 'grown up' in a rather conventional world for whom being queer was of little account. 'It's not what you do. It's how you do it,' she told me once.

Now she was dead. Pippo, Franco Zeffirelli's boyfriend, was staying in her spare room at the time and together we carried the body over to the bed. Her jaw was hanging open. Natasha called the doctor, and he told us to tie it up with a scarf. I went guiltily to the chest of drawers where strange ribbed brassieres and complicated girdles lay in neat stacks. It felt wrong to be going through her drawers. I chose a green chiffon scarf and wound it around her head. The mouth shut with a clatter that made me smile: it was the first and last time Maria would be open-mouthed. We brushed her hair and made the bed around her. We began to arrange her precious Russian icons around her body. I would put one in a certain position. Pippo would look at it and move it somewhere else. This went on until the mourners arrived and we went downstairs leaving Maria shrouded in flowers and icons and candles.

When death comes into a house something strange happens. Maria had kept her house alive with her incredible energy. Now the life had gone out of it, flown out of the bedroom window with her spirit. I noticed for the first time the peeling wallpaper, the threadbare carpets. A strange group assembled every night for psalms around the body with the Russian priest.

Like Lady 'Bubbles' Rothermere, her great friend, she had been an unremarkable actress who married into the aristocracy. Both ladies were viewed with the deepest suspicion in post-war Belgravia, and both ladies had managed to lose their pasts in a mist of juggled dates and make-believe. It was worse for Bubbles. She was immortalised on film. She would never be able to change that scene in *Reach for the Sky*. Maria's performances were all on the stage. Even if, as her detractors claimed, her brother drove a bus, or worse, her father drove a tugboat, it didn't make any difference in the end, because Maria was as grand as they came. If it *was* a performance then it was one without cracks, right down to the dowager's underwear in her chest of drawers. Who cared anyway? – *Debrett's* needed the soubrettes.

I remember once reading a book by Mollie Weir, a now forgotten Scottish character actress, who wrote about an actress called Little Mary. They were both dancers in the West End in the fifties. Little Mary was going out with a lord, and she and Molly would go to the hospital – even then, in hospital, poor Peter – in their costumes from the show to cheer him up. At the end it says that 'Little Mary got her lord, and I hope she is very happy.' I don't think she was ever happy. She was Russian. She loved and hated too fiercely.

But she was loved back by the curious throng of guests who arrived at the house in the days after her death. They had drinks in the drawing room. Vanessa Redgrave. Elizabeth Harris-Harrison (Damian's mother), Prince and Princess Galitzin. John Gielgud, Franco Zeffirelli. The Russian priest arrived, and everyone was given a candle. Then we went upstairs where Maria lay, cosily tucked in, the room flickering and jumping in the candlelight, the air thick with the smell of flowers and death and wax. We stood around the bed and the priest sang in Russian. The girls looked vacantly at the mother who had made their lives hell, but without whom it was hard to imagine living. Such is the irony of life and love. She had dragged this family of slowcoaches into the twentieth century and had died trying. As the priest sang we all looked at Maria (her jaw had never looked firmer), still marvelling that she would not spring up and say something squashing.

She was laid out in the Russian church in an open coffin before the funeral and then she was buried between Froggy Footman, the pug, and Mishka, the retriever, in the dogs' graveyard at Wilbury. Maria may have gone over to the other side, the next world, but some girls of her age had new boyfriends and were going on tour.

I met Joan Collins through her ex-boyfriend Robin, who was several years younger than she. It was generally agreed, however, despite the chasm between their ages, that they were ideally suited. They adored each other. But Robin was afraid to venture out in public, and this was the only sore spot in a rather good arrangement. Joan needed someone to get her from book launch to political rally, from Swifty Lazar's Oscar party to Valentino's fashion show. Robin wouldn't play. Actresses are actresses. One day the wind changes and, like Mary Poppins, they fly off to nurseries new. Joan unceremoniously dumped Robin and took up with a much younger man, theatre manager Percy Gibson. A lot of people took Robin's side until the wedding bells began to peal, at which point, realising that they would be missing an event of considerable magnitude – Rank's last shout – everyone began to revise and defrost. Percy was in the business. They could work together, etc, etc.

I was on Robin's side, and Joan had not invited me to the wedding. But one night we were at dinner with Valentino, and we had it out.

'Now look here, Rupert,' said Joan, deadly serious. 'I'm not twenty-five. I can't show up to awards and fashion shows on my own. I want my man to be with me. If he feels embarrassed or compromised, or whatever it was he felt, then fair enough, but too bad. It's a bore always having to rely on a queen friend to get from A to B. It wasn't fair.'

I had to agree. 'I'd love you to come to the wedding,' she continued. 'We've been neighbours in the South of France. We've had a lot of laughs. So pull yourself together.'

I did.

The night before the nuptials, I'd been invited to a birthday party at Trade, a legendary and lethal club in Clerkenwell. I'd no intention of going, but Jamie came round to do my roots after dinner and one thing led to another so that by the time Joan's wedding day dawned I was still only halfway through my evening, writhing around the dance floor, squeezing five into a toilet, and lunging at passing beauties until about two o'clock in the afternoon, when I left the club with eyes like saucers, drenched in sweat, and staggered into a taxi with several complete strangers. I had completely forgotten about Joan's nuptials. Back in the hotel where I was staying, the party continued until Ruby Wax arrived to take me to the wedding.

'Are you on acid?' said Ruby when she saw me.

'Probably,' I replied.

'How many faces do I have?'

'Two.'

'Okay, let's go!'

Inside Claridge's, there was a line to greet the newlyweds. I could hardly speak and for some reason was walking diagonally like a crab. Joan's tiny publicist swished up to us. 'Joan and Percy would love to do a picture with you both.'

'Uhhhh?'

'This way.'

Suddenly we were in a makeshift studio with lights, assistants, make-up and hair (for Joan and Percy). I was standing between them. Percy was kilted. Ruby was playing up, doing high kicks and cracking jokes. I could only just stop my eyes from popping out.

Joan, on the other hand, looked sensational. Nothing suited her quite so well as a good wedding; this was her fifth. She looked like a portrait by Gainsborough, newly painted for the set of a Rank film: décolleté with a lavender train.

I was at a table with three of my favourite monsters, Ruby Wax, Wendy Stark and Lynda La Plante. Roger Moore was also there with his new wife. And of course no party was complete that year without Cilla Black. From the Shadow Lounge to the Shadow Cabinet, Cilla seemed to be everywhere.

The bridegroom sat between Joan and a little old lady with white hair – his mother, who was several years younger than the bride. Shirley Bassey came to sit on my knee halfway through the evening. I wasn't sure whether she was a hallucination or not.

'It's actually happening!' confirmed Ruby, laughing.

Shirley and I hit it off and vowed to make an album together. She was wearing a pair of red satin trousers with a beret and she suddenly slid to the floor like a slippery fish and disappeared. Everyone laughed, but then the toasts began and we forgot all about her until a few minutes later a manicured hand clasped the edge of the table and she hauled herself back on to my knee. Neither of us remembered having met before. Now the band was playing and she wanted to sing for Joan who arrived at that moment.

'Joan, it's fantastic. Shirley wants to sing,' I said. Joan looked worried.

'Don't encourage her,' she said firmly.

Soon we understood why. Shirley clambered onto the bandstand. The polite conductor, evidently thrilled, leant into the mike. 'Ladies and gentlemen, Miss Shirley Bassey!' We all sat up ready for 'Goldfinger', but Shirley had other ideas: free-flow a capella.

'Joanie,' she warbled, arms reaching across the ballroom. 'Oh oh oh oh. I have known you since time was a baby boy . . .'

When I left she was still up there. No one could get her off.

Last year, I visited Elizabeth Taylor's house once more, eight years after Roddy McDowall's death. The occasion was her annual Easter egg hunt. I was in LA performing my seventeenth career revival plan to a fairly empty house. It was Easter 2005 and the three-day weekend stretched out before me like a tunnel. I don't know why, but LA often made me miserable. I could never shake off the feeling of being an outsider, a boy on his first day of school. And so when Candice Bergen invited me to go with her to Miss Taylor's party, I accepted with alacrity. Elizabeth Taylor was one of the ideals that had not been knocked off its pedestal for me, as was Candice, for that matter. (By the way, I call her Elizabeth, but please don't think I pretend to know her. I don't. I am merely her fan.)

It was a sunny day. The garden was no longer the white funeral bower of Roddy McDowall's memorial. Now it resembled a fruit salad. Its herbaceous borders were crammed with phlox and tobacco plants. A little pen on the lawn contained a family of lambs, a sweet black dwarf pig and a duck. Their agent hovered discreetly behind a tree. Veronique Peck, Gregory's widow, arrived, looking more beautiful than ever, in a flowing see-through coat and a wide-brimmed hat. Arnie Klein, the famous LA collagen doctor, sat with a group of daddy bears around a table by the pool. He wore a bracelet with 'Botox' inscribed in diamonds. It was his nurse who had mothered poor Michael Jackson's children. Would *he* be there? Candy and I wondered as we drove up the driveway towards the house. (Probably not: he was busy fighting for his life in the Santa Maria courtroom, celebrating Easter more traditionally, by being strung up and crucified for all America to watch.) But Carrie Fisher was there with her daughter, and Nastassja Kinski was there with hers.

By four o'clock Elizabeth still had not come down, although Bob Daly, the former chairman of Warner Brothers, informed us that her make-up and hair were already done, but that she had suddenly decided to take a bath. (Aha, I thought, the old Bianca Jagger technique: do your make-up and then soak in a moderately warm bath for that special glow.) Finally José, hairdresser to the stars, came down in a cowboy hat and a bag bulging with tricks of the trade to tell us she would be down presently. If I was starting over and was crazy enough to try this business again, José's job would be ideal, I thought out loud. The others didn't agree.

Half an hour later she made her entrance in a wheelchair. She had black spiky hair this time and more glorious jewels hung around her neck. No wonder she had a wheelchair; the weight of the Burton ring alone probably warranted a Zimmer frame. She looked tiny, like the sheep and the little duck, but when her eyes locked briefly with yours there was intense electricity. I should think there was not much point pretending with Elizabeth. Those eyes bored right through you. They were full of experience but also compassion. This was the only woman who dared give Aids its public face way back in the grim Reaganite eighties. Ronnie never mentioned the word during eight years of office. She fought tirelessly and forced the world to look when everyone else would have happily brushed it under the carpet.

Unlike many stars Elizabeth's act never looked manufactured. All actors act. They can't stop themselves. They have given everything to it, after all, but in many cases there was not much to give. The great thing about Elizabeth Taylor was that she had a great life force. She had lived spontaneously in front of the popping flashbulbs and there was no subterfuge, no filter in those famous eyes. Even on Easter Day, late for her own party, in a wheelchair, there was nothing faked, although the performance was stunning. At one point she valiantly decided to get out of her chair to chat. A hundred arms shot out and pulled her up as if she were a little baby being lifted out of her paddling pool. Everyone adored her and it was sweet to watch. On her feet she was tinier than ever, and finding herself simply standing and chatting, she slipped back into her chair after a few seconds as if it were a nearby couch.

CHAPTER 50

Goodbye, Hollywood

I was staying in the abandoned Deco tower on Sunset that I used to break into all those years ago when I was starting out. Like me, it had been through several incarnations since those days. Now it had been renovated by Paul Fortune and called the Argyle. Every foreign trader has their hotel in LA and mine had always been the Beverly Hills, but suddenly the smell of canned flora had lost its charm. The ramshackle Polo Lounge, that strange clumsy extension, no longer conjured up Sharon Tate or Jacqueline Susann, even though, that spring of 2005, I had my last tête-à-tête with Gavin Lambert there before he died. We talked about Roddy, John Schlesinger and Krishnamurti, a philosopher I loved.

'What was he like?' I asked.

'Wonderfully worldly,' said Gavin. 'I once went to one of his lectures in a new pair of shoes, and afterwards Krishnaji said: "I very much liked your shoes. Are they new?"'

'Do you think he could have been the Messiah?' I asked.

'Oh, if anyone was, it was he,' replied Gavin.

Peter Finch had his fatal heart attack on the red carpet leading from the valet parking to the foyer at the same hotel. Every time I checked in, I said a silent prayer for that brilliant actor who gasped his last breath as excited guests came and went. It was not often you got the chance to watch a Hollywood legend croak and this was one of the roadside stupas in front of which we made the sign of the very cross and kissed our fingers; there but for the grace of God . . .

I wanted a change so I moved into the penthouse suite at the Argyle with a very motivating deal brokered by Paul. Things had come full circle. It was funny to finally return to the top of that old tower. The dank smell of piss, the boarded-up windows, the peeling walls and the split mattress had vanished beneath a thousand coats of paint, the smell of new fitted carpet and a king-sized orthopaedic bed. Shiny glass glistened in the sun's rays, and the city fell about beneath like the huge encrusted skirts of a giantess. The terrace wrapped around the entire building. Truman Capote, Claudette Colbert, Errol Flynn and, of course, Montgomery Clift, had all stood there and watched a thousand dusks fall. According to legend John Wayne kept a cow out there, but everything had been painted over now, in thick layers of Paul's signature oatmeal. The Hollywood hills rose sharply behind, with their mad houses perched on stilts, roads like razor slashes cut into the crumbling sand, and below the cities of the plain stretched into the haze.

Twenty years ago I wanted to own this view, although I knew I never would. My heart raced just to stand above it. My imagination summoned Monty from the grave, and we stood there together looking at the city, him behind, leaning his chin on my shoulder. Like the little boy in the bedroom cupboard, I hid in a fantasy world. With a joint in one hand and a can in the other, lying in a dusty ray of light on the old mattress, I pretended I was shooting a film with Elia Kazan, living with Monty, and leaving for dinner with Elizabeth and Roddy, and maybe James Dean. I was so successful in this dream that I was on the very verge of breakdown, drinking vodka and painkillers with Monty just to keep sane.

'Monty,' I'd say. 'Sometimes I just want to run away. Be a traffic controller at some little airstrip on the Keys.' Monty would look at me, with his vacant dilated eyes.

'Old chum,' he'd say. 'You've got to get back out there. You're the best actor we've got.'

Monty wasn't the only ghost I knew in LA. Years later, in another momentary embrace with Hollywood in 1994, I was starring in a kids' movie *Dunston Checks In*. My co-star was a brilliant young orang-utan called Sammy. He was my favourite scene partner and acted to hand signals. (If only some of the others had!) I was renting Tony Perkins' house from his widow, my friend Berry Berenson. It was hidden in the hills off Woodrow Wilson Drive. The family hadn't lived in it since Tony had died of Aids, and there was a tomblike atmosphere along the long corridor flanked with framed family snapshots that led past the bedrooms to the room where he died. The family dog, Charlie, a sweet old collie, had been left in the house, and became slightly demented with loneliness, but he loved us and we loved him. Sometimes he would career from Tony's bedroom up the corridor to the large barn of a sitting room, running round and round some unseen thing, jumping up and nipping at thin air. Mo watched with his head to one side, and once the french windows burst open. It was very weird, but not scary. I slept in the bed in which Tony died and soon I was possessed. Actually it was quite magical. A family of possums lived underneath the floor and played tag at night: above an owl stood guard on the roof and hooted until dawn. Mo and I lay on the bed with our ears pricked. When the moon was full it literally flooded into the room, and my dog was a silver ghost and Tony Perkins was there. Soon I would find myself talking to him, or else I was going mad. Anything was possible in the Hollywood hills.

Tony was practical and quite tough. 'You're not going to get it,' he said, as I leafed through a new script sent by ICM.

'Shut up, Tony!' I replied to an empty room.

'They're just sending it to keep you quiet and they know you're not a very fast reader. Did you ever see so many *long* scripts?'

He had a point.

On my way to auditions, lost on the freeway and late, verging on tears, he was my air traffic controller. 'Pull yourself together, queen. Turn left.'

At dinner one night with Tony's best friend, the photographer Paul Jasmin, I described what was going on. 'That's Tony,' he said. 'I get it too. He was quite tough. Fearless in a way. Once, quite near the end, he asked me: "What would you say if the grim reaper arrived now?" I said I had no idea. 'What would you do?' I asked him. He was silent for a moment. Then he replied: "I'd say, "Gimme five minutes.""'

Now it was all ghosts sitting on the terrace high above the city, and I felt undead as I joined the stream of rush-hour traffic before dawn each morning on my way to Manhattan Beach where *Boston Legal* was shot. I was reunited with Candy Bergen and James Spader and *Boston Legal* was another turning point for me. It was strange seeing Jim after all the years. He had been friends with Eric Stoltz and John Philbin in the days when we all lived at Hollywood Boulevard in the early eighties. Jim and I steadfastly refused to go to acting class. We both belonged to the 'just do it' school. Now he was at the peak of his form, and *Boston Legal* was the best show on TV. They filmed eight pages of dialogue a day, whole court cases in one shot. The others were all brilliant at it but I was out of my depth. In one scene Candy was the prosecuting lawyer and I was the defence. It was a far cry from Morgan Le Fay and Lancelot du Lac, although she gave me a second great piece of advice. In a break between takes she sidled up and whispered, 'One of your shoulders is all hunched up. It looks weird.' She was right. I was twisted like a tree in a storm. In the next take I managed to lose the hump. Afterwards Candy winked at me from across the courtroom. She won the case, but I was losing the plot. I felt like a silent star making a sound movie, bewildered by the microphone flying through the air. I fluffed my lines, missed my marks and nearly crashed every day on my way to work. Twenty years of experience simply melted away and I was back at the beginning. No technique, no charisma and, worse, no drive to kickstart them all into action. It felt like live burial.

The night before I returned to Miami, I had dinner with Gore Vidal, Gavin Lambert and Wendy Stark. Here was the Hollywood I loved. We went to an eccentric restaurant on Santa Monica called Dan Tanners. Gore and Gavin were on brilliant form, full of life, deeply anarchic, and of course hysterically funny. The other tables of pimps and working chicks, executives and starlets, were sullen and speechless, lost in anaesthetic by comparison, but ours was raucous, competitive, tipsy and overflowing with affection. It was like eating in hall at a brilliant university. Everyone raised their voice to be heard above the others. Opinions were aired and squashed. ('You do have some terribly silly views, don't you, dear!') Entire careers were polished off in a sentence. ('She couldn't act and she couldn't fuck.') Others were enhanced by some extraordinary revelation. ('She had an extended clit that you could chew.') Gavin and Gore had known them all. It was a magical evening and we closed the restaurant.

Back at the hotel, I stood, drunk, on the terrace; the ghosts were all out on the streets of West Hollywood, men flitting through the shadows looking for sex, rats watching from palm trees. Somewhere down there the next blockbuster was being written by a lonely tech geek hunched before a computer, the next actress was going through her moves in front of a mirror, and the next dead hairdresser from the sixties was being unloaded into Cunningham O'Grady's all-night mortuary on Fairfax. Strands of streetlights shimmered in the misty desert night, mile after mile, as unimaginable as the universe, and all of us up there on that terrace looked down in wonder. Truman, Claudette, the Duke, Errol, Monty, me and the cow . . .

I felt an explosion of sheer peace as another door slowly closed and I tiptoed to my room.

CHAPTER 51

Wilma

Hurricane Wilma arrived on Miami Beach during the early hours of a Monday morning in late October 2005. She was the biggest storm in history according to the talking heads on American TV. She sat over the Yucatán peninsula for two days while the whole of Florida braced itself for a repeat of the latest episode of America's skydiving sitcom: *The Kiss of Katrina*. The first gusts began as dusk fell; little bursts of warm air punched at you in the breeze. In the mauve sky a vast bank of cloud curved high above South Point in a semicircle. On Washington Avenue the Cubans were hammering boards to the windows of their shops. People laden with emergency supplies hurried home. All the bodegas and hardware stores had been cleaned out in the panic that Americans have come to feel empty without. Everyone barricaded themselves into their houses, and as darkness fell the streets were suddenly deserted.

Suddenly South Beach felt like an old-fashioned out-of-season sea resort – I wandered towards the beach, intoxicated by the wind which had now become strong enough that you could lean your whole body against it and not fall to the ground. All the bars on Ocean Drive were open but empty. Their calypsos and salsas could just be heard in snatches as the roar of the wind briefly subsided. Against the coloured lights of these establishments – Johnny Rockets, Wet Willie's, The Surfcomber – the silhouettes of palm trees were already bent double in the gale. They were loving it. And so was I.

The best thing about Miami has always been the wind. It blows at you from across a vast expanse of sea. It diffuses the light on the beach with dust and salt. It smells of all the scented flowers of the Caribbean. It wakes you up and empties your head. I walked over the dunes onto the beach and battled my way towards the sea, and stayed there until about half past three when I was nearly killed by a flying coconut. During the walk home the storm suddenly took hold, and knocked me off my feet. For a moment I had to grab onto some railings like one of the nasty old nannies from *Mary Poppins*. A sheet of metal bounced past me like a feather. A palm tree snapped across the street.

I finally got home and lay in bed as the windows bent inwards and a weird pressure built up that made my ears pop. It is at moments like this that all the windows in a room can dramatically shatter. Mr Greenwald, the developer, said mine were hurricane resistant; for once he was right. Wilma moaned, shrieked and hammered at them but they stood their ground. The lights flickered and cut out. Some queen off her face called from New York, but after a few minutes my phone went dead. Now I was all alone.

Soon after dawn, Wilma reached her peak with a thunderous medley of micro-tornadoes, at which point one of the last old abandoned fleapits on Ocean Drive flew apart, leaving a skeleton of beams under a tumbled roof. The rest of it bounced off towards 5th Street. There was nothing to do but wait. Bizarrely, as I sat there inside my rattling flat, it felt incredibly peaceful. I woke at noon and the storm was over. It was completely silent. No wind. No birds. No air-conditioning. No cars. No voices. It was extraordinary. The sea was calm. I walked out into the dark passage outside my apartment and began the most curious seven-floor descent down a pitch-black staircase.

Outside, the city was trashed. Trees were all over the roads. Pylons had fallen; wires leant dangerously over the street. Cars had been smashed. Windows were blown out in some of the swanky new high-rises and gaped like missing teeth. People were walking around in a kind of daze. Car alarms and sirens began to whine.

Night fell and America turned into Guatemala. The surface glamour of South Beach had simply been ripped away, exposing the bare bones of a corrupt city. Only nature had the nerve to hold a mirror up to the rotting face of America. The darkness was impenetrable that night. No street lights. No moon. Crowds stood around the bodega on Washington, which the Cubans couldn't resist opening. People were allowed in one by one for fear of looting and were held at bay by armed police, all in the ghostly light thrown from a kerosene lamp inside the shop that turned the crowd into a prehistoric tribe, hiding in the trees around the campfire of an imperialist explorer. They were menacingly curious. Only Spanish was spoken. The white folk had stayed at home. Cars drove slowly through the streets, headlights on full beam, catching for a second the mad eyeballs of the wandering mass.

Only South Beach's homeless went on with their lives undisturbed and surveyed us blankly from doorways and bus stops. The little old hunchbacked lady who compulsively swept the streets stood under a tree with her broom, wearing a rather smart new raincoat. The black lady covered with tumours was already asleep beside her wheelchair on the corner of Washington and Lincoln. And the Cuban priest who had arrived fifteen years ago on a raft was playing his flute quietly outside the Versace mansion that stood silent and boarded up on Ocean Drive. I sat down on the steps where Gianni had been gunned down and listened to the trills and nursery songs of this homeless Papageno. There had been ten hurricanes since Gianni had been shot and the gilt Medusas on the railings were peeling. Was Gianni stuck for eternity at the door to his palace like a character from a Jacobean tragedy? That would have been punishment indeed. I searched the atmosphere for a trace of him, but there was nothing. I was the one who was stuck, the Brigitte Bardot of South Beach, still there after everyone else had left or died. The Cuban priest stopped playing and shuffled away down the empty boulevard. He had a suitcase on wheels. As he disappeared it looked like a black dog at his heels.

In the old days Mo would bound ahead and wait expectantly at the gates of the Versace house, wagging his tail. I would laugh, secretly proud, and anyone we were with thought we were unbearably chic. I swear that dog knew he was funny. Sometimes we would bump into Gianni and Antonio on their way to the beach, like a couple of Italian ladies laden down with folding chairs, straw baskets, magazines and books. I laughed out loud remembering that when Naomi Campbell tried to lay a flower on the steps after Gianni's murder she was nearly arrested.

There was no food anywhere so I went to the Raleigh. A hopeless candle burnt in the foyer. There was nobody behind the desk. I sat down in an armchair and was engulfed by the darkness. Twenty minutes later I said, 'Excuse me,' to a passing waiter, who gave a little shriek of terror before shining a torch at me and asking me to leave.

'I'm a friend of the hotel,' I said lamely.

'Only hotel guests can eat,' he said, and stuck rigidly to his guns.

In the huge lounge that had once been a kosher restaurant for hundreds of elderly Hassidic Jews, two marooned groups of guests sat huddled around candles, their faces caught in the flickering light like portraits by Rembrandt. They briefly looked up. They were eating a gloomy makeshift meal, and I could tell that tempers were frayed. The staff of the hotel sat around another table outside on the terrace with candles and beer. They were having a party . . . Nothing had ever changed in this hotel. It was under new ownership and had been renovated, but it was still as stumbling and useless as it had always been. Once that had been a part of its charm but now the Italian group at the next table were not so sure. They had been clucking away in lowered Venetian about how all the lights were on in the Delano, and soon when the manager arrived, the little white-haired leader of the group jumped up and flashed his torch in the face of the bewildered man.

'We must have some beautiful candles,' he sang in a voice chillingly like Gianni Versace's: high pitched, and threatening.

'I don't think we have any candles, sir,' came the feeble reply.

'No candles? Is not possible. Geeeve me *now* some beautiful candles!'

'Sir, there has been a hurricane.'

'I know. Thanks God we are in pieces one. But this one is the hotel. We must have ambient to laugh at this things. We *need* to laugh. I am *dépriment. Dépriment.*'

'We're doing everything we can, sir. Everything.' Even though this means fuck off and leave me alone in Floridian, the little white-haired man was appeased. He had said his bit and seemed happier as he huffed back into his chair to translate and exaggerate his confrontation for the benefit of the ladies of his party. As he flashed his torch around the huge dark hotel foyer, I got the giggles. In the old days Kenny would have told him to go fuck himself, which would probably have been the better approach, because now the Italians were never going to be happy. Once you had seen through the appalling amateurishness of South Beach, there was no looking back. You either moved there, or you got the hell out.

There was something final in the air that night. Leaving the Raleigh, I walked towards Flamingo Park. Police cars with flashing lights roamed the streets. One stopped. A round face with little malicious eyes and thin blond hair peered at me from behind the disco lights of the squad car, entitled and insolent.

'There's a curfew. What are you doing?'

'How do I know there's a curfew?' I asked.

'Watch the TV.'

'But I don't have electricity. How can I watch TV?'

The policeman looked at me menacingly. For the purposes of this book, incarceration would have provided a marvellous twist, a stunning finale, and so I stared back knowingly. Plus there might at least be hot water and electricity in the police station.

'Just go home, okay,' he said and drove on, much to my disappointment.

Historically, queers can always be counted on to go out as soon as there is a crisis. Riots and wars, power cuts and blizzards are all an excuse for a night out. Disaster makes us feel horny and connected, and anything illegal like a curfew brings out a rebellious streak that lies just below the surface of most of us. One fabulous old Parisian fairy I knew (now dead) once told me that he had had sex in only two periods of his life: the first during the Second World War and then not again until the student riots of 1968.

'You must have got a bit frustrated in between,' I reasoned.

'Not a bit. For me nothing could ever be as intense as the embrace of two people who thought they were about to be slaughtered. After the war it was all fireworks – no bombs. Until '68.' (The French word for fireworks is *feu d'artifice*, which literally means artificial fire.)

So I expected the west side of Flamingo Park to be jumping. But there was *no one there*. Just three police cars lying in wait in case any queers got the wrong idea. Oh no! Even the queers had been broken by the New America. We had become spineless virtual geeks. Cruising on line for a chemical fuck, or holding hands in a mega-church praying for forgiveness. There was nothing in between except maybe cardio and weight training.

Suddenly, and with total clarity, I knew it was time to leave.

CHAPTER 52

Goodbye, Miami

Christmas was upon us, and Miami tried to straighten herself up for the oncoming season. Someone held a party for the homeless and had given them all a Father Christmas outfit. On my last cycle ride down the beach, the low coral wall dividing the park from the dunes, where the homeless spent the day, was now dotted with miserable careworn Santas, sitting glumly in their fake-fur-trimmed hats. Only in America could such a breathtaking vision be seen. Even the mad old Hari Krishna monk was gobsmacked. He, too, sat alone on the beach wall, momentarily drained of faith and disciples. In high season, three or four regretful drug casualties might dance behind him past Wet Willie's on Ocean Drive, clashing their little cymbals in the faces of the hip hop kids who drank Sea Breezes out of paper cups. But they always went back north in summer with the bums, and each year the mad monk seemed to edge closer to the sea wall, which was a kind of dividing line between society and the vagabond world, his coral robe bleached white and ragged. He knew that once you moved out of your room for that first night huddled among the dunes, there was no turning back. Our world became an impenetrable screen in front of which they sat.

It was a cartoon world, and I had become a part of it. Out of the blue, Jeffrey Katzenberg offered me the voice of Prince Charming in *Shrek 2*, a role I would never get in a live-action film. I was ecstatic; I loved *Shrek*. It is a strange fact that America is only prepared to look at herself through the safety of cartoons: *Shrek*, *South Park* and *The Simpsons* hold the mirror to society. Only the titles of live-action films give you any indication about the absurd state of our world: *Mission Impossible*, *Failure to Launch*, *Maid in America*. (Professor in Guatemala.)

Being the gay guy in films was another cartoon. There was only so far I could go before being run over by the steamroller. Now I was walking flattened. I would pop back out, but only to be knocked on the head by the giant hammer, because now the winds were changing. In the aftermath of *Brokeback Mountain* and *Transamerica*, two excellent and beautifully performed films, one paper reported that Brad Pitt had told his agent to find him a gay part. Another one said that while gay actors were good for comedic gay roles, straight guys were better as the serious queers. The hairdryer has been grabbed from my hands. Now Tom will present it to Russell in a fireman's outfit on the edge of some burning skyscraper at the emotional clinch before the final abseil to freedom. ('My ex gave me this after the White Party, before this whole mess started. Remember me, buddy, when you backcomb our kids. Now *jump!*')

Hey-ho. Does that mean that I will play the serious straight role? Possibly not, I think, as I ride in the taxi over the causeway for the last time. An escaping Father Christmas is walking by the side of the freeway, trying to make it back downtown. Behind him a row of gigantic Norwegian liners sit in the harbour. They are beautiful and lethal. They have killed the reefs that surround America.

Yesterday it all felt huge but this evening, as the sun sets over the skyline that coke built, downtown Miami, I feel weightless, as if I had shed my skin. I am going to disappear. In the airport, I sit at La Carretta. It was at this stool, years ago, that I discovered I had been living with a bigamist. Difficult in the gay world, you might say. But I managed. That day I had sat frozen as flight after flight came and went, unable to move from the bar. Now, I begin to laugh. A drunken English tourist with a chubby red face is watching me.

'You were a bit of okay in *Maurice*,' he says expansively. 'And *Four Weddings and a Funeral* is my daughter's favourite film.'

At this stage in my career, there seems to be little point in correcting the small error, and so I graciously acquiesce. 'Thank you. I loved making both those films,' I say modestly.

Bad move. He moves to the stool next to me and surveys me with bloodshot eyes. In the bubble between destinations, we are suddenly best friends.

'But then you went off the boil, right?' His face is very close. 'What happened, mate?' He puts his giant paw on my shoulder.

'I have a very small willie,' I say. Very Hugh reply, I think, but he pays no attention.

'Yeah. That film with Julianne what's-her-face. Nine and a half . . .?'

'Months, *Nine Months*. Moore.'

'There you go again. Mumbling. It's your trademark isn't it?'

The flight to São Paulo is announced. I get up. He grabs my arm. 'Sign something for me before you go.' It is a command. He gives me his ticket folder.

I write inside it with a gothic flourish:

Drop dead!
  Love,
    Hugh Grant XXX